Employment, Stress and Family Functioning

WILEY SERIES ON
STUDIES IN OCCUPATIONAL STRESS

Series Editors

Professor Cary L. Cooper
Manchester School of Management
University of Manchester
Institute of Science and Technology

Professor S. V. Kasl
Department of Epidemiology
School of Medicine
Yale University

Further titles in preparation

Employment, Stress and Family Functioning

Julian Barling

Queen's University
Kingston, Ontario

JOHN WILEY & SONS
Chichester · New York · Brisbane · Toronto · Singapore

Other Wiley Editorial Offices

John Wiley & Sons, Inc., 605 Third Avenue,
New York, NY 10158-0012, USA

Jacaranda Wiley Ltd, G.P.O. Box 859, Brisbane,
Queensland 4001, Australia

John Wiley & Sons (Canada) Ltd, 22 Worcester Road,
Rexdale, Ontario M9W 1L1, Canada

John Wiley & Sons (SEA) Pte Ltd, 37 Jalan Pemimpin #05-04,
Block B, Union Industrial Building, Singapore 2057

Library of Congress Cataloging-in-Publication Data:

Barling, Julian.
    Employment, stress, and family functioning / Julian Barling.
        p.   cm.—(Wiley series on studies in occupational stress)
    Includes bibliographical references.
    ISBN 0 471 91773 7
    1. Work and family. I. Title. II. Series.
    HD4904.25.B37   1990
    306.85—dc20
                                                    89-38905
                                                        CIP

British Library Cataloguing in Publication Data:

Barling, Julian
    Employment, stress and family functioning. – (Wiley series
    on studies in occupational stress).
    1. Personnel. Stress
    I. Title
    158.7

    ISBN 0 471 91773 7

Printed and bound in Great Britain by Biddles Ltd., Guildford, Surrey

Contents

Editorial Foreword to the Series

The Wiley Series on Studies in Occupational Stress has made a major contribution to the literature in the field of occupational and organizational stress over the last decade. The main objective of this series was to help review existing work in the field, and to map out the future of research in this burgeoning and increasingly important area of organizational behavior and occupational health. The early books set the stage in trying to develop an understanding of various occupational groups, such as blue collar workers, white collar and professional workers, health care professionals, etc. Gradually the emphasis shifted to important conceptual issues such as control and autonomy in the workplace, coping with stress, and the link between stress and health. These early books tended to be edited volumes of discrete, integrated topics, which were appropriate at the time, given the 'state of the art' of occupational stress research. As more and more research is being pursued and published in the journals, it is important that we now begin to consolidate this literature, and to provide more comprehensive and in depth accounts of particular topical concerns in the field. The books which will follow, therefore, will be author written books which focus on an issue or topic of interest, in a more pragmatic sense, and are directed towards people in the workplace: managers, trade unionists, occupational psychologists, occupational medics, and the myriad of others involved in the health and well-being of people at work. This book represents this new dimension to our series.

CARY L. COOPER
University of Manchester, UK

Preface

When the initial commitment was made to write this book at the beginning of 1987, the motivation was unambiguous: neither family nor work roles exist in a vacuum. Instead, there is a growing realization that they do affect each other, and the need to understand their interaction is critical. Below are several major reasons why a project of this nature is justified.

First, there is widespread concern about possible negative effects on the family arising from the growing number of employed wives and employed mothers. For example, one analysis attributes brutal crime among teenagers at least partially to the increasing attention parents (and especially mothers) place on their employment, concluding that 'many youngsters lack attention and supervision in part because their parents are too busy making a living.' (*Time*, June 12, 1989, p 58). Because of the policy implications that may follow from such conclusions, it is crucial that their scientific merit be subject to close empirical scrutiny.

Second, organizations and unions are expressing practical interest in the interface between work and family. Within-company child care centres are being established under the assumption that organizations, employees and their families will benefit, as are other organizational interventions such as flexible work schedules and employee assistance programmes. Not all such ventures are taking place solely at the behest of management. In a widely publicized union-management contract in 1989, the Communication Workers of America and AT&T reached an agreement just prior to the beginning of the strike that provided significant non-employment related benefits to employees. These benefits included financial assistance with adoption of children and prolonged leave to care for terminally ill members of the extended family. In a separate programme co-sponsored by the Canadian Auto Workers union, Chrysler Canada, Ford of Canada, General Motors of Canada and the Ontario government, a child care centre will be established in 1989 primarily to assist shift workers, and will be open from 5.30 a.m. until 1 a.m.

The central thesis of this book is that it is people's positive and negative experiences of employment (and unemployment) that explain the relationship between employment and the family, not simply whether they are employed or not. The central aspects that are considered in *Employment, Stress and Family Functioning* include bidirectional effects between work and family, the role of subjective employment experiences and objective employment characteristics, the effects of husbands' and wives' employment on their own and their spouses' marital functioning, a focus on the interdependence of fathers' and mothers' employment on children, and the effects of unemployment on the family. This book also includes a consideration of some policy implications.

Acknowledgements

As is surely the case with all such efforts, this book could not have been completed alone. In one sense, the groundwork, research and writing of this book has been enhanced by the contributions of Clive Fullagar, Steve Bluen, Sally Grant and Michele Laliberte who at various stages took the time to comment on some portions of the book, or allowed me to share some thoughts with them. Karyl MacEwen made a special contribution in this sense by reading (and re-reading!) the entire manuscript. Her comments, critiques and support throughout the entire project were always more than appreciated. Lori Gilham smiled calmly and met any unrealistic demands that I made to provide me with secretarial support. In an indirect sense, many individuals contributed over the past few years by making my work more meaningful and providing me with the sort of work environment that organizational psychologists dream about: Dan O'Leary, Clive Fullagar, Karyl MacEwen, Steve Bluen, Ricky Mauer and 'Prof' Jack Mann. I also express my gratitude to the Social Sciences and Humanities Research Council of Canada and Imperial Oil for their financial assistance for some of the research I have reported in the book. Finally, I thank my wife Janice, and my children Seth and Monique, for the motivation, support and understanding that made writing this book worth while and a realistic possibility.

Chapter 1
Work, Employment and Family Functioning

In today's society, concern is frequently expressed regarding the possible interdependence of work and family life. More specifically, there is widespread apprehension that there is an overlap between work and family, that work exerts a unidirectional effect on family functioning, and that any effects of work on family functioning are inevitably negative. These concerns are sufficiently pervasive to warrant an extensive examination of the conceptual and empirical status of the link between work and family. In addition, there are assumptions underlying the relationship between work and family life that by themselves provide sufficient motivation to scrutinize this relationship. Specifically, there are some pervasive assumptions about this relationship which guide our thinking and determine the way in which we pose our research questions. The following example illustrates just how our assumptions both motivate and limit our research. Approximately three decades ago, Gurin, Veroff and Feld (1960) conducted their landmark study on mental health in a national probability survey in the United States of America. In this study, Gurin *et al.* (1960) questioned both males and females about their mental health, and about the factors presumed to influence their mental health. To understand the causes of mental health for these two samples, they asked men about aspects of their *work* lives, yet questioned women about their *home* and *family* lives. They deliberately chose to ask men and women different questions, operating under the assumption that psychological aspects of the work role are pertinent to men's mental health, while psychological characteristics regarding the homemaker role are relevant for women's mental health. This assumption limited the questions they asked, the data they collected, the results they obtained and the conclusions that could be drawn from their study.

Current assumptions about the relationship between work and the family will now be outlined briefly, after which an overall plan of the text will be presented. Before that, however, a condensed history of research and thinking on work and family functioning in the twentieth century is in order.

WORK AND FAMILY FUNCTIONING IN THE TWENTIETH CENTURY: AN HISTORICAL SYNOPSIS

Without doubt, the nature and consequences of the relationship between employment and family functioning has attracted considerable attention since the

1

mid-1970s. It would not be difficult to argue that this surge in interest by academics, policy makers and the lay public parallels the increase in the number of married couples in which both spouses are employed, and in the number of employed mothers. Kanter's (1977) *Work and Family in the United States: A Critical Review and Agenda for Research and Policy* was influential in setting an agenda for relevant research on work and the family. One indicator of the influence of any text is the extent to which it is cited. A computer search of the Social Science Citation Index shows there were 184 citations to Kanter's text in journals from the time of its publication until February 1989. However, the notion that 'it has only been in the past decade that researchers have become interested in the relationship between paid work and family' (Burke and McKeen, 1988, p. 1) ignores empirical research conducted on this topic since the late 1920s and early 1930s. To illustrate this point, research that has focused both on the effects of employment conditions on marital functioning, and the consequences of maternal employment for children's behaviour, are considered. For example, Hoppock (1935), Friend and Haggard (1948), Locke and Mackeprang (1949), Aberle and Naegele (1952), Gover (1963) and Dyer (1956) all investigated the relation between employment and marital or family functioning. Following Mathews's (1934) early study, the effects of maternal employment have been studied extensively (e.g. Essig and Morgan, 1946; King, McIntyre and Axelson, 1968; McCord, McCord and Thurber, 1963; Payne, 1956; Williamson, 1970). Early studies even investigated the possible effects of father occupation on their sons' career choice (e.g. Jensen and Kirchner, 1955; Nelson, 1939). These studies will not be described at this stage, but will be described more fully in the relevant sections throughout the text. The point that must be emphasized here is that empirical studies investigating the relation between work and the family have been conducted at least since the late 1920s. However, it is only within the last decade that this relation has received sustained attention on an integrated basis from academics representing diverse disciplines.

Given that empirical research on the interdependence of work and family has been conducted for at least 60 years, it is worth contemplating what differences exist between the research currently conducted and that reported earlier. First, the question of the interdependence of work and family functioning has been legitimated as an issue of major importance in its own right (Gutek, Nakumara and Nieva, 1981; Kanter, 1977; Piotrkowski, Rapaport and Rapaport, 1987; Voydanoff, 1987). Second, there are more attempts currently to consolidate research and theorizing on work and family into an integrated framework, in contrast to earlier studies.

From an historical perspective, one of the first issues that should be highlighted is that the presumed relationship between work and family roles has been of general interest for at least as long as empirical studies have been conducted. Assumptions about the strength and causal direction of this relationship, however, have been inconsistent over time. An examination of social science theorizing during the late 1940s and early 1950s supports this observation.

If some of the earlier writings within organizational psychology are considered, it is clear that suggestions that work and family functioning affected each other had emerged by the 1930s. As early as 1935, Robert Hoppock reported in his book, *Job Satisfaction*, that data from his empirical study of 500 teachers showed that family factors influenced job satisfaction. Interest in, and apprehension about, the relationship between work and the family continued in the 1940s, as illustrated by Friend and Haggard's (1948) study published by the *American Psychological Association*. Friend and Haggard (1948) went as far as to suggest that: 'Basic to effective adjustment of the worker to the job, is an appreciation of the extent to which workers' family experiences penetrate their attitude to their jobs' (p. 146). Thus, by the 1950s, numerous sources assumed that work and family functioning were interdependent (Bullock, 1952). Moreover, both Friend and Haggard (1948) and Hoppock (1935) assumed that the causal direction in this relationship was such that family functioning influenced work. At the same time, concern was also being expressed regarding the possible negative effects of maternal employment on children (Bossard and Boll, 1966; Mathews, 1934).

Although the pervasive assumption during the 1950s was that work and family were interdependent, divergent opinions were emerging. There were suggestions in the 1950s that work and family systems were independent. For example, Parsons (1959, pp. 262 and 263) postulated the existence of a rigid structural differentiation between individuals' different roles. Parsons stated that:

> Broadly speaking, there is no sector of our society where the dominant patterns stand in sharper contrast to those of the occupational world than in the family. .... Clearly for two structures with such different patterns to play crucially important roles in the same society requires a delicate adjustment between them. The direct integration of occupational function with the kinship system, as it occurs in many nonliterate and peasant societies, is quite impossible ... and it is noteworthy that his (the father's) familial and occupational roles are sharply segregated from each other.

This perspective is reinforced by data from Aberle and Naegele's (1952) study conducted at the same time. They found that the men they interviewed believed that there was little overlap between their family and work roles.

However, by the early 1970s, there was uniformity in the assumption that work and family roles were intertwined. Hall (1972) suggested that while society expected wives and mothers to enact their various roles (e.g. mother, wife, employee, self) simultaneously, fathers and husbands were afforded the luxury of fulfilling those roles sequentially (e.g. the roles of worker, parent, and spouse). This meant that while fathers were at work, they were not expected to concern themselves about family issues. Yet when mothers were at work, they would be expected to concern themselves not only with job-related tasks, but also with any relevant family issues. The extent of the overlap between work and family is further evident from two different surveys. Based on her interviews with a randomly selected sample in a Boston suburb, Crosby (1984) reports: 'To our question "What creates a happy work life?" came the surprising answer, A full home life' (p. 46). Employees themselves now see work and family as linked. Burke (1988, p. 184) points to the following incident:

> Recently some of my colleagues and I were involved in developing a culture for a large organization. As part of the development stage, we asked representative members of the organization to add to our list of culture dimensions what they thought should be surveyed. To my surprise. . .they added, among other dimensions, the work–family–self relationship. . .I do not think I will be surprised again and, in fact, given a chance in the future, will include this dimension in our next culture survey.

Today, there is considerable agreement that there is an overlap or spillover between work and family for most individuals (e.g. Crosby, 1987; Kanter, 1977; Voydanoff, 1987), and the available data would suggest that this is true for both men and women (Barling, 1986a; Barling and Jannsens, 1984; Crosby, 1984; Herman and Gyllstrom, 1977). While it is beyond the scope of this discussion to speculate on the reasons for this, it is reasonable to accept the contributing role of the influx of large numbers of mothers into the labour force (see Chapter 7). This influx was stimulated at least partially by the necessity of female employment during the Second World War, and maintained thereafter.

Having focused briefly on the course of research investigating work and family, we now turn to a consideration of three pervasive and current assumptions inherent in theorizing on this topic.

ASSUMPTION 1: UNIDIRECTIONAL EFFECTS OF WORK ON FAMILY LIFE

The belief that there is considerable overlap between work and family life is now widespread, and has become evident in a variety of presentations in different media over the past decade. On one level, the number and titles of books appearing on this topic reflect the assumption of an interdependence between work and family life: *Must success cost so much?* (Bartolome and Evans, 1980), *Families that Work: Children in a Changing World* (Kamerman and Hayes, 1982), *Work and Love: The Crucial Balance* (Rohrlich, 1980), *Workaholics: Working with Them, Living with Them* (Machlowitz, 1980), *The Executive Parent* (Hersch, 1977), *Married to their Careers: Career and Family Dilemmas in Doctors' Lives* (Gerber, 1983) and *Tradeoffs: Executive, Family and Organizational Life* (Greiff and Munter, 1980a). Likewise, there have also been innumerable articles in various magazines aimed at the lay public. For example, *Newsweek* has published at least two cover stories on the topic ('The superwoman squeeze', 19 May, 1980; and 'A mother's choice', 31 March, 1986). The *New York Times Magazine* published a major article by Shreve entitled 'Careers and the lure of motherhood' (21 November, 1982) while an article entitled 'Executive guilt: Who's taking care of the children?' appeared in

Fortune (16 February 1987). An article by Maslach and Jackson (1979) appeared in *Psychology Today* entitled 'Burned-out cops and their families', and Walker (1976) published '"Til business us do part?' in the *Harvard Business Review*. In addition, several motion pictures have focused on this issue. For example, *Nine to Five* portrays the spillover between the worlds of work and family, while the potential effects of husband/father unemployment and associated role-related changes on the family were depicted in *Mr Mom*. These articles and movies must be considered as significant given their wide audience: even if their content does not influence beliefs, they certainly reflect widespread social beliefs.

These books, articles and movies are important. As many of their titles alone indicate, they reflect what Kanter (1977) calls 'economic determinism', according to which it is assumed that work-related factors, such as excessive work involvement and work-related stressors, exert unidirectional effects on the family. This unidirectional assumption is prevalent throughout the social sciences and probably society as a whole. Yet other directional assumptions remain equally plausible: For one, it may be that family factors influence work performance. Indeed, earlier writings on the interdependence of work and family postulated that it was family functioning that influences work performance (e.g. Friend and Haggard, 1948; Hoppock, 1935). A more recent example derives from the research of Salkever (1980, 1982), who provides data showing that a sick child at home negatively influences a mother's work performance. In addition, Crouter (1984a) found that mothers with young children are likely to report that family factors spill over into the work situation. Finally, Kriegsman and Hardin (1974) and Gutek, Repetti and Silver (1988) question whether there are particular conditions under which family functioning influences work, such as whether experiencing a divorce would exert a negative impact on work performance. Accordingly, there are sound reasons to question the validity of the assumption of 'economic determinism'.

ASSUMPTION 2: WORK EXERTS AN INEVITABLY NEGATIVE EFFECT ON FAMILY LIFE

A close examination of the literature reveals the pervasive assumption that any effect of work on the family is inevitably negative. However, current research suggests that the assumption that it is work that negatively influences the family may not be supported. For example, while it is widely assumed that frequent job-related mobility exerts a negative impact on marital adjustment and children's behaviour (e.g. Greiff and Munter, 1980a; Packard, 1972), an examination of the empirical data suggests this may not be the case. Rather, there is evidence that both children (Brett, 1982) and university students (Mann, 1972) who have experienced frequent mobility may function better than their counterparts with fewer experiences of mobility. This effect may be intensified in the long term (Brett, 1982). Likewise, while maternal employment was widely believed to exert negative effects on the mother herself, the marital relationship and any children, the extensive data collected over the past few decades suggest that such concerns are simply not justified (Hoffman, 1986, 1989).

The general point has already been made that our assumptions shape the issues we choose to investigate. Our assumptions may exert additional effects; specifically, they may even limit the results we eventually obtain by proscribing the questions we ask in the first instance. With respect to the presumed negative effects of work on the family, this tendency can be readily illustrated. For example, two national surveys in the United States have recently focused on the potential effects of maternal employment on the family (General Mills American Family Report, 1981; Lauer, 1985). Both of these surveys asked questions concerning possible *detrimental* effects of maternal employment on the family. Yet neither survey included any questions regarding any *beneficial* consequences that may accrue to the family from maternal employment.

ASSUMPTION 3: SEX BIASES IN THE LINK BETWEEN WORK AND FAMILY LIFE

In addition to adopting the assumption that work negatively affects family functioning, much of the literature further adopts a sex-biased view of the work/family relationship. A close examination of the literature reveals the following widely held assumptions. On the one hand, mothers who are employed are widely believed to exert detrimental effects on their children, their spouses and their own well-being. On the other hand, fathers who are employed are assumed to exert beneficial effects on their children, their spouses and their families. Fathers who are unemployed are presumed to exert negative effects, but mothers who are not employed are assumed to exert positive effects on their children, their marriages and themselves, because they are readily available to fulfil family and marital obligations. Thus, mothers who are employed exert negative effects, while fathers who are employed exert positive effects. In addition, Hall's (1972) argument about the way in which inter-role conflict is experienced differentially by mothers and fathers also implies a sex bias in the relationship between work and the family. Specifically, it is assumed that fathers do not have to concern themselves with their family roles and responsibilities while at work, yet mothers are not afforded the same luxury.

THE IMPORTANCE OF STUDYING WORK AND FAMILY FUNCTIONING

The Contribution of Work and Family to Psychological Well-Being

One major reason for examining the influence of work on the family is to assess whether there is any support for the previously mentioned assumptions. A second reason for analysing the interaction between work and family life is the critical role that each fulfils in general psychological well-being (Kahn, 1981). Freud himself considered both work and love as essential for mental health (cf. Aring, 1974), a notion that was accepted within early psychoanalytic theorizing (Lantos, 1943; Robbins, 1939). In other words, although the focus of this book is on work and family variables, both of these major roles occur in a wider context and wield broader implications for general psychological well-being. Indeed, as will become apparent throughout the text, there are numerous situations were an understanding of the interdependence between work and family functioning is enhanced through a consideration of global psychological well-being or its specific components such as depression (e.g. Barling, Tetrick and MacEwen, 1989).

More recently, research conducted at the Institute for Social Research at the University of Michigan has documented consistently that experiences related to work and the family constitute the two most powerful contributing factors toward individual well-being (Campbell, Converse and Rodgers, 1976; Kahn, 1981; Veroff, Douvan and Kulka, 1981). Further support for the role of work and family factors in psychological well-being can be deduced from the role family and work stressors fulfil in negative life experiences. For example, family, work and combined family/work stressors constitute substantial proportions of the chronic life stress items within Holmes and Rahe's (1967) *Social Readjustment Scale*, and Sarason, Johnson and Siegel's (1978) more recent *Life Experiences Survey*. Likewise, if we examine the 53 items of DeLongis, Folkman and Lazarus's (1988) revised *Daily Hassles Scale*, we could classify at least 23 of their items as assessing events occurring in these two domains.

The Need for an 'Open Systems' Approach to Understanding the Link Between Work and Family Life

As will become apparent, none of the three commonly held assumptions presented above is consistently supported by empirical data. It remains for any assumptions concerning the relationship between work and family to be subjected to strict scrutiny. Whether correct or not, these assumptions guide and direct current research and thinking on the work/family interface, and both personal and policy decisions depend to a large extent on these widespread beliefs. Thus, there is a need for an integrative review focusing specifically on this topic. In this book, an attempt will be made to evaluate critically the empirical research on the work/family relationship within an open systems framework (Katz and Kahn, 1978). Such a framework permits an evaluation of unidirectional and reciprocal relationships between work and family functioning, and includes other relevant variables outside of the domain of work and family, which impinge on the work/family relationship. An open systems perspective is widely accepted within both the organizational sphere (Katz and Kahn, 1978; Schein, 1980; Trist *et al.* 1963) and the family context (Bronfenbrenner and Crouter, 1982). Within such a framework, it is accepted that inputs or imbalances in any subsystem (e.g. job transfer or impending divorce) exert a ripple effect throughout the rest of the system (e.g. child behaviour problems or the quality or quantity of work performance). Stated differently, an open system perspective posits the interdependence of all subsystems. Therefore, a change in one system requires change in the others if homoeostasis is to be achieved. Another process that is critical in the adoption of an open systems perspective is the notion of 'throughputs' or 'transformations' which link the inputs into the system and outputs arising from the systems. In studying the link between work and family systems, a focus on throughputs or transformations facilitates an understanding of the factors that mediate the relationship between work and family. In other words, these throughputs constitute the mediating factors linking work and family that are so essential for a comprehensive understanding of why a relationship emerges between work and family.

There is one impediment to the adoption of an open systems framework. While implicitly acknowledging the utility and validity of an open systems perspective, psychologists and social scientists have constructed artificial boundaries around their own disciplines and sub-specialties, restricting their focus to one context (either work or family). There are numerous examples of this phenomenon, all of which exert a cumulative restrictive effect on the gathering of knowledge. Research focusing on the interaction between work and the family has been conducted primarily by clinical, developmental or family psychologists. Thus, while the resulting focus on the family is usually adequate, their analyses of the work environment and the employment experience remain limited (cf. Gutek *et al.*, 1981). For example, it is clear that some assumptions made by non-organizational psychologists regarding the state of knowledge within organizational psychology totally ignore the results of other research findings. For example, Heyns (1982, p. 259) maintained that '... job satisfaction influences the effectiveness of mothering and the activity of children... *Yet we do not know what aspects of a job lead to satisfaction*' (italics added). Yet job satisfaction is arguably the most widely researched aspect of organizational psychology: Locke (1983) estimates that more than 3350 empirical studies and conceptual chapters focusing on job satisfaction had been published by 1983, and there is a considerable body of research findings and knowledge specifically isolating variables that result in job satisfaction (Locke, 1983; Nord, 1977). Thus, there is an interesting contradiction here: we are told by non-organizational psychologists that we know little about the determinants of job satisfaction, even though this may be one area where organizational psychologists have contributed most. This reflects the negative consequences of the continued existence or maintenance of self-imposed barriers between various disciplines in psychology and the social sciences, and the resulting lack of information exchange between clinical, family and developmental psychology on the one hand, and industrial/organizational psychology on the other.

In addition, when the effects of maternal employment have been studied, the typical study has contrasted groups of employed and non-employed mothers (cf. Hoffman, 1986), even though the most appropriate psychological focus would be the quality of the employed mothers' work experiences (Barling, Fullagar and Marchl-Dingle, 1988; Barling and Van Bart, 1984; Hoffman, 1986). Likewise, most attempts to understand the effects of unemployment on family functioning have typically relied on between-group analyses, and accordingly have contrasted individuals who are employed with their counterparts who are unemployed. Yet, like the research that contrasts employed and non-employed mothers, this dichotomy focuses only on employment status (i.e. whether one has a job or not), and totally ignores the qualitative experience of employment or unemployment (e.g. Jahoda, 1982). Within this framework, it is assumed that *(a)* there is a marked similarity in terms of work experiences *within* employed individuals on the one hand, and unemployed (or non-employed) individuals on the other hand, and *(b)* considerable variation *between* the experiences of these groups. Recent research, focusing on the nature of employment see (Chapters 3–6), non-employment (Chapter 7) and unemployment (Chapter 9), suggests that this assumption is inappropriate. Given the inattention to the subjective nature of the employment or unemployment experience, the fact that the conceptualization of work-related experiences by non-organizational psychologists frequently reflects conceptual confusion should not be surprising. This tendency is illustrated when distinct phenomena such as job satisfaction and organizational commitment are equated (Riesch, 1981).

It must the noted that industrial/organizational psychologists are not immune from committing a similar error. They have been equally remiss in their neglect of the overlap between work and family factors. For example, while the quality of *work* life has understandably been well researched (e.g. Goodman, 1979; Lawler, Nadler and Cammann, 1980), the effects of work experiences on the quality of *family* life have not received the same attention (Zedeck, 1987). Likewise, the effects of family functioning on organizational performance have been neglected. The costs of such neglect can be gleaned from recent findings showing the effects of family factors (e.g. having a sick child) in work disruptions such as absenteeism. Second, projections regarding the future of work have generally failed to consider the interaction between work and the family (e.g. Dunnette, 1973). Third, on a more specific level, even the consideration of the effects of women's paid employment on their own general well-being has been restricted. Despite research suggesting the contribution of family functioning towards general psychological well-being (e.g. Campbell *et al.*, 1976; Veroff *et al.*, 1981), the interdependence between work and the quality of the marital relationship has been ignored in some major reviews of women's paid employment (e.g. Warr and Parry, 1982a).

Knowledge that could be gained from disciplines within psychology other than one's own specialty is missed all too frequently. Moreover, this trend towards increasing specialization (e.g. Kazdin, 1975) is continuing. For example, Meier (1987) took psychologists to task in this respect after examining the citation practices in a special issue of the *American Psychologist*. He showed that only 6% of the references in a special issue of that journal on a single topic represented a cross-fertilization of ideas in psychology. Similarly, Zedeck (1987) devoted his presidential address to the Division of Industrial and Organizational Psychology of the American Psychological Association to a plea for clinical and organizational psychologists to realize the extent to which they could learn from each other, and just how much our knowledge of our own areas could advance with a more intensive and extensive understanding of the theories, methodologies and findings of other specialties. As just one example, Zedeck (1987) cites the similarities between the processes underlying individual withdrawal from different systems, namely divorce within the family context and organizational turnover within the organizational framework.

Consequently, it is within an open system framework that the examination of work and the family will take place throughout this text. Within such a framework, it is accepted that the most comprehensive understanding of the interdependence between work and the family must come from an analysis of the divergent literatures available on this topic within various disciplines of psychology and the social sciences. In this sense, the contents of this text deliberately travel in the opposite direction to this trend towards specialization.

OUTLINE OF THE TEXT

Before sketching the contents of the ensuing chapters, some issues concerning the general orientation followed throughout this text are considered. First, the focus throughout this text is on the nuclear family. Although family theorists have focused on the extended family in some detail, the vast majority of research and theorizing on the link between work and the family has focused on the nuclear family. Second, while previous research and speculation on work and family has been based largely on a clinical or family perspective, the aim in this text is to redress this imbalance by explicitly including any relevant material from the realm of organizational psychology. Third, the orientation throughout this book is on an evaluation of the available *empirical* data. There is no shortage of speculative and anecdotal articles in magazines or books regarding the interdependence between work and the family (which should be apparent from the titles already listed throughout this chapter). Likewise, there are books which outline a research agenda (e.g. Kanter, 1977). However, the aim of the present book is to go beyond this *speculative* literature and examine the available *empirical* data on the relationship between work and the family.

Precisely because the term 'empirical' is beset with so many meanings, it is necessary to delineate the nature of the empirical research upon which the ensuing discussions will be based. While the term 'empirical' sometimes refers to data collected from experience or instructed observations, the meaning that is more common in the behavioural sciences will be followed. Specifically, the empirical data that will be subjected to investigation are of both a quantitative and a nomothetic nature.

In Chapter 2, a framework for understanding the process that links the family and employment systems is offered. In addition, conceptual and definitional aspects of both the employment and family systems relevant to this text are introduced. Chapters 3 and 4 focus on the relationship between marital functioning on the one hand, and objective and subjective work factors on the other. Because much of the available literature has focused separately on husbands and wives, the literature considered in these two chapters deals with the link between work and family for husbands. Chapters 5 and 6 deal with the relationship between the marital functioning of women, and objective and subjective work-related aspects respectively. The effects of parental employment on children will be dealt with in Chapters 7 and 8. Again, because the vast majority of research has segregated the effects of mothers' and fathers' employment on their children, the relationship between maternal employment and their children's behaviour will be considered in Chapter 7. Thereafter, the relationship between fathers' employment and child behaviour will be considered separately in Chapter 8. The issue of how parental unemployment (primarily fathers' unemployment) influences family functioning will be taken up in Chapter 9. Last, the three assumptions listed in this chapter will be re-evaluated in light of the empirical data presented in Chapters 3–9. Also, based on the preceding discussions, Chapter 10 will contain an agenda for further research and theorizing concerning work and the family, and will close with a consideration of social and treatment implications.

Chapter 2
Work, Employment and Family Functioning: Conceptual and Definitional Issues

Before delving into empirical research addressing the interface between work and family functioning, it is necessary first to define concepts underlying the research to be discussed in subsequent chapters. In addition, it is necessary to reiterate the open systems view of work and family functioning adopted throughout the book. This open systems perspective is necessary if one is to consider the possibility that work and family affect each other. It acknowledges that everyone functions in several contexts or systems, work and family being just two of them, and that events or experiences in one system affect experiences in any other system. Once it is accepted that experiences in one system affect those in another, it is necessary to devise a framework for understanding and predicting what effect experiences in one system will exert on adjacent systems. A general description of such a framework is presented below. Thereafter, the various subsystems inherent in the work and family systems will be outlined.

AN 'OPEN SYSTEMS' APPROACH TO UNDERSTANDING EMPLOYMENT AND FAMILY FUNCTIONING

In describing the overall framework within which to consider the interdependence of work and family (see Chapter 1), the need to adopt a general open systems perspective was emphasized. Within this framework it is accepted that events occurring within one system exert ripple effects on other systems. To understand this, three processes are important. These include inputs into the system (i.e. the initial events), how the system transforms these inputs or events (i.e. mediating processes), and subsequent outputs from the system (Katz and Kahn, 1978). This means that events occurring within the family may have an impact on work, and vice versa. For example, having a sick child at home (the initial event) may result in a mother's absence from work (the output). The factors that enable some mothers to attend work under such circumstances (e.g. availability of alternative child care) reflect the transformations or mediating factors. The two major systems studied in this book are work and family. Within each, there are several subsystems. For example, within the family, individuals can also be part of a marital subsystem, and if there are children, a parent/child subsystem. Likewise, within the organization,

12

individuals can be part of several subsystems simultaneously, such as peer/social groups, task oriented groups, and unions. Thus, all individuals are members of several systems and subsystems simultaneously. A comprehensive understanding of any single family member's behaviour can best be achieved with reference to the total context in which the behaviour is enacted. Given the continual interactive nature of these subsystems, the prediction of the intensity and duration of any event is critical. Thus, a framework for classifying, understanding and predicting the nature and effects of various events and/or stressors is offered.

CLASSIFYING EVENTS AND THEIR OUTCOMES: STRESSORS, STRESS AND STRAIN

Since the late 1970s and early 1980s, there has been a tremendous increase in interest in, and empirical research on, psychological stress (Pratt and Barling, 1988; Staw, 1984). However, despite the abundance of literature on stress, critical questions remain unanswered that are central to an understanding of the interdependence between work and the family. For example:

(1) Why does the duration of the consequences of different stressors vary so widely, ranging from same day only effects (DeLongis *et al.*, 1988), effects that endure for a few days or less (Barling, Bluen and Fain, 1987), to those that linger for five years or more (Davidson and Baum, 1986)?
(2) Do different types of stressors require different types, sources or levels of coping resources, such as social support?
(3) How do different stressors (e.g. daily and chronic) interact?

Such questions remain unanswered largely because there is no framework offering predictions about how any given event or stressor will effect a given individual. The framework adopted here is based on the idea that there are different categories of events or stressors which predict the duration of any effects and the effectiveness of individual coping.

Differentiating Between Stressor, Stress and Strain

Kahn *et al.* (1964) initially proposed a conceptual distinction between the terms stressor, stress and strain, that has been followed by some researchers, but ignored by most researchers (Pratt and Barling, 1988). Indeed, although vast numbers of people seem to suffer from daily (Warr and Payne, 1983a) or chronic (Kahn *et al.*, 1964) stressors, there is confusion as to what exactly stress is (Bailey and Bhagat, 1987). This confusion is described in numerous sources. For example, Ivancevich and Ganster (1987) suggest that if we were to ask 100 people what they understood by the term stress, we would probably get 100 different answers.

Any attempt to refine the concept of 'stress' must also consider the terms 'stressor' and 'strain', as there is considerable confusion in the way in which these terms are used. Within Kahn *et al.*'s (1964) widely cited framework, stressors are defined as objective environmental characteristics or events. These events are quantifiable and their occurrence can be verified objectively. Stress refers to the subjective interpretation or experience of stressors. The distinction between stressors and stress in crucial, because not all individuals who experience the same event interpret or perceive it in a similar manner. Finally, strain refers to the individual's affective, behavioural, or physiological response to their subjective experience of stressors. In other words, strain is the result of negatively perceived stressors or stress, and is the last stage in the total 'stress process' (see Figure 2.1). In following Kahn *et al.*'s (1964) framework, Eden (1982, p. 313) clearly describes stressors as '... events [that] are verifiable independently of the individual's consciousness and experience', stress as environmental properties '... as they are experienced by the person and represented in his consciousness' and strain as '... an individual's maladjustive psychological and physiological response to stress'.

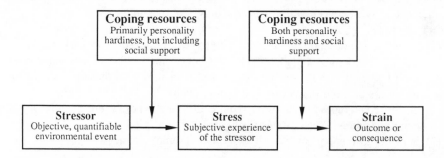

Figure 2.1   Framework for linking stressors, stress and strain

Differentiating Between Types of Psychological Stressors

Differentiating between various types of stressors is important, because different types of stressors may result in different outcomes (Keenan and Newton, 1985; Payne, Jick and Burke, 1982) may require different coping strategies (Payne *et al.*, 1982), and the duration of strain may depend on the nature of the initial stressor (Barling *et al.*, 1987; Pratt and Barling, 1988). Although Payne *et al.* (1982) pointed to the importance of distinguishing between types of stressors, they provided no guidelines for doing so, and the situation has not changed radically since then. For example, House (1987) and Beehr and Franz (1987) are still calling for a framework for differentiating between acute and chronic stressors. Moreover, Pratt and Barling (1988) conclude that few studies mention the specific nature of the stressor being investigated.

Three types of stressors are discussed in the literature: chronic, acute and daily stressors. It is suggested that these different stressors can be distinguished on the

basis of three orthogonal dimensions: the duration of the stressor, the specificity of
its time of onset and its likelihood of recurrence.

As shown in Table 2.1, chronic stressors last a long time, are highly repetitive,
and it is usually difficult to specify the exact time of their onset. Frequently cited
examples of chronic stressors include intra-role stressors (i.e. role conflict, role
ambiguity and role overload) and inter-role stressors (i.e. conflict between work
and family), job insecurity, noise on the shop floor, lack of control (e.g. on an
assembly line), or having a terminally ill child or spouse. Daily stressors have
a specific time of onset, are of short-term duration (by definition, they endure
no longer than a single day), and occur infrequently. Although daily events or
stressors may well recur in the future, they do not occur repeatedly day after day.
(If the same stressor did occur day after day, it would be classified as a chronic
stressor.) Examples of daily stressors include criticism for poor job performance or
tardiness, conflict with peers or supervisors, experiencing difficulties with a client
or friend, losing or misplacing things at work or at home, or an argument with one's
spouse or children. Acute stressors also have a specific time of onset, and are of
short-term duration (but could endure longer than a day). Unlike daily stressors,
however, acute stressors occur extremely infrequently and have a low likelihood of
recurrence. Examples of acute stressors that have been studied include involvement
in a short-term strike, a shooting in the case of police officers, getting fired or laid
off, a job change, or workplace disaster. The death of a close relative would also
constitute an acute stressor.

Table 2.1 Differentiating between daily, acute and chronic stressors

Type of stressor	Duration of stressor	Specific time onset of stressor	Likelihood of recurrence of stressor
Daily stressor	Short term	Yes	High
Acute stressor	Short term	Yes	Low
Chronic stressor	Long term	No	High

Two issues arise out of this proposed framework. First, there are no definitive
guidelines separating each of the orthogonal dimensions. For example, although
a daily event can endure no longer than a single day, there is some ambiguity
surrounding the temporal limits separating an acute from a chronic stressor. For
example, the *DSM-III-R* (1987) defines an acute stressor as any event enduring
for six months or less, yet there are suggestions that acute stressors have a far
shorter duration than this (see Pratt and Barling, 1988). However, none of the three
orthogonal dimensions offered in this framework is meant to define any event
or stressor in isolation. Rather, it is only through a simultaneous consideration
of the three dimensions that the different stressors will be classified appropriately.
Second, the same event can serve as a different type of stressor in different contexts.
Two examples of this will suffice. For some individuals, inter-role conflict might

constitute a chronic stressor. For others, inter-role conflict might not be present on an enduring, long-term basis. Rather, as different issues emerge (e.g. sickness of a child), inter-role conflict could manifest as a *daily* stressor (e.g. Alpert and Culbertson, 1987). Second, for some individuals, commuting to and from their workplace is clearly a chronic stressor that must be confronted each and every day on a continuous basis. For others, however, commuting may pose a problem that is encountered infrequently.

Now that a framework for distinguishing between types of stressors has been presented, the usefulness of the framework in addressing the questions posed at the beginning of this chapter will be discussed.

THE EFFECT OF STRESSOR TYPE ON THE DURATION AND NATURE OF STRAIN

Campbell, Daft and Hulin (1982) maintain that guidelines for choosing temporal lags between causally related variables remain one of the most frequently neglected topics in research on organizational psychology. Their observation applies equally to most other areas of the social and behavioural sciences (e.g. Gollob and Reichardt, 1987). When a distinction is made between the three kinds of stressors, the choice of the temporal lag between the stressor and strain becomes clearer.

The independent research programmes of Stone and Neale at New York State and Lazarus and Folkman in California provide a clear indication of the timing and duration of the consequences of daily stressors. In a series of studies investigating the relationship between daily stressors and mood, same-day effects on mood emerge (e.g. Caspi, Bolger and Eckenrode, 1987; DeLongis *et al*., 1988; Eckenrode, 1984; Jandorf *et al*., 1986; Stone, 1987). Caspi *et al*. (1987, p. 184) note that 'Some days, everything seems to go wrong, and by day's end, minor difficulties find their outlet in rotten moods'. However, two exceptions to this pattern should be noted. Stone, Reed and Neale (1987) have shown that when the outcome or strain is physical symptoms rather than mood, same-day effects do not emerge. Rather, their longitudinal data showed that daily stressors increased *three days* prior to the onset of the physical symptoms (e.g. upper respiratory tract infections). Stone *et al*. (1987) suggest that the process operative here can still be interpreted as one in which daily stressors exert an immediate effect. Specifically, the lagged relationship between daily stressors and symptoms emerges because there is an immediate effect on the secretory immune system in general, and more specifically on secretory IgA. It then takes some time (three days) for this immune dysfunction to translate into an upper respiratory tract infection. Second, in terms of the duration of the strain, most of the effects of daily stress dissipate on the same day. Occasionally, however, mood effects carry over to the following day (e.g. Caspi *et al*., 1987).

Two recent studies provide examples of the duration of psychological strain following a chronic stressor, in this case unemployment. First, Dew, Bromet and Schulberg (1987) showed that levels of psychological distress remained elevated for a period of three years following unemployment. Again, from the area of unemployment, Fryer and Warr (1984) have shown that cognitive difficulties, an indicator of strain in their study, are positively associated with the length of unemployment. Consequently, knowing the nature of a stressor not only enables the prediction of how and when the strain will occur, but also how long it will last.

If we examine studies that focus on acute stressors, a different pattern emerges regarding the duration of strain. Loo (1986) retrospectively investigated the responses of 56 RCMP officers in Canada who had been involved in a shooting incident in the previous 20 years. A shooting represents an acute stressor for this group: it is of short-term duration and has a specific time onset, but unlike a daily stressor, it is of extremely low frequency and has a low likelihood of recurrence. Loo's (1986) interviews with these officers revealed that the effect of the acute stressor was evident immediately, and most of the strain associated with the stressor had dissipated within a week of the event.

A second study focusing on an acute stressor was conducted by Barling *et al.* (1987), who investigated the effects of a fatal explosion at the world's largest dynamite factory in which 14 people were killed. The subjects in that study were tested within two weeks of the disaster. There were no significant differences in either personal functioning (marital satisfaction and psychological distress) or organizational functioning (organizational commitment and job satisfaction) between workers physically exposed to the blast and workers in either of the two quasi-experimental control groups (those performing a different job function at the same plant, and those performing the same function at a different plant). This pattern was replicated two months following the blast. Consistent with Loo's (1986) study, Barling *et al.* (1987) found no evidence of any negative effects of the acute work stressor two weeks following the disaster.

In some situations, acute stressors may exert long-term effects. Three employment-related examples can be cited. First, the accident at Three Mile Island (TMI) in March 1979 was an acute stressor. The actual nuclear incident lasted only a short while, had a very specific time of onset, and is unlikely to occur frequently. However, as Baum *et al.* have noted, a 'low point' has not yet been reached at TMI. In other words, concern persists that the possible effects of the incident are not yet over. As a result, negative behavioural, physiological and biochemical consequences still linger five or more years later (e.g. Davidson and Baum, 1986). Second, involvement in a short-term strike (i.e. three weeks) by community college teachers represented an acute stressor (Barling and Milligan, 1987). However, in that study negative psychological functioning (but not marital functioning) was still evident six months after the end of the strike, which is *not* typical of an acute stressor. What transpired was that the teachers were legislated back to work without a new contract, and the initial conflict endured for months. Third, most workers facing a potential strike do not believe it will last a long time, and do not make any financial plans to cope with a dramatic drop in family income (Gennard, 1981). When strikes do last a long time, therefore, chronic financial stress results. Thus, the guiding principle is that the duration of the strain will endure as long as the *stress* itself (Pratt and Barling, 1988). In other words, the duration will endure as long as there is any concern that the effects of the stressor are still present, or that a recurrence of the stressor is possible. Of course, the timing and severity of the strain will also depend on the effectiveness of different coping strategies the individual may choose to mobilize and utilize.

ARE DIFFERENT COPING STRATEGIES REQUIRED FOR DIFFERENT STRESSORS?

Another reason for differentiating between different types of stressors is that coping effectiveness may depend on the nature of the stressor (Pratt and Barling, 1988). An examination of two types of coping resources that are frequently studied as buffers against the negative effects of stressors, namely personality hardiness and social support, will illustrate this issue.

Hardiness is a personality construct comprised of three dimensions: namely, a sense of commitment to something (rather than alienation); perceiving events as challenges (rather than threats); and experiencing a sense of control over events in one's life (rather than a lack of control) (Kobasa, 1982). As a personality resource, hardiness is stable and always available to the individual. Both daily and acute stressors have a sudden onset, and occur infrequently and irregularly. As a result, when they do occur, they demand immediate coping. Because personality hardiness is a resource that is stable over time, it is immediately available to aid in coping with the sudden impact of a daily of acute stressor. Social support, on the other hand, operates differently. As a social resource external to the individual, it takes time to seek, receive and then utilize social support (Dunkel-Schetter, Folkman and Lazarus, 1987). Hence, social support may only be effective in situations where chronic (rather than daily or acute) stressors are encountered. Unlike acute or daily stressors, where immediate coping is demanded, individuals exposed to chronic stress have sufficient time to elicit support.

There is some foundation in the literature for these propositions. In two separate studies of acute stressors, the receipt of social support was not associated with enhanced psychological functioning, although personality resources were (Hobfoll and London, 1986; Hobfoll and Walfisch, 1984). Caspi *et al.* (1987) found that social support did not moderate the effect of stressors and social support on same-day mood, but there was a significant interaction between same-day stressors and social support on the following day's mood, Caspi *et al.* (1987) suggest that the one day lagged effect represents the time taken to mobilize and utilize available social supports. Alternatively, support may be mobilized immediately, but only utilized at a later stage. In either event, the guiding principle is that the process of seeking, mobilizing and utilizing social support is time consuming. Hence, social support is useful only when individuals confront chronic stressors. Unlike social support, personality resources may be effective in moderating the effects of chronic, acute and daily stressors.

INTERACTIONS BETWEEN DIFFERENT TYPES OF STRESSORS

It is unclear whether and how different types of stressors interact. For example, the relationship between daily stressors and mood may be different for individuals currently experiencing chronic stressors than for those not experiencing chronic stress. Caspi *et al*. (1987) showed that chronic stressors, namely ongoing concerns about neighbourhood quality (what they referred to as chronic ecological stress) and major life events both moderated the relationship between daily stressors and same-day mood. However, their effects on the daily stressor/mood relationship were different. Chronic ecological stress aggravated this relationship, but the effect of daily stressors on mood was reduced in the presence of chronic life stressors.

The interaction of different stressors is of some importance in considering the link between work and family. Daily life is such that many individuals experience more than one type of stressor simultaneously, very likely from different sources or domains. Moreover, consistent with an open systems perspective, these simultaneous stressors are probably interdependent. For example, perceived financial strain following from job loss probably exacerbates the effects of objective income loss following job loss. Likewise, going through a divorce might decrease both spouses' social network size and the frequency and intensity of arguments, which then exert interactive effects on the individual concerned. On a daily basis, commuting problems to or from work could cause scheduling problems, and result in conflict with one's boss or spouse. Hence, it is important to investigate the nature and effects of simultaneously occurring stressors.

CLARIFYING THE TERM 'WORK'

The *Oxford English Dictionary* lists 39 different meanings for the word 'work' (Jahoda, 1982), and *Webster's New Collegiate Dictionary* (1977) offers eleven major meanings of the term 'work'. In both cases, only one of the meanings offered conveys the popular usage of the term 'work': namely, performing a task or holding a job *for financial gain*. In almost all other cases, the primary meaning conveyed is that of concerted individual or group effort or action towards a particular goal, or the outcome of such action. Yet when work or work stressors are considered in the literature, the term 'work' is used to denote *the performance of a task for financial gain*. However, work does not necessarily imply task performance for financial gain. A more accurate term for such activity is employment. Because it is important to distinguish between tasks performed for financial gain and those enacted without any chance of financial reward, the terms employment, unemployment and non-employment will be introduced now and used subsequently. Ignoring the distinction between employment, unemployment and non-employment would be of no consequence if there were no conceptual and research implications associated with the distinction. However, there are critical distinctions and implications, and these terms will now be differentiated.

When speaking of employment, there is an implicit assumption that employment is dichotomous: people are either employed or unemployed. However, such a dichotomy does not do justice to the complexities and the differing experiences associated with each of these terms. Employment refers to the performance of a task for which there is a financial reward. Unemployment implies the loss of employment, and the current absence of financial reward for tasks performed. In contrast to unemployment, non-employment does not imply the loss of employment. Instead, non-employment refers to the absence of financial reward for work currently performed. Thus, it should be emphasized that virtually everyone works, whether or not they are employed. For example, becoming unemployed typically does not mean being 'out of work'. On the contrary, being unemployed means confronting new kinds of work in the home and with children, and losing much of this work on regaining employment (Shamir, 1986a). Furthermore, homemakers perform work in the home, yet are classified as non-employed because they receive no financial compensation for their work. As such, the description of unemployed or non-employed individuals as being 'out of work' is inaccurate and an insult to the quantity of work and associated responsibility that many non-employed people shoulder.

EMPLOYMENT AND EMPLOYMENT STRESSORS

Even though most people experience some level of job stress, confusion still exists about the definition of job stress. For example, the data from Kahn *et al.*'s (1964) classic study showed that at least one-third of the employees in their American sample experienced occupational stress at any one point in time. More recently, Warr and Payne (1983a) found that 15% of men and 10% of women employed full-time in Britain reported experiencing some job-related strain strain the previous day. However, we would be implying an overly pessimistic and unnecessarily narrow perspective of the experience of employment if we focused solely on the stressful nature of employment. There are data suggesting that certain job characteristics are positively associated with psychological well-being (e.g. Broadbent, 1985). Accordingly, it is important to discuss those job characteristics that are associated with psychological well-being, in addition to those associated with negative effects of employment.

Several models specifying various job characteristics have been posited, and three will be discussed here: Hackman and Oldham's (1980) job characteristics model; the recent suggestions of Warr concerning principal job features that are central to mental health (Warr, 1987a, b); and the manifest and latent functions of employment identified by Jahoda (1982). The purpose, however, is not to evaluate the relative validity of each of these models. Rather, the central purpose is to describe characteristics or features of jobs which are important in understanding the link between employment and family functioning.

Hackman and Oldham (1980) suggested that if three critical psychological states are fulfilled by a job, internal motivation and satisfaction will result. These three critical psychological states are feelings of personal responsibility, experienced meaningfulness and a knowledge of the results of one's job performance. Hackman and Oldham (1980) further specified five 'core job dimensions' that, if implemented, ensure fulfilment of the three psychological states. Feedback from the job itself, and from supervisors and peers leads to a knowledge of the results of one's work. Providing autonomy both to schedule work and decide on the procedures to optimize task performance heightens responsibility. Experiencing meaning on the job is enhanced if there is sufficient skill variety, task identity and task significance. When these three critical psychological states are present, mental health is enhanced (Broadbent, 1985; Warr, 1987b).

Warr (1987a, b) suggests that there are nine principal job features, all of which are associated with job-related and general mental health. Because Warr's framework is based on the job characteristics model to some extent (Warr, 1987a, p. 256), there is some overlap between these two models. Warr's features of the 'opportunity for skill use' and 'variety' correspond with Hackman and Oldham's 'skill variety', while 'environmental clarity' parallels 'feedback'. Likewise, 'opportunity for control' in Warr's model is consistent with 'autonomy' in Hackman and Oldham's model. More important here are the four unique features of employment identified by Warr (1987a, b) which are of special importance to an understanding of the interdependence of employment and family. These four characteristics focus on *extrinsic* job features, whereas Hackman and Oldham focused only on *intrinsic* characteristics. Intrinsic job characteristics describe involvement in, and completion of, the job itself. Examples include the opportunity for meaningful work, autonomy, participation in decision making and the chance for extensive skill utilization. In contrast, extrinsic job characteristics refer to features of employment other than the task or the job itself. Pay level and pay equity, supervision, the possibility for promotion, social interactions with peers and company policy are all examples of extrinsic job characteristics.

In one extrinsic job feature, the 'availability of money', Warr (1987b) includes not just the objective amount of money available, but also perceived pay inadequacy and perceived pay inequity. Indeed, Warr (1987b) suggests that perceived pay inadequacy and perceived pay inequity provide a better prediction of mental health than either the amount of money available, or satisfaction with pay (see Chapters 3, 4 and 9). The second extrinsic feature emphasized by Warr but omitted by Hackman and Oldham is the physical security inherent in the job, which embraces the right not only to be protected from any physical threat but also to be provided with a safe working environment.

A third extrinsic job feature that contributes to mental health is the opportunity for social contact provided by employment (Warr, 1987a, b). Only positive social contacts enhance mental health. Jahoda (1982) suggests that social contacts available through employment are different from those offered by the family. Family contacts and relationships are more emotional in nature, while job-related social contacts provide more informational support. The fourth extrinsic job feature relevant to the link between employment and the family is Warr's (1987a, b) notion of a valued social position. Employment can offer a sense of esteem, because varying levels of social status are associated with different jobs, and self-esteem is positively associated with the quality of job performance (Jans, 1982). Similarly, Jahoda (1982) suggests that employment provides a valuable source of information on which to base judgements of personal worth and identity. This is relevant to the effects of employment on the family, because mothers' self-esteem is associated with psychological maltreatment of children (Garbarino, Guttman and Seeley, 1986).

One dimension that Warr (1987a, b) discusses in a very different manner from Jahoda (1982) concerns temporal aspects of employment. Warr (1987a, b) states that holding a full-time job consumes about 35 to 40 hours per week, and that the amount and distribution (e.g. shift work) of this time is negatively associated with mental heath. Jahoda (1982) views the temporal aspects of employment differently. She proposes that employment offers individuals the opportunity for structuring their days, noting that greater temporal structure is associated positively with mental health. Thus, in contrast to Warr, Jahoda proposes that the temporal structure afforded by regular employment is associated with mental health. As will become apparent throughout this text, there is research focusing on both these issues.

Fitting intrinsic and extrinsic job characteristics into the framework outlined earlier permits better predictions of the timing and duration of their effects, and provides an indication of how individuals might best cope with these job characteristics. Intrinsic and extrinsic job characteristics can typically be accommodated within a chronic model. This is because these job characteristics are far more likely to be of an enduring nature, that is, relatively stable. If present, intrinsic job characteristics such as autonomy and responsibility will probably persist over time. Likewise, extrinsic job characteristics such as financial resources or physical security are also likely to be present on a stable basis. However, as the research of Lang and Markowitz (1986) makes clear, there are particular situations in which employment experiences typically considered to be of a chronic nature (e.g. role overload) can exist on a more episodic basis. As a result, it remains important to delineate those situations in which job features or characteristics depart from an enduring, stable state. This would allow for a more precise prediction of the timing and duration of any outcome, and for understanding how individuals cope with unfavourable job characteristics. In this sense, such a delineation would enable a more specific understanding of the link between employment and the family.

As already stated, if we are to achieve an understanding of the interdependence of employment and family functioning, we must first describe these two systems.

The aim now is to provide the basis for an understanding of what exactly is meant by family functioning.

FAMILY FUNCTIONING

An open systems perspective is critical for an appreciation of how employment affects family functioning, and vice versa. An open systems perspective is also useful in accounting for interactions between subsystems within the family, and between the family and other systems.

The nuclear family is made up of different individuals. In broad terms, there is one adult and his or her spouse, and their child(ren). It is the link between these individuals that makes up the different subsystems. For example, the relationship between the two adults comprises the marital subsystem, while that between either parent and a child comprises the parent/child subsystem. These two subsystems will be described, and their relevance to a consideration of the interdependence of employment and the family outlined.

Bidirectional effects are not only possible within the family, they are inevitable. It is not only parents who influence children's behaviour; children also exert an effect on their parents individually, or on the marital relationship (Emery *et al.*, 1983). A related point is that not only are the subsystems within the family interdependent, but the family system interacts with other macro-systems, and itself is part of the extended family. Second, even though the prevailing assumption is that employment exerts negative effects on the family, it is critical to go beyond an examination of any negative consequences for the family, and explicitly examine benefits of employment for family functioning.

Marital Functioning

As will become apparent in Chapters 3–6 and Chapter 9, the range of marital activities that have been studied empirically is extremely wide. In searching for a way of categorizing these marital activities, at least two options are available. They could be categorized strictly in terms of whether they are behavioural (e.g. verbal or physical aggression, frequency of sexual contact, marital role performance), affective (e.g. feelings towards one's spouse, relationship satisfaction) or cognitive (e.g. commitment to the marriage). An alternative approach emphasizes marital quality, that is the positive or negative nature of the marital activity. The first approach is adopted for several reasons. First, findings presented in the marital literature show that these three components exert different effects on global marital satisfaction (e.g. Broderick and O'Leary, 1986). Second, this categorization is consistent with the way in which marital activities have been conceptualized in research on employment and marriage. Although this framework has not been adopted explicitly, the possible effects of different job characteristics and employment experiences on marital behaviours, cognitions and affect have been studied. Third, despite the fact that Johnson *et al.*'s (1986) data suggest the adoption of a two-dimensional approach to marital quality, the discussion throughout this text will not be limited to their two dimensions (viz. a positive and negative dimension of marital quality). They excluded some important marital variables from their analysis (e.g. they did not focus on communications, sexual satisfaction or psychological and physical aggression), and their dimensions may reflect a continuum ranging from poor to high quality marital relationships.

Divorce is frequently viewed as the ultimate indication of poor marital functioning. However, divorce is an inadequate indicator of marital functioning. All marital behaviours have multiple determinants, but other unique factors affect the likelihood of obtaining a divorce. Some individuals may choose to remain married because of religious proscriptions against divorce even though their marital relationship may be characterized by considerable dissatisfaction. Likewise, there are legislative differences specifying the amount of time individuals are required to be separated before divorce is a legal option. Two interesting consequences relevant to an understanding of employment and family emerge from legislative and religious proscriptions on divorce. Given that there are factors outside of the employment and family systems that determine the likelihood of obtaining a divorce, employment (or unemployment) characteristics or experiences must be expected to account for less of the variance in divorce than they might in other marital activities. A further reason for exercising caution in interpreting divorce as an outcome of employment factors is that values regarding divorce may be more important than marital dissatisfaction in predicting who will ultimately divorce.

In considering the utility of divorce as a criterion of marital functioning, it is important to differentiate between divorce and marital instability. Divorce has numerous determinants outside of the marriage and represents the objective end point of a process. Marital instability reflects both a cognitive component (e.g. considering whether the marriage is in trouble or thinking about a separation) and a behavioural component (e.g. whether the individual has spoken to anyone about a divorce or taken any steps to dissolve the marriage).

One further clarification regarding marital functioning is necessary. The term marital *quality* is often taken to be synonymous with others such as marital satisfaction, adjustment and happiness. Spanier and Lewis published two seminal reviews of the marital quality literature (Lewis and Spanier, 1979; Spanier and Lewis, 1980). According to them, marital quality represents 'the subjective evaluation of a married couple's relationship on a number of dimensions and evaluations' (Lewis and Spanier, 1979, p. 269). Spanier and Lewis (1980, p. 826) elaborate further, stating that marital quality:

... reflects numerous characteristics of marital interaction and marital functioning. High marital quality, therefore, is associated with good adjustment, adequate communication, a high level of marital happiness, integration, and a high degree of satisfaction with the relationship. The definition does not convey a fixed picture of discrete categories, i.e. a high versus low-quality marriage, but rather suggests the existence of a continuum ranging from high to low.

Redundancy between terms such as satisfaction, happiness, adjustment and quality pervades the marital literature. Different writers may use different terms (e.g. satisfaction and adjustment) to reflect the same concept, or use inaccurate terms to describe the concept under study. A brief and non-random examination of some recent empirical articles shows that, at best, adjectives describing the quality of the marital relationship are used interchangeably, and at worst they are used in a manner implying there are no conceptual differences between them (see Table 2.2). Accordingly, the term 'marital quality' will be avoided in this text. In its place, marital functioning and family functioning will be used as generic terms to describe the subjective evaluation of specific aspects of the marriage (e.g. behavioural, affective and cognitive components) and family.

Parent–Child Interactions

Consistent with an open systems perspective, parent–child interactions could be conceptualized in a number of different ways. Specifically, these interactions could be viewed as resulting from job-related experiences, a mediating factor between job experiences and children's behaviour, an influence on the experience of employment, or the result of children's behaviour. The literature on employment and the family has focused primarily on the first two functions of parent–child interactions.

Parental Experiences and Children's Behaviour

The notion that a link exists between parental experiences such as marital discord and child behaviour problems has long been acknowledged, and adherents to psychodynamic, family systems and behavioural approaches to therapy all accept the existence of this link (O'Leary, 1984). There is a considerable body of empirical data showing a relationship between marital conflict and child behaviour problems in general. A number of issues concerning this link should be highlighted. First, the relationship between marital discord and child behaviour problems emerges in clinic-referred (whether for child behaviour problems or marital discord) and community samples. Second, with the exception of very young children (Jouriles, Pfiffner and O'Leary, 1988), marital discord is typically associated with conduct problems or externalizing behaviours for boys, and withdrawal for girls. Marital conflict is even associated with conduct problems in toddlers as young as 18 months (Jouriles *et al.*, 1988). There is a need to understand the coping mechanisms and resources available within the family system that prevent parental stressors from affecting children negatively, or that determine why boys and girls react differently to the same stressor. Last, most research and theorizing on the link between marital discord and child behaviour problems assumes that marital discord causes child behaviour problems, although there is little empirical research focusing on causality in this relationship. There are valid reasons for assuming that in some

Table 2.2   Correspondence between aspects of marital quality studied[1]

Author(s)	Aspect of marital functioning *purportedly* measured	Aspect of marital functioning *actually* measured
Barling (1984)	Marital satisfaction	Marital adjustment
Barling (1986a)	Marital functioning	Marital adjustment
Barling and Rosenbaum (1986)	Marital aggression[2]	Marital aggression
Bell, Daly and Gonzalez (1987)	Marital quality/ Marital satisfaction	Marital adjustment
Broderick and O'Leary (1986)	Marital satisfaction	Marital adjustment
Callan (1987)	Marital quality/ Marital adjustment	Marital adjustment
Emery and O'Leary (1982)	Marital discord	Marital adjustment and overt hostility
Hooley *et al.* (1987)	Marital distress	Marital adjustment
Houseknecht and Macke (1981)	Marital adjustment	Marital adjustment
Kalin and Lloyd (1985)	Marital adjustment	Marital adjustment
Lockhart (1987)	Marital aggression	Marital aggression
MacEwen and Barling (1988a)	Marital adjustment	Marital adjustment
Martin *et al.* (1987)	Marital aggression	Marital aggression
Peyrot, McMurray and Hedges (1988)	Marital satisfaction	Marital satisfaction
Prinz *et al.* (1983)	Marital disturbance	Marital adjustment Overt hostility Aggression
Schumm and Bugaighis (1986)	Marital quality	Marital satisfaction
Snowden *et al.* (1988)	Marital satisfaction	Marital adjustment
Steinberg and Silverberg (1987)	Marital satisfaction	Marital satisfaction
Suchet and Barling (1986)	Marital functioning	Marital adjustment Communication
Thomas, Albrecht and White (1984)	Marital quality	Intimacy in the relationship
Weller and Rofe (1988)	Marital happiness	Marital satisfaction and tension

[1] Decisions regarding the nature of the marital variable purportedly measured were made on the basis of the description in the title of the article or the abstract.

[2] Different adjectives are typically used in the literature to describe inter-partner violence (e.g. spouse abuse, marital violence, marital aggression). We will use the term 'marital aggression' throughout this table, which is consistent with the fact that the same questionnaire is typically used in all these studies, namely Straus's (1979) *Conflict Tactics Scale*.

cases, children's behaviour problems strain the marital relationship (Emery *et al.*, 1983).

In the same way that research findings document a significant link between marital discord and child behaviour problems, there is also empirical support for a link between maternal depression and children's functioning. Two points warrant attention. First, there are data showing that depressed mothers manifest significantly less positive interactions with their infants (aged 3–6 months) than do non-depressed mothers (Field *et al.*, 1988). Second, this tendency generalized beyond the mother–child dyad, because infants of depressed mothers also interacted more poorly with strangers than did infants of non-depressed mothers.

Consistent with assumptions (1) that it is primarily employment experiences that affect family functioning, and (2) that this effect is primarily negative, it is not surprising that most research investigating the effects of parental employment experiences has conceptualized child problem behaviours as outcomes. Nonetheless, child behaviour problems may fulfil other functions in the family systems. First, it is equally plausible that children's positive social behaviours are causally associated with parental employment experiences. Second, there are data showing that children's behaviour also affects their parents' experiences (e.g. Emery *et al.*, 1983). Thus, diverse children's behaviours will be investigated both as direct outcomes of their parents' employment, as consequences of parent–child interactions, as well as possible predictors of their parents' employment experiences.

GOING BEYOND THE FAMILY AND EMPLOYMENT SYSTEMS

Consistent with the central principle of an open systems perspective, namely that adjacent systems impinge on one another, it must be assumed that systems outside of the family and employment systems also influence the relationship between these two systems. This means that any discussion of the interdependence of employment and the family that only considers these two systems must be incomplete. For example, recent research suggests consistently that negative affect or depression is associated with marital discord (Beach and O'Leary, 1986) and child behaviour problems (Field *et al.*, 1988), and predisposes individuals to perceive work events as stressful (Brief *et al.* 1988; Watson, Pennebaker and Folger, 1987). Consequently, in trying to understand the interdependence of employment and the family, it would be appropriate to examine the effects of personal factors such as depression on family functioning and employment experiences. As a result, whenever there are relevant data available, factors occurring outside of the employment and family systems will be considered throughout this text if they influence either the family or employment, and hence the relationship between employment and the family.

CONCLUSION

In this chapter, conceptual and definitional issues relevant to the link between employment and the family were outlined. The terms stressor, stress and strain were disentangled, daily, acute and chronic stressors were defined, work was distinguished from employment, and employment, non-employment and unemployment were differentiated. Because an exclusive focus on employment stressors would portray an inaccurate picture of the range of employment experiences, the benefits of focusing on intrinsic and extrinsic job characteristics in understanding how employment interacts with family functioning were discussed. The need to focus on the various systems within the family and to accept a multidimensional approach to understanding family functioning that takes account of both positive and negative behaviours, was highlighted. Lastly, the importance of going beyond an examination of the employment and family systems to understand their interaction was emphasized.

Chapter 3

Objective Employment Characteristics and Marital Functioning

The following two chapters will focus on the influence of objective and subjective employment characteristics on marital functioning. Two major concerns have motivated research on the relationship between objective employment characteristics and marital functioning. The first of these is whether the amount and/or scheduling of time devoted to employment negatively affects marital functioning. The second concern centres around the issue of whether job-related mobility has negative effects on the marriage and the family. Two points are worth noting: temporal aspects of employment have received far more empirical attention than have the possible effects of job-related mobility; also, there has been more research on objective rather than subjective employment characteristics.

TEMPORAL EMPLOYMENT CHARACTERISTICS AND MARITAL FUNCTIONING

Of all the assumptions regarding the relationship between employment and marital functioning, perhaps none has been as pervasive as that concerning the effects on marital functioning of the amount and scheduling of time spent in employment. Briefly stated, it is assumed that the more time spent on the job, the greater the negative effect on marital functioning. The first section of this chapter will examine the data that address the effects of temporal characteristics of employment on marital functioning.

The *amount* of time spent at work is not the only temporal dimension of importance. Two other temporal characteristics that may be important in influencing marital functioning are *when* work is completed, that is, the shift schedule that the individual works, and the flexibility in scheduling the work. Two basic work schedules exist: one involving the scheduling of which *days* are worked each week; the other involving the scheduling of the *hours* worked each day. The second dimension along which time at work can vary is its flexibility. Flexibility is reflected in one of two ways: first, whether individuals have the right to vary their arrival and departure at work; and second, the extent to which they perceive that they have some control over the amount and scheduling of their job time.

What follows is a review of the empirical data focusing on the relationship between these three temporal characteristics of employment (the amount of time, its scheduling and flexibility) and marital functioning. First, it should be noted that this discussion is based predominantly on the effects of husbands' employment time on marital functioning. As will become apparent in Chapter 5, there are different expectations regarding the effects of husbands' versus wives' employment time on family functioning. Theoretical explanations concerning the relationship between employment time and marital functioning are gender specific. Nonetheless, the separate discussion of the possible effects of husbands' and wives' employment time on marital functioning is not meant to imply or foster any sexist bias in the way in which husbands' and wives' employment is considered. It simply reflects the different literatures that have developed for men and women.

EMPLOYMENT TIME AND MARITAL FUNCTIONING

There has been a consistent trend, during the course of the twentieth century, for the number of hours devoted to employment by men each week to decrease. The reasons for this are varied, ranging from concerns regarding workers' health, changes in the composition of the labour force and the effects of unions. Also, there is now considerable variation in the number of hours spent on the job, such that the '40-hour workweek' is probably more mythical than factual. For example, Voydanoff (1987) estimates that in 1979, American non-agricultural workers spent an average of 38.5 hours on the job each week (down from 58.4 in 1901, 40.9 in 1948 and 39.1 in 1968). In contrast, Bartolome (1983) estimates that the 'average' individual spends approximately 45 hours per week at the office, and an additional 10 hours in the pursuit of job-related commuting. Reasons for individual variations in the number of hours devoted to the job each week include so-called 'workaholism' (Machlowitz, 1980), the work involvement of the Type A behaviour individual (e.g. Friedman and Rosenman, 1974) or the hypothesized obsessive compulsive nature of the job-involved individual (Schwartz, 1982). The conventional wisdom here is that time devoted to the job is negatively related to marital functioning, because it detracts from the time available for one's spouse and family. Another possible basis for this relation is that people who are dissatisfied at home seek additional gratification at work. This has been referred to as the 'compensation hypothesis' (Zedeck, 1987) and will be considered in more detail in Chapter 4.

The logic underlying the presumed relationship between the amount of time spent on the job and marital functioning is as follows. It is assumed that occupational success demands considerable personal investment, which requires an additional time commitment over and above that normally expected for fulfilment of job demands. This detracts from time available to spend with one's spouse. Husband availability is assumed to be directly and negatively related to the amount of time devoted to employment, and availability is held to be either a sufficient factor by itself, or a necessary but insufficient factor, for positive marital functioning. This 'availability hypothesis' equates the number of hours the employed husband has available for the family and the marriage after job-related time has been excluded with marital and family functioning.

There are other employment-related characteristics that will detract from the total amount of time an individual has available for the marriage. These include commuting time, periodic short-term business trips that require time away from the family, and more regular, prolonged periods away from the family (i.e. a couple of months). Each of these three cases will be discussed in terms of whether they influence marital role performance, interfere with employment and family roles or with subjective marital satisfaction. Consideration of these three facets of marital functioning follow from suggestions that the amount of time devoted to the job and the scheduling of that time may influence these aspects of marital functioning differently (e.g. Staines, 1986; Staines and Pleck, 1984).

Marital Role Performance

Marital role performance consists of those formal and informal activities that are necessary to ensure that marital responsibilities are fulfilled, and include spouse support, child care and household responsibilities. The hypothesis is that the more hours spent on the job, the less time available for the performance of one's various marital roles (e.g. spouse support, household and financial chores). Using the data derived from the 1977 Quality of Employment Survey, Staines and Pleck (1984) showed that there was indeed a significant negative relationship between the total number of hours spent at work and the amount of time devoted to household responsibilities.

Clark, Nye and Gecas (1978) extended the notion of marital role performance. They questioned whether extensive 'work involvement' (i.e. the amount of hours devoted to work per week, which they reduced to six discontinuous categories, 1–14 hours, 15–39 hours, 40 hours, 41–48 hours, 49–59 hours and 60 or more hours) would influence not only the number of role behaviours that husbands completed, but also how adequately they were completed. Included in their measure of role behaviours was the extent to which husbands provided support for their spouses (which Clark *et al.*, 1978, referred to as the the 'therapeutic role'), and the way in which husbands fulfilled their sexual relationship. Clark *et al.* (1978) found no support for the hypothesis that there is a direct negative relationship between the time spent working and quantitative or qualitative role performance within the household. One significant relationship did emerge, though: the amount of time that husbands devoted to employment was negatively associated with the extent to which they shared in recreation with their spouse.

In their study of 468 employed parents, Voydanoff and Kelly (1984) assessed the effects of the number of hours, the amount of overtime worked, and the number of hours spent moonlighting during the average week on the *satisfaction* that husbands expressed with the amount of time they had available for family activities. Although the relationships that emerged from their multiple regression analyses were statistically significant, the magnitude of the obtained relationships was small enough for the meaning of these three relationships to be put into question. None of the three predictors accounted for more than 1.3% of the variance in satisfaction with family activities. A similar issue was addressed by Jackson, Zedeck and Summers (1985). Over and above the number of *regular* hours committed to employment, Jackson *et al.* (1985) investigated whether the number of *overtime* hours worked per week exerted any effect on the satisfaction husbands expressed with the amount of time available for the fulfilment of family roles. Included in the family roles they investigated were the amount of time available for discussion on family and personal problems, assisting with household activities, and joint activities such as shopping and visiting. No significant relationship emerged between the amount of time spent in employment and satisfaction with the time available for family activities in their sample of 95 power plant operators and their spouses.

Thus, where significant, the magnitude of the relationships in these studies was low, and may have been reduced further because of attenuation in both variables studied. The average number of household roles fulfilled by husbands and the amount of time spent on such activities per week is low.

Interference Between Employment and Family Roles

In the previous section, the central issue was whether the amount of time spent on the job exerted an effect on a quantitative and objective index of the amount of time available for marital role performance, and the satisfaction with that time. We now turn to the extent to which either spouse perceives interference between completion of employment and family roles as a function of temporal aspects of employment. There has been some research investigating whether the amount of time committed to employment interferes with the fulfilment of, and balance between, employment and family roles. Studies have operationalized the amount of job time in various ways, but perhaps the most logical method would be to sum the total number of hours devoted to paid employment per week. Such an approach has not been followed often, however, possibly because there is little variation in the number of hours spent on the job each week by husbands. A related approach is to divide the number of hours on the job into sub-categories. This approach of arbitrarily sub-categorizing the data has been followed in at least three separate studies (Clark *et al.*, 1978; Greenhaus, Bedeian and Mossholder, 1987; Pleck, Staines and Lang, 1980). Although different sub-categories of the number of hours worked were used in these studies, they demonstrate a significant, although modest, positive relationship between number of hours worked an interference with the employment–family role. It should be noted again, however, that sub-categorizing the data may artificially reduce the magnitude of the relationship between the number of hours committed to employment and employment–family role interference. First, sub-categorizing the amount of time devoted to paid employment or housework results in range restriction. Second, most of the variance in the amount of time on the job emerges after the individual has worked approximately eight hours per day. Yet the way in which the categories were defined in these studies fails to take this into account. In all these studies, there is a limited number of categories to describe the number of hours worked over and above what is often regarded as the 'norm', namely 40 hours per week. Also, the diversity in the way in which job-related time is categorized across studies limits the comparisons that can be drawn between studies. Third, Shamir (1983) has shown that the amount of job time does not interfere with employment–family roles as long as the individual devotes nine hours or less to his or her job per workday (i.e. is not involved in overtime work). Thus, even though support exists for the notion that the amount of hours spent on the job each week does interfere with the performance of employment–family roles, the magnitude of this relationship may have been underestimated in the research cited.

Marital Adjustment

Amount of regular time spent on the job

The third dimension of marital functioning which may be affected by the amount of time committed to employment is marital adjustment. Several studies have been conducted focusing on this issue, and a close examination of these studies shows that there is no direct relationship between the amount of time devoted to employment and marital adjustment.

In one of the few studies evaluating the effects on marital functioning of the amount of job time Greenhaus *et al.* (1987) showed that although the univariate relationship between an individual's time commitment to employment and his or her own marital adjustment was statistically significant, the amount of variance explained in marital adjustment was marginal. Perhaps more importantly, the relationship between the number of hours spent on the job per week and marital adjustment was not statistically significant after the effects of subjective work experiences (e.g. job performance, role conflict) had been excluded statistically. Clark *et al.* (1978) also showed that there was no relationship between the amount of time husbands committed to employment and a global measure of their *wives'* marital satisfaction or a specific measure of sexual behaviour. Although a significant relationship emerged in one study between the number of hours worked per week and marital dissatisfaction and negative marital behaviours (Burke, Weir and DuWors, 1980a), the large number of correlations computed together with the modest relationships yielded suggest that the findings may have been due to chance.

Taken together, these findings suggest that the amount of time itself exerts no meaningful influence on the quality of either spouse's marital functioning. In evaluating the effects of the amount of time spent on the job, the only study showing what may be regarded as a clinically significant impact (Beckman, Marsella and Finney, 1979) did not investigate marital satisfaction directly, and may not be generalizable because Beckman *et al.* (1979) used military wives as subjects.

It is possible that there is an indirect relationship between the total amount of time devoted to employment and marital adjustment (Mortimer, 1980). Findings from the studies discussed above suggest that while there is no direct relationship between the amount of time committed to the job and marital adjustment, such time does interfere with the completion of employment–family roles. In turn, there are data showing that the conflict experienced between the employment and family roles is consistently associated with marital adjustment for both males (Barling, 1986a) and females (MacEwen and Barling, 1988a; Suchet and Barling, 1986). Also, there is a significant relationship between husbands' and wives' perceptions of the distribution of housework and marital satisfaction, regardless of the wives' employment status (Yogev and Brett, 1985a). Thus, the amount of time committed to job-related activities influences inter-role conflict, which in turn is negatively associated with marital adjustment. This process model (which is depicted in Figure 3.1) becomes all the more plausible because MacEwen and Barling (1988a) collected data over a three-month period, and found that inter-role conflict predicted subsequent change in marital adjustment, but that the rival hypothesis that marital adjustment causes changes in inter-role conflict could be excluded. Accordingly, any relationship between the amount of time spent on the job and marital adjustment is probably indirect, and research might well focus on the variables that mediate this relationship.

Figure `3.1   Hypothesized indirect relationship between job-related time demands and marital dissatisfaction

Mortimer (1980) tested such a process model of the relationship between the amount of job time and marital adjustment. Instead of focusing solely on a direct relationship, Mortimer assessed whether there is an indirect relationship between the amount of time devoted to employment and marital adjustment. Mortimer (1980) hypothesized that excessive time demands from husbands' jobs would increase employment/family conflict. In turn, this family conflict would decrease the wives' supportive behaviours, which would then decrease the husbands' marital satisfaction. Mortimer's (1980) data supported her model. There was no direct relationship between time demands and marital adjustment. More importantly, as can be seen from Figure 3.2, the results of Mortimer's (1980) path analysis showed that this relationship was mediated by employment/family conflict and wives' supportive behaviours. Mortimer's (1980) data show that the relationship between job-related temporal demands and marital satisfaction is somewhat different from that of the relationship between socioeconomic status and marital adjustment (see Chapter 5). While job-related temporal requirements only exert an indirect effect on marital adjustment, socioeconomic status exerts both a direct and an indirect effect on marital adjustment. In general, therefore, Mortimer's (1980) data suggest that the effects of the amount of time spent on the job directly influence the interference between employment and family roles. In turn, employment–family role interference exerts a direct and negative effect on marital adjustment.

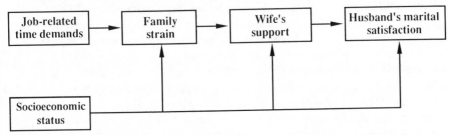

Figure 3.2   Indirect effects of husbands' job-related time demands on marital satisfaction in Mortimer's (1980) study

Job-related absence

Perhaps the most dramatic manifestation of the amount of time taken up by one's job occurs when one spouse is absent for protracted periods of time. The literature on the effects of family separation on marital functioning can be traced at least to the Second World War (Grossenbacher-Boss, McCubbin and Lesteram, 1979). Since that time, two forms of husband-related absence have been noted: absence as a short-term, periodic phenomenon, and long-term absence (typically in the military). Aside from the rhetoric concerning the wife as a 'corporate casualty' of her executive husband's job-related absences (e.g. Seidenberg, 1973), it could be predicted either from an open systems approach (Grossenbacher-Boss *et al.*, 1979) or from role theory, that rapid changes (i.e. husbands' work separations and reunions) would impose demands on the family and marriage that necessitate role readjustment, both at the time of departure and return. In addition, it has been suggested that other aspects of marital functioning would also be threatened by business-related travel (e.g. sexual relationships). Interviews with individuals involved in frequent business-related travel and their spouses, as well as data collected from small, non-representative samples provide anecdotal support for these concerns (Culbert and Renshaw, 1972; Renshaw, 1976). However, aside from these two studies, there are no empirical data testing any hypotheses regarding frequent business-related travel.

Unlike husbands' brief absences because of business-related travel, some job-related absence can be prolonged. Before considering prolonged absences, one point should be made. There are considerable data available on the effects of husband absence on the marriage. In most cases, however, the results of such studies are not relevant here because the husband's absence is not job related (e.g. due to death, divorce, desertion), and therefore may have different consequences (e.g. grief, anger, financial strain) than job-related absences.

A number of reports concerning the relationship between job-related husband absence and marital functioning have been reported within the military context. Frances and Gale (1973) speculate that husband absence places a strain on the marital relationship in general and the sexual relationship in particular. Their experience in providing treatment for military families led them to believe that it is usually the wife who would present as the patient. This is not surprising, because women present at mental health clinics more than men, a phenomenon that may be exacerbated in the military situation where men may be less willing to admit any kind of psychological difficulties. Bey and Lange (1974) conducted interviews with the wives of individuals serving tours of duty in Vietnam. The problems these wives experienced ranged from numbness, shock and disbelief when their husbands first received orders of their impending tour of duty, to housing problems, separation problems, and difficulties associated with their husbands' return. These included concern as to whether their husbands have changed, and whether their husbands would accept the changes they themselves (i.e. the wives) had experienced during the one-year absence. MacIntosh (1968) contrasted a group of 63 military wives who were separated from their husbands and were receiving out-patient psychiatric treatment, with a group of 113 military wives who were not separated from their husbands, but were receiving out-patient psychiatric treatment at the same clinic. Presumably, any differences between the two groups with respect to psychiatric problems would be due to job-related absence of the husband. However, aside from the finding that wives whose husbands were in the army as a career functioned better than those whose husbands were draftees, no other differences emerged between the two groups that offer any insights into the consequences of work-related husband absence.

Beckman *et al.*'s (1979) study investigating job-related husband absence provides data that are relevant to marital functioning. In a longitudinal study, Beckman *et al.* (1979) investigated 24 Navy wives' depression under conditions of husband presence and husband absence in a cross-over design. Their focus on depression has implications for marital functioning, because clinical depression is significantly associated with marital distress (e.g. Beach and O'Leary, 1986). Using two measures of depression, they showed that wives' depression was significantly higher when their husbands were away for three-month tours of duty in a nuclear submarine that when their husbands were at home. What is most important about Beckman *et al.*'s (1979) findings is that wives' depression scores on the Zung Depression Scale ($M = 52.92$) during conditions of husband absence indicated the presence of clinical levels of depression, while the level of depression under conditions of husband presence (M = 43.13) indicated an absence of clinical symptoms. Rosen and Moghadam (1988) suggested that there is a negative correlation between the amount of time husbands spend training away from home and the psychological well-being of wives. They reasoned that the more time spent in active training, the greater wives' concern about the occurrence of a potentially dangerous incident. Although their results did not support this hypothesis, they showed that the level of social support that wives received, including support from husbands, significantly moderated the relationship between the amount of time spent training and wives' psychological well-being. When wives received support, there was no relationship between stress and well-being; when they experienced what Rosen and Moghadam (1988) refer to as 'no support' (but which more accurately reflects the receipt of *low* levels of support), there was a statistically significant relationship between the stress the wives experienced as a function of their husbands' job-related absence and their own psychological well-being.

The extent to which the above findings are generalizable to non-military husbands' absence might be limited. Military wives suffer different stressors from corporate wives, such as fear of physical harm befalling their husband. First, having a husband in active military duty (e.g. Bey and Lange, 1974; Hobfoll and London, 1986), undergoing military training (Rosen and Moghadam, 1988) or on nuclear submarines (Beckman *et al.*, 1979) results in a different set of subjective stresses and concerns for the waiting wife than would the absence of the husband due to non-military reasons. Second, the prolonged absence typical of the military may be more analogous to a chronic stressor, while the short-term absence more typical of non-military organizations is more similar to an acute stressor. The question of whether job-related husband absence due to more conventional business or organizational environments influences marital functioning remains to be assessed.

Amount of overtime worked

Another way in which the effects of the amount of job time may become manifest is when individuals spend additional time on the job on an irregular basis over and above that normally required, that is, when individuals engage in overtime work. Jackson *et al.* (1985) assessed whether there was a relationship between the average amount of overtime per week and the spouse's self-reported family functioning, but no significant relationship emerged between these two variables. Ridley (1973) also investigated the amount of overtime rather than regular time on the job. Ridley (1973) did not use an objective measure of overtime. Rather, his 'job involvement' variable reflected the amount of time devoted each day to reading, writing, talking and thinking about the job during non-job hours. Although Ridley (1973) suggests that 'some support was found for this hypothesis' (p. 235), that is there is a relationship between marital adjustment and his measure of 'involvement' in neither case were the relationships statistically significant. Indeed, Ridley (1973) himself concludes later that 'Most of the respondents in this study were more than moderately successful at preventing their job involvement from interfering with marital adjustment' (p. 236). It would appear from these two studies, therefore, that there is no empirical support for the hypothesis that the amount of overtime worked is *directly* associated with marital adjustment. This conclusion would be consistent with Staines and Pleck's (1983) multivariate analysis of their data from the 1977 Quality of Employment Survey that staying at work overtime is not associated with marital satisfaction. In evaluating the effects of overtime on marital functioning, however, two factors mitigate against obtaining significant results. First, only a limited number of people work overtime, and second, there is a limited amount of time that people can actually work overtime. Thus, range restriction in the measure of the amount of overtime work completed would limit the extent to which a statistically significant relationship could be detected.

Time spent commuting

In practical terms, the amount of time actually spent on the job provides a conservative estimate of the amount of time individuals spend away from their families for employment-related purposes. This is because of the time it takes to get to and from work each day, especially in larger metropolitan areas. Indeed, one consequence of the movement of families away from city centres towards the suburbs has been increased commuting time to and from work each day. Obviously, the longer it takes to get from home to work, or back home after work, the less the available family time. It would be interesting, therefore, to assess whether the amount of time actually spent on the job and amount of time spent commuting to and from work exerted independent effects on marital functioning. As is becoming increasingly evident, commuting to and from work in large urban areas is a stressful experience. An extreme example is the number of incidents of highway shootings in the greater Los Angeles area in 1987 that reflected and exacerbated the stress of commuting (Work *et al.*, 1987). Studying the effects of commuting time would be particularly interesting from a conceptual perspective, as it is conceivable that time spent on the job and time spent commuting to and from work, involve different psychological stressors (e.g. chronic vs daily).

Using an interesting procedure, Stokols *et al.* (1978) collected data on the effects of job-related commuting. For several days each week, as soon as their subjects arrived on the job in the morning, data on their blood pressure and mood were obtained. Task performance was assessed later the same day. Their data showed that the duration, distance and speed involved in the daily commute were associated with systolic and diastolic blood pressure and subjective reports of tension and nervousness. In a subsequent re-analysis of the same data set, Novaco *et al.* (1979) showed there was a significant positive association between the time and distance involved commuting, and the desire to change residences.

There do not appear to be any specific studies investigating the effects of commuting on marital or family functioning. However, other studies focusing on the amount of time devoted to employment and marital functioning have included measures relevant to commuting. As part of their study of work schedules and family disruption, Jackson *et al.* (1985) obtained an index of the time spent commuting each day (an average of 55.35 minutes per person per day in their study), which was significantly associated with their measure of dissatisfaction with the congruence between the employment and family roles. However, this finding was not replicated in a separate study. The 1977 Quality of Employment Survey included two items assessing the effects of different aspects of commuting (time and commuting-related problems) on employment–family conflicts. In an analysis of this data set, Pleck *et al.* (1980) found no association between either of their two items and any of four aspects of conflict between employment and family roles (all conflicts combined, excessive work time, scheduling conflicts and fatigue and irritability).

One reason for these seemingly inconsistent findings could be the existence of moderating factors. In other words, the relationship between commuting stress and the outcome of interest could be dependent on a third variable. Schaeffer *et al.* (1988) investigated this issue in a quasi-experimental design. They showed that although commuting stress was associated with increases in blood pressure and decreases in performance on a proofreading task, these relations were most pronounced under two conditions: when individuals travelled a stressful route to work, and were passengers in a car pool (rather than drivers) thereby relinquishing control over relevant decisions (e.g. the route taken, environmental conditions in the interior of the car). Another reason for differences in the findings of studies on commuting is that the amount of time spent commuting may be different across studies. However, this possibility cannot be addressed because Pleck *et al.* did not report the amount of time their subjects spent commuting.

Nonetheless, given the inconsistent results, the question of whether commuting influences marital functioning remains open, particularly because most of these studies did not focus specifically on marital functioning as the outcome. This issue will probably increase in importance, given predictions that the urban gridlock associated with commuting will worsen (Work *et al.*, 1987). A different approach to the conceptualization of commuting as a stressor may be required to examine the relation between commuting and marital functioning. Both Jackson *et al.* (1985) and Pleck *et al.* (1980) operationalized commuting as a chronic stressor. Commuting may be a chronic stressor if getting to and from one's workplace is a problem each day. Alternatively, commuting may only present occasional problems, and would represent a daily stressor. This distinction is important, because individuals may adapt to the persistent and predictable nature of any commuting difficulties, and only become unsettled by unexpected events during their daily commute. To test this, a daily stressor model would be more appropriate. Daily studies would provide an interesting extension to Novaco *et al.*'s (1979) and Stokols *et al.*'s (1978) studies. Instead of assessing people's blood pressure, mood and so forth when they get to work, outcomes that may influence marital and family functioning might be measured as people arrive *home* at the end of each work day. This research strategy might yield interesting results about the effects of commuting on marital and family functioning, especially if the description provided in *Time* magazine (Smilgis, 1987) captures the essence of the stressful nature of commuting: 'Your body releases more adrenaline, your blood vessels constrict, your pressure rises.... You're still wound up three or four hours later' (pp. 62–3).

SHIFT WORK AND MARITAL FUNCTIONING

A second temporal aspect of employment is the *scheduling* of job-related time. The meaning of shift work for the day-to-day functioning of workers and their families cannot be underestimated. In short, in addition to shift work's impact on the shift worker, the non-shift working members of a family must undergo continual changes and sacrifices because of the shift work pattern. For example, when the shift worker is asleep during the day, other family members must be especially quiet, the non-shift working spouse has to prepare meals at unusual times of the day, and may experience decreased contact with relatives and friends because their social and leisure schedules do not coincide with that of the shift worker (Walker, J., 1985). Also, J. Walker (1985) suggests that some wives of shift workers might be nervous and/or lonely at night, and may encounter increased childrearing responsibilities while their husbands are involved in the late afternoon or evening shift, as a result of which wives would be less free to participate in social activities during the evening. Dunham (1977, p. 627) identified two early studies in which a higher incidence of sexual problems was noted among shift workers than regular day workers, and one study in which shift work was associated with a higher divorce rate than individuals employed on a regular shift. J. Walker (1985) suggests all these difficulties would be exacerbated in poor and overcrowded housing conditions and larger families. Yet common assumptions about the effects of employment on the family are often not supported when subjected to empirical scrutiny. For example, Rutenfranz *et al.* (1977) suggest that shift work may also exert positive effects on the family because of the increased amount of time available to the shift worker during the day, or because of having several consecutive week-days free. Consequently, it is important to analyse empirically the effects, if any, of shift work on marital functioning.

Prevalence of Shift Work

To understand the potential scope of the relationship between shift work and marital functioning, it is worth noting briefly the prevalence of shift work. Shift work is by no means a recent phenomenon. Individuals have participated in shift work schedules ever since there was a need for the health profession, policing, the military, sailors and so forth. By the late nineteenth century, two twelve-hour shifts were extremely common in heavily industrialized centres because of the need for greater levels of productivity, and the costs and disruptions involved in continually starting up and shutting down heavy machinery (Meadow, 1988). Kogi (1985) estimates that within industrialized countries, between 15% and 30% of industrialized workers are now engaged in some form of shift work. Kogi's (1985) estimate converges with many other frequently cited statistics concerning the prevalence of shift work. For example, Shamir (1983) suggests that approximately 20% of the workforce in both the United States and Western Europe is employed on some sort of shift schedule. Dunham (1977) estimates that approximately 25% of the manufacturing sector is employed on a shift schedule in the United States, and Zedeck, Jackson and Summers (1983) cite the same statistic for the labour force in North America. Based on data from the 1980 Current Population Survey, Presser (1986) estimates that slightly fewer employed mothers than fathers are involved in shift work, regardless of whether they are employed on a full-time or part-time basis. Given that most estimates of the number of people employed in some kind of shift work converge at approximately 20% or more, an analysis of how, if at all, marital functioning is influenced by shift work is essential. In considering this issue, the effects of different shift work schedules (e.g. pattern of days worked and pattern of hours worked) on the three aspects of marital functioning previously considered (namely, marital role performance, interference in employment–family roles, and marital adjustment) will be discussed. This allows a comparison of the relative effects of different shift work schedules on the same criteria of marital functioning. Thereafter, the subjective meaning of shift work will be considered.

Marital Role Performance

As already noted, marital role performance concerns the extent to which formal and informal activities required for the successful maintenance of the household are accomplished. Not surprisingly, marital role performance is considered to be one of the major negative consequences of engaging in shift work. Based on the various analyses on the 1977 Quality of Employment Survey by Staines and Pleck (1984), it would appear that the direction of the effects (i.e. beneficial or detrimental) is dependent on whether the shift schedule consists of a pattern of hours or days. A regular shift schedule that includes days worked on weekends is associated with 2.4 hours *less* time spent on housework per week by husbands (e.g. cooking, cleaning, repairs, shopping, yard work, finance; Staines and Pleck, 1984). There is no comparable reduction in hours spent each week on marital role performance when wives are involved in weekend shift work. There are also decreases in the amount of household responsibilities completed associated with participation in rotating shifts (Mott *et al.*, 1965).

When the pattern of hours, rather than days, is considered, a different perspective emerges. Staines and Pleck (1984) showed that involvement in the afternoon or night shift resulted in substantially *more* time per week (6.2 hours and 4.0 hours, respectively) devoted to household responsibilities. This is consistent with Mott *et al.*'s (1965) findings that individuals on shift work (as opposed to day work) reported that it was easier to help with household responsibilities. Staines and Pleck (1984) speculate that this increased involvement in housework emerges because individuals who work a night shift have been shown, on average, to sleep between five and ten hours less per week. Together with being awake for longer periods, being available in the house when no other family members are present increases the amount of time available to the shift worker for involvement in household responsibilities.

One work schedule that would affect both the pattern of hours and the pattern of days is involvement in the 4/40-hour workweek. A focus on the 4/40 hour workweek is informative as it provides an opportunity to separate the effects of the amount of work from its scheduling, because the number of hours worked per week remains constant, while the scheduling of those hours changes. Essentially, in return for fewer days (namely, four) at work per week, workers accept longer working hours (namely, ten) each day. Maklan (1977) showed that there were no substantial differences between husbands engaged in four-and five-day weeks and traditionally female gender-typed behaviours (such as cooking, shopping, washing dishes and clothes). Substantial differences did emerge, however, when more traditionally male-oriented household responsibilities (e.g. home repairs and maintenance, non-grocery shopping) were considered: husbands on the four-day week engaged in substantially more of these behaviours than their counterparts working five days a week.

Interference Between Employment and Family Roles

The assumption that shift work interferes with successful completion of employment–family roles is plausible given the lack of synchrony between the temporal demands of the job and role responsibilities of the family (Meadow, 1988). Being employed either non-standard or variable days or hours removes shift workers from the family context at those very times when their presence is most required. The results from studies in Israel (Shamir, 1983) and the United States (Staines and Pleck, 1984) support this hypothesis. For example, working on the job either at weekends or holidays (Shamir, 1983; Staines and Pleck, 1984) is associated with increased employment–family role interference, possibly because these are usually viewed as times set aside for familial and social activities. The value placed on evenings and weekends can be inferred from the manner in which individuals working during the evening or at the weekend are provided with additional monetary compensation (Wedderburn, 1981). This additional compensation offered cannot be explained simply in terms of the physical inconvenience of working night shifts: one of the crucial determinants for the additional compensation offered is the disruption to the familial and social schedules, as is evidenced by the compensation offered for day work on a Sunday (200%) compared to night work during the week (120%).

There are also data investigating how shifting patterns of paid work over days (i.e. including Saturday and Sunday) affect employment–family interference. J. Walker (1985) found from interviews with wives whose steel worker husbands were involved in shift work that what the wives resented most was the inability to enjoy weekend activities together with their husbands. These findings were replicated and extended by those of Young and Willmott (1973), who found more reports of employment–family role interference among shift workers than among weekend workers or regular day workers. The empirical data available regarding the way in which the pattern of hours interferes with employment–family roles is consistent with these observations. Several studies have shown that the afternoon shift interferes most with these roles (Hood and Golden, 1979; Shamir, 1983). Likewise, working two shifts (i.e. twelve hours) is associated with increased employment–family role interference (Walker, J., 1985), presumably because involvement in two shifts requires attendance at work in the late afternoon and early evening, those times during which there are so many family responsibilities.

Thus, an irony emerges in the way in which marital role performance and perceived employment–family role interference are influenced by working the afternoon shift. While it has been shown that the amount of time spent on marital role performance *increases* when the individual is on the afternoon (or evening) shift, this may increase scheduling conflict for spouses, because employment–family interference is greater when the individual works afternoon shifts. Thus, as Staines (1986) notes, what might transpire (especially if the wife is employed on regular day shift) is that shift workers are available for completion of family roles at inappropriate times. In other words, the schedules of spouses (and probably also the children) do not coincide, as a result of which shift workers report greater schedule conflict and inter-role conflict.

Of the two studies reported that have focused on the effects of the 4/40 workweek on the family, only one assessed its effects on interference between employment–family roles. Dunham, Pierce and Castaneda (1987) conducted a longitudinal study in which they investigated the effects of changing from a 5/40 to a 4/40 week. Their results showed that involvement in the 4/40 schedule significantly decreased interference between family and social activities, although their measure did not differentiate the effects of the 4/40 week on family and social activities.

One issue has not been investigated, but may yet exert a substantial impact on marital role performance. By its very nature, shift work may augment the trend in society towards integrated and shared roles between spouses when the wife is a shift worker. Specifically, as will be seen in Chapters 6–9, simultaneous with the introduction of large numbers of mothers into the labour force, there has been a move towards more egalitarian role allocation and responsibilities between spouses. Yet this trend may be strengthened when spouses are involved in different shifts and completion of certain roles (e.g. making dinner, child care during the evening) cannot be completed by the wife because of her shift work involvement.

Marital Adjustment

The third aspect of marital functioning against which the effects of shift work have been considered is marital or family adjustment. Before proceeding, differences between marital and family adjustment as the outcome of interest are worth noting. In some studies, the outcome of interest is family satisfaction, which is typically measured with questions focusing on satisfaction with the marriage *and* children. It is important to differentiate between marital satisfaction and family satisfaction, as they may be unrelated in some circumstances, and probably involve different causes and consequences. Besides resentment from wives whose husbands are engaged on the job during the weekend (Walker, 1985), Staines and Pleck (1986) reported data from the large-scale 1977 Quality of Employment (which focused on an unweighted sample of 1090 people) that involvement in a variable schedule of days was associated with lower family adjustment (which was derived from self-ratings of marital and family satisfaction, and marital happiness).

There are also data, however, addressing the relationship between the pattern of hours worked and marital adjustment. Mott *et al.* (1965) showed in their study that marital adjustment was greatest for individuals employed on a day shift. However, Staines and Pleck (1986) failed to find support for a relationship between pattern of hours worked and marital adjustment. Nonetheless, despite their large sample size and its representiveness, problems with their measure of marital adjustment may have limited the extent to which their results are comparable to those of Mott *et al.* (1965). They used a three-item measure of *family* adjustment (in which two of the items assess marital adjustment; 'All in all, how satisfied would you say you are with your marriage?', 'Taking everything together, how happy would you say your marriage is?', and 'All in all, how satisfied would you say you are with your family life?'). Yet one problem is that different results are frequently yielded depending on whether global or specific satisfaction scales are used. As Allen and Keaveny (1979) note, people frequently report high levels of job, marital or life satisfaction on global indices of satisfaction. Yet problems are uncovered for the same individuals when more specific aspects of satisfaction are used.

Maklan (1977) compared the marital adjustment of individuals in a four-day and five-day workweek. Although Maklan (1977) found no differences between the two groups regarding either global marital adjustment or specific satisfaction with marital role performance, there were interesting distributional differences in marital adjustment. Specifically, individuals involved in the 4/40 workweek tended to provide far more extreme responses (both positive and negative) than their counterparts engaged in a more regular five-day workweek.

In summarizing the meaning of the above literature, three issues emerge. First, it is apparent that shift work exerts a different effect on the quantity and quality of marital functioning. Specifically, while working non-day shifts allows more time for involvement in the marital role (an index of the *quantity* of marital functioning), it is also associated with increases in greater conflict between employment and family roles (an index of the *quality* of marital functioning). Second, aside from Shamir's (1983) study, there appears to be little research investigating rotating shifts where the hours worked vary. This may be an important omission, if, as it is often suggested, it is the *irregularity* of the shift pattern that is most detrimental to family functioning (Bosch and de Lange, 1987). Third, a common aspect throughout all the studies cited above concerns the way in which shift work is operationalized. Specifically, in all these studies, objective data are used to classify the individual into a group (evening shift, weekend shift, and so forth). Yet this ignores what may be an equally important dimension of shift work, namely, the subjective meaning of shift work to the individual. On a methodological level, the difference between these two general approaches to studying shift work reflects a between-group approach (e.g. contrasting shift workers with non-shift working controls) and a within-group approach (focusing on the different meanings of, and satisfactions with, shift work). But the importance of this distinction is more than merely methodological. An exclusive focus on between-group designs assumes consistency in the effects of shift work across workers, and that any effects of shift work are negative. The within-group approach implies an acceptance of variation between individuals regarding the meaning of the same objective shift work schedule. There are some data that address the relationship between the subjective meaning of shift work and marital functioning, and it is towards a consideration of this literature that this discussion now turns.

Subjective Meaning of Shift Work

The importance of understanding the subjective meanings of shift work emerges when it is realized that there are considerable variations in the level of expressed dissatisfaction with shift work (Dunham, 1977). In addition, shift work dissatisfaction is associated with family difficulties independent of the nature of the scheduling (Walker, J., 1985). In perhaps the first large-scale ($N = 732$) study on satisfaction with attributes of shift work, Zedeck *et al.* (1983) showed that the strongest predictor of shift work satisfaction was the expressed satisfaction with time for family activities ($r = 0.50$). Inspecting and reanalysing the data from Zedeck *et al.*'s (1983, p. 302) study supports such an interpretation, because satisfaction with family activities was a stronger predictor of shift work satisfaction than intrinsic, extrinsic or overall job satisfaction ($M\ r = 0.38$) or any of eleven perceived work environment attributes ($M\ r = 0.24$), current feelings such as enthusiasm, tension, tiredness and irascibility ($M\ r = 0.31$) or physical health symptoms (digestion, muscle pain, heart problems; $M\ r = 0.18$). Likewise, dissatisfaction with family activities also emerged as the strongest predictor ($r = 0.32$) of an individual's stated preference for a change in shift.

In a later report, Jackson *et al.* (1985) used the same data to analyse whether any effects of shift work carried over on to the non-shift working spouse. Jackson *et al.* (1985) contrasted two aspects of shift work, namely the structural interference induced by shift work (i.e. objective conditions related to shift work), and the emotional outcomes (i.e. physical health, psychological mood and behavioural adjustment) specific to the shift work experience. Their results again suggest that there is an important distinction between the effects of shift work on the quantity and quality of marital functioning. Structural interference associated with shift work was correlated with employees' self-reported dissatisfaction with family *involvement*, but not associated with the spouse's self-reported quality of marital interactions or family life. Jackson *et al*.'s (1985) results further reinforce the importance of taking a within-group approach that accepts differences in the meaning of shift work for individuals, and focusing on the correlates or effects of differing levels of shift work satisfaction.

Individual Differences in Shift Work Adjustment

One issue raised by Zedeck *et al*.'s (1983) study that has yet to receive sufficient empirical attention is the possibility that there are individual differences in the relationship between shift work adjustment and marital functioning. There are a number of indications in the literature that some variables (such as marital status and work schedule flexibility) moderate the relationship between shift work and marital functioning, and others moderate the effects of shift work on outcomes relevant to marital functioning for example, self-selection into and out of shift work (Frese and Okonek, 1984), job satisfaction and stress, type of job, and whether community resources are available to shift workers during off-shift periods, or 'community synchronicity'.

Perhaps the most obvious moderator variable is marital status: Bosch and de Lange (1987) showed that married nurses suffer more negative effects from shift work than do their unmarried counterparts. From these data it could be suggested that the number of dependants might also exacerbate the effects of shift work, given that one of the most frequent outcomes studied concerns employment–family interference. Another variable that might fulfil a moderating role is the perceived flexibility of the work schedule, a variable to be discussed in greater detail later in this chapter.

One major determinant for leaving shift work is family related problems and dissatisfactions (Frese and Okonek, 1984; Zedeck *et al*., 1983). General work stress and job satisfaction might also moderate any negative effects of shift work: Shamir (1983) found that individuals who were less satisfied with their jobs in general and experienced more stressors (independent of the type of shift worked) experience more inter-role conflict. Bosch and de Lange (1987) contrasted shift work in health care and in industry. In health care, night duties consist mainly of monitoring tasks performed by reduced numbers of staff. In contrast there are no differences in duties in industry across the various shifts, with the result that equal numbers of workers are on duty completing the same tasks. This implies that the social context remains constant across shift changes in industrial settings, but is fragmented in the night shift in health care situations. This difference may have a significant effect on the way individuals experience both their jobs and social relationships, which in turn may moderate how shift work is experienced.

A final moderator variable that must be considered is that of community synchronicity (Bosch and de Lange, 1987; Dunham, 1977; Zedeck *et al.*, 1983). Dunham (1977) studied two groups of individuals performing the same job function for a large corporation in the midwestern United States. The first plant was located in small town, in which virtually no other community members worked shifts. Accordingly, the community itself was not oriented towards serving the needs of shift workers (e.g., in terms of when shops, restaurants, and recreational facilities were open). In contrast, the second plant was located in a larger community in which a majority of members were involved in shift work, as a result of which the non-job needs and requirements of shift workers were fulfilled through non-standard opening times of shops, libraries and so forth. Dunham (1977) conducted separate analyses on the two plants. In the smaller, non-shift work oriented community, employees on the day shift registered most satisfaction with different aspects of the job, with their counterparts who worked night shifts registering the lowest job satisfaction. No such differences emerged in the larger community. Moreover, membership in a group participating in shift work explained 24% of the variance in job satisfaction in the first plant, but only 11% in the second. Dunham (1977) suggests that the negative effects of shift work might be reduced if we *increase* the frequency of shift work so that the same community and recreational facilities that are available to the day worker are available to all. This logic might be extended to the question of whether negative effects of shift work on a spouse could be reduced substantially if both partners work the same shifts. From the above discussion on shift work and marital functioning, the following general conclusions can be drawn. First, shift work does not necessarily exert direct negative effects on marital functioning, and its influence on the quantity (i.e. number of marital roles fulfilled) and quality (i.e. interference between work and family roles, marital satisfaction) of marital functioning is not uniform. Rather, working night or afternoon shifts increases involvement in marital role performance, but also increases employment–family role interference (scheduling or role conflict). Second, and related to this, there are marked differences in the way in which individuals perceive and react to their shift work. Indeed, paraphrasing Dunham (1977), we might suggest that community or psychological rhythms are as important as circadian rhythms in determining the social and marital functioning of shift workers.

THE 'FAMILY WORK DAY'

Before addressing the issue of work schedule flexibility and marital functioning, the concept of the 'family work day' (Kingston and Nock, 1985; Nock and Kingston, 1984) should be considered. According to Kingston and Nock, any focus on individual spouses' job-related time or schedule ignores the fact that the 'traditional' family in which the husband is the breadwinner and the wife the homemaker has become atypical (see Chapter 7). Thus, what Nock and Kingston call for is a focus on the couple (rather than two separate spouses) as the unit of analysis when considering the effects of the amount and scheduling of time on marital functioning. Such a consideration is important, given the results of the 1980 Current Population Survey of the United States. Of families with at least one child and both spouses employed, 10% of the couples were involved in different shifts that did not overlap at all (Presser and Cain, 1983). Consequently, a comprehensive understanding of the time and scheduling of work patterns must examine *both* spouses *simultaneously*, that is, the *family* work day. It is the interaction of the two spouses' separately on the job times and schedules that will determine the amount and scheduling of the time available for employment and family activities.

Nock and Kingston (1984) first set out to establish the frequency of three temporal characteristics of the family workday. The first characteristic, *total family work time*, reflects the total number of hours during which *either* of the partners was engaged in his or her job. The second characteristic is *the length of the family work day*, which provides an index of the total amount of time either one or both spouses are involved in paid employment activities. Thus, the length of the family workday is the later of the two times either of the spouses ends his or her work minus the earlier of the two starting times. (If there is any intervening period during which neither spouse works, as may well be the case if both partners are involved in shift work, the time would be subtracted accordingly.) The third temporal characteristic associated with the family work day is *the amount of off-time scheduling*, which reflects the amount of time during the day when only one spouse would be employed.

To investigate temporal characteristics and family consequences of the family workday, Nock and Kingston (1984) re-analysed data from the 1977 Quality of Employment Survey. Their results suggest that a truncated perspective of the amount of time available for marital or family roles may be provided when employed *individuals* rather than employed *couples* are the unit of analysis. The median total family work time (16. 95 hours) is consistent with the total individual work times for males (8.8 hours) and females (8.2 hours). However, when the length of the family work day is considered, it is clear that the total amount of time that couples have available *for each other* is less than that remaining at the end of the individual work days. Specifically, the median length of the family work day (9.9 hours) indicates that just under ten hours per day are taken up with one or both partners being at work, and therefore unavailable for marital activities. Moreover, Nock and Kingston (1984) reported that the length of the family work day was more than twelve hours for just over 20% of their sample. Only 8.5% of their sample reported no off-scheduling. The median amount of off-scheduling per day was 2.65 hours and 25% of the sample reported more than five hours per day during which only one spouse was on the job.

Nock and Kingston's (1984) conceptualization of the family work day would be important if it contributed to our understanding of how the amount and scheduling of time on the job affects family functioning over and above the results from research treating the individual as the unit of analysis. Their use of data from the Quality of Employment Survey allows for a comparison of the effects of the family work day with that of the individual work day. In other words, it allows for a comparison of the couple as the unit of comparison with that of the individual.

Clearly, Nock and Kingston's (1984) earlier analyses show that a consideration of the amount time devoted to work by two separate spouses provides us with a different index compared to that obtained from the notion of the family work day. More importantly, the total number of hours committed to employment during the family work day was significantly associated with the extent to which employment interferes with both family and free time, although only for women. For women, the length of the family work day was positively associated with the amount of time they spent on chores, their free time, time spent with husbands, feeling they had insufficient free time, and the extent to which their jobs interfered with free time. Also, there were no significant effects for men, off-scheduling was not related to marital role performance or employment–family interference, and none of the measures of the family work day was associated with marital satisfaction. Last, it should also be noted that the amount of common family time available is determined not just by parents' job schedules, but also by their children's timetables (Volger *et al.*, 1988). Consequently, while providing an interesting perspective, there is insufficient information at this stage to argue that family work time exerts consistent effects on marital functioning over and above the amount and scheduling of each individual's work time.

FLEXIBLE WORK SCHEDULES AND MARITAL FUNCTIONING

The notion of flexible work schedules was probably first introduced in West Germany in the late 1960s. Initially, the rationale prompting the implementation of flexible schedules was two-fold: first, flexible work schedules represented an attempt to attract greater numbers of skilled mothers back into the active labour force at a time when there was a skilled labour shortage. It was hoped that the nature of flexible work schedules would enable mothers to become re-employed, and simultaneously fulfil their other role responsibilities. A second reason underlying the introduction of flexible work schedules was the need to overcome problems of urban congestion (i.e. commuting and parking problems) that arose from having so many individuals descending on city centres at the same time each day (Anand, 1975; Winett and Neale, 1980a). By 1980, it was estimated that 2.5 million West German workers, 35% of workers in France and 40% in Switzerland were engaged in some form of flexible work schedule, and that 13% of organizations in the private sector in the United States (involving approximately 3 million workers) were participating in flexible work schedules (Kim and Campagna, 1981; Winett and Neale, 1980a).

In one sense, predictions as to how marital and family functioning would be influenced by flexible work schedules run counter to those regarding the effects of the amount of time and non-standard work schedules. Specifically, flexible work schedules were introduced with the purpose of allowing mothers to complete their various roles more satisfactorily while being employed, and alleviating employment–family role interference. Thus, it has been predicted that there should be a positive association between involvement in a flexible work schedule and at least one aspect of marital functioning, namely work/family role interference or conflict.

There is no shortage of research focusing on the effects of flexible work schedules. This is probably due to the fact that in the late 1970s, legislation appeared in the United States mandating federal agencies to investigate the possible effects of flexible work schedules. Yet the degree to which these data can increase understanding of the effects of flexible work schedules on marital functioning remains questionable. Most of this research has been conducted on federal employees, much of it remains unpublished, and the most frequently investigated outcome has been organizational consequences of flexible work schedules (see Winett and Neale, 1980a, pp. 417–23).

In considering the effects of flexible work schedules, it should first be noted that two different aspects of work schedule flexibility have been considered. Most studies have followed an objective approach, and examined the consequences for individuals employed on a flexitime work schedule. Within this approach, contrasted group studies have typically been conducted (i.e. individuals on flexitime are contrasted with their counterparts who are not) as have pre-test/post-test designs (wherein individuals are contrasted before and after the implementation of a flexitime programme). Staines (1986) makes the point, however, that there is also a subjective component to the notion of flexibility. This subjective component concerns the extent to which individuals perceive themselves to be in control of both the amount and scheduling of their work time, irrespective of whether they work on flexible schedules. Both of these approaches will be evaluated in this section, again in terms of how they influence marital role performance, interference between employment and family roles, and marital adjustment. Related issues such as the extent to which commuting time is influenced will also be considered briefly.

Marital Role Performance

Data from three separate studies support the prediction that individuals on flexitime work schedules are more involved in marital role performance than their counterparts who work on standard schedules. Winett and Neale (1980a, b) conducted two quasi-experimental longitudinal studies in which both males and females on flexitime were contrasted with individuals from the same federal agencies who were not employed on a flexitime schedule. In both these studies, individuals engaged in flexible work schedules spent more time with their spouses and families. This finding is consistent with the data of Bohen and Viveros-Long (1981), who also studied individuals at two different federal agencies, but did not separate their samples by sex. In these samples, individuals on flexitime devoted significantly more of their non-work time to household responsibilities than did their counterparts engaged in regular work schedules. Workers involved in flexitime work schedules may have more time available to them (e.g. because of reduced commuting time). Data from Winett and Neale's (1980a, b) research also provide some basis for understanding why individuals in a flexible schedule have more time available for family interactions. For individuals in the flexitime group, the number of minutes spent commuting decreased slightly, while the number of minutes spent commuting by their counterparts in the regular hours group increased marginally. Hicks and Klimoski (1981) found that individuals involved in flexitime schedules reported fewer difficulties associated with commuting and parking.

However, a different pattern of results is obtained when the perceived control over the scheduling of job time is studied. As part of the 1977 Quality of Employment Survey, respondents were asked two questions to ascertain how flexible they perceived their work schedule to be ('How hard do you think it would be to get the days you work changed permanently if you wanted them changed?' and 'How hard do you think it would be to get the hours you work changed permanently if you wanted them changed?'; Staines and Pleck, 1984, p. 517). The index created from summing these two items was not associated with the amount of time the respondents devoted to household responsibilities. Thus, marital role functioning (specifically, the quantity of household responsibilities) is positively and significantly associated with an objective measure of whether the individual is participating in a flexitime work schedule, but not directly associated with perceived flexibility. In a later analysis, Staines and Pleck (1986) showed that perceived schedule flexibility exerts a different effect on marital role performance. They hypothesized that the relationship between non-standard work schedules and marital functioning would be moderated by perceived schedule flexibility. That is, non-standard work schedules would exert their most detrimental effects on the marital functioning of individuals who believed they exerted little or no control over their work schedule. Their analyses support this hypothesis. Moreover, they also hypothesized that any positive moderator effects would be greatest for females, and analysis of their three-way interactions showed that the beneficial, indirect effects of perceived schedule flexibility were indeed greatest for females. This gender effect may emerge if, as Hall (1972) hypothesizes women are required to enact their various roles simultaneously, while men enact their roles sequentially.

Interference with the Employment–Family Role

Consistent with the nature of flexitime schedules, it could be argued that individuals employed on such schedules would be afforded greater opportunities to control the scheduling of their personal and family activities. Thus, it might be predicted that employees who participate in flexitime schedules would suffer less interference between their employment and family roles. A number of empirical studies contrasting employees on flexitime schedules with those on standard schedules have been conducted to assess this issue. The results from these studies suggest that individuals afforded the opportunity of participating in a flexitime schedule do indeed perceive less interference between their employment and family roles (e.g. Barling and Barenbrug, 1984; Hicks and Klimoski, 1981; Winett and Neale, 1980b). Only one study has been reported in which no support was found for this hypothesis (Dunham *et al.*, 1987). They reported that there was no association between *change* into a flexitime schedule (they used a pre-test/post-test design) and interference with activities with family and friends. However, their dependent variable was different from those investigated in the previous studies mentioned (Barling and Barenbrug, 1984; Hicks and Klimoski, 1981; Winett and Neale, 1980b), in that it did not separate interference with family roles from interference with social activities. As a result of this, Dunham *et al.*'s (1987) findings cannot be compared with those of the three other studies.

The relationship between schedule flexibility and employment–family role interference parallels that of the relationship between involvement in a flexitime schedule and marital role performance. Thus, unlike its effects on marital role performance, Staines and Pleck (1984) found that perceived controllability of the schedule was negatively associated with the total conflict experienced between employment and family roles. (Voydanoff, 1988, reports the same finding. However, because both studies analysed data from the 1977 Quality of Employment Survey, this cannot be taken as similar findings from independent studies.) In other words, the greater the perceived controllability over the schedule, the less the perceived conflict between employment and family roles. As a result, both objective involvement in a flexible schedule as well as the belief that one has control over the amount and timing of one's schedule are significantly and negatively correlated with interference between work and family roles.

Marital Satisfaction

There is no research addressing the direct relationship between involvement in a flexitime schedule and marital satisfaction. The data from the 1977 Quality of Employment Survey also do not permit a specific examination of the relationship between perceived controllability over scheduling flexibility and marital satisfaction. However, information on family satisfaction (rather than marital satisfaction) was obtained in that survey, and two of the three items in this index specifically assessed marital satisfaction. Staines and Pleck (1984) showed that perceived schedule flexibility was positively associated with this index of family satisfaction.

In concluding this section on the time spent in employment and marital functioning, it is appropriate to question just how meaningful the time spent in employment is to individuals. On the basis of data collected from five representative national samples, Lacy, Bokemeier, and Shepard (1983) found that the number of hours spent on the job was ranked as the *least* important job characteristic (after the meaning of work, promotion, income and security). This is somewhat consistent with the results of Keith and Schafer's (1983) findings in a study of depression in two-job families. They compared the effects of husbands' objective work characteristics (e.g. hours worked per week, objective income levels) and subjective employment characteristics (e.g. job satisfaction, work orientation) in predicting their spouses' depression levels. Their results suggest that husbands' subjective employment characteristics were more important in predicting wives' depression than were temporal or objective employment characteristics. Consequently, an examination of the consequences for marital functioning of the amount of time devoted to employment may provide a limited perspective of the effects of the full range of employment-related stressors on marital functioning.

JOB-RELATED TRANSFERS AND MARITAL FUNCTIONING

As stated at the beginning of this chapter, there are two main objective job characteristics that are assumed to be negatively associated with marital functioning. The first concerns temporal aspects of employment; and these have now been discussed. The second objective characteristic, widely believed to be negatively associated with marital functioning, is the mobility associated with job-related transfers.

The Nature of Job-Related Transfers and Geographic Mobility

If we are to understand what is meant by job-related mobility, the first step is to separate the notion of job-related mobility from that of a job change. The factors differentiating these two events are the level of involvement for the family, whether the individual remains with the company and to a lesser extent career advancement. First, job-related transfers resulting in geographic mobility directly involve the nuclear family in the move, while job changes frequently occur without any change in residence. This distinction is important and underlies much of the concern regarding mobility. Baum and his colleagues have shown that the negative stress associated with a natural or technological disaster is exacerbated when people are uprooted from their communities (Baum, Gatchel and Schaeffer, 1983). Second, in most cases, individuals stay within the same organization when experiencing a job-related transfer, with the implication that the job-related transfer would lead either immediately or at a later stage to promotion within the organization. Third, job-related transfers are typically offered to successful employees, and if the individual refuses to move, his or her career advancement in the organization would be jeopardized, perhaps permanently. Thus, job-related mobility differs from a job-related change in terms of its meaning both for the individual as well as for the members of the nuclear family. As such, the consequences of job-related transfers would be greater for marital functioning.

Prevalence of Job-Related Transfers

Although it is difficult to isolate one statistic that would indicate the extent of geographic mobility as a function of job-related transfers each year, there are data suggesting that this experience is frequent in North America. For example, Brett (1982) estimates that over 100 000 employees and their families are likely to be transferred each year in the United States alone. In 1984, Gault quoted statistics from the Employee Relocation Council which suggested there are between 300 000 and 500 000 supported relocations for home owners each year. Even this is probably an underestimate of the extent of job-related mobility, because it ignores those relocations where the transferee was not a home owner. Sell (1983) reported data from the 1973 to 1977 Annual Housing Surveys in the United States suggesting that approximately 800 000 household heads were relocated annually by their companies, and that this figure had doubled since the early 1960s. Carruthers and Pinder (1983) also suggest that nearly 800 000 people are transferred to a new geographic location each year for job-related reasons.

Perhaps the highest estimate of job-related mobility comes from Gault (1984) who reported Internal Revenue Service data in the United States indicating that 1.5 million taxpayers report some kind of job-related relocation expenses each year. Thus, although the exact level of employee relocation and job-related mobility is difficult to isolate, it is clear that job-related mobility is frequent. Even if we exclude from these estimates any factors that may overinflate the apparent extent of geographic mobility, for example, individuals moving to retirement communities or students moving away from home, the level of employee-related mobility remains high. Clearly, therefore, substantial numbers of families are subject to job-related transfers annually, and it remains for the empirical data to be considered in assessing whether such mobility is negatively associated with marital functioning.

Concern About the Negative Effects of Job-Related Transfers

With the increasing levels of job-related transfers during the 1970s, widespread concern was expressed about the consequences of such mobility for the individual concerned, the spouse and children in the family. Perhaps the concern over the possible negative effects of job-related mobility can be appreciated if the work of Seidenberg (1973), and Packard (1972), are considered. Both Seidenberg (1973) and Packard (1972) maintain that loneliness for the spouse is one of the negative consequences of geographical mobility that follows from job-related transfers. For example, Seidenberg maintains that 'Wives suffer because their identities and sense of self worth are shattered by continual moves' (1973, p. vii). Seidenberg's statement reflects a widespread belief that may no longer be accurate, namely that it is inevitably the husband who is employed and the wife who is non-employed and who must uproot herself. This perspective is no longer appropriate: many wives are now offered transfers, and employees are refusing offers of within-company mobility in increasing numbers even if negative career implications do ensue.

Although Packard (1972) devotes one chapter of his book, *A Nation of Strangers*, to the possible benefits arising from geographic mobility, all the remaining chapters detail the negative consequences that the individual, the non-mobile spouse and the children may experience. Packard (1972) includes divorce, marital infidelity and sexual problems among the marital problems likely to emerge from geographical mobility, even though if present, such problems could have existed before the move. In support of his assertion, Packard (1972) quotes data suggesting that marital instability and divorce are far higher in mobile communities, mobile counties and mobile states in the United States of America than in those communities, states or provinces where mobility is less prevalent. On a more individual level, Packard (1972) points out that the assassins of John Kennedy, Robert Kennedy and Martin Luther King were highly mobile, lonely individuals who constantly changed their jobs or residences. Packard is suggesting that geographical mobility can result in mindless acts of aggression. Yet, this argument is flawed. It assumes that mobility causes negative consequences, rather than considering that there may be certain personality types who are more prone to both geographical mobility as well as such senseless aggression. Second, Packard's analogy ignores the fact that these individuals chose to move, probably because they were unsuccessful and lonely. Yet individuals involved in job-related mobility are relocated by their organizations, frequently because of their job success. Third, the mobility patterns of assassins do not cause their aberrant behaviours; rather, their aberrant behaviours are most likely a consequence of mental disorder.

Given the concern that a link exists between mobility and family breakdown (Packard, 1972; Seidenberg, 1973), two questions must be answered. First, why does job-related geographic mobility continue at such high levels if mobility exacts such a high personal and familial price? One plausible answer to this first question can be gleaned from Weissman and Paykel (1972), who, like many others, point out that 'career advancement in many professions and in academia often depends on the individual's willingness to move to a better job' (p. 27). Hence, individuals may accept such transfers because of the implied negative consequences of refusing to move. A second and more fundamental question is whether the concern expressed is consistent with the empirical data available focusing on the relationship between job-related transfers and marital functioning. Since Packard (1972) and Seidenberg (1973) expressed their concern early in the 1970s, and the incidence of geographical mobility has increased since then, there has been an increasing number of empirical studies investigating specifically whether there are any negative effects for marital functioning associated with the geographic mobility that follows from job-related transfers.

Empirical Studies on the Effects of Job-related Transfers

One assumption inherent in the concern regarding geographical mobility is that individuals whose mobility is involuntary will fare worse than their counterparts who choose to move. Using data from a nationally representative sample in the United States between 1966 and 1969, Butler, McAllister and Kaiser (1973) examined this issue. They compared groups of non-mobile and mobile individuals. However, they further subdivided the mobile individuals into two groups, according to whether their move could be considered voluntary or not. Contrary to the concern frequently expressed, Butler *et al.*'s (1973) data generally suggest that involuntary residential mobility exerts little if any negative effect on the social behaviour of the spouses. In fact, if anything, the data suggest that males who moved, whether voluntarily or not, are *less* likely than non-mobile males to self-report any kind of mental disorder. Thus for males, when any impact of mobility is present, the data from Butler *et al.*'s (1973) nationally representative sample contradicts popular concerns. Specifically, mobile males are less likely than their non-mobile counterparts to be alienated, they are less likely to report any kind of mental disturbance and less likely to report poor medical health. A slightly different pattern emerged for females, however, in that mobile females were more likely to report symptoms of disturbance. One exception to this pattern for women emerged. Women who had just moved experienced less alienation than those who had not. Visiting within the community provides a good index of post-mobility adjustment, because of frequently voiced concerns that moving to a new community as a function of a husband's job-related transfer would increase the wife's loneliness and alienation (Packard, 1972; Seidenberg, 1973). To focus on the issue of post-mobility social visiting patterns, McAllister, Butler and Kaiser (1973) used a data set consisting of a group of women who paralleled a general cross-section of married American women during the years 1966 to 1969. McAllister *et al.* (1973) investigated whether the visiting frequency of these women changed following their mobility experience. Again, the results obtained contradict previous assumptions. McAllister *et al.* (1973) found that following mobility, women experience increased social interactions in their new places of residence, and that this interaction is typically local in nature.

McKain (1973) also investigated post-mobility adaptation among wives whose husbands had been transferred, but he used a smaller sample of army families. Essentially, McKain (1973) investigated the functioning of 200 families both three and twelve months following the transfer. The effects of mobility were such that marital problems were significantly associated with general alienation three months following the move, but there was no significant association between marital adjustment and alienation one year after the move. This suggests that the negative stress associated with job-related mobility is chronic, in that it lasts more than a few days. However, its effects dissipate within the first year. Nonetheless, McKain's (1973) results are limited by the military nature of the sample. Even though (or perhaps because) military families experience considerable geographical mobility, the generalizability of findings based on military samples cannot be taken for granted.

Jones (1973) replicated McKain's (1973) findings in that she found that any strain following mobility does not endure for long periods of time. Jones (1973) also found that any negative strain varies with the stage of the moving process, and varies between individuals. Jones (1973) studied a group of 500 families selected from those who had been clients of a major moving company in the United States. Jones's (1973) results suggest that there are no long-term negative effects associated with mobility. For example, she found that wives experienced no decrease in social relationships associated with the number of times they had moved, and Jones (1973) concludes that most women certainly are able to make a very positive adjustment.

Moderators of the Effects of Job-Related Mobility

Some studies have progressed beyond the examination of whether a linear relationship exists between mobility and personal or marital functioning to investigate what factors moderate this relationship. One such study is that reported by Jones (1973) who went beyond others, identifying factors that may moderate whether the move is experienced positively or negatively. In other words, Jones (1973) identified individual differences that may moderate the relationship between geographical mobility and subsequent strain, including the amount of information (i.e. informational support) people have available to them prior to the move. Jones (1973) found, for example, that where wives had no information prior to the move, they were far more likely to be unhappy after the move. Moreover, wives who were unhappy after the move said that they could have used more information in the planning stages, prior to the move. Wives were more likely to be unhappy in the new community if their husbands had taken the decision to move on a unilateral basis with little or no consultation with them. These findings suggest that marital functioning before the move, and perhaps especially the communication between the spouses, may predict marital satisfaction after the move is completed. Two related studies support aspects of Jones's (1973) findings. First, Komarovksy (1940) found that the effects of unemployment on marital functioning could be predicted from the level of marital functioning prior to the layoff (see Chapter 9). Second, in their study of the chronic stress resulting from the Three Mile Island incident, Chisholm, Kasl and Mueller (1986) showed that psychological functioning some time after the disaster could be predicted on the basis of the amount and accuracy of information that residents and workers received at the time of the disaster.

A second important moderating factor or individual difference is the age of the individual. Jones (1973) suggests that age may be the single most important predictor of crying (one indicator of depression or a feeling of loss) in the first two weeks following the move. In her study, no individual 60 years or older reported crying. However, these people may not have been moving because of job-related transfers and therefore may not be relevant in the present context. Individuals in the 40–49 age group reported crying most frequently immediately following the move. Again, however, any negative effects tended to dissipate within a few weeks, a trend similar to results obtained from other studies on acute stressors (Barling *et al.*, 1987; Loo, 1986). Consequently, the results obtained by both Jones (1973) and McKain (1973) suggest that any negative effects following mobility do dissipate fairly rapidly, and for most people, job-related mobility may be an acute stressor.

One problem with the studies of Jones (1973), McKain (1973), McAllister *et al.* (1973) and Butler *et al.* (1973) is that they are all based on data collected almost two decades ago. Attitudes towards moving have changed substantially since then. Employees may be more accepting of job-related mobility because of current high levels of job-related transfers, and such mobility may now be viewed as a regular job requirement. If this is the case, job-related mobility may now exert positive effects. There is some support for this argument from the literature on unemployment. Negative effects associated with unemployment such as increased risk of mortality and marital functioning are lessened considerably in communities with unusually high rates of unemployment (see Iverson *et al.*, 1987; Kessler, Turner and House, 1987; respectively). Consequently, recent studies conducted by Brett (1982), Fox and Krausz (1987), and Brett and Reilly (1988) should be examined in some detail. Brett (1982) contrasted large groups of mobile people with comparison groups of non-mobile or stable people drawn from a random sample of the American population. Brett's (1982) study extends previous research by measuring mobility in two ways: first, she conducted a contrasted-groups analysis with the three non-mobile groups; second, she conducted a within-group analysis in which she took the total number of moves the individual had ever experienced as the predictor or independent variable, and assessed whether it was associated with current psychological functioning. More important, unlike most other studies which focused on the effects of mobility on a variety of indices of psychological well-being, Brett (1982) also provides data on marital and family satisfaction as outcomes of geographic mobility.

When focusing on either the men or women in the transfer or mobile sample, Brett (1982) found no correlation between the total number of moves and either marital or family satisfaction. However, there were statistically significant differences between the marital and family satisfaction of the transfer group when compared to the randomly selected samples. Mobile groups were significantly more satisfied with both their family and their marriages, and this difference held true both for men and women. Brett concludes that mobile men and women 'are more satisfied with their family lives and marriages than are stable men and women' (1982, p. 460). However, the differences between mobile and non-mobile couples was not replicated when focusing on non-family social relationships, because non-mobile individuals functioned significantly better in terms of social relationships and community satisfaction. Thus, although Brett does not suggest that people experience no difficulty associated with mobility, her data suggest the consequences

of mobility need not be as dire for the marriage and the family as previously feared.
The results to date suggest, therefore, that contrary to the concerns expressed
early in the 1970s, the consequences of mobility may not be negative for the
marriage. Fox and Krausz (1987) extended this notion to investigate the role of
the family in supporting and assisting its members who were about to undergo
a company-wide relocation. In the study reported by Fox and Krausz (1987), a
government department in Israel was about to relocate, and they focused on the
relocation intentions of the 155 workers who agreed to participate in their study.
While all the other studies cited so far focused on the consequences of mobility for
the family, Fox and Krausz (1987) focused on the role of the family in helping the
individual to cope *prior* to the move. Fox and Krausz's (1987) hypotheses were
based on the assumption that it is the spouse and children's attitudes that determine
the consequences of the move, and how the family unit copes with it. Their results
showed that the attitudes of the spouse and the children towards the impending
move were the most important determinants of the intention to relocate, and of
positive reactions to the relocation. Job prospects for the spouse in the new area
were also significantly correlated with the intention to relocate. Their results also
provide a revealing perspective on the relative role of family- and employment-
related variables in this situation. While family variables predicted the intention to
relocate, current job satisfaction and job involvement were unrelated to the intention
to relocate. In a subsequent longitudinal study, Brett and Reilly (1988) showed that
spouses' support was also the best predictor of job-related mobility. Consequently,
Fox and Krausz's (1987) and Brett and Reilly's (1988) data support the notion
that family processes fulfil a significant role in relocation and relocation intention,
and the anticipation of strain following the relocation. Yet spouses' employment
status did not predict the willingness to accept the offer of job-related mobility
in Noe, Steffy and Barber's (1988) study. Taken together, what all these results
suggest is that objective employment characteristics are not associated with job-
related mobility (Noe *et al.*, 1988), yet subjective family processes are (Brett and
Reilly, 1988; Fox and Krausz, 1987).

It would appear from the studies cited above that geographical mobility
associated with a job change does not necessarily exert negative effects on the
family. Indeed, the results of these studies suggest just the opposite: although there
may initially be short-term negative strain for some individuals, marital and family
satisfaction may later be enhanced. A question that must be addressed, therefore,
is why the results of these studies differ so markedly from the predictions put
forward regarding a negative relationship between job-related transfers and marital
functioning (e.g. Packard, 1972; Seidenberg, 1973).

Job-Related Mobility: Continuing Concern vs Empirical Data

A number of factors contribute to an understanding of why the results from
empirical studies differ from the concerns expressed previously. Specifically, the

level at which the analysis is conducted, the type of methodology used, and possible ideological biases may be important factors. If we take the level of analysis as the first factor, it is clear that Packard (1972) used the community group as his level of analysis. Indeed, Packard's (1972) analysis is based on observations of community phenomena and community trends. For example, if we again examine Packard's (1972) notion that divorce is a function of mobility, it is clear that his conclusion is based entirely on the assumption that divorce rates vary between communities, and that those communities in which divorce rates are high are typically characterized by high mobility rates. Nonetheless, it should be emphasized again (see Chapter 2) that divorce is an inadequate criterion of marital functioning, and of the effects of job-related stressors.

The reasons for the marked differences between the concerns expressed about the negative effects associated with job-related mobility and results based on empirical data go further than the level of analysis. The typical methodologies used may also account for the differences. The empirical studies suggesting mobility is not associated with subsequent negative strain have often been based on representative or random populations. The studies reinforcing the concern have typically been based on samples from which any kind of generalization is hazardous. For example, in suggesting that there is a link between mobility and depression, Weissman and Paykel (1972) identified a group of clinically depressed women, and noted that among this group there was a high proportion of people who self-reported a close temporal relationship between mobility and depression. Packard's (1972) conclusions are also based on a non-representative sample. As Packard himself notes, his conclusions and concerns are based on the following general strategy:

> ... I made a number of trips to towns and cities in the United States that attracted my curiosity and briefly for comparative information I visited four cities from countries abroad. Typically in America I would fly into the town or city to be visited, rent a car and drive around for a day or two to get the feel of the area, and then begin talking to people about their life patterns. I would also talk with people who might have special knowledge such as local officials, reformers, professors, social workers, school officials, businessmen, realties, and union officials to get their impressions. There were many group discussions. ... Also in my research I conducted samplings involving a few hundred people in four communities. ... The exploration led me to believe that at least 40 million Americans now lead feebly rooted lives.
>
> (Packard, 1972, p.2)

Predictably, Packard (1972) has been severely criticized for his research methodology. He has also been taken to task for his version of American society that romanticizes the past, but is overly pessimistic about the present and the future (e.g. Gans, 1972). Gans (1972) also criticizes Packard for his selective use of studies which ignored the fact that family and personal changes following mobility are not necessarily negative. In contrast, Gans (1972) suggests that mobility experiences may offer the family unit and the individuals concerned the opportunity for development, growth and enhanced resilience and satisfaction.

Thus, an examination of the empirical data suggests that the concern expressed regarding the inevitably negative effects of geographical mobility is misplaced. As Brett (1982) notes, however, this does not mean that all individuals or families experience few difficulties with job-related transfers. These findings should alert us to three factors. First, the perception of the family as vulnerable and at the mercy of external events does the family a disservice. Instead, the family and its members are more resilient than the pessimistic picture painted so frequently in the literature. Second, it might be worthwhile for future research to examine how families cope with job-related transfers. Lastly, it should be noted that there is a gender-bias in the research on the effects of mobility: consistent with the notion that it is the husband who is employed and the wife who is the homemaker in 'normal' families, research invariably focuses on the effects of husbands' job-related mobility on their own and their spouses' marital functioning. There are no corresponding studies investigating any effects on marital functioning when it is wives who are offered the chance of job-related mobility.

OBJECTIVE EMPLOYMENT CHARACTERISTICS AND MARITAL FUNCTIONING: CONCLUSION

In this chapter, the effects of four objective employment characteristics on marital functioning were considered. The first three concerned temporal aspects of employment. Essentially, neither the amount of time spent on the job nor the scheduling of that time exerts a direct influence on marital satisfaction. However, indirect effects emerge. The relationship between job-related time demands and the scheduling of that time on the one hand, and marital satisfaction on the other, is mediated by family–employment role interference. In contrast, being employed on a flexible work schedule, and perceiving control over the schedule, results in decreases in conflict between employment and family roles. Finally, although some individuals experience problems in the short term following job-related geographic transfers, studies show that marital and family satisfaction may be enhanced in the longer term.

Chapter 4

Subjective Employment Experiences and Marital Functioning

In previous research on the interdependence of employment and family factors, researchers have frequently conceptualized and operationalized employment as dichotomous, that is individuals are employed or not. In Chapter 3, the relationship between objective aspects of employment and marital functioning was investigated. The present chapter examines whether experiences of employment have an equal or greater effect on marital functioning than employment. As Aldous (1969a, p. 708) stated:

> ... once one goes beyond the simple dichotomy of employment and unemployment, the characteristics of the job the man holds in the occupational structure can have profound effects on his marital and parental role performance.

Employment characteristics can be categorized in several ways. The framework that is followed here describes employment characteristics in terms of whether they are objective or subjective. Subjective employment characteristics reflect individuals' perception of their employment experiences, and their affective response to their employment. Subjective employment characteristics include job stress, perception of and need for autonomy and responsibility in the workplace, and job satisfaction. These subjective aspects of employment can be clearly differentiated from the temporal employment characteristics that were discussed in Chapter 3, and which focus on observable and quantifiable characteristics, such as the amount of time spent on the job, shift work patterns, flexible work schedules, and job-related geographic mobility.

There are several reasons for discussing the relationship between subjective employment characteristics and marital functioning separately from the relationship between temporal aspects of employment and marital functioning. First, research on this topic has treated the relationship between objective and subjective employment characteristics and marital functioning separately. Second, scant theoretical and empirical attention has been paid to differentiating effects of subjective and objective employment characteristics on marital functioning. Yet it is important to compare the relative contribution of objective and subjective employment characteristics to marital functioning. There are data suggesting that the subjective perception of employment (e.g. job stress, participation in decision making) rather than objective or temporal characteristics (e.g. work schedules and the amount of time spent on the job) determine the size and direction of any relationship with marital functioning (e.g. Pratt and Barling, 1988). Certainly, data from five separate random surveys in the United States showed that when contrasted with the meaning of work, promotion, income and security, the amount of time spent on the job was rated consistently as the least important attribute of employment (Lacy *et al.*, 1983).

Subjective employment characteristics can be subdivided into several categories. For the purposes of this discussion, they will be divided into individual difference variables (e.g. job stress, job satisfaction, job involvement, Protestant work ethic, dimensions of Type A behaviour) and structurally determined characteristics (e.g. participation in decision making, perceptions of the organizational climate). In contrast to structural characteristics, individual difference variables are attitudinal, and have predictors that exist outside of the organizational context. For example, Brief *et al.* (1988) show how factors extraneous to the organization, like general negative affectivity, predispose individuals to experiencing negative job stress. Structural characteristics of employment are a function of the structure and functioning of the organization, and include such characteristics as opportunity to participate in decision making.

JOB STRESS AND MARITAL FUNCTIONING

Much concern has been expressed regarding the possible detrimental effects of job stress on marital functioning among academics, columnists and practitioners (see Chapter 1). Similar concerns are now being voiced by jobholders. For example, Maslach and Jackson (1979) quote a police officer from New York City as saying:

> You change when you become a copy. You become tough and hard and cynical ... And sometimes, without realizing it, you act that way all the time with your wife and kids. But it's something you have to do, because if you start getting emotionally involved with what happens at work, you'll wind up in Bellevue (a psychiatric hospital).

Thus, it is surprising that so little empirical research has focused specifically on job stress in this particular context. A number of trends are apparent in the available literature. First, the nature of the job stressor is frequently not specified (i.e. whether it is acute, daily or chronic), as a result of which we cannot predict the duration of any stressor, stress or strain. Second, where a relationship emerges between job stressors and marital functioning, it is typically modest in size. This suggests that marital functioning is multiply determined, and the effect of job stressors on marital functioning should be examined relative to other causes of marital functioning. Third, the research is invariably derived from self-report data. This raises questions as to whether validity is compromised by confounding perceived job stress and other variables such as mood (e.g. Brief *et al.*, 1988) or social desirability. Fourth, because the research is invariably cross-sectional, inferences about causality remain hazardous (Barling *et al.*, 1987). Lastly, the research often focuses on 'special' or 'atypical' populations. For example, Hageman (1978) focused on the police, Martin and Ickovics (1987) focused on military wives and MacEwen and Barling (1988b) focused on individuals within the first eighteen months of their marriages. As a result of the concentration on these atypical populations, the generalizability of any results remains an empirical question.

Where research has been concerned primarily with establishing the size and direction of the relationship between job stressors and marital functioning, it is not unusual to find a significant but low relationship (e.g. Hageman, 1978; Martin and Ickovics, 1987). Specifically, the greater the job-related stress, the lower the self-reported level of marital functioning. In considering this body of research, we will contrast the effects of acute and chronic job stressors on general measures of marital satisfaction, and where the availability of the data permits, we will also consider specific aspects of marital functioning.

Chronic Job Stressors

The studies that have been conducted in this area have either focused on chronic role stressors or chronic job stressors. Two studies were located focusing on the link between chronic job-related role stressors and marital satisfaction. The three forms of role stress that have been investigated in this context are role conflict, role ambiguity and role overload. Two forms of role conflict (namely, intra-role conflict and inter-role conflict) will be discussed frequently throughout the text and need to be differentiated. *Intra-role conflict* (frequently referred to as role conflict) occurs when the individual experiences conflicting pressures or messages concerning performance of a single role (Kahn *et al.*, 1964). *Inter-role conflict* occurs when the individual experiences pressures arising from the performance of different roles (e.g. spouse, employee, mothers; Greenhaus and Beutell, 1985).

In one study of administrators in a provincial penitentiary system, Burke *et al.* (1980a) investigated the relationship between husbands' role conflict and role ambiguity, and their wives' marital functioning. While neither role conflict nor role ambiguity was associated with wives' positive marital behaviours (e.g. laughed or shared a joke, spent an evening chatting), both role conflict and role ambiguity were significantly associated with wives' negative marital behaviours (e.g. not showing love, irritating personal habits). Like most of the findings relating job stressors to marital functioning, however, these results should be interpreted cautiously, because *(a)* the size of the relationships is modest, *(b)* the data were obtained at one point in time only, and *(c)* the number of correlations computed was large, increasing the possibility that individual correlations were significant by chance.

More recently, Greenhaus *et al.* (1987) investigated the relationship between several employment experiences (including role conflict), job performance and marital satisfaction in a large group of accountants. Whereas Burke *et al.* (1980a) found no relationship between husbands' role conflict and wives' marital satisfaction, Greenhaus *et al.* (1987) found that role conflict was significantly and negatively associated with marital adjustment. Greenhaus *et al.* (1987) also showed that role conflict was significantly associated with employment–family conflict. Again, however, the size of these relationships, while statistically significant, was modest, indicating that role stressors must be considered as only one facet of the many variables impinging on marital satisfaction.

Greenhaus *et al.* (1987) extended their study to examine an additional function served by role conflict. Specifically, they examined whether role conflict moderated the relationship between job performance and marital satisfaction, and found that there was no direct relationship between job performance (a performance rating by one's supervisor) and marital adjustment. However, role conflict did moderate the relationship between job performance and marital adjustment. For individuals experiencing high levels of role conflict, high job performance was associated with lower levels of marital adjustment. Conversely, there was no association between job performance and marital adjustment when role conflict was low. It can be concluded from Greenhaus *et al.*'s (1987) data that while high job performance need not be viewed as a potential risk factor for marital distress, under certain stressful employment conditions (in this case, role conflict), job performance is associated with poorer marital adjustment.

Most research assessing the effects of chronic job stressors on marital functioning has focused on global marital satisfaction. One dramatic and specific index of marital functioning that will be considered frequently throughout this text is family violence (see Chapters 5, 7 and 9). Consistent with the notion that stress is one of the major predictors of family violence (e.g. Farrington, 1986), attention has turned to the question of whether job stress predicts family violence. Most of this research has focused on whether job stress is associated with child abuse, or whether unemployment stress is related to family violence in general. However, there are two studies addressing the relationship between job stress and spouse abuse.

Barling and Rosenbaum (1986) contrasted the levels of job stress in three groups: maritally satisfied men, maritally dissatisfied but non-abusive men, and men currently undergoing treatment for spouse abuse. They found significant differences between these three groups in terms of job stress; abusive husbands reported significantly more job events, and perceived these events more negatively than either of the other two groups. Three aspects of this study warrant attention. First, Barling and Rosenbaum (1986) note that while the occurrence of job-related events and the negative perception of those events was associated with spouse abuse, the positive perception of job events was not associated with spouse abuse. This suggests that negative job-related stress is associated with spouse abuse. Second, by including a maritally dissatisfied but non-abusive group, Barling and Rosenbaum (1986) could infer that the association between job-related stress and spouse abuse was independent of marital dissatisfaction. Third, Barling and Rosenbaum (1986) replicated previous research (Hageman, 1978; Martin and Ickovics, 1987), because the significant relationship between job stress and marital dissatisfaction was modest in magnitude.

MacEwen and Barling (1988b) investigated the effect of total life stress measured six months after marriage (i.e. job stress together with general life stress) on spousal violence twelve months later in a large sample of 275 newly married couples. Moreover, MacEwen and Barling (1988b) obtained reports of aggression from both partners to minimize biased reporting of marital aggression. Contrary to expectation, MacEwen and Barling (1988b) showed that after accounting for prior levels of marital aggression, there was no relationship between total life stress and spouse abuse one year later for men. However, there was a slight but significant association between total life stress and spouse abuse for women, even after prior levels of aggression were controlled. MacEwen and Barling's (1988b) use of global stress as the predictor precluded a contrast of the specific effects of job stress and life stress. They provide one intriguing suggestion concerning the failure to find support for the hypothesis that stress in general predicts spouse abuse. They suggest that the small effect of stress on spouse abuse may be due to the long time lag between the measurement of stress and spouse abuse, and that a daily or acute stressor framework should be used. This emphasizes the need to focus on the nature of the subjective employment experience, and the nature of the job stressor. Lastly, spouse abuse may be more likely to occur when there is congruence between the source of the stress and the outcome. Hence, spouse abuse may result more from family stress than from job-related stress.

Acute Job Stressors

As discussed in Chapter 2, acute stressors occur more suddenly, less frequently and demand more immediate coping than chronic stressors. Two studies have explicitly investigated effects of acute job-related stressors on marital satisfaction. Both these studies involved longitudinal analyses of the effects of an acute job stressor on marital satisfaction.

In the first of these two studies, Barling and Milligan (1987) addressed the effects of participation in a 22-day strike by 7200 community college teachers. Short-term strikes may affect the family for several reasons. Aside from financial strain, Vispo and Shine (1985) note from their study of an eighteen-day strike of correction officers that family members may find themselves aligned with opposite sides in intense strikes. Barling and Milligan (1987) investigated whether the stress associated with industrial relations events affected marital satisfaction and psychological well-being, during the strike and again two and six months after legislation compelled the striking teachers to return to their jobs. Two results from this study are noteworthy. First, immediately as the strike was terminated, the stress associated with striking was significantly and negatively associated with marital satisfaction. Second, negatively perceived industrial relations stress was not associated with change in marital satisfaction either two or six months following termination of the strike. This study suggests that any effects of acute negative job stressors on marital satisfaction may not be long-lasting if the strike is of a short-term duration. When a strike endures for some time, the family suffers considerable financial strain (Gennard, 1981). Under such conditions, chronic stress may be generated, and long-lasting effects on marital functioning may develop.

A second study conducted to investigate the effects of an acute job stressor on marital satisfaction focused on the effects of an acute workplace disaster (Barling *et al.*, 1987). In 1985, an explosion involving 1.5 tons of explosives occurred in the nitroglycerine issuing house of the world's largest dynamite factory. The consequences of this blast were devastating in terms of human life and physical property. Fourteen people were killed, and fourteen suffered serious burns and other injuries, and the buildings in which the blast occurred were annihilated. The marital satisfaction of the 40 survivors was contrasted with that of workers in two quasi-experimental control groups. Assessment took place during the second week following the blast, and again two months thereafter. It was predicted that individuals who had experienced the disaster would suffer psychological effects because of the perceived severity of the disaster, which would be manifested in poorer marital functioning, life satisfaction, job satisfaction and organizational commitment. Contrary to expectation, there were no differences between any of these three groups either during the second week following the blast or two months thereafter. Barling *et al.* (1987) suggest that the acute nature of the work-related disaster accounts for this. The negative consequences of an acute job stressor dissipate as soon as people believe there is no longer any likelihood the event will recur, or any concern that the effects of the stressor still linger (Barling and Milligan, 1987; Jones, 1973; Loo, 1986). If this is the case, then it is possible that the acute job disaster exerted a temporary influence on marital satisfaction that had dissipated by the time the survivors were tested.

EMPLOYMENT EXPERIENCES AND MARITAL SATISFACTION

As enumerated in Chapter 2, there are various job characteristics and employment experiences that lead to greater psychological well-being if present in the job. For the purposes of this discussion, the possible effects of career salience, participation in decision making, perceptions of the organizational climate, and job involvement on marital functioning will be evaluated.

Career Salience

There has been some research focusing on the relative salience or importance of one's job and marital satisfaction. Aldous (1969a) initially questioned whether excessive job salience would exert a detrimental effect on marital functioning. The research focusing on this question has produced contradictory findings. On the one hand, Gaesser and Whitbourne (1985) showed that work salience was not associated with marital adjustment. On the other hand, Mortimer's (1980) data suggest the degree of occupational involvement was indirectly associated with marital satisfaction. However, the different meanings assigned to the constructs of work salience and occupational involvement may partially account for these differences in findings. Likewise, their measures of marital functioning also differed.

Participation in Decision Making

Since the 1970s, one of the most frequently debated yet least understood topics within organizational psychology has been the nature and effects of participation in decision making. As Schweiger and Leana (1986, p. 147) observe:

> Few topics in the field of organizational behavior have held the attention of researchers with as much persistence as the issue of subordinate participation in decision making (PDM). For over fifty years, numerous researchers have investigated PDM in settings ranging from controlled laboratory conditions to a wide variety of organizational contexts. Yet our ability to make accurate predictions regarding the overall effects of PDM remains rather negligible.

Consistent with the general concern that employment influences non-job functioning, there is now interest in whether participation in decision making on the job has any effect on marital and family functioning. Price (1985) suggests that participation in decision making increases workers' feelings of autonomy and power, and that those feelings generalize to areas beyond their employment. Although participation in decision making is investigated frequently in the organizational context (Schweiger and Leana, 1986), the question of whether its effects spill over to the family are not considered. Indeed, there are only two studies that investigate the effects of a participatory work environment on family functioning. Piotrkowski (1979) studied the effects of non-participation in decision making among a sample of blue collar workers. She found that when employees had little chance of exerting control, and the job was experienced as boring and non-demanding, it was associated with patterns of non-participation in the family. This supports Price's hypothesis that there is a causal relationship between participation in decision making and participation in the family.

Crouter (1984b) conducted a qualitative study to investigate the relationship between participation in decision making and family functioning. She predicted that access to a participative work environment would lead to enhanced family functioning, including greater effectiveness as a spouse and a parent. The results of her in-depth interviews with 55 blue-collar and supervisory personnel suggest that participation in decision making can yield both positive and negative effects on family functioning. For example, the potential benefits of participation in decision making on family functioning are evident from the comments of one employee, who stated that:

> Working here takes more time away from my personal and family life, but it has helped in terms of dealing with my family. I'm more willing to get their opinions. We hold 'team meetings' at home to make decisions.
>
> (Crouter, 1984b, p. 82)

Detrimental effects on the family following participation in decision making on the job can be inferred from the following two comments.

> My husband can't understand why I like it here so much and why I'd want to work later (longer hours). He thinks I've become terribly independent. It bothered him at first . . . I felt a part of my team. He had trouble understanding that and felt left out.
>
> (Crouter, 1984b, p. 80)

Participation in decision making on the job may also interact with other factors, such as gender role beliefs, in predicting marital functioning. One of Crouter's (1984b) subjects said of her husband:

> My husband got to the point where he didn't want to hear about my work. He's a little threatened by my learning new things. . . . He felt like he was stupid and I was smart, and he wanted to keep up with me (p. 80).

Before considering explanations for these findings, one aspect of these findings is noteworthy. Specifically, increased independence and assertion following participation in decision making on the job may have positive consequences for one spouse, but negative consequences for the other.

One explanation for these findings is that for some individuals, the additional responsibility and time commitment required by participation in decision making results in higher levels of personal strain (Crouter, 1984b; Jackson, 1983). This increased arousal would obstruct or frustrate optimal performance in other life domains such as marital functioning. Another explanation for the negative effects of participation on family functioning is that for any spillover to be positive, the expectations held regarding one system (e.g. employment) must be congruent with those in another (e.g. the family). Clearly, the democratic ethic implied by participatory work environments may be inconsistent with the authoritarian climate of many blue collar marriages (Komarovsky, 1987). Crouter (1984b) suggests that a participatory employment environment for one spouse may exert negative consequences for the marriage if the partner's employment environment is not consistent with the marital environment. Of course, this in no way implies that wives should be denied opportunities for participating fully and equally on the job because of possible negative side-effects on the marriage. To do so would be akin to the oft-quoted story of Golda Meir, then Prime Minister of Israel, being asked to place a curfew on all women in a major Israeli city during a period when the number of rapes had increased! Rather, if there is any policy-related implication from this finding at all, it speaks to the importance of equality of decision-making power within the marriage.

Because the results from Crouter's (1984b) study suggest that both positive and negative relationships can emerge between participation in decision making and marital functioning, it is important to examine moderators of the relationship between participation in decision making and family functioning. The moderating factors include spouses' tolerance for ambiguity and changes in routine, social skills, age, extent of formal education and general intelligence. For example, the need for tolerance for ambiguity increases with the introduction of participation in decision making (Jackson, 1983). Consequently, the positive relationship between participation in decision making and marital functioning may be greater for workers with a high tolerance for ambiguity. A negative relationship between participation in decision making and marital functioning would be evident in workers manifesting a low tolerance for ambiguity and less formal education.

Perceptions of Organizational Climate

Closely related to participation in decision making is the employee's perception of the psychological climate on the job. Indeed, participation in decision making is one of the job characteristics contributing to global perceptions of organizational climate. There are two studies assessing the relationship between perceptions of organizational climate and marital satisfaction. One study focuses on the relationship between accountants' perceptions of their organizational climate and their marital functioning (Greenhaus et al., 1987), and the other focuses on the relationship between husbands' perceptions of organizational climate and their wives' marital satisfaction (Barling, 1984).

Barling (1984) assessed whether there was a relationship between men's perceptions of organizational climate and their wives' marital adjustment. Using a global scale of perceived organizational climate, Barling (1984) found a significant relationship between husbands' perceptions of organizational climate and their spouse's marital satisfaction. Greenhaus et al.'s (1987) study focused on the relationship between four dimensions of 336 accountants' perceptions of the organizational climate (reward inequity, autocracy, pressure and the extent of support they perceived to be available in the environment), and two aspects of marital functioning (marital adjustment and employment–family conflict). They were able to isolate which of the four dimensions were related to each aspect of marital functioning. Specifically, no significant relationships emerged between autocracy and pressure on the job and either marital satisfaction or the extent of employment–family conflict. Reward inequity, however, was associated with employment–family conflict but not marital adjustment, while the extent to which the job environment was perceived as non-supportive was associated with both marital dissatisfaction and employment–family conflict. The results of this study extend those of Barling (1984) in isolating which specific dimensions of perceived organizational climate contribute to the overall effect on marital functioning.

The results of both these studies, therefore, suggest that perceptions of the organization's climate are associated with marital satisfaction. More importantly, it is possible to isolate which specific perceptions of organizational climate are associated with marital functioning (reward inequity and a non-supportive employment environment) and which are not (an autocratic environment and perceived pressure). What remains unanswered, however, is just why such a relationship would be expected.

Job Involvement and Job Commitment

In the industrial/organizational psychological literature, conceptual distinctions are usually drawn between job satisfaction and job involvement. As already noted, job satisfaction typically reflects the *outcome* of an individual's evaluation of his or her job. On the contrary, within this framework there are two independent components of 'job involvement'. The amount of time devoted to employment, and individuals' identification with the process of work. The relationship between job involvement as a temporal characteristic and marital functioning was considered in Chapter 3, where it was concluded that there is minimal support for a link between temporal employment characteristics and marital functioning. The discussion in this chapter is based on a conceptualization of job involvement consistent with definitions in organizational psychology (e.g. Brooke, Russell and Price, 1988), as an identification with intrinsic characteristics of the job. Some studies still confuse the notion of involvement with commitment, despite their being clearly differentiated in the organizational psychological literature (e.g. Barling and MacEwen, 1988; Brooke *et al.*, 1988). Nonetheless, it is still not possible to assess the separate effects of job involvement and occupational commitment on marital functioning for two reasons: first, there are relatively few studies in this area; and second, among those studies that do exist the two concepts of job involvement and occupational commitment are not adequately differentiated.

A relationship between job involvement and marital functioning has been the focus of speculation for some time. For example, on the basis of nearly two decades of clinical observations, Johnson and Masters (1976) maintain that high levels of involvement on the job, or high levels of adherence to the (Protestant) work ethic, are obtained at the expense of a fulfilling interpersonal and sexual relationship. Taking a somewhat different approach, Holman (1981) proposes that the relationship between employment involvement and marital functioning is curvilinear. He suggests that the data support the 'success constraint' theory put forward by Aldous, Osmond and Hicks (1979), from which it follows that marital functioning will be poorest under extremely low or extremely high conditions of employment involvement. If this specific hypothesis is supported, a curvilinear relationship between job involvement and marital functioning would emerge. Nonetheless, despite such assertions, there is no empirical support for the existence of a linear or a curvilinear relationship between the psychological identification with one's job and marital functioning. For example, Barling (1984) assessed whether a husband's job satisfaction, perceived organizational climate and job involvement were associated with his wife's marital satisfaction. After controlling for the effects of job satisfaction and perceived organizational climate, job involvement was not associated with marital satisfaction.

Another study focused on the relationship between occupational commitment and marital adjustment. Ladewig and McGee (1986) analysed their data separately for males and females, and showed some gender-specific effects. For husbands, there was no direct relationship between their occupational commitment and marital adjustment, but there was a significant negative relationship between wives' occupational commitment and husbands' marital adjustment. This pattern was reversed for women: while there was no relationship between husbands' occupational commitment and wives' marital adjustment, wives' occupational commitment was negatively associated with their own marital adjustment. Thus, as Ladewig and McGee (1986) point out, the results show that both husbands and wives agree that husbands' occupational commitment is not associated with marital adjustment, but higher levels of occupation commitment by wives is negatively associated with husbands' and wives' marital adjustment. The pattern of findings for wives and husbands also differs in that the relationship between occupational commitment and marital adjustment for wives was mediated by their perceptions of a supportive family environment, but a similar mediating influence did not emerge for husbands. The causal direction underlying these relationships could not be determined, however.

Ladewig and McGee's (1986) results are interesting despite the fact that there is some confusion regarding their definition of occupational commitment. To measure occupational commitment, they used items incorporated in some scales of job involvement (e.g. 'I live, eat and breathe my job'; Lodahl and Kejner, 1965), some that are similar to items assessing employment role commitment (e.g. 'I would probably keep working even if I didn't need the money'; see Jackson *et al.*, 1983) and others that clearly assess job satisfaction (e.g. 'The major satisfaction in my life comes from my job'). Thus, it is not possible to conclude that their findings are specific to occupational commitment. It is still critical to specify which employment experiences predict which aspects of marital functioning. One final aspect of Ladewig and McGee's (1986) findings is interesting. On the basis of their results, they question whether one model of employment and marriage can be generated for husbands and wives. This will be considered further when discussing whether similar or divergent models are most appropriate for understanding the effects of maternal and paternal employment on children (see Chapters 7 and 8).

JOB SATISFACTION AND MARITAL SATISFACTION

The preceding section focused on the association between intrinsic job characteristics and marital functioning. The question of how marital functioning is associated with job satisfaction is now considered.

Job satisfaction differs from intrinsic job characteristics in at least one major respect. While intrinsic job characteristics typically refer to the *process* of subjective employment experiences, job satisfaction reflects the *outcome* of these employment experiences (Barling and Van Bart, 1984). According to Locke (1983), job satisfaction may be defined 'as a pleasurable or positive emotional state resulting from the appraisal of one's job or job experiences' (p. 1800). If Locke's (1983) definition is followed it can be seen that job satisfaction also differs from job stressors or job stress as they were defined in Chapter 2. Briefly, while job satisfaction is a response following from an appraisal of one's job, job stressors are objective job-related events, and job stress is the individual's subjective perception of those events. This distinction is supported by empirical data, as *(a)* there is no consistent empirical relationship between measures of job stress and job dissatisfaction (e.g. Barling and Rosenbaum, 1986), *(b)* some individuals who report experiencing considerable negative job stress remain satisfied with their jobs (e.g. McGee, Goodson and Cashman, 1987), and *(c)* individuals experiencing the stress associated with a job-related disaster do not necessarily report lower levels of job satisfaction (Barling *et al.*, 1987).

There are important differences between the literatures dealing with the relationship between intrinsic job characteristics and marital functioning on the one hand, and job satisfaction and marital satisfaction on the other. Specifically, the literature on the relationship between intrinsic job characteristics and marital functioning consists of a number of empirical studies that do not share any unifying theoretical or conceptual framework. Instead, this literature is a collection of studies focusing on direct relationships between job characteristics and different aspects of marital functioning. In contrast, there has been an attempt to consolidate the results from studies on the relationship between job satisfaction and marital satisfaction into a unified conceptual framework.

In trying to understand the relationship between job satisfaction and marital functioning, two observations can be made. First, virtually all studies in this area have focused on marital satisfaction, and second, this research forms part of larger endeavour to understand the relationship between job and non-job (i.e. marital, family, leisure) satisfaction. Accordingly, the relationship between job satisfaction and marital satisfaction will be reviewed first. Thereafter, the literature on job–non-job satisfaction will be examined briefly to determine whether there are any aspects of this more general literature that are germane to the question of job and marital satisfaction.

Perhaps the earliest study conducted on the relationship between job satisfaction and marital satisfaction was reported by Dyer (1956). Despite suggestions that there was a tendency in the 1950s to view employment and family roles as separate (see Chapter 1), Dyer (1956) noted that he conducted his study because of reports of an overlap between these two roles. In his report, Dyer (1956) did not present any data pertaining to a global measure of marital satisfaction, but focused instead on specific facets of marital satisfaction. He constructed two groups on the basis of the husband/father's job satisfaction (satisfied vs less satisfied). From an examination of the item scores, it is clear that there are consistent differences between the two groups of husbands. Specifically, husbands who were satisfied with their jobs reported fewer marital disagreements and believed that their wives were proud of them and their jobs. Based on wives' self-reports, the husbands in Dyer's (1956) study may well be accurate in their self-perceptions: wives of husbands who were satisfied with their jobs were more likely to enjoy talking to friends about their husbands' jobs, and take their friends to show them their husbands' work. In general, therefore, Dyer's (1956) data suggested that husbands' job satisfaction is associated with both their own and their wives' marital satisfaction. One limitation to Dyer's interpretation of his results is the socioeconomic status confound inherent in this study. Higher socioeconomic status individuals were significantly more likely to be satisfied with their jobs than their counterparts with lower socioeconomic status. Thus, the possibility that it is really perceived financial strain or socioeconomic status that is associated with marital dissatisfaction cannot be excluded on the basis of Dyer's (1956) study alone.

Since Dyer's (1956) early study, numerous investigators have focused on the relationship between job satisfaction and marital satisfaction. Although the focus on the link between job satisfaction and marital satisfaction was not the major focus of the study in most cases, Dyer's (1956) results were typically replicated, in other words, a positive relationship emerged between job satisfaction and marital satisfaction. For example, Haavio-Mannila (1971) showed a positive relationship between job satisfaction and marital satisfaction. The fact that Haavio-Mannila's (1971) data were collected from subjects who were selected randomly from the Finnish population excludes the possibility of a socioeconomic factor limiting the generalizability of these findings.

More recent studies have provided additional support for the existence of a positive relationship between job satisfaction and marital satisfaction (e.g. Barling and Rosenbaum, 1986). Barling *et al*. (1987) studied the effects of an acute work-related disaster on personal and organizational functioning, and found that there was a significant, positive relationship between job satisfaction and marital satisfaction. Gaesser and Whitbourne's (1985) multivariate analysis suggested a refinement of the finding of a link between global job satisfaction and marital satisfaction. In their small, non-random sample of 40 husbands from families in which the husband was the breadwinner, they showed that only extrinsic job satisfaction was positively associated with marital adjustment. Intrinsic job satisfaction, on the other hand, was not associated with marital adjustment. Finally, Barling (1984) found that a positive relationship existed between husbands' job satisfaction and wives' marital satisfaction. One point should be made regarding these positive correlations. As was the case with the research relating job stress to marital satisfaction, the magnitude of the significant relationships reported is modest. Clearly, job satisfaction is but one of the many predictors of marital satisfaction.

There are also studies reported in the literature in which no relationship emerged between job satisfaction and marital satisfaction. For example, Ridley (1973) studied female teachers, and found that there was no relationship between job satisfaction and marital satisfaction. In fact, in Ridley's (1973) study one-third of the women who experienced job dissatisfaction were satisfied with their marriages. Using a different approach, Kemper and Reichler (1976a) showed no significant relationship between university students' perceptions of their fathers' job satisfaction and marital satisfaction.

It is apparent, therefore, that there is no consistent relationship between job satisfaction and marital satisfaction. Rather, some studies yield a positive relationship between marital satisfaction and job satisfaction, others do not. An examination of the general literature on the relationship between job and non-work satisfaction suggests some explanations for these seemingly contradictory findings, and it is towards an understanding of these explanations that we now turn.

Some Explanations for Inconsistent Relationships Between Job and Marital Satisfaction

As indicated previously, research has focused on whether a relationship exists between job satisfaction and different aspects of non-work satisfaction, such as marital, life or leisure satisfaction, rather than how such a relationship might be mediated. The research conducted on job satisfaction and marital satisfaction has typically focused only on the size and direction of any relationship between employment and family factors. On the contrary, the research focusing on job satisfaction and other facets of non-work satisfaction has also considered the conditions under which such a relationship might emerge. Extensive reviews of this research reveal inconsistencies among studies on the link between job satisfaction and marital (or life) satisfaction. In some cases, for example, significant positive relationships emerge between job satisfaction and life (or non-job) satisfaction (e.g. Iris and Barrett, 1972; London, Crandall and Seals, 1977; Rousseau, 1978). In other cases, significant negative relationships have emerged between job satisfaction and leisure satisfaction (e.g. Miller and Weiss, 1982). Finally, in some of these same studies in which a significant relationship emerged between some aspects of job satisfaction (e.g. supervision, pay or promotional satisfaction) and life satisfaction, no significant relationship emerged between other aspects of job satisfaction (e.g. co-workers' satisfaction or intrinsic satisfaction) and life satisfaction (e.g. Iris and Barrett, 1972). Because marital satisfaction is considered to be one aspect of non-job satisfaction in this research, an understanding of why inconsistent relationships emerge between marital and job satisfaction will be advanced from analysing these more general findings on job and non-work satisfaction.

Extending the early theorizing of Wilensky (1960), six different hypotheses have now been posited to account for the different relationships that emerge between job satisfaction and marital satisfaction (Bartolome and Evans, 1980; Near, Rice and Hunt, 1980; Staines, 1980; Zedeck, 1987): the spillover, instrumental, integrative, compensation, conflict, and segmentation hypotheses. Each of these hypotheses addresses a different type of relationship between job and non-job satisfaction (positive, negative or null), and suggests different reasons for the emergence of the specific relationship.

The spillover, instrumental and integrative hypotheses are directed towards an understanding of why positive correlations emerge between job satisfaction and life or marital satisfaction (see Table 4.1). The spillover hypothesis has probably received most empirical support (Staines, 1980), and suggests that positive job-related reactions literally spill over or are transferred to non-work situations. Likewise, feelings of job dissatisfaction also spill over to non-work situations, resulting in marital, life or leisure dissatisfaction. This process is reflected in the following statement by a Californian police officer's wife:

> I can't understand how seemingly normal husbands turn into such 'machos'. Arguments end in 'Because I told you so'. Our children feel as though they really can't discuss problems with their father because he relates in terms of the law and logic, not the emotions involved. Sometimes I feel that if I don't do as he wants, I'll be arrested.
>
> (Maslach and Jackson, 1979, p. 59)

An important point that emerges from this is that the spillover hypothesis is meant to account for the positive nature of the statistical relationship, and in this respect accounts for spillover of both positive and negative emotions.

Unlike the spillover hypothesis, the instrumental hypothesis suggests that a positive relationship exists between job and non-work satisfaction, because one role (e.g. employment) is used as a means of satisfying the other (e.g. leisure satisfaction or marital satisfaction). For example, individuals may put more effort into their jobs to obtain a financial incentive that is used to obtain some other valued outcome, such as a family vacation. The meaning of the instrumental hypothesis is reflected in John Mason Brown's observation that 'Most people spend most of their days doing what they do not want to do to earn the right, at times, to do what they may desire' (Jackman, 1984, p. 226). The integrative hypothesis is also based on the existence of a positive relationship between job and non-job satisfaction, but the rationale offered here is that the roles and behaviours required for success in both domains are so similar that it would be unnecessary, if not impossible, to separate them. Therefore, a positive relationship between job satisfaction and marital satisfaction could be the result of three very different causes.

Unlike these three hypotheses, both the compensation and conflict hypotheses are offered to account for those situations in which negative correlations are yielded between job and non-work satisfaction. The compensation hypothesis suggests that a negative relationship emerges because an individual lacking gratification in one domain (e.g. job satisfaction) will seek fulfilment in another (e.g. marital or leisure satisfaction). The conflict hypothesis suggests that a negative relationship emerges because the activities and behaviours involved in successful completion of one role

Table 4.1 Classifying the relationship between job satisfaction and marital satisfaction

Nature of the relationship	Direction of the relationship	Hypotheses underlying the relationship
Spillover	Positive	Positive feelings in one domain spill over into others
Instrumental	Positive	One role is used as a means of satisfying others
Integrative	Positive	Requirements for success in different roles are fundamentally similar
Compensation	Negative	Fulfilment sought in one role because of lack of gratification in others
Conflict	Negative	Activities required for success in one role incompatible with success in others
Segmentation/Independence	No	Job and family roles are completely unrelated

(e.g. employment) are in direct competition with the other role under consideration (e.g. marriage). Finally, the segmentation or independence hypothesis is meant to account for the emergence in some studies of no relationship between job and non-work satisfaction. The explanation offered in this instance is that job and non-work roles and activities are entirely separate entities of an individual's life, as a result of which no relationship should be expected.

The question that emerges, then, is whether any of these six hypotheses can be used to understand the relationship between job satisfaction and marital satisfaction. More specifically, the issue is whether these six hypotheses can help us to understand and predict the conditions under which a positive, negative or null relationship will emerge between job satisfaction and marital satisfaction. In addressing this issue, two sources of data are examined. First, one study contrasted the spillover and compensation hypotheses (Pond and Green, 1983). Second, the research already discussed in which either a positive relationship (e.g. Barling, 1984; Barling and Rosenbaum, 1986; Barling *et al.*, 1987; Dyer, 1956; Gaesser and Whitbourne, 1985; Haavio-Mannila, 1971) or no relationship (Kemper and Reichler, 1976a; Ridley, 1973) has emerged between job satisfaction and marital satisfaction (or other indicators of marital functioning) will be re-examined.

Pond and Green's (1983) study did not provide consistent support for either the spillover on the compensatory hypothesis. Pond and Green (1983) found a positive correlation between marital and job satisfaction for husbands whose wives were employed. However, the corresponding correlation between job satisfaction and marital satisfaction for employed wives, and for husbands whose wives were not employed, was not significant. Pond and Green (1983) then extended their within-spouse analysis to a between-spouse analysis. There were no significant correlations between the job satisfaction of the employed spouse, and the marital satisfaction of his or her partner. Thus, no support is provided for the compensatory hypothesis, and Pond and Green (1983) note that there is limited support for the spillover hypothesis. Because most of the correlations (i.e. five out of six) were not significant, the segmentation or independence hypothesis receives most support. However, an alternative explanation is that support for the independence or segmentation hypothesis may be premature: it is possible that no predictable relationship will emerge between job satisfaction and marital satisfaction until the appropriate moderator variables are identified and operationalized.

It is doubtful whether the inconsistencies among studies on job satisfaction and marital satisfaction can be understood solely on the basis of the spillover or independence hypothesis. This is because an examination of those studies suggests no consistent factors that account for the positive correlations, or any consistent factors in the studies yielding null relationships between job satisfaction and marital satisfaction.

The major reason for presenting these six hypotheses is to assess whether they contribute to an understanding of the relationship between job satisfaction and marital satisfaction. To do so requires that some features of the six hypotheses by highlighted. First, virtually all the research on which these six explanations are based have used cross-sectional designs (Staines, 1980). Yet cross-sectional designs are limited in the extent to which they are useful in resolving causal issues, and each of the six hypotheses specifically addresses causal issues. Second, given the existence of six rival hypotheses to account for the same phenomenon, at best only one of the explanations can be correct, but they could all be incorrect. Yet, as already noted, there is empirical support for the existence of a positive, negative and null relationship between job and non-work satisfaction. Perhaps the error here is to assume that there is a direct relationship between job and non-job (including marital) satisfaction, ignoring the role of moderator variables. Moderator variables determine the direction of any relationship between job and life satisfaction. Other methodological problems with research on the relationship between job satisfaction and marital satisfaction include problems of monomethod bias (sole reliance on self-report data emanating from questionnaires). What is required, therefore, are studies making *a priori* predictions about the strength and direction of the link between job satisfaction and marital satisfaction based on situational moderating factors.

PERCEIVED FINANCIAL STRAIN AND MARITAL FUNCTIONING

The relationship between marital functioning and family income has received considerable empirical attention within the sociological literature. For the purposes of the present chapter, it is important to emphasize that any discussion of the relationship between objective level of pay and marital functioning on the one hand, and perceived financial strain or financial security and marital functioning on the other hand, will be treated separately, individuals' appraisals of their financial situation are treated as a separate issue from their objective wage level. First, objective income levels and perceived financial strain are conceptually distinct: income levels are objective and readily quantifiable, whereas perceived financial strain reflects the subjective appraisal of the extent to which income level is perceived as sufficient to meet current needs. Hence, the distinction between income level and perceived financial strain parallels that between stressors and stress. At least two studies point to this distinction between wage level and perceived financial strain. In a community sample of older adults, Krause (1987) showed that the relationship between objective income and perceived financial strain, while significant, is only moderate ($r = 0.26$). Second, it has been argued that perceived financial strain exerts lasting effects, and there are data showing that perceived financial strain is related to multiple dimensions of depression (i.e. depressed affect, somatic and retarded activities and decreased positive affect) in adults in general (Ross and Huber, 1985) as well as in samples of older adults (Krause, 1987).

Consistent with this distinction, income level and perceived financial strain can be predicted to exert different effects on marital functioning. However, there is very little empirical research that has investigated the relationship between perceived financial strain and marital satisfaction. The relationship between wages or socioeconomic status and marital functioning or marital dissolution has received the most examination. Wage level is consistently and negatively associated with the likelihood of marital dissolution (cf. Cherlin, 1979). Furthermore, Mortimer (1980) found that men's socioeconomic status (a summated measure of income, education and occupational prestige) was associated with their own job–family strain, their wives' supportive behaviours and their own marital satisfaction.

Objective wage level also influences marital functioning in a moderating manner. Draughn (1984) showed that wage level was a significant moderator of the relationship between husbands' perceived competence on the job and perceived competence in the role of husband. Second, Mortimer (1980) found that while husbands' socioeconomic status is directly associated with their own marital satisfaction, this relationship is mediated by family strain and wives' support behaviours. Thus, Mortimer (1980) suggests that socioeconomic status exerts both a direct and an indirect effect on marital satisfaction. This process was illustrated in Figure 3.2.

In one study focusing on the relationship between perceived financial strain and marital satisfaction in a small sample of army wives, perceived financial well-being was positively associated with marital satisfaction (Thoresen and Goldsmith, 1987). Another study provides data from which it is possible to contrast the relationships between objective pay level and marital satisfaction, and financial strain and marital satisfaction. Specifically, Voydanoff and Kelly (1984) showed that while there was no significant relationship between total family income (obtained by cumulating total household income, subjects' income, unemployment benefits or contributions from older adults) and the amount of time devoted to family activities, 'income inadequacy' (measured by items such as 'we don't have enough money for all of our needs' and 'we can't save money for future needs') was significantly and negatively correlated with one aspect of marital functioning, namely family activity time. As a result, this study is consistent with others (e.g. Keith and Schaffer, 1985) which suggest that subjective employment experiences are more important determinants of marital functioning than objective employment characteristics.

Of some relevance here is the increasing focus in the literature on farm stressors. One of the major sources of stress within this occupation is perceived financial strain. Events that would precipitate perceived financial strain for farm owners and workers include droughts, falling prices and disease outbreaks (Olson and Schellenberg, 1986). One consequence for family functioning of perceived financial strain for this group is the need for one member of the family to go outside of the farm and obtain employment.

Pooyan and Eberhardt (1987) studied the relationship between different sources of stress and psychological well-being in a random sample of farmers in North Dakota. Even though their study did not assess the effects of farm stressors on marital functioning, two findings are of some relevance, particularly given the random nature of their sample. First, the most stressful aspect of farming was personal financial problems, which included difficulties in loan repayment and low market prices for livestock and crops. Second, personal financial problems were significantly and substantially associated with life satisfaction (which itself is consistently related to marital satisfaction) and emotional strain, and significantly but moderately correlated with illness frequency and job satisfaction.

In conclusion, therefore, research has focused separately on the effects on marital functioning of objective income and perceived financial strain. Most of the research has focused on level of income, and shows a consistent link between income level and marital functioning. The results of recent research suggest that perceived financial strain exerts an equal if not greater effect on marital functioning than does income levels.

TYPE A BEHAVIOUR AND MARITAL FUNCTIONING

The Nature of Type A Behaviour

Following publication of Friedman and Rosenman's *Type A Behavior and Your Heart* in 1974, there has been a tremendous amount of research and theorizing on both the nature and the consequences of Type A behaviour. In their classic text, Friedman and Rosenman (1974) noted how the Type A behaviour style is associated with an elevated risk for coronary heart disease. In recounting the development of Type A behaviour, they point to earlier research focusing on the occurrence of coronary heart disease that could not be linked to traditional causes such as diet and cholesterol levels. They point to one incident which they ignored at the time of its occurrence, but which suggested that coronary heart patients may well *behave* differently.

But now, in retrospect, we are a bit abashed when we recall one particular incident that took place about then. We had called in an upholsterer to fix the seats of the chairs in our reception room. After inspecting our chairs, he asked what sort of practice we had. We said we were cardiologists and asked why he wanted to know. 'Well', he replied, 'I was just wondering because it is so peculiar that only the front edge of your chair seats had worn out.' Had we been sufficiently alert, we might have thought about the chance remark and what it indicated about the behaviour pattern of our coronary patients.

(Friedman and Rosenman, 1974, p. 55)

The Type A individual has since been recognized as being highly competitive, having a high achievement orientation and excessive sense of time urgency, an unrelenting drive to achieve at continually higher levels, explosive speech patterns, rapid motor movements and polyphasic thinking (i.e. focusing on several different topics or issues at the same time). The Type A person is restless, irritable, impatient and aggressive, and is continuously involved in the quest to achieve greater quantitative and qualitative goals. In contrast, the Type B individual manifests few of these characteristics and was believed to be at less risk of developing coronary heart disease than Type A individuals.

One question that must be asked at this stage is why the link between Type A behaviour and marital functioning is considered in this chapter. The reason for this is the assumption that the characteristics of Type A individuals are most pronounced in job-related contexts. One important aspect of the Type A behaviour personality that numerous writers have commented on is their excessive involvement in, and preoccupation with, their jobs. This excessive involvement is presumed to occur at the expense and neglect of other life domains (Machlowitz, 1980). Thus, Type As are frequently described as being work addicts, with an unreasonable work ethic, who set unrealistic expectations of what they feel they must accomplish. They work long, hard hours and force themselves to endure conditions that their Type B counterparts would find noxious and avoid. Consistent with the influence and interest of Friedman and Rosenman, both cardiologists, it is not at all surprising that the earlier research on Type A behaviour focused almost exclusively on the effects of Type A behaviour on coronary heart disease and other related health issues.

Type A Behaviour and Marital Satisfaction

Given the nature of Type A behaviour, it is not surprising that researchers began to focus on whether Type A behaviour exerts a negative effect on the psychosocial aspects of an individual's life. If we consider the hard-driving and competitive nature of the Type A individual, together with his or her anger, hostility and aggression, and if these behaviours generalize beyond the employment situation, negative effects for marital functioning could be predicted. Indeed, Friedman and Rosenman (1974) observed that Type A individuals devote less time to their marital and family relationships, and tend to be more distant from their family members than their Type B counterparts. Since then, research has contrasted the social relationships of Type A and Type B individuals. The results show that Type A individuals cooperate less, compete and dominate more, and devote less time to social relationships than Type B individuals (e.g. Ditto, 1982).

One question that has since been addressed is whether Type A behaviour is associated with marital dysfunction. In what was probably the first series of studies focusing on Type A behaviour and marital functioning, Burke and his co-workers focused on this relationship in a group of senior administrators from Canadian Correctional institutions. In their first study, Burke, Weir and DuWors (1979) showed that the overall Type A behaviour of 85 employed husbands was associated with marital dissatisfaction of their spouses. Burke *et al.* (1979) also reported significant correlations between husbands' Type A behaviour and positive and negative marital behaviours of wives. There was also a significant correlation between the self-reported Type A behaviour of employed husbands and the extent to which wives reported that husbands' jobs exerted a negative influence on the family. Also, the greater the self-reported level of Type A behaviour of husbands, the fewer social contacts and friends wives reported having and the less their sense of belonging to a social network from which to obtain social support. Like much of the other research already discussed concerning the relationship between marital functioning and either job stress or intrinsic job characteristics, the magnitude of these correlations was modest (all r's < 0.30), even though they were significant.

Burke and Weir (1980) obtained similar results when the relationship between husbands' Type A behaviour and marital dissatisfaction was studied. Specifically, when Burke and Weir (1980) surveyed 85 senior correctional institution administrators, they again showed that significant correlations existed between husbands' Type A behaviour and marital dissatisfaction. As with the analyses conducted with husbands' Type A behaviour and their wives' marital dysfunction, husbands' Type A behaviour correlated significantly with the extent to which they reported negative interference between employment and family life. Once again, the size of these relationships was small.

In a third study, Burke, Weir and DuWors (1980b) considered whether the extent to which the employed husband's spouse perceived him to manifest Type A behaviours was associated with her own marital dissatisfaction. As in the two previous studies, a significant relationship again emerged between Type A behaviour and marital dissatisfaction. Specifically, Burke *et al.* (1980b) showed that the extent to which the wife perceived her husband to manifest Type A behaviour was associated with marital dissatisfaction, and with the extent to which wives perceived husbands' jobs to interfere with the balance between employment and family life. As was the case with husbands' self-reports (Burke *et al.*, 1979), there was also a significant negative correlation between the extent to which the wife perceived her husband as being Type A and the number of good friends she reported having, an index of the size of her social network. One deviation exists from the previous results, however. No correlation emerged in this third report between the extent to which the wife perceived her husband as manifesting Type A behaviours on the one hand, and either her positive or negative marital behaviours, or the frequency to which she reported visiting friends with or without her spouse on the other hand. Nonetheless, it is clear that the results of Burke and his colleagues' three analyses show that an association exists between Type A behaviour and marital dissatisfaction.

Keegan *et al.* (1979) also report results from a study conducted in Canada, in which significantly more Type A individuals in their study reported being dissatisfied with their marriages than did Type B individuals. In addition, Keegan *et al.* (1979) noted that Type A's preferred receiving respect and recognition from their spouses, whereas their Type B counterparts favoured love from their spouses. This may be somewhat consistent with the Type A individual's focus on more extrinsic, tangible and visible goals, while their Type B counterparts aspire more towards intrinsic and emotional concerns.

However, there is one major difference between Keegan *et al.*'s (1979) study and the three studies reported by Burke and his colleagues. The subjects in Keegan *et al.*'s research were drawn from a cardiologist's practice: 50 of the 60 subjects had been referred for cardiovascular assessment by their family physicians, the remaining ten were referred for assessment prior to participation in a coronary prevention exercise programme. Any individual who had suffered a minor cardiac infarction within three months of the evaluation was not included in the study. Thus, it should be noted that Keegan *et al.*'s (1979) results are based on individuals who had referred themselves to a physician. On the contrary, although non-randomly selected, the subjects in Burke *et al.*'s research programme had no identifiable coronary heart disease. Thus, although the relatively small number of non-Type A subjects in Keegan *et al.*'s (1979) study might suggest that some caution would be appropriate if generalizing from their results alone, the fact that the association between Type A behaviour and marital dissatisfaction is consistent across groups of presumably healthy individuals in Burke *et al.*'s research programme and the coronary heart patients in Keegan *et al.*'s (1979) research enhances the generalizability of the relationship between Type A behaviour and marital dissatisfaction.

Kelly and Houston (1985) also investigated the relationship between Type A behaviour and marital adjustment. Their sample again differs markedly from those on which the previous four studies were based. Specifically, Kelly and Houston (1985) studied a middle class sample of employed women in the United States. In one respect, Kelly and Houston's (1985) results diverge from those already mentioned, as they showed that Type A and Type B females did not differ in their evaluation of their own marital relationships, even though they used the same criterion of marital functioning (viz. Orden and Bradburn's Marital Happiness questionnaire) that had been used by Burke and his colleagues in their three reports. However, like the study by Burke *et al.* (1980b), Kelly and Houston (1985) did show that a significant relationship existed between wives' perceptions of the level of their husbands' Type A behaviour and their own marital dissatisfaction.

Data also emerged concerning the relationship between Type A behaviour and marital adjustment in the Framingham study on coronary heart disease (Haynes *et al.*, 1978). This study is probably one of the more extensive attempts yet conducted to understand the development, correlates and consequences of coronary heart disease, Since 1949, 2282 men and 2845 women who were initially free of any coronary heart disease were followed biannually. From 1965 to 1967, data were also collected on the marital relationships of 1822 members of the original Framingham heart study. Correlations were computed between Type A behaviour and two indices of marital functioning: marital disagreements and marital dissatisfaction. There was a significant correlation between Type A behaviour and marital disagreements, yet the correlation between marital dissatisfaction and Type A behaviour was not significant, possibly because the questionnaire assessing marital disagreements measured a wide variety of specific marital issues, whereas the marital dissatisfaction scale only contained three global items focusing on the general extent of dissatisfaction, (e.g. 'Everything considered how happy would you say your marriage has been?'). Haynes *et al.*'s (1978) results must be considered to be reliable given the large number of subjects used ($N = 1822$), the normative nature of their sample, and the fact that their results largely replicate those of Burke and his co-workers, Kelly and Houston (1985) and Keegan *et al.* (1979)

While most of these studies have focused mainly on the effects of Type A behaviour and marital dissatisfaction, Becker and Byrne (1984) investigated the effects of Type A behaviour on the weekly frequency and duration of marital communication and sexual activity in sixteen young married couples. Husbands' Type A behaviour was significantly and negatively related to the frequency of their communications with their spouses. However, no significant relationships emerged between husbands' Type A behaviour and the average frequency of sexual activity. For wives, there were no significant relationships between Type A behaviour and either of the marital behaviours. The results of this study, however, may not be generalizable. First, Becker and Byrne (1984) used a rather small sample ($N = 16$). Second, focusing only on young married couples may provide an incomplete picture of the marital relationship, because marital satisfaction tends to decrease over time (O'Leary *et al.*, 1989).

A number of issues should be noted regarding the research findings on the relationship between Type A behaviour and marital dissatisfaction and dysfunction. First, all the studies cited above are cross-sectional. Even though it may not be plausible to suggest that marital dissatisfaction leads to the manifestation of Type A behaviour, longitudinal data are required for a true test of the causal inference that Type A behaviour leads to marital dissatisfaction. Second, Matthews (1982) has suggested that the hostility displayed by Type A individuals would obstruct the development of fulfilling interpersonal interactions. Thus it would have been surprising had no relationship emerged between Type A behaviour and marital dissatisfaction. Third, the relationship between Type A behaviour and marital dissatisfaction is moderate. In none of the studies cited above is more than 10% of the variance in marital dissatisfaction explained by Type A behaviour. Perhaps one characteristic common to all the studies cited can account for this. Specifically, each of these studies utilized a global index of Type A behaviour, despite research (e.g. Spence, Helmreich and Pred, 1987) suggesting that Type A behaviour is a multidimensional construct. For example, Spence *et al.* (1987) showed that Type A behaviour consists of *irritability–impatience* and *achievement striving*. Research findings show that the irritability–impatience dimension is most closely associated with health outcomes (Barling and Charbonneau, 1989; Spence *et al.*, 1987) whereas the achievement striving dimension is most closely associated with performance (Barling and Charbonneau, 1989; Spence *et al.*, 1987; Spence, Pred and Helmreich, 1989). Subsequently, impatience–irritability has also been shown to predict depression (Bluen, Barling and Burns, in press).

Based on the framework provided by Spence *et al.* (1987), and Booth-Kewley and Friedman's (1987) meta-analysis which suggest that the various dimensions of Type A behaviour influence diverse outcomes differently, Barling, Bluen and Moss (1988) contrasted the separate effects of impatience–irritability and achievement striving on marital dissatisfaction. Barling, Bluen and Moss (1988) hypothesized that it would be the impatience–irritability dimension rather than achievement striving that would be associated with marital dissatisfaction. A test of this hypothesis might hold important implications. At least some of the concern regarding the possible effects of employment on the family centres around the question of whether the achievement striving nature inherent in the Type A pattern must be attained at some personal and marital cost to the individual and her or his spouse. Barling, Bluen and Moss (1988) chose to investigate this issue among medical practitioners and their spouses, because of suggestions that medical practitioners experience considerable and divergent job stressors, yet remain highly involved in their jobs (Gerber, 1983). Based on analyses from three different samples, their results showed that while husbands' impatience–irritability was associated with both their own and their wives' marital dissatisfaction, correlations between achievement striving and global Type A behaviour with marital dissatisfaction in these two samples were not significant. These results suggest that it is not the job-involved nature of the Type A construct that is associated with marital satisfaction. This is consistent with Barling's (1984) finding that husbands' job involvement is not related to their wives' marital satisfaction. Such results suggest that it may be possible to continue to engage in achievement striving without compromising one's own or one's spouse's marital satisfaction.

One issue that might still be investigated further is *how* Type A behaviour (or its components) affects marital dissatisfaction. In other words, research might focus on what behaviours mediate the relationship between Type A behaviours and marital dissatisfaction.

Compatibility of Spouses' Type A Behaviour and Marital Functioning

Most research conducted on Type A behaviour and marital functioning has focused on the relationship between Type A behaviour and marital dissatisfaction. Another issue that has attracted some empirical attention is whether Type A or Type B individuals tend to marry either the same or opposite types. Neither of the two studies conducted found a tendency for Type As or Type Bs to marry within their own type (Kelly and Houston, 1985; Robinson and Heller, 1980). Kelly and Houston (1985) extended this study and examined whether certain combinations of Type A and Type B within a marriage are associated with more marital tension or dissatisfaction. They found that for the employed women and their husbands, there was no husband/wife combination of Type A and Type B characteristics that was associated with greater marital dissatisfaction. However, Blaney, Brown and Blaney (1986) obtained a different pattern of results. In their non-random sample of 101 coupled described as consisting 'primarily of friends or acquaintances of the researchers and friends or acquaintances of theirs' (Blaney *et al.*, 1986, p. 494), Blaney *et al.* (1986) found a significant 2 × 2 (spouse × A/B Type) interaction. Specifically, marital satisfaction was significantly lower when a Type A husband was paired with a Type B wife. Whether the results of the studies conducted by Kelly and Houston (1985) and Blaney *et al.* (1986) are comparable is questionable: Blaney *et al.* (1986) used couple data as the criterion rather than the focus on individual self-reports of marital satisfaction, as had Kelly and Houston (1985), and some questions about the generalizability of Blaney *et al.*'s (1986) sample remain. Also, Kelly and Houston (1985) focused on female subjects only.

Wives' Perceptions of Their Husbands' Type A Behaviour

One final question that has been addressed in the research is whether wives can estimate accurately the extent to which their husbands manifest Type A or Type B behaviour. In one study (Becker and Byrne, 1984), husbands' self-reports and wives' reports on husbands Type A scores were not related. However, these results may not be generalizable: Becker and Byrne (1984) used a small sample of young, married couples, and their results are atypical. In three other studies, positive correlations between husbands' and wives' Type A scores have been obtained. Both Kelly and Houston (1985) as well as Burke *et al.* (1980b) showed that wives agree with their husbands' self-reported Type A behaviour. More recently, Barling, Bluen and Moss (1988) have shown that the highly significant correlations obtained between wives and husbands' ratings of global Type A behaviour are retained when the correlations between specific Type A dimensions, namely impatience–irritability and achievement striving, are computed.

If we accept Spence *et al.*'s (1987) two-dimensional approach to understanding the nature of Type A behaviour, an issue alluded to earlier is re-emphasized. Specifically, Type A behaviour is more a lifestyle characteristic than a specific job-related behaviour. Thus, again, it should not be surprising that some relationship emerges between specific components of Type A behaviour and marital dissatisfaction given the manifestation of Type A behaviours across diverse situations, and their possible effects on behavioural interactions between spouses. This also implies that there should be less emphasis attached to Type A behaviour as an employment stressor, or a specific employment experience, and a re-emphasis on Type A behaviour as a personal style that permeates all areas of individual functioning. One shortcoming in this research is the lack of any consideration in individual differences that may moderate the relationship between Type A behaviour and marital dissatisfaction. This will be considered further in the final chapter.

SUBJECTIVE EMPLOYMENT EXPERIENCES AND MARITAL FUNCTIONING: CONCLUSION

In concluding the discussion of subjective employment experiences and marital functioning, it is apparent that positive employment experiences such as job satisfaction, participation in decision making, job involvement, and perceptions of the organizational climate, are all positively associated with marital functioning. On the contrary, negative job stress is correlated with marital dysfunction. Although this conclusion is based on an extensive body of empirical research, scant attention has been paid to three critical issues: namely, the direction of causality in these relationships; the clinical vs statistical meaning of the significant findings; and the mediating factors that might account for the correlations that do emerge. Finally, any evaluation of the conclusion that there is a positive association between subjective employment experiences and marital functioning takes on added significance in contrast to the general lack of a consistent relationship between objective employment characteristics and marital functioning (see Chapter 3). It is still likely that subjective employment characteristics are more important determinants of family functioning than objective employment characteristics. Accordingly, these issues will be considered further in the final chapter.

Chapter 5

Wives' Subjective Employment Status and Marital Functioning

In the preceding two chapters, the association between both objective and subjective employment characteristics and marital functioning was explored. A close inspection of the studies citied would reveal that the majority examined the effects of the husbands' job characteristics and experiences on their own and wives' marital functioning. One assumption underlying that discussion is relevant to an understanding of the effects of wives' employment on the marital functioning of both partners. Consistent with the 'husband availability' hypothesis, it is assumed that the amount of time husbands devote to their jobs (including overtime) and the extent of job-related husband absence are associated with both spouses' marital functioning. Simply stated, this hypothesis postulates a positive relationship between the amount of time the husband devotes to the marital relationship and marital functioning. This 'availability' hypothesis is even more pertinent when focusing on the link between wives' employment and either of the spouses' marital functioning. While the 'husband availability' hypothesis has only partially guided, directed and sustained the literature relating husbands' employment to their marital functioning, it has been far more influential in the literature on wives' employment. An additional hypothesis driving the research on wives' employment and marital functioning proposes that wives' power base in the marriage relative to that of their husbands influences both partners' marital functioning, and that this distribution of power is directly related to wives' employment status. It is the aim of the present chapter to detail and evaluate the effects of different aspects of wives' employment status (i.e. employed or homemaker) on marital functioning. The effects of wives' subjective employment experiences on both partners' marital functioning will be discussed separately in Chapter 6. Before considering the consequences of wives' employment status for marital functioning, the historical and current social context within which such research has been conducted will be highlighted. This is important because societal assumptions limit the questions posed and the way in which research is conducted.

Most of the research in this area has contrasted employed and non-employed wives and their spouses, assuming that employment is harmful to women's marriages. This research has been motivated by the societal stereotype that the 'good' wife does not seek employment; instead, she remains available at home to care for her husband (and her children) whenever they need her. Thus, this literature is yet another instance of how our research agenda has been shaped and maintained by societal beliefs and prejudices. As Laws (1971, p. 496) states so succinctly in her critique of the marital literature:

> In the research literature on working mothers we find the scientists investigating the disingenuous hypothesis of the laymen. The literature on working wives and working mothers, though distinct, shares assumptions with which we are by now familiar. Given the premise that a woman's primary obligation/glory/identity is defined by her unique biological potential, the nature of the research hypotheses may be predicted. ... A woman who wishes to give primacy (or equal emphasis) to some other area of concern in maladjusted, inadequate, immature, in flight from her femininity ....

Despite the fact that Laws (1971) made this observation some two decades ago, it is apparent from recent magazine articles that such beliefs and stereotypes continue unabated. For example, Amiel (1985, p. 8) argues that: 'The difficulty comes when women set their sights not just on a job but a career. ... Frankly, it is difficult enough for two people who both want high-powered careers to be married at all, let alone have children.'

The notion that non-employed wives remain in an unequal power relationship relative to their spouses and other employed wives has different consequences for husbands and wives. First, it is assumed that husbands whose wives are employed will manifest poorer marital (and personal) functioning than husbands whose wives are homemakers. Second, it is assumed that the marital (and personal) functioning of employed wives will be qualitatively better than non-employed wives because of the more egalitarian power relationship between the spouses. The implications of this are that employed wives exert positive effects on themselves but a negative effect on their husbands.

Not surprisingly, the development of empirical research focusing on the consequences for both spouses when the wife is employed reflects the belief that there are basic differences between employed and non-employed wives. However, as will be seen, there is now some movement way from this stereotype. For example, earlier research almost uniformly contrasted employed wives with their homemaker counterparts. The assumption guiding this research was that differences would emerge because of the negative consequences arising from the relative time available for marital role fulfilment to employed and non-employed wives, and the power wives might derive from their employment (e.g. through their increased contribution to family finances). In other words, researchers initially expected substantial differences between these two groups, but minimal variation within each group. Subsequently, findings from numerous studies started to converge, suggesting that differences within the group of employed wives on the one hand, and non-employed wives on the other, may be at least as important as any differences between these two groups. As a result, there was increased effort to understand factors predicting within-group differences, and empirical studies started to examine the role of moderator variables such as age, educational level and race. More recently, with the confirmation that there is considerable systematic variation within the group of employed wives, studies have begun to focus only on employed wives, investigating the subjective work-related experiences of employed wives. As a result, the research has broadened its focus from the correlates and consequences of wives' employment status (whether she is employed or not) to include the correlates and consequences of wives' subjective employment experiences.

To continue focusing separately on the relationship between marital functioning and husbands' and wives' employment perpetuates the ideological position that spousal availability and power are differentially associated with marital functioning for husbands and wives. However, wives' and husbands' employment and their marital functioning must be treated separately here. From a purely practical perspective, most of the literature has dealt with the effects of husbands' employment and wives' employment as two separate issues. Their separate treatment in this text merely reflects that practical reality. Second, there has been some question based on previous research findings (Ladewig and McGee, 1986; Sekaran, 1985) as to whether similar conceptual models can apply to both husbands and wives (see Chapters 3 and 4). This is an empirical issue that will be addressed later.

There is now an extensive literature on dual career couples (e.g. Aldous, 1981; Sekaran, 1985). However, it is suggested that the findings from research on dual *career* couples may not be generalizable to all couples. Dual *career* couples differ from dually *employed* couples in several respects. Individuals holding a 'career' rather than a 'job' are of a higher socio-economic level, and have greater occupational demands placed on them. Perhaps more importantly, social prejudices may be greater against career rather than employed, non-career wives. As Amiel (1985, p. 5) states, 'A career differs from a job in that it requires a dedication to the labor force and a stream of energy outside regular working hours that is virtually incompatible with married life, let alone motherhood'. There are also empirical findings showing that differences in aspects of the sexual relationship between partners depend on the extent of their 'career' orientation (e.g. Avery-Clark, 1986). The very term 'dual career couples' has become so widely used that it is in danger of losing its conceptual foundations. Accordingly, the unquestioning use of the term 'dual career couple' is avoided (Spitze, 1988), but employment and marital experiences when both partners are employed will be examined.

The present chapter first focuses on the effects of wives' employment on the quality of both their own and their husbands' marital functioning. Wherever relevant in this discussion, the research that examined factors that moderate this relationship will also be considered. The final section will deal with the possible effects of the relative occupational status of wives' and husbands' occupational characteristics and prestige.

WIVES' EMPLOYMENT STATUS AND MARITAL FUNCTIONING

As will be the case when considering the relationship between wives' employment and their husbands' marital functioning, the present discussion of the relationship between wives' employment status and their own functioning is divided into three sections. Specifically, we will consider the relationship between wives' employment and (1) their own general psychological well-being, (2) global marital adjustment or satisfaction and (3) specific aspects of marital functioning. It is possible to support both positive and negative effects of wives' employment status on their own psychological well-being and marital functioning (see Krause, 1984). One could predict a positive relationship because employment provides wives with the opportunity for a more equitable marital relationship, partially because of their increased contribution to family income. Also, employment provides wives with the means for exerting greater control over their own lives, greater control within the marital relationship, and achieving self-esteem. As Stokes and Payton (1986, p. 300) note, employment provides:

> ... a source of challenge and satisfaction to many women. Women who would feel confined and isolated as full-time homemakers may gain a sense of accomplishment from employment outside the home, and they may enjoy the increased interpersonal contact such employment provides.

On the other hand, it could be argued equally plausibly that the continuing social opprobrium directed against the employed wife and mother (e.g. Amiel, 1985) would increase her feelings of guilt and role ambiguity, and decrease her psychological well-being. Also, despite the increasing number of women entering the labour force, women employed outside the home continue to occupy jobs usually high in stress, low in opportunity and high in pay inequity compared to jobs held by men (Terborg, 1985).

Wives' Psychological Well-Being

One psychological factor that has been investigated as a possible outcome of wives' employment status is depression. Although depression is not itself part of the domain of marital functioning, depression affects the marital relationship, especially for women (Beach and O'Leary, 1986).

Data contrasting depressive affect of employed wives and homemakers derive primarily from large random or non-random samples. Data from random samples of the United States population suggest that employed wives are less depressed than homemakers. Kessler and McRae (1982) interviewed 2440 adults and found that employed wives suffered less depression, and had higher self-esteem than full-timer homemakers. These differences remained even after Kessler and McRae

(1982) controlled statistically for the effects of husbands' earnings, and the number and ages of children. Other studies have replicated and refined Kessler and McRae's (1982) findings. Warr and Parry (1982b) showed that employment was associated with less depression in a sample of lower socioeconomic status women. Warren and McEachren (1983) studied 499 non-randomly selected and well-educated women, and also found that non-employed women suffered more depression than their employed counterparts. More importantly, however, Warren and McEachren (1983) also showed that employment status interacted significantly with perceived control over their lives in predicting wives' depressive affect. Specifically, wives who were not employed and who held a perception of low control over life events manifested the greatest depression.

This again points to the importance of progressing beyond simple comparisons of employed and non-employed wives, towards a more comprehensive understanding of wives' subjective experience of employment. Although it is clear from the studies cited here that being employed (as opposed to a homemaker) is associated with less depressive affect, specific conditions of employment (e.g. job dissatisfaction), life stress (e.g. perceptions of a lack of control) or demographic characteristics (e.g. lower socioeconomic status) might contribute further to elevated depression among employed wives. Some of these factors that increase the risk of depression among employed wives may be correlated. For example, membership in a lower socioeconomic status group may result in perceptions of a lack of control. Krause and Geyer-Pestello (1985) provide data in support of this argument. From a random telephone survey of 300 women in Akron, Ohio, they showed that pay dissatisfaction and employment/home conflict significantly predicted the level of depression among employed wives.

Between-group differences also emerge when other indices of psychological well-being are measured. For example, Stokes and Peyton (1986) analysed data collected from 6033 adults during 1982 in a national probability sample. In their study, homemakers reported slightly lower self-esteem than employed wives, more conservative values than employed wives, as well as more traditional perceptions of the role of women. Thus, even though it must be noted that homemakers reported slightly more supportive family environments and less overall life dissatisfaction in Stokes and Payton's (1986) study, the preponderance of data continue to suggest that employed wives fare better than their non-employed counterparts in terms of mental health or psychological well-being.

One problem with all these studies, is that it is assumed that there is homogeneity *within* each of the employed and non-employed groups. Yet as a group, employed wives differ with respect to their satisfaction with their jobs, their commitment to the role of employed wife, and their beliefs about appropriate female behaviour.

Employed Wives Global Marital Satisfaction

As already noted, there is some discrepancy between conventional wisdom and empirical data relating wives' employment to their husbands' marital satisfaction. Specifically, unlike the assumptions pertaining to husbands of employed and non-employed wives, it is frequently assumed that employed wives evidence greater marital satisfaction than their non-employed counterparts (e.g. Houseknecht and Macke, 1981).

Burke and Weir (1976) showed that employed wives are more satisfied with their marriages than non-employed wives. However, it should be noted that the magnitude of the difference between employed and non-employed wives (113.39 vs 108.98) was again too small to have any clinical significance. Most studies have shown no differences between the global marital satisfaction of employed and non-employed wives. Whether randomly selected samples (Allen and Keaveny, 1979; Locksley, 1980; Orthner and Axelson, 1980) or samples of convenience (Meeks *et al.*, 1986) are used, no differences in global marital satisfaction are yielded. In addition, this pattern of results was replicated in Smith's (1985) statistical cumulation of previous findings focusing on this issue. The few studies which have found that employed wives have lower marital satisfaction than non-employed wives (Bowen, 1987) were confined to specific groups (e.g. military husbands and their wives) or specific situations. For example, Houseknecht and Macke (1981) found that the relationship between wives' employment status and marital adjustment was moderated by the extent to which their husbands supported their employment. Employment was negatively associated with marital satisfaction only when husbands were not supportive of their wives pursuing employment outside the home. Interestingly, this finding replicates others showing similar moderating effects where husbands hold negative attitudes towards their wives' employment role (Spitze and Waite, 1981). Staines *et al.* (1978) showed that years of education and number of children moderated the relation between wives' employment status and marital functioning. Specifically, employed wives with less than twelve years of education and more children wished they had not married and thought of divorce more frequently than housewives. Staines *et al.* (1978) suggest that women with less than twelve years of education are more likely to hold jobs that are dissatisfying, and that allow for little participation, autonomy and responsibility. Thus, it may be the nature of employment experiences more than educational level that functions as the moderator of the relationship between employment status and marital satisfaction. Likewise, because the negative relationship between wives' employment and marital satisfaction was limited to those wives who were mothers of preschool children, role overload may also be a moderator variable.

The absence of any consistent effects of wives' employment status on their own marital satisfaction is surprising, given what Locksley (1980) refers to as the 'extensive controversy over the significance of this phenomenon'. One possibility is that assumptions about the effects of wives' employment status are incorrect. This issue will be considered in more detail in Chapter 10. A second possibility is that specific aspects of dissatisfaction are not revealed when global measures of satisfaction are used (Allen and Keaveny, 1979). Consequently, data that contrast specific aspects of marital functioning between employed and homemaker wives are now considered.

Specific Aspects of Wives' Marital Functioning

Power balance between spouses

Perhaps the first facet of the marital relationship that should be assessed is the power relationship between the spouses, because of the hypothesis that one of the primary benefits of employment for wives is a more egalitarian power structure within the marital relationship. Characteristics of such a structure would include joint decision making and an equitable sharing of household tasks. Indeed, any change in the power balance towards a more egalitarian relationship is frequently regarded as the most important positive effect of employment for wives. Two ways in which the power relationship between spouses has been reflected is in terms of the division of household responsibilities, and financial decision making. An issue of ideological importance is raised here. Even if husbands of employed wives were to lose some of the power they currently possess within the marital relationship, this in itself would not mean that such changes are negative. Instead, any such changes should be seen in the larger context of a redistribution of power in an effort to obtain a more equitable power balance.

An examination of the literature on wives' employment and the power balance yields a consistent picture. On the one hand, there has traditionally been a substantial discrepancy between the number of household tasks performed by employed husbands and employed wives. Although employed wives complete somewhat fewer household chores than non-employed wives, employed wives still complete substantially more of the housework than their husbands, perhaps six times as much according to Moore and Hofferth (1979). Moreover, although the majority of the research was generated in the United States, similar patterns have emerged in other countries (e.g. Australia; Presland and Antill, 1987). Thus, the notion that employed husbands and employed wives share household tasks equally can be discounted, no matter what job the wife holds (Yogev, 1981), even though there has been some change in the overall distribution of household roles. However, Maret and Finlay's (1984) data contrasting changes in household responsibilities for employed and non-employed wives between 1974 and 1976 clearly suggest that although statistically significant, any change was small. In addition, employed wives still fulfil a secondary role to their spouses regarding financial decision making within the marital relationship, even though they contribute more to the total family income than do wives who are non-employed (Blood and Hamblin, 1958; Presland and Antill, 1987). Yogev (1981) provides one explanation as to why the power imbalance remains between employed husbands and employed wives.

She shows that dual career couples do not share role responsibilities. Rather, role expansion occurs for the employed wife. In other words, while the employed wife assumes a greater role in financial decision making, she adds these new roles without relinquishing her other roles. Thus, when assuming the employed role, the wife is merely accumulating additional role responsibilities.

Sexual functioning

Another specific aspect of employed wives' marital functioning that has been investigated is sexual dysfunction. Based on their clinical impressions and observations, Johnson and Masters (1976) suggested that sexual dysfunction is associated with wives' employment status. This is a topic that has attracted some attention, partially because it is widely believed that the changing power structure between spouses affects their sexual relationship and functioning. For example, in a report in *Newsweek* (1987, p. 66), entitled 'Not tonight, dear', it is argued that:

> In two-career marriages, particularly, there may be an underlying power struggle that spills over into the bedroom. Northwestern's Knopf tells of one such couple who are currently her patients. The two had an unwritten 'contract', she says, agreeing that both should work; but it was implicit the man should have the better job. When the wife took a superior job, the husband, threatened and angry, lost his desire for her. Then the wife also lost desire: although she liked her work, she felt guilty about straying from the traditional role. Sometimes, inhibited desire can be an unconscious stratagem for maintaining the upper hand by withholding sexual gratification.

Avery-Clark (1986) makes the point that most research focusing on the relationship between wives' employment status and sexual dysfunction has been based on personal statements of single individuals seeking or receiving treatment, or small and non-representative samples, and from research where control groups are absent (e.g. Johnson, Kaplan and Tusel, 1979). Avery-Clark's study is the only empirical investigation of the relationship between sexual dysfunction and wives' employment. In a retrospective analysis, Avery-Clark (1986) examined the files of women who presented themselves for treatment of sexual dysfunction at the Masters and Johnson Institute in St Louis, Missouri between 1 January 1979 and 1 March 1985. She classified the 218 women who met her criteria (married, employed, neither of the spouses was a student or retired, and the problem was one of sexual dysfunction or disorder, *not* marital distress) into one of three groups: a 'career' group, a 'job' group, and an 'unemployed' group. Wives in the career group had a high commitment to employment, reflected by the amount of time they had devoted to obtaining job-related education and currently devoted to employment, the emphasis in their job on the development of responsibility and long-term goals, and employment for personal development rather than for financial reasons. Wives in the job group did not evidence as high a degree of commitment to employment, their employment was focused on short-term goal achievement and they were more likely to be employed for purely financial reasons. It is important to note that wives in Avery-Clark's (1986) 'unemployed' group should be described as 'non-employed'; they were involved in homemaking and volunteer activities for which there was no direct financial compensation, and had not lost a job. This distinction between non-employment and unemployment is important: as will become apparent in Chapters 7 and 9, unemployed and non-employed spouses experience very different stressors. Lastly, Avery-Clark (1986) used DSM III as the basis for diagnosing wives' sexual dysfunction, thereby enhancing the generalizability of the findings.

After controlling for wives' age in the sample, one significant difference emerged between the three groups. Career women were significantly more likely to present with problems of inhibited sexual desire or vaginismus. There were no other significant differences between the three groups in terms of aversion, dyspareunia, and inhibited orgasm. Avery-Clark (1986) explains the findings in terms of the stressors that employed wives, and career women in particular, experience. Nonetheless, it remains unclear why it is specifically vaginismus and inhibited sexual desire that is associated with wives' employment status, and not any of the other sexual dysfunctions. Future research should investigate whether specific employment experiences (e.g. shift work, job satisfaction, participation in decision making, job-related alienation) are associated with sexual dysfunction. Finally, as Avery-Clark (1986) notes, the data presented above are derived from women who self-presented at a clinic for specific sexual dysfunction. It remains to be seen whether the pattern of findings revealed above also characterizes the experiences of non-clinical groups of employed women, or groups of employed men who present for treatment of sexual dysfunction. This is particularly important because other alternative explanations remain feasible. For example, employed wives may have had more money to spend on such treatment, leaving the sample studied non-representative. Also, employed wives may have felt more free to refuse sexual relations with their partners because of their increased feelings of independence and power.

One final point concerns the assumptions from which the link between wives' employment and sexual dysfunction is proposed (Avery-Clark, 1986; Johnson et al., 1979). Specifically, it is assumed that any change in the power balance between spouses will emerge because of the wife's increased independence and participation in job-related decisions. It is also assumed that these changes will result in conflict between the spouses. Yet there are reports showing that increased participation in decision making for the employed wife can exert positive effects on the marital relationship under certain circumstances (Crouter, 1984a). As a result, it remains possible that for some individuals, wives' employment may enhance sexual and marital functioning, and it may be beneficial to investigate what factors predict whether employment for the wife is associated with sexual problems within the marital relationship.

Divorce

Perhaps the final criterion against which to evaluate the possible effects of wives' employment is marital disruption or divorce. An examination of the available literature suggests that these two terms are used interchangeably in this context. This is partially an attempt to increase sample sizes (as not too many divorces occur in the typically short time period of the studies cited) as well as an attempt to reflect the notion that common law marriages are also studied. In terms of the specific aspects of marital functioning that may be influenced by wives' employment status, divorce is considered last because it is the final link in the process of marital dissatisfaction. Having said that, however, arguments already raised (see Chapter 2) against using divorce as a criterion of poor marital functioning should be borne in mind (e.g. differing legislation as to the reasons for which a divorce can be obtained, when a divorce can be obtained, and religious differences as to whether divorce is permissible).

Even if we were to ignore any conceptual reasons positing a link between wives' employment and divorce, or any empirical data supporting such a link, the conventional wisdom asserting the existence of such a relationship together with the sheer volume of popular articles is so pervasive that this issue is worthy of empirical scrutiny (see Barling, in press). As one example among many, Tuthill (1980) entitled her article 'Marriage and a career: no easy choices and a good chance of divorce'. Throughout the discussion on wives' employment and marital dissolution, one issue should be emphasized that has both ideological implications and again leads to questions about the adequacy of divorce as a criterion of marital functioning. In the literature that presupposes a link between wives' employment and marital dissolution, it is assumed that should such a link emerge, this would constitute evidence of one of the extremely detrimental effects of wives' employment. This assumption is based on the belief that divorce and its consequences are inevitably negative. Yet this may not be the case. Instead, in many instances, marital dissolution that follows chronic marital distress may be positive for the spouses as well as any children in the family. Indeed, there are empirical data to support this alternative view, especially where intrafamily conflict has been high prior to and during the divorce process (Long *et al.*, 1988). This again points to the difficulty of accepting divorce as the extreme criterion of negative marital functioning: divorce is certainly indicative of poor marital functioning, but is not necessarily worse than the continuation of a poor marital relationship.

In their 1979 literature review, Moore and Hofferth concluded that there was no consistent support for any link between wives' employment status and divorce. Rather, some studies have provided support for a positive relationship, others for a negative relationship. The reasons advanced for the emergence of a positive correlation between wives' employment and divorce include the disruption to traditional homemaker roles and the corresponding role readjustments required by individual family members, and the increased stress placed on the marital and family system. It has also been argued that a relationship exists between wives' employment and divorce because of the increased financial resources that employment provides. Employment increases wives' financial independence and social contacts. Therefore, employed wives would be more able to support themselves (and their children) following a divorce than would homemakers.

Since Moore and Hofferth (1979) published their review, a number of longitudinal studies using large, randomly drawn samples in the United States have examined the link between wives' employment status and divorce (e.g. Booth *et al.*, 1984; Cherlin, 1979; Mott and Moore, 1979; Spitze and South, 1985). One finding that is replicated consistently is the positive relationship between wife's income and the likelihood of marital dissolution (Booth *et al.*, 1984; Cherlin, 1979). This finding led to the 'independence hypothesis': as the ratio between husbands' and wives' earnings approaches unity, divorce will become more likely. The reasoning underlying this hypothesis is that when wives are employed, they have more resources at their disposal which facilitate personal and financial independence following divorce. Support for this hypothesis emerged in all four of the studies mentioned above (namely, Booth *et al.*, 1984; Cherlin, 1979; Mott and Moore, 1979; Spitze and South, 1985). Findings such as these, however, are placed in a wider perspective by Mott and Moore (1979) and Cherlin (1979), who note that economic factors are only one facet of the numerous factors that facilitate divorce. Indeed, Cherlin (1979) notes that the relationship between income and divorce is remarkable more because of its consistency than its magnitude.

Therefore, while consistently associated with marital dissolution, economic factors are by themselves insufficient for an understanding of the relationship between wives' employment status and divorce. Spitze and South (1985) argue that even excluding the role of economic factors in divorce, the amount of time the wife devotes to employment each week will be associated with divorce. First, consistent with the 'availability hypothesis', Spitze and South (1985) suggest that the greater the amount of time devoted to employment, the less the amount of the time available for marital interactions. Second, Spitze and South (1985) suggest that even when wives devote large amounts of time to employment, the ratio of husbands' time in housework to that of their wives remains about 1:6, thereby increasing the wives' perceptions of inequity regarding the sharing of household responsibilities. Based on pooled data of 5774 wives, the number of hours wives spend in employment each week was positively associated with the likelihood of divorce occurring in the future after controlling for standard economic predictors. Also, the relationship between the amount of time spent in employment and divorce is greatest amongst middle-class couples and when the husbands disapprove of their wives' employment. Under both these conditions, Spitze and South (1985) argued that the burden of household chores and roles on the wife would increase.

Instead of solely contrasting employed and non-employed wives, Booth *et al.* (1984) also conducted a within-group analysis of employed wives, and examined the direct and indirect effects on marital instability of the number of hours spent on the job each week. They found that any effects of job-related time demands on marital instability are indirect (see Figure 5.1). Instead, consistent with Spitze and South's (1985) two hypotheses, Booth *et al.*'s (1984) analyses showed that the amount of time wives spend on the job each week is associated significantly and directly with the division of labour in the household between spouses. Moreover, the division of labour between spouses also directly predicts spousal interactions, although neither of these two factors themselves directly predict marital instability. Rather, spousal interactions are negatively and directly associated with marital disagreements.

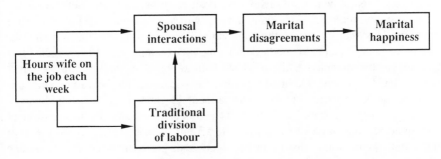

Figure 5.1   Indirect effects of wives' time on the job and marital happiness in Booth *et al.*'s (1984) study

Subsequent research by Yogev and Brett (1985a) provides an explanation for the emergence of a relationship between the number of hours devoted to employment and the division of household chores. For dual earner wives, marital satisfaction is associated with the division of household chores when the wife perceives equity in the number of household responsibilities completed by each spouse. For instance, Ruble *et al.* (1988) have shown, using both cross-sectional and longitudinal data, that a wife's positive feelings towards her husband decrease when her expectations concerning the division of household labour are violated following the birth of the first child. On the contrary, for husbands whose wives are employed, marital satisfaction is associated with the perception of themselves doing *fewer* household chores than their employed wives. This model may also apply to homemakers or to men. Specifically, when wives spend far greater amounts of time in the homemaker role than they expect to, the division of labour within the family will become even more marked, further heightening wives' perceptions of inequity. There may also be a relationship between the amount of time non-employed wives spend in the homemaker role and marital interactions. Likewise, when men find themselves more involved in household tasks than they would want, a similar process may be initiated even if the relationship is still not equitable.

One omission in all these studies, however, is that the partner who seeks or initiates the divorce is never identified. Instead, it is assumed that it is only the wife who wishes to dissolve the relationship. Yet it may be the husband or both partners making this decision. If it is not the wife who seeks to terminate the marital relationship, alternative interpretations may be required. Future research should isolate which partner seeks the divorce. There is one further context in which having a job makes it easier for the wife to leave the relationship. Strube (1988) notes that, in general, many battered wives continue with the relationship. However, wives' employment status predicts whether they will leave a violent relationship. Specifically, employed wives are far more likely to leave a violent relationship than are non-employed wives. This may be one area where any ambiguity as to whether the effects of employment on divorce are positive or negative are minimized.

In summary, the results of studies linking wives' employment status to divorce or marital instability suggest the following. There is consistent support for the economic 'independence' hypothesis relating wives' employment to divorce. Over and above this hypothesis, the amount of time spent in employment by wives is associated with the likelihood of divorce occurring in the future, and this relationship is primarily indirect. The amount of time devoted to employment influences marital instability through its consecutive effects on the division of household responsibilities and marital interactions. Nonetheless, perhaps the most important observation is that no matter which data set is analysed, the magnitude of the effects of wives' employment (whether employment status or time in employment is analysed) on divorce remain modest. Perhaps this should not be surprising. As Mott and Moore (1979, p. 364) conclude:

> If men and women marry largely for noneconomic reasons, it is not inconsistent that large proportions of persons who dissolve their marriages should have similarly noneconomic motivations.

WIVES' EMPLOYMENT STATUS AND THEIR HUSBANDS' MARITAL FUNCTIONING

The original impetus for research on the consequences of employment for wives was the fear that this would lead to detrimental effects for the husband. Two streams within the research of wives' employment status and husbands' marital functioning can be identified. First, there is a body of research focusing on the psychological well-being of husbands whose wives are employed. Second, concern that wives who accept employment outside of the home exert harmful effects on their husbands has resulted in a focus on the effects of wives' employment on husbands' global marital adjustment or satisfaction, as well as on specific aspects of marital functioning (e.g. power relationships, dependency and so forth). These two issues will now be considered.

Wives' Employment Status and Husbands' Psychological Well-Being

In considering husbands' well-being within this context, research has focused on several outcome criteria, including life satisfaction, job satisfaction, depression and psychosomatic symptoms. Specifically, there are no indications that husbands of employed wives have a higher level of psychological functioning than their counterparts whose wives are homemakers. Some studies have found no differences in psychological functioning between these two groups, and others have found that husbands of employed wives fared significantly worse than husbands whose wives are not employed. To investigate such inconsistencies, Fendrich (1984) conducted a meta-analytic study of the relationship between wives' employment status and husbands' psychological well-being. The results of this meta-analysis suggested that there was no relationship between these two variables. However, this finding may not be generalizable given that Fendrick (1984) included only five studies in the meta-analysis, and the results of these studies were not consistent. In addition, in one of the studies on which the meta-analysis was based (Rosenfield, 1980), wives' employment exerted a *detrimental* effect on husbands' well-being. In three of the other studies (Booth, 1979; Burke and Weir, 1976; Kessler and McRae, 1982), the effects of wives' employment were not consistent across measures of well-being. Because the results of the studies and the meta-analysis remain equivocal, Fendrich (1984) then re-analysed the data from the *Quality of American Life* survey (Campbell *et al.*, 1976). Based on the data from this randomly drawn database, Fendrich (1984) also showed that there was no *direct* relationship between wives' employment and husbands' psychological well-being. Fendrich (1984) suggested that this relationship may be moderated by husbands' income, or husbands' perceived adequacy in the role of family breadwinner.

In a separate study, Kessler and McRae (1982) found that husbands of employed wives were significantly more depressed than those of non-employed wives. They speculated that such differences might emerge as a function of the husbands' objective earnings, and therefore controlled statistically for this factor (as well as the number and age of all children). However, the difference between these two groups of husbands remained after removing any effects of income and number and age of the children, thereby lending empirical support to the notion that differences between the groups were a function of wives' employment status, not husbands' earnings.

Staines, Pottick and Fudge (1985) investigated the relationship between wives' employment and husbands' job and life satisfaction. They used survey data from a national sample of workers, and found that husbands whose wives were employed registered significantly poorer job satisfaction and life satisfaction than those whose wives were homemakers. In a separate report, Staines, Pottick and Fudge (1986) further analysed this same data set in an attempt to understand why such a negative effect of wives' employment status emerged. They found that when they controlled for the effects of the husbands' perceived adequacy as the breadwinner, there was no longer a significant relationship between wives' employment status and husbands' well-being. This strongly suggests that it is not the *objective* level of husbands' earnings that moderate the relationship (as Kessler and McRae found), but the *subjective* perceptions concerning their adequacy in the role of breadwinner. Interestingly, this finding is consistent with Fendrich's (1984) suggestions regarding the role of the breadwinner. This finding replicates other research (see Chapter 4) suggesting that perceived financial strain is a better predictor of marital functioning than is objective wage level. Differences in the effects of objective income level and perceived financial adequacy parallel the distinction between stressors and stress. Objective income level is quantifiable and verifiable independently of individuals' perceptions, and perceived financial adequacy represents individuals' beliefs that they have sufficient financial resources to meet their needs.

These studies show, therefore, that there is no consistent support for the notion that husbands of employed wives fare significantly worse in terms of mental health than those whose wives are not employed. Rather, only under certain conditions (e.g. the husbands' perceived ineffectiveness as the breadwinner; Staines *et al.*, 1986) does a relationship exist. Also, the size of any relationships is typically modest, suggesting that by itself, employment status is not a sufficient predictor of mental health.

Husbands' Marital Functioning

As Locksley (1980) and many others have observed, the employed wife is also presumed to exert detrimental effects on her husband's marital functioning, for example, his feelings of adequacy and sexual impotence. A number of empirical studies have contrasted the marital functioning of husbands of employed and non-employed wives. These studies can be classified according to whether they focused on global (e.g. marital adjustment or satisfaction) or specific indices (e.g. power relationships) of marital functioning.

Global marital satisfaction

Initial fears that wives' employment exerts a detrimental impact on husbands' marital satisfaction were prompted by ideological beliefs concerning the role of wives. These fears may well have been maintained by the results of an earlier study. Burke and Weir (1976) showed that husbands of employed wives did report less marital satisfaction than their counterparts whose wives were homemakers. However, there are important elements inherent in Burke and Weir's (1976) methodology and analyses which seriously limit the extent to which their results can provide information regarding the effects of wives' employment status on husbands' marital satisfaction. First, the magnitude of the difference in marital satisfaction between the two groups was too small to attach any clinical or predictive significance to the results. Second, when Burke and Weir (1976) focused on more specific marital variables, the trend for husbands of employed wives to fare worse was not replicated. Third, when inspecting their results, it becomes clear that there is no uniform pattern suggesting that husbands with employed wives are 'at risk' of marital dissatisfaction. For example, Burke and Weir (1976) report that husbands of employed wives communicated more frequently with their wives about their feelings than husbands of non-employed wives. Without some knowledge of the specific content of the communication, the direction of this effect is ambiguous. Fourth, because Burke and Weir's (1976) sample consisted only of professional engineers and accountants, the generalizability of their results remained questionable. Finally, subsequent studies have failed to replicate Burke and Weir's (1976) findings.

In contrast to Burke and Weir's (1976) study, Staines and his co-workers (Staines *et al.*, 1978) showed that there was no relationship between wives' employment status and husbands' global marital satisfaction based on survey data from two nationally representative samples obtained in the United States. Locksley (1980) also based her findings on data drawn from a randomly selected, large sample in the United States. Her results replicated those of Staines *et al.* (1978), again showing that there are no differences between husbands of employed and homemaker wives in terms of marital satisfaction. Orden and Bradburn's (1969) results showed a similar pattern, with one exception. Their data suggested that when there are preschool children in the home, husbands of employed wives are less satisfied with their marriages than husbands of homemakers.

Booth (1979) investigated the same issue using a stratified probability sample of families residing in Toronto, Canada. He found that wives' employment status did not contribute to husbands' marital dissatisfaction. Greater confidence could have been placed in these results had Booth's (1979) measurement of wives' employment status and marital functioning referred to the same time period. Instead, while he asked wives about their employment status over the past week, husbands were asked whether they had an argument with their spouse over the past twelve months, or whether either spouse had threatened to leave home during the past 24 months. It is by no means certain that the wives remained employed over these two years. Thus, even though the question being addressed was whether employment status influenced marital functioning, we cannot be sure whether wives were employed or not at the time their marital satisfaction was being assessed.

Additional support for the notion that wives' employment status exerts no effects on husbands' marital satisfaction emanates from Smith's (1985) analysis of previous findings. Smith (1985) showed that of 27 previous studies (involving 1066 husband–wife comparisons), 93% yielded no differences between the marital satisfaction of husbands of employed and non-employed wives. This pattern held true even when husbands' educational level and stage in the life cycle were controlled statistically. To summarize then, there are no consistent differences between husbands of employed and non-employed wives in terms of global marital satisfaction. However, differences may still emerge between these two groups when they are contrasted on specific measures of marital satisfaction. It would not be unusual for people to report moderate levels of global job, life or marital satisfaction, with indications of dissatisfaction emerging when more specific facets of job, life and marital satisfaction are considered (Allen and Keaveny, 1979).

Specific Aspects of Husbands' Marital Functioning

An examination of the literature reveals that there has been fairly extensive consideration of the possible effects of wives' employment status on three specific aspects of the husbands' marital functioning: The power relationship between husband and wife, the extent to which the husband participates in household tasks and responsibilities, and the extent of communication and companionship within the marital relationship.

Power balance between spouses

Power distribution between spouses has been assumed to be more equitable when the wife is employed, and because that would be a change from the 'traditional' male/female relationship, it may be perceived as a threat by some husbands. In one of the earlier investigations of this issue, Blood and Hamblin (1958) hypothesized that wives' employment would have a beneficial effect on the power relationship between spouses. Specifically, they hypothesized that the power relationship between spouses would become 'less traditional' and more egalitarian when the wife accepts employment outside the home.

The empirical data do not support Blood and Hamblin's (1958) hypothesis. First, Blood and Hamblin (1958) report that husbands of employed wives become more egalitarian, while husbands of homemakers move more in the direction of traditional authority relationships. However, a close examination of the data presented in their Table 1 (Blood and Hamblin, 1958, p. 350) shows that these differences are not statistically significant. Second, it is unclear how Blood and Hamblin (1958) arrive at their conclusions concerning *change* in expectations given the cross-sectional nature of their data. Third, these authors also report on an index of the power relationship between spouses, namely the extent to which husbands use suggestions offered by their wives. Blood and Hamblin (1958) proposed that employed wives would have more of their suggestions accepted by their husbands than homemakers, because of the greater egalitarian nature of their marriages. Yet, contrary to their suggestions, no such differences resulted. One explanation for these findings is that they collected their data in 1958 or earlier. It is possible that if their study were to be repeated today, the results would now support their hypotheses. In other words, it is possible that change has occurred in attitudes and beliefs about wives' role in the marriage following the introduction of large numbers of women into the labour force since 1960 (see Chapter 7).

Aldous (1969b) analysed the consequences of wives' employment status in a lower socioeconomic group of black and white husbands. She found that the direction of the relationship between wives' employment status and the pattern of decision making between spouses was different for black and white men. Specifically, white husbands' decision making in the marriage was not dependent on their wives' employment status. As such, the findings for the white sample replicate those of Blood and Hamblin (1958). On the contrary, black husbands whose wives were employed participated *less* in decision making than black husbands whose wives were not employed. Aldous (1969b) offers an intriguing explanation for her findings, relating the different pattern of findings for the black and white groups to the experience of discrimination that blacks have had to endure in the United States, and the consequent socialization differences between black and white children. This explanation will be discussed in more detail later in conjunction with the results of wives' employment status on husbands' marital role performance.

Household responsibilities

The above analyses suggest that wives' employment status *per se* is not associated consistently with the power of the husband within the marriage. Nonetheless, there are differences between the husbands of employed and non-employed wives with respect to the division of households responsibilities. The relative extent to which husbands and wives contribute to household tasks is related to, if not a function of, the power relationship between the spouses. Before discussing this particular aspect of marital functioning, it should be noted that the issue being considered here is not the extent to which husbands and wives contribute to household responsibilities. The data show consistently that wives are substantially more involved in household chores than their husbands. Moreover, it has been apparent for some time that most wives, irrespective of their employment status, would prefer their husbands to be more involved in household responsibilities (Blood and Hamblin, 1958; Pleck, 1985). What is under consideration here is the extent to which husbands' contribution to household tasks is influenced by their wives' employment status.

Blood and Hamblin (1958) assumed that husbands of employed wives would participate more in housework than husbands whose wives were homemakers. This assumption was predicated on the belief that employed wives could demand greater equality in the marital relationship because of their economic contribution to the family. Their data show that husbands of employed wives certainly complete a greater proportion of housework than their counterparts whose wives are not employed. Three points should be noted concerning these data. First, Blood and Hamblin (1958) excluded any housework completed by children. Second, the proportion of household chores completed either by the husbands of employed wives or husbands of homemakers was still substantially less than 50%. Third, Blood and Hamblin (1958) noted another interpretation of their results: perhaps the proportion of household chores completed by husbands whose wives are employed is greater because the total amount of housework completed in dual earner marriage decreases (e.g. husbands and wives decide to do fewer chores, or pay for them to be done). However, the total amount of time devoted to housework did not depend on wives' employment status. It would appear from Blood and Hamblin's (1958) early study, therefore, that wives' employment status positively affects husbands' participation in household tasks. Since then, numerous investigators have focused on this issue. The majority of these studies have shown that husbands of employed wives do indeed participate more in household responsibilities, although the magnitude of the difference varies between investigations (e.g. Blood and Wolfe, 1960; Ybarra, 1982).

One study has been reported in which the findings deviated from this pattern. As already noted, Aldous (1969b) investigated the effects of wives' employment status on husbands' task performance in the family in a sample of lower socioeconomic black and white men. Among the group of black husbands, husbands whose wives were employed *were less active* in household chores than their counterparts whose wives were homemakers. White blue collar husbands whose wives were employed did not participate less in household chores and family chores. These differences between black and white husbands held true even after Aldous (1969b) controlled statistically for the age and number of children in the family. Aldous (1969b) suggests that race *per se* is an inadequate explanation of this phenomenon. Rather, race functions as a 'marker' variable, denoting that some other important psychological process underlies the difference between these two groups. She suggested that such differences are a function of past prejudice and discrimination against blacks in the United States, as a result of which black children are socialized to view the employed wife as a threat to the husbands' power in the marriage and the family. On the other hand, white children are socialized into a system where children view the father as the breadwinner, irrespective of the wife's employment role status. To Aldous, this implies that any positive change in socialization patterns must be achieved by the provision not only of employment opportunities for black husbands and fathers, but *equal* employment opportunities at an equitable wage that allows the husband/father to assume a role similar to that enjoyed by their white counterparts.

Companionship and communication

A third aspect of the marital relationship which may be associated with wives' employment status is marital communication and companionship. Locksley (1980) investigated a variety of aspects of companionship, such as the amount of leisure time spouses spend together, and the frequency and content of communication between spouses. There were no differences at all between the husbands of employed and non-employed wives across any of these dimensions. In reviewing previously published data on companionship (which involved a total of 285 respondents in 13 studies), Smith (1985) showed that most studies found no differences between husbands whose wives were employed and those whose wives were homemakers. Thus, it would appear that husbands' reports of companionship do not depend on their wives' employment status. The findings regarding marital communication are not as clear. Smith's (1985) review of previous research suggests that there are no differences in interspousal communication between husbands of non-employed wives, and husbands of homemakers. Nonetheless, differences have been found in some studies. First, Burke and Weir (1976) showed that husbands of employed wives were more satisfied with their marital communication than their counterparts whose wives were homemakers. It is important to note, however, that the magnitude of the difference between the two groups was sufficiently small (62.96 vs 60.32 respectively) to question the clinical or predictive utility of this finding.

In summary, therefore, there is little support for the notion that husbands of employed and homemaker wives differ in terms of global marital satisfaction. However, the division of labour between spouses is more equitable where wives are employed rather than homemakers; nonetheless, husbands of employed wives still do not participate equally. Given this pattern of findings, one further possibility should be explored. It is possible that while there is no direct relationship between wives' employment status and husbands' marital functioning, factors such as the division of household labour or inter-role conflict mediate this relationship. This would be consistent with the findings regarding indirect effects of the amount of time husbands' spend on the job and marital functioning (see Chapter 3). Parasuraman *et al*. (1989) investigated whether employment/family conflict, time committed to the job and satisfaction with child care mediated the relationship between wives' employment status and husbands' marital functioning. Like other studies, Parasuraman *et al*. (1989) found no direct relationship between wives' employment status and husbands' marital functioning. Their hypothesis concerning the mediating role of inter-role conflict was not supported, because it was not associated with wives' employment status. On the contrary, the amount of time husbands committed to the job did mediate the relationship between wives' employment status and husbands' marital functioning, presumably because husbands of employed wives spent less time on the job. Lastly, Parasuraman *et al*. (1989) noted that although the results for satisfaction with child care were marginally significant, their effects intensified when there were young children in the home, Thus, Parasuraman *et al*.'s (1989) study puts into perspective previous findings regarding wives' employment status and husbands' marital functioning. There is no direct relationship between these latter two variables; however, there is an indirect relationship, and research should now identify the indirect paths through which wives' employment status influences husbands' marital functioning.

STATUS INCOMPATIBILITY: RELATIVE OCCUPATIONAL STATUS OF SPOUSES

As can be seen from the preceding discussion, the initial research on wives' employment focused on employment status (i.e. employed vs homemaker), and the possible effects of employment status on wives and their husbands. More recently, the concept of wives' employment has progressed beyond a unidimensional consideration of wives' employment status. The question that is raised with this alternative framework is whether the wife's occupational achievements *relative to her husband* exert any effects on marital functioning for either herself or her spouse. The relative occupational achievements within the marital dyad are important, as they guide expectations about each spouse's behaviour. Consistent with a social context in which an inequitable power relationship between spouses is the norm, it was hypothesized that negative effects on marital functioning result when the wife's occupational achievements exceed those of her husband. A number of studies have now been reported that investigate this hypothesis, contrasting the effects of relative occupational attainments with different aspects of marital functioning (Richardson, 1979).

In the first large sample study investigating the effects of wives' employment and occupational status, Richardson (1979) analysed data from the 1972–77 cumulative surveys of the National Opinion Research Council. Classifying the levels of relative occupational attainments into three categories (namely, wives higher, equal to or lower than their husbands), Richardson (1979) focused on the effects of relative occupational attainments on marital satisfaction. No support was yielded for the hypothesis that marital dissatisfaction was greater when wives held jobs similar or greater in occupational prestige than those of their spouses.

Richardson's study has been criticized on methodological grounds. Mugford (1980) questions its generalizability because of the way in which Richardson operationalized relative occupational prestige and marital satisfaction. First, because he used archival data, Richardson was constrained to use the data in the form that they had already been collected; and marital satisfaction scores were presented as a simple dichotomy ('very happy' or 'not happy'), and therefore the results are not sufficiently sensitive to isolate differences between groups. Second, with regard to relative occupational prestige, Mugford (1980) points out that categorizing occupational prestige into three groups, namely low prestige (0–29), medium prestige (30–49), and high prestige (50–89), presents interpretive difficulties. For example, where a husband's prestige score was 47 and his wife's was 51, she was ranked as higher in prestige (even though the absolute difference is only four points). Yet a wife who obtained a prestige score of 47 would be ranked as equal in occupational prestige when her husband obtained a prestige score of 31. Thus, in the first instance, fairly similar scores would be represented as significantly different, whereas in the latter case, significantly larger differences would be coded as similar. Consequently, a large number of classifications of occupational prestige in Richardson's (1979) study are imprecise.

Hornung and his colleagues (Hornung and McCullough, 1981; Hornung, McCullough and Sujimoto, 1981) conducted two studies in which they overcame the methodological problems in Richardson's (1979) study. In both these studies, the effects of relative status inconsistency and status incompatibility on marital functioning were investigated. In considering these two studies, we will focus only on status incompatibility. Status inconsistency occurs when an individual's own educational level and occupational prestige are at variance. As such, status inconsistency is a within-person construct. Status incongruency emerges when marital partners differ significantly on either educational level or occupational prestige. In this respect, status incongruency emerges within the context of a dyad. However, wives are only at higher risk of spouse abuse when their status exceeds that of their husbands. Our interest is whether characteristics of wives' employment status in the context of the marital dyad (i.e. relative to her husband) influence marital functioning.

In their first study, Hornung and McCullough (1981) showed that status incongruency is associated with marital satisfaction. A number of aspects of this relationship are worth noting. First, although the magnitude of the effect for status incongruency was not very high, its effects were significantly greater than the effects of each individual's occupational prestige taken in isolation. This supports the notion of investigating occupational prestige as a relative factor between spouses rather than an intraindividual factor. Second, this effect is particularly pronounced for wives who are determined to advance in their careers and jobs. Third, Hornung and McCullough (1981) note that their results probably provide a conservative test of the hypothesis that status incongruency is negatively associated with marital functioning. Because only those marriages that had successfully weathered the stress of occupational incongruency and remained intact were included in their sample, any severe effects of status incompatibility that may have resulted in the dissolution of the relationship would be missed.

In their second study, Hornung et al. (1981) investigated the relationship between status incongruency and spouse abuse in a large random sample. They argued that status incongruency between spouses leads to stress, and that this stress predisposes spouses to abusive behaviour. Specifically, they investigated the incidence and prevalence of three forms of spouse abuse: psychological and physical aggression, and life-threatening behaviour. Prevalence refers to the extent of aggression across couples, while incidence reflects the frequency of violent acts within couples. Thus, a low prevalence rate combined with a high incidence rate suggests that violence occurs within very few marriages, but when it does, it occurs frequently. On the contrary, a high prevalence rate together with a low incidence rate would indicate that spouse abuse occurs in many couples, but on an infrequent basis.

Hornung et al. (1981) documented a consistent effect of status incongruency across all indices of marital aggression. With regard to the prevalence and incidence of spouse abuse, Hornung et al.'s (1981) data suggest the following pattern. Each of the three forms of spouse abuse is more prevalent in those marital dyads where either spouse holds a blue collar job. Also, wives who occupy managerial positions or own small businesses are at higher risk for spouse abuse than wives whose jobs provide less prestige. Indeed, there was a substantially greater probability of life-threatening violence occurring within the marriage when the wife, but not the husband, held a managerial position than when the husband held a managerial position. When the incidence rather than the prevalence of the three forms of aggression was considered, status incongruity exerted its greatest effects on life-threatening behaviour, then on physical aggression, and less of an effect on psychological aggression. In fact, where a women's occupational prestige is higher than that of her spouse, she is more than twice as likely to experience life-threatening behaviour from her husband than women who are equal to their spouses in occupational prestige.

Three points should be noted in evaluating the results of Hornung *et al.*'s (1981) study. First, consistent with the results of Hornung and McCullough's (1981) study, the relative occupational status of spouses was a more significant predictor of risk for spouse abuse than the prestige of either of the individual spouses' occupations considered in isolation. Second, the fact that significant effects emerged in terms of life-threatening behaviour may be evidence of a substantial effect: there are suggestions that the measure of life-threatening behaviour that they used in their study is not sufficiently sensitive to be able to detect differences because of the low base rate of this behaviour in many non-clinical populations (Barling *et al.*, 1987). As this would reduce the likelihood of significant effects emerging, the fact that significant findings emerged in Hornung and McCullough's (1981) study is notable. Third, the effects of status incongruency on spouse abuse paralleled those from their earlier study on marital dissatisfaction, despite the fact that different samples were used in the two studies.

Ironically, the most recently published article concerning the effects of relative occupational achievements on marriage used the oldest data set. Philliber and Hiller (1983) used data from the 1967 and 1974 National Longitudinal Surveys to assess the effects of relative occupational achievements on divorce. In their retrospective analysis, Philliber and Hiller (1983) considered marital separation to have occurred if a woman reported some change in marital status during any of the 1968, 1969, 1972 or 1974 surveys after respondents had reported being married in 1967. Respondents were considered never to have separated if they reported being married across these interview phases. Thus, whether individuals were married to different partners at the two interviews and had separated in the interim cannot be determined.

Philliber and Hiller (1983) found some evidence for negative effects of status incongruency. However, while significant, the magnitude of the effect of status incongruency on divorce was modest, and the numerous problems associated with utilizing divorce as a criterion of marital functioning against which the effects of employment characteristics can be considered should be borne in mind. Nonetheless, the direction of this trend is consistent with other data showing that the closer to unity the ratio between husbands' and wives' wages, the greater the likelihood of marital dissolution (Cherlin, 1979; Mott and Moore, 1979). Moreover, Philliber and Hiller's (1983) data showed that the strongest occupational characteristic associated with subsequent divorce was whether the wife held a non-traditional job. They found that there were two consequences of wives occupying a traditional sex-typed job. First, there was a direct effect in reducing the likelihood of divorce. Second, and perhaps more importantly, a moderating role was served where wives occupied a traditional job such that any impact of status incongruency between the spouses was reduced.

Finally, in evaluating the possible effects of status incongruency, the hypothesis that negative effects ensue for status incongruent marriages was supported across three marital behaviours, namely marital dissatisfaction, spouse abuse and marital instability or divorce (Philliber and Hiller, 1983). Nonetheless, two issues remain. First, third variable effects might account for the relationship between status incongruency and marital functioning, thereby raising questions of causality. For example, it is possible that non-traditional women are more likely both to seek a divorce as well as hold jobs that go against traditional role prescriptions. Second, the data for all studies showing empirical support for a status incongruency effect were generated some time ago. Specifically, Hornung and McCullough's (1981) data were derived from the 1973 and 1974 General Social Surveys of the National Opinion Research Council. The data on which Hornung *et al.* (1981) based their analyses were initially reported in 1979. Finally, Philliber and Hiller's (1983) data on status incongruency and marital dissolution were collected as part of the 1967 and 1974 National Longitudinal Surveys. However, major societal changes since these three data sets were collected may have changed the meaning of status incongruency. Specifically, the influx of a large number of wives into the labour force over the last two decades and parallel emphases on employment equity for women have contributed to the situation where dual earner marriages are now the norm, representing 60% of all marriages (see Chapter 7). At the same time, it is likely that changes in social values have made it more likely that wives will report incidents of spouse abuse. Consequently, it is likely that the effects of status incompatibility on marital functioning were specific to a set of social attitudes and expectations, and it would be important to see whether similar effects prevail today.

WIVES' EMPLOYMENT STATUS AND MARITAL FUNCTIONING: CONCLUSION

The discussion in this chapter has focused on wives' employment status, in other words, whether wives are employed or not. The first issue considered was whether the marital functioning of husbands or wives depends on the wives' employment status. Although husbands of employed wives participate more in household tasks, wives' employment exerts no other consistent effect on their husbands. In contrast, employment provides wives with certain benefits. Specifically, employed wives manifest greater psychological well-being and less depression. This is important, because it is possible that psychological well-being mediates the relation between employment and marital functioning. Although employed wives are more likely to divorce, divorce should not necessarily be viewed as a negative outcome. The research suggests that employment provides wives with greater financial resources and more perceived power within the marriage, which may enable them to dissolve an unsatisfactory marriage. The last issue considered in this chapter was the consequence of status incongruency for marital functioning: when wives' occupational prestige or educational attainments exceed those of husbands, the likelihood of the wives being abused increases.

We have not yet considered how wives' subjective experience of their employment might influence marital functioning. Yet Parry (1987) notes that if we are to understand women's psychological functioning more fully, we need to go beyond analyses that merely contrast employed and non-employed wives, and supplement such analyses with a focus on their own employment attitudes and experiences. Stated somewhat differently, the focus on wives' employment status must be broadened to include a consideration of the meaning of employment to the wife. It is to a consideration of this issue that we now turn in Chapter 6.

Chapter 6
Wives' Subjective Employment Experiences and Marital Functioning

In Chapters 3 and 4, the effects of husbands' objective and subjective employment experiences on marital functioning were considered. In the previous chapter, the effects of wives' employment status on marital functioning were considered. We now turn our attention to the effects of wives' subjective employment experiences on their own and their husbands' marital functioning.

Before starting this discussion, a few points are worth noting. First, the fact that employed wives' job-related experiences and attitudes are discussed separately from those of their husbands might appear to suggest that husbands and wives experience their jobs differently. This is not necessarily the case. Instead, the effects of wives' employment experiences are considered separately in the present chapter only because that best reflects the current state of the literature. Second, focusing on the relationship between wives' subjective employment experiences and their marital functioning necessitates a different research design from the one used to contrast employed wives with wives who are homemakers. Specifically, the typical research design described in the previous chapter, where the marital functioning of two groups of wives is contrasted, relies on between-group analyses. This approach assumes that there is considerable variation between these groups, yet substantial similarity within each of the two groups. As opposed to this, focusing on wives' subjective employment experiences assumes that there will be considerable systematic variation within the group of employed wives. Third, consistent with the hypothesis that the relative presence or absence of the wife in the home influences marital functioning, most research in this area has contrasted the marital functioning of employed and non-employed wives. There are very few studies focusing on the job-related experiences and attitudes of employed wives. Fourth, where wives' employment-related experiences and attitudes have been of interest, most research has focused on the conflict between the roles of wife and worker, that is, on inter-role conflict. However, even when inter-role conflict is studied, most of this research has not focused on marital functioning as the outcome variable. Accordingly, as was the case in the previous two chapters, our discussion is limited either to those studies that have focused directly on marital functioning, or to any studies that have focused on outcomes that would be of special relevance to marital functioning, such as depression (Beach and O'Leary, 1986; Beach, Nelson and O'Leary, 1988).

Lastly, one question that emerges when considering wives' subjective employment experiences and marital functioning is whether the employment experiences and attitudes are specific to wives, or whether the results are generalizable to other groups as well (e.g. homemakers or employed fathers).

WIVES' JOB EXPERIENCES AND PSYCHOLOGICAL WELL-BEING

As discussed in Chapter 4, Crouter (1984b) explored how involvement in a participatory system at work influenced marital functioning. She showed that increased participation in decision making on the job exerted neither uniformly positive nor negative effects on marital functioning. In a separate study, Clegg, Wall and Kemp (1987) investigated the relationship between work on an assembly line on the one hand, and job satisfaction, absenteeism and mental health on the other. Clegg *et al.* (1987) found in their sample of blue collar women that the extent to which someone felt she could use her full abilities on the job moderated the relationship between assembly-line work and mental health.

Neither of these two studies focused on an outcome directly relevant to marital functioning. One study was located that was relevant to the relationship between wives' general employment experiences and marital functioning. Krause and Geyer-Pestello (1985) investigated which specific job experiences or attitudes were a source of depressive affect for employed women. Their results showed that pay dissatisfaction predicted depression among employed women. Yet two factors inherent in this study detract from the conclusion that employed women's pay dissatisfaction causes their depression. It is possible that depressed individuals are more likely to experience dissatisfaction with their pay. Even then, it may not be pay dissatisfaction that was associated with depression. Krause and Geyer-Pestello's (1985) single item measure of pay dissatisfaction 'The income that I earn is just about right for the job I have' may be described more accurately as a measure of pay equity, questioning the construct validity of their findings.

Two interrelated difficulties arise in interpreting the findings of these three studies in terms of the specific job-related experiences and attitudes of employed wives. First, the employment experiences investigated in these studies (namely, participation in decision making, involvement in assembly-line work, and pay dissatisfaction) are by no means gender specific. Second, there are no reasons to suspect that similar findings would not emerge if samples of employed husbands were to be studied. Just because the title of an article suggests that the findings are specific to employed wives (e.g. Clegg *et al.*, 1987; Krause and Geyer-Pestello, 1985; Long and Haney, 1988) typically denotes only the composition of the sample, and not necessarily the specificity of the findings to employed women. In the present chapter, however, we will concentrate our attention on those issues that are specific to employed wives. We will begin by investigating one employment-related experience that was initially studied to comprehend more fully the meaning of employment for women, rather than men.

THE MANY ROLES OF EMPLOYED WIVES

Multiple Roles of Employed Wives

The first approach to understanding the meaning of employment for wives was based on investigating how the number of social roles they hold influences functioning. Within this approach, it was assumed that irrespective of the quality of role fulfilment, the number of roles enacted is associated with marital functioning. Two opposing hypotheses have been proposed to account for the effects of multiple roles on marital functioning (Baruch and Barnett, 1986a; Marks, 1977). First, the 'scarcity' hypothesis predicts that holding multiple roles will be negatively associated with psychological and marital functioning. This hypothesis is based on the belief that individuals have a finite amount of time and resources available to them for successful completion of their various roles. Opposed to this is the 'enhancement' hypothesis, which predicts that the number of roles held by employed wives will be positively correlated with marital and personal functioning. The rationale underlying this assumption is that exposure to multiple roles provides wives with greater access to a variety of social resources and support systems, and more opportunities for personal fulfilment and personal security. Thus, although holding fewer social roles may diminish the conflict between roles, this could also cause social isolation, boredom and depression. Much of the literature on multiple roles has assumed that there are two primary roles, namely those of homemaker and employed wife. It is also possible to provide a more finite categorization of these roles. Holahan and Gilbert (1979a, b) specify four roles, for example spouse, parent, employee and self, and indeed numerous roles are identified in the literature. Pietromonaco, Manis and Frohardt-Lane (1986) studied five different roles (viz. worker, partner, parent, volunteer and student).

In examining the literature, it is clear that not much research has been conducted addressing the effect of holding multiple roles on marital functioning. Rather, research has focused on physical health and/or general psychological well-being as outcomes, finding that involvement in multiple roles is associated with increased physical health for both men and women (Verbrugge, 1983). There are also studies in which involvement in multiple roles is associated with increased self-esteem and job satisfaction (Pietromonaco *et al.* 1986). At the same time, there have been reports in the literature suggesting that there is no relationship between multiple roles and self-esteem (Barnett, 1982).

There is only one study assessing whether a relationship exists between multiple roles and marital and family satisfaction. Pietromonaco *et al.* (1986) collected data on a group of non-randomly selected employed wives, who were either graduates of the University of Michigan or had recently sought information from that university concerning course work. Pietromonaco *et al.* (1986) found no relationship between the number of roles (ranging from one to five) these employed wives held and either their marital/partner satisfaction or the satisfaction they received from their children. Nonetheless, the obvious non-random nature of their sample (95% of the respondents participating in their study had received a university degree) questions the generalizability of these results.

In general, therefore, research findings on the effects of multiple roles provide some support for the role enhancement hypothesis when personal functioning is the outcome of interest. There were no studies on multiple role and marital satisfaction from which generalizable findings have emerged.

One objection to the concept of multiple roles is that it ignores the employed wife's experience of her various roles, in particular the subjective stress that may arise from holding conflicting roles. Indeed, research findings confirm that it is the qualitative experience of an individual's role, instead of merely the number of roles, that is the primary contributor to psychological distress (Baruch and Barnett, 1986a). As such, the role accumulation hypothesis may not account for the relationship between holding multiple roles and marital functioning. To appreciate the consequences for employed wives of holding several roles, it is necessary to go beyond a consideration of the number of roles held. In this sense, focusing on the number of roles held is similar to a focus on objective stressors. The number of roles any individual holds is objective and quantifiable. How individuals perceive these roles and the interaction of these roles parallels the notion of stress. As such, it is predicted that role experiences will be a more significant predictor of personal and marital functioning than the number of roles held. What is required, therefore, is an examination of the effects of the subjective meaning of different roles.

Inter-role Conflict

There has been considerable research focusing on the experience of one's roles. Most of this research has focused on the notion of inter-role conflict, which can be traced back to the work of D.T. Hall. In 1972, Hall suggested that employed wives and husbands experience the interface between work and family roles differently. Specifically, Hall (1972) suggested that while employed mothers are expected to fulfil the demands of their work and family roles *simultaneously*, employed fathers are afforded the luxury of fulfilling the same two roles *sequentially*. This means that in terms of everyday behaviour, employed mothers are required to deal with problems relating to their employment role while at home and their home role while at the job. On the other hand, employed fathers complete the demands of their employment and home roles sequentially, with primacy being accorded to the work role. This means that while on the job, husbands are not expected to concern themselves with the family or home role. Thus, issues concerning the home, husband or parent role would not be allowed to interfere with successful completion of their employment role. If the logic underlying Hall's (1972) differentiation is pursued, it follows that employed mothers should experience more psychological stress and conflict concerning successful completion of their employment and family roles than would employed husbands. On the basis of this argument, the notion of inter-role conflict gained considerable popularity, and subsequent research focused considerably more on employed wives' inter-role conflict than on employed husbands' inter-role conflict.

Two different approaches to inter-role conflict have been suggested in the literature. The first, from an historical viewpoint, was that of Holahan and Gilbert (1979a, b). They suggested that if we consider four different roles that the employed wife fulfils, namely spouse, employee, mother and self, there are then six different types of inter-role conflict. These six types of inter-role conflict represent all possible conflicts between each of the individual roles, namely spouse vs employee, spouse vs mother, spouse vs self, employee vs mother, employee vs self, and mother vs self. In their research, conflicts between these different roles were shown to be associated differentially with outcomes such as self-esteem, life satisfaction and marital satisfaction. However, subsequent research has suggested that these six areas of inter-role conflict are highly interrelated (Barling, 1986a; Suchet and Barling, 1986). Indeed, an exploratory factor analysis of these six areas of inter-role conflict yielded only one factor of general inter-role conflict (Barling, 1986a). This means that contrary to Holahan and Gilbert's assumptions, employed wives do not experience these types of conflict as independent. Instead, it is more likely that they experience conflict between several of their roles simultaneously. As a result, in considering the effects of inter-role conflict on marital functioning, we will focus our attention primarily on global inter-role conflict, i.e. conflict between all these roles.

A second approach to understanding the nature of inter-role conflict considers types of conflict with respect to resources that are strained (Greenhaus and Beutell, 1985). Time-based conflict emerges when the individual does not have sufficient time to complete successfully the different roles. Behaviour-based conflict occurs when behaviours required for successful completion of one role are incompatible with those required for successful completion of another role. For example, it is often assumed that independence, aggression, assertion and self-reliance are necessary for females' managerial success, yet negatively associated with their marital functioning. In their place, empathic and nurturant behaviours are assumed to contribute to marital functioning. The third type of inter-role conflict is strain-based conflict. This occurs when strain resulting from performance in one role negatively affects performance in a different role. Thus, for example, strain-based conflict would exist when employment stressors cause such personal distress that there is considerable interference with marital functioning. Despite suggestions that there are three different forms of inter-role conflict, there is no research assessing their relative contribution to global inter-role conflict, or their relative consequences for the individual. Indeed, research consistently focuses on the overall experience of inter-role conflict (Kopelman, Greenhaus and Connolly, 1983).

The final point that is worth noting is that the present discussion will focus on the consequences of inter-role conflict. In previous chapters, there has been some consideration of the factors that predict inter-role conflict, such as participation in shift work schedules (see Chapter 3). On the contrary, in the remainder of this chapter, we will focus first on the effects of inter-role conflict on aspects of personal functioning that may in turn affect marital functioning. We will then consider the effects of inter-role conflict on global and specific aspects of marital functioning. Finally, the effects of multiple roles and inter-role conflict on marital functioning will be contrasted, as will the consequences of inter-role conflict for husbands and wives.

Inter-role Conflict and Psychological Well-being

There is a belief that juggling multiple roles exerts negative effects on personal and marital functioning. In this section, the relationship between inter-role conflict and global indices of personal functioning such as self-esteem and life satisfaction will be examined. Thereafter, we will examine the relationship between inter-role conflict and depression.

The results of studies conducted to assess the influence of inter-role conflict on personal functioning have used different techniques for assessing role conflict. Nonetheless, all these studies provide support for the role scarcity hypothesis (which postulates that holding multiple roles would exert negative effects because individuals have a finite amount of time and resources at their disposal), because inter-role conflict is negatively associated with diverse indices of personal functioning. Pietromonaco, Manis and Markus (1987) investigated three groups of women from a large, national random sample in the United States. Within each group, they investigated the extent to which their subjects' cognitive orientation to paid employment (career oriented versus non-career oriented) was consistent with their employment status (full-time employed, part-time employed and non-employed women). Pietromonaco *et al.* (1987) equated an inconsistency between employment status and cognitive orientation with inter-role conflict. Pietromonaco *et al.*'s (1987) results suggest that, by itself, employment status does not predict self-esteem and life satisfaction. Specifically, after controlling for age, educational attainment and marital status, there were no differences between the three employment status groups in terms of self-esteem and life satisfaction. However, there were significant differences in terms of self-esteem and life satisfaction *within* these groups. For example, career oriented, employed women manifested higher levels of self-esteem and life satisfaction than non-career oriented, employed women.

Other studies have measured inter-role conflict directly, rather than inferring its presence when employment status and employment attitudes are not consistent. Hall and Gordon (1973) found that conflict between roles was negatively associated with general happiness for full-time employed women and homemakers. In Parry's (1987) sample of working-class mothers in the United Kingdom, inter-role conflict was associated with anxiety. In a study of 293 employees in an American organization, Burden (1986) showed that the conflict experienced between employment and family roles was highly associated with decreased life satisfaction. It should be noted, however, that Burden (1986) combined data for males and females. This is important, because the results from other research suggest that the correlation between inter-role conflict and psychosomatic health problems is highly significant for women, but not for men (Barling and Janssens, 1984). In a sample of employed wives, Barling and MacEwen (1989) showed that inter-role conflict was associated with cognitive difficulties, an index of psychological well-being. The consistent association between inter-role conflict and personal functioning has emerged beyond both first-world or industrialized countries and urban settings. Khaleque, Wadud and Chowdhury (1988) found that the conflict experienced between employment and home roles was associated with psychological well-being in a sample of employed mothers in Bangladesh. Second, Mertensmeyer and Coleman (1987) investigated the correlates of inter-role conflict in a group of young urban and rural mothers and fathers in the United States. Their results showed that inter-role conflict was significantly and negatively associated with self-esteem in both the urban and the rural groups. These two studies are of particular interest, because the overwhelming majority of research findings on the interdependence of employment and the family has been generated on first-world, urban individuals.

Sekaran (1985) has provided the most sophisticated analysis of the influence of inter-role conflict on psychological well-being. She investigated the direct and indirect effects of the stress associated with multiple role involvement on job satisfaction, life satisfaction and mental health in a sample of 166 dual career couples across different regions of the United States. Sekaran (1985) also analysed whether the same model of inter-role conflict applies to men and women. In the sample of employed wives, multiple role stress was directly and indirectly associated with all three aspects of psychological functioning. Specifically, multiple role stress was directly linked with life satisfaction, which itself was directly associated with mental health. Multiple role stress also exerted a direct effect on job satisfaction. For the employed husbands, Sekaran (1985) showed that multiple role stress only exerted an indirect effect on mental health, instead of a direct effect on mental health as with employed wives. Specifically, multiple role stress was associated with life satisfaction and job satisfaction, both of which were associated with mental health.

These studies show that the conflict or stress between multiple roles is consistently associated with lower levels of life satisfaction and psychological well-being. On the basis of her data, Sekaran (1985) notes that multiple role stress affects not only life satisfaction and mental health, but also predicts job dissatisfaction for both spouses. Sekaran's (1985) findings support the notion of an 'open systems' perspective, in that inputs or imbalances in one system can spill over into other systems. Sekaran's (1985) study also suggests that consequences of employment-role experiences may be gender specific, and this specific issue is discussed further in Chapter 10.

The second aspect of personal functioning that may be associated with inter-role conflict is depression. The results of studies examining the relationship between inter-role conflict and depression suggest consistently that the experience of inter-role conflict is associated with depression. These results hold even when different questionnaires are used to assess both inter-role conflict and depression, thereby reducing the possibility that the emergence of such a relationship across studies is a function of the questionnaires used. In two studies already discussed relating to inter-role conflict and psychological well-being, significant correlations also emerged between inter-role conflict and depression. Specifically, both Parry (1987) and Burden (1986) found that inter-role conflict was associated with depression. Keith and Schafer (1985) also showed that role dissatisfaction and disagreements over role performance were associated with depression for both homemakers and employed women. Finally, perhaps most credibility can be placed on Krause and Geyer-Pestello's (1985) findings. They assessed 129 individuals from a random sample of 300 women who were employed in Akron, Ohio. After controlling statistically for the influence of pay and job dissatisfaction, full-time or part-time work status and commitment to the employment role, Krause and Geyer-Pestello (1985) showed that conflict between employment and home roles for these women was still associated with global depression and specific aspects of depression (e.g. somatic difficulties, lack of positive affect, depressive affect).

Consequently, it can be concluded that the relationship between inter-role conflict and depression mirrors that between inter-role conflict and general psychological functioning. The next question that emerges is whether inter-role conflict is associated with marital functioning.

Inter-role Conflict and Marital Functioning

Like assumptions concerning the relationship between inter-role conflict and personal functioning, there is a pervasive belief that high levels of inter-role conflict exert negative effects on marital functioning. As can be seen from an examination of the non-empirical literature on the nature of this relationship, it is assumed that holding multiple roles inevitably leads to the experience of inter-role conflict. For example Neuman (1979, p. 302) entitled her article 'Wife, mother, teacher, scholar and sex object: role conflicts of a female academic'. Moreover, it is widely assumed that experiencing inter-role conflict exacts an inevitable cost on marital functioning. This can be seen clearly from an examination of the titles of articles that have appeared in popular journals. For example, Harris (1979, p. 44) states in the sub-title of her article that 'The combined demands of jobs, home and children can strain the two-income family'. Greiff and Munter (1980b, p. 40) ask the question: 'Can a two-career family live happily ever after? Maybe, but only if certain "tradeoffs" are made'. Finally, the message that inter-role conflict has a detrimental impact on marital functioning is obvious from the title of an article that appeared in *Time* magazine (Toufexis, 1985): 'The perils of dual careers: married couples who work are crowding therapists' offices'.

Inter-role conflict can be measured either directly, as it is in most studies, or indirectly. It is measured indirectly when conflict between major roles is inferred from incongruence between a role and attitudes to or acceptance of that role (e.g. Barling, Fullagar and Marchl-Dingle, 1988). Gross and Arvey (1977) used this approach to infer the effect of conflicts between roles on marital satisfaction in a group of employed wives. Their results provide some support for the hypothesis that inter-role conflict is associated with marital satisfaction, because wives' employment status alone was not associated with their marital satisfaction. Instead, employment status interacted with the satisfaction employed wives experienced with the homemaker role in predicting marital satisfaction. Most research in this area, however, has assessed inter-role conflict directly via questionnaires.

Consistent with findings from research focusing on the relationship between inter-role conflict and psychological well-being, and the findings of Gross and Arvey (1977), inter-role conflict is consistently associated with marital dissatisfaction. For example, Suchet and Barling (1986), Pleck *et al.* (1980), Mashall (1985) and MacEwen and Barling (1988a) all showed that inter-role conflict was positively associated with marital dissatisfaction, even though these studies were conducted in different countries (South Africa, the United States and the latter two studies in Canada) using different measures of inter-role conflict. Kopelman, Greenhaus and Connolly (1983) also showed that inter-role conflict was associated with *family* (rather than *marital*) dissatisfaction in two separate studies. The research focusing on the effects of inter-role conflict on specific aspects of marital functioning produces similar results. For example, inter-role conflict is correlated with spouse support (Holahan and Gilbert, 1979b; Suchet and Barling, 1986) and with family support (MacEwen and Barling, 1988a).

Research focusing on inter-role conflict and marital functioning has moved beyond the assessment of linear relationships, the use of cross-sectional designs, and the exclusive conceptualization of inter-role conflict as a chronic stressor. One of the most important and consistent trends in the literature on psychological stress has been to de-emphasize linear relationships between stressors and strains (Barling *et al.*, 1987), and to focus instead on moderators. Much of this research has investigated the role of social support as a possible moderator. Simply stated, social support serves a moderator function when the relationship between inter-role conflict and marital functioning varies significantly across different levels of social support. Holahan and Gilbert (1979b) provided some early support for the moderating role of social support, because the effects of self vs spouse or self vs parent conflict for employed women was dependent on the level of social support. Suchet and Barling (1986) specifically investigated the moderating effect of spouse support on the relationship between inter-role conflict and marital satisfaction. They showed that under conditions of low inter-role conflict, spouse support had no effect on marital satisfaction, verbal communication or non-verbal communication. However, when inter-role conflict was high, the employed wives in their sample who received low levels of support from their spouses fared significantly more poorly in terms of marital satisfaction, verbal and non-verbal communication. Their findings achieve added importance because not only are they statistically significant, they are also of some applied or clinical significance. Employed wives experiencing high inter-role conflict who received high spouse support obtained an average score of 107.27 on the Short Marital Adjustment Test (Locke and Wallace, 1959), a score indicative of a satisfactory marriage. Yet employed wives in this study who were experiencing high inter-role conflict and reported receiving low levels of spouse support yielded an average score of 79.67, and scores below 90 on this questionnaire are indicative of a marriage 'at risk' (O'Leary and Turkewitz, 1978).

Nonetheless, it should be noted that like the research on job stress and social support (Beehr, 1985), social support does not always serve positive moderating functions on the relationship between inter-role conflict and marital satisfaction. In a subsequent study, MacEwen and Barling (1988a) investigated whether family (rather than spouse) support moderated the relationship between inter-role conflict and marital satisfaction. Their results showed that family support exerted a negative buffering effect on the relationship between inter-role conflict and marital dissatisfaction. Employed mothers experiencing high inter-role conflict who received high levels of family support experienced greater levels of marital dissatisfaction than employed mothers experiencing high levels of inter-role conflict together with moderate levels of family support.

These discrepant findings suggest that when the moderating function of inter-role conflict is investigated, the type of the support needs to be considered. Suchet and Barling (1986) and Houseknecht and Macke (1981) used a spouse support scale that focused predominantly on instrumental support from the husband (e.g. help with housework and children). They found that this type of social support fulfilled a positive moderating role. On the contrary, MacEwen and Barling (1988a) measured emotional support from the family, and found that emotional support served a negative buffering effect. In other words, the negative effects of inter-role conflict on marital functioning were exacerbated for individuals receiving high levels of emotional support. Other studies confirm that the type of support is critical in predicting the nature of the moderating function served by social support (e.g. Barling, MacEwen and Pratt, 1988; Krause, 1987). Likewise, the extent to which the source of the support is consistent with the source of the stressor will determine the nature of the moderating function (Pratt and Barling, 1988). In any event, these findings confirm that the linear relationship between inter-role conflict and marital functioning may be less important than the strength and direction of this relationship under different conditions.

Unlike most research on employment and the family, the assumption that the cross-sectional relationship between inter-role conflict and marital dissatisfaction implies a unidirectional causal effect of inter-role conflict on marital dissatisfaction has been challenged. For example, MacEwen and Barling (1988a) tested the hypothesis that marital dissatisfaction may exacerbate inter-role conflict. They found that inter-role conflict predicted increases in marital dissatisfaction over a three-month period. but that marital dissatisfaction did not predict change in inter-role conflict over time.

All the research on the relationship between inter-role conflict and marital functioning discussed so far has implicitly accepted a chronic model of inter-role conflict. More recently, there has been some interest in the daily experience of inter-role conflict. In one study, Killien and Brown (1987) investigated the nature of the inter-role conflict hassles or stressors that are experienced on a daily basis in a group of 92 women. The women in this study completed daily diaries, from which data concerning daily inter-role conflict hassles were extracted. Their results showed two interesting findings. First, they conducted a content analysis of the nature or source of inter-role conflict stressors, assessing which specific roles contributed most frequently to the experience of daily inter-role conflict. Their results showed that by far the most frequent role source was that of 'self', constituting 28.7% of all the reports across seven role sources. In descending order of frequency, the other roles reported were child and co-worker (both 15.6%), miscellaneous (14.3%), work/activities (13.0%), partner (9.8%) and household (4.5%). When they analysed the source of the inter-role stressor by the primary role group each of the mothers represented, they found that self remained the most significant type of stressor for homemakers, single working mothers and married working mothers. This trend was broken only for employed wives without children, for whom the job was reported as the most frequent source of daily inter-role conflict stressors, with the self emerging as the second most important. To some extent, their results on the importance of the role of self parallel those of Holahan and Gilbert (1979a). Holahan and Gilbert (1979a) found some evidence that employed mothers experienced most inter-role conflict when either the worker, parent or spouse role competed with the self role.

Second, Killien and Brown (1987) found that there were fewer reports of daily inter-role conflict stressors than they had predicted. Specifically, over the 30-day period of the study, a total of 492 hassles were reported by the 92 respondents. Sixty per cent of the women in the sample reported between one and five inter-role conflict stressors, and 16.7% did not report experiencing any such stressors, resulting in an average of 3.6 inter-role conflict stressors per person. Although this low frequency may reflect the absence of inter-role conflict stressors, it could also be a function of the way that Killien and Brown (1987) structured their question. They note that asking respondents to report 'What went wrong today?' may limit the nature and amount of information that will be obtained. Even if the frequency of inter-role conflict stressor were under-reported in their study, conceptual and methodological implications still emerge. On a conceptual level, stressors associated with inter-role conflict are not necessarily experienced every day, and therefore may be amenable not only to a chronic stressor model, but also to a daily stressor model. On a methodological level, the need to move from cross-sectional to longitudinal or time series designs in studying inter-role conflict stressors is emphasized.

Killien and Brown's (1987) study was not intended to provide any information concerning the relationship between daily inter-role conflict and marital functioning. However Bolger *et al.* (1989) recently reported a preliminary analysis of a data set that focuses on the daily experience of inter-role conflict, and its effects on personal and marital functioning. To date, their study provides the only test of the consequences of daily inter-role conflict. Bolger *et al.* (1989) studied 166 married men and women from the metropolitan Detroit area, who completed daily diaries for 42 consecutive days. In their preliminary report, they only describe the influence of daily inter-role conflicts on mood; they do not present any findings on marital functioning. However, they suggested that the inter-role conflict model predicts that conflicting demands between two simultaneous roles have an added or interactive effect. In other words, conflicts both on the job (e.g. with a supervisor) and at home (e.g. with one's spouse) have an additive negative impact on mood. Although they found no support for this hypothesis, it is possible that assessing conflict on the job and conflict at home as they did is not conceptually consistent with the notion of inter-role conflict, which reflects conflicts *between* job and family demands. If we adopt Greenhaus and Beutell's (1985) perspective, inter-role conflict exists only when employment-related conflicts *prevent* a spouse from fulfilling his or her role obligations at home. In other words, it is not the mere presence of simultaneous conflicts relating to separate roles that constitutes inter-role conflict, but rather the fact that role fulfilments in one domain are incompatible with role fulfilments in a second domain. Like Killien and Brown (1987), Bolger *et al.* (1989) also show that inter-role conflict is not necessarily experienced on a chronic basis, and that role stressors can also occur on a more episodic or acute basis.

In conclusion, therefore, the data consistently confirm that employed wives' inter-role conflict has a detrimental effect on both personal well-being and marital functioning. Moreover, our knowledge of this relationship has been refined by recent research isolating conditions under which the relationship between inter-role conflict and marital dissatisfaction is exacerbated or lessened. Furthermore, some research has attempted to isolate the causal relationship between inter-role conflict and marital functioning. From this research, there are indications that inter-role conflict leads to increased marital dissatisfaction, while marital dissatisfaction does not necessarily increase inter-role conflict. Lastly, there are indications that the relationship between inter-role conflict and marital dissatisfaction holds true whether a chronic model or a daily model of inter-role conflict is studied.

Inter-role Conflict: Employed Husbands and Wives

So far, the discussion in this chapter has traced the effects of employed wives' subjective employment experiences, with close attention to the deleterious effects of inter-role conflict on personal functioning and marital functioning. This focus on employed wives' inter-role conflict and the avoidance of husbands' inter-role conflict is consistent with early assumptions about how men and women experience their multiple roles (e.g. Hall, 1972). Specifically, it is assumed that employed husbands and employed wives experience their various roles differently (i.e. sequentially vs simultaneously), and that because of this, employed wives are at greater risk for inter-role conflict than employed husbands.

Because there has been some social change since Hall's (1972) observations, as indicated by the influx of such large numbers of mothers into the labour force, husbands may now be participating more in family activities. If so, they would then experience similar levels of inter-role conflict to their wives. Three issues relevant to employed husbands' and employed wives' inter-role conflict will be examined: *(a)* whether levels of inter-role conflict differ for employed wives and husbands; *(b)* whether inter-role conflict has different correlates and consequences for employed wives and employed husbands; and *(c)* whether there are different societal pressures on employed husbands and wives that result in their experiencing inter-role conflict differently.

There is little research contrasting the level of inter-role conflict experienced by employed husbands and employed wives. However, where such data do exist, there are indications that husbands and wives experience similar levels of inter-role conflict. This finding has been obtained across a number of studies using both specific and general measures of inter-role conflict in different countries. Holahan and Gilbert (1979a) studied 28 dual career couples at a large university in the southwestern United States. They found no differences between husbands and wives in terms of any of the six types of inter-role conflict they investigated (e.g. spouse vs parent, worker vs spouse). Herman and Gyllstrom (1977) obtained similar results with a sample of dual career couples at various levels of the organizational hierarchy within a university. Voydanoff (1988) also found no differences in her study of a large sample of men ($n = 757$) and women ($n = 270$) in the United States. Barling and Janssens (1984) replicated Herman and Gyllstrom's (1977) and Holahan and Gilbert's (1979b) studies, finding no difference in the level of inter-role conflict between employed husbands and wives. Likewise, Buik (1988) showed no difference between husbands and wives regarding general inter-role conflict in a small sample of Canadian physiotherapists and their spouses. The findings of these studies do not appear to be limited to dual 'career' couples. Barling and Janssens's (1984) sample consisted of individuals employed at a bank or a government transport organization, and again no differences were found in the level of inter-role conflict between men and women. Also, while the previous studies mentioned all contrasted the inter-role conflict of husbands and wives within the same dyad, Barling and Janssens (1984) and Voydanoff (1988) contrasted levels of inter-role conflict between employed wives and employed husbands who were not related.

Even if employed husbands and wives do experience similar levels of inter-role conflict, this does not preclude the possibility that the inter-role conflict experienced by employed wives and employed husbands has different causes and consequences. Indeed, there are clear indications that the personal consequences of inter-role conflict differ for employed men and women. As already noted, Sekaran's

(1985) path analysis suggested that inter-role conflict (which she measured as the subjective stress associated with holding multiple roles) exerted different effects on husbands and wives in dual career couples. Specifically, although inter-role conflict was directly associated with job satisfaction and life satisfaction for husbands and wives, multiple role stress exerted a direct effect on mental health for employed wives, and not for their employed husbands. Barling and Janssens (1984) showed that inter-role conflict was significantly associated with psychosomatic symptoms for employed women ($r = 0.59$) but not for employed men ($r = 0.14$). These findings emerged even through there were no differences in the level of inter-role conflict between employed wives and employed husbands (M: 25.73 vs 27.9 respectively).

Only one study has focused on the effects of employed husbands' inter-role conflict on their marital satisfaction. Barling (1986a) investigated this issue in a group of 67 white, employed fathers in South Africa representing different socioeconomic levels. The results of this study showed a significant relationship between inter-role conflict and marital dissatisfaction ($r = 0.49$). Barling (1986a) also investigated whether personality hardiness moderated this relationship (see Chapter 2). Numerous retrospective and prospective analyses had found a positive moderating effect of personality hardiness on the relationship between job-related stress and illness (e.g. Kobasa and Puccetti, 1983). Consistent with these findings, Barling (1986a) showed that personality hardiness moderated the relationship between inter-role conflict and marital dissatisfaction. Specifically, the relationship between employed fathers' inter-role conflict and marital dissatisfaction was significantly greater for individuals low in personality hardiness than their counterparts higher in personality hardiness. Two important issues emerged from this study. First, the relationship between inter-role conflict and marital dissatisfaction for these employed fathers (i.e. $r = 0.49$) closely parallels that found for the 64 employed mothers (i.e $r = 0.45$) in Suchet and Barling's (1986) study. Second, as with Suchet and Barling's (1986) study, the results from Barling's (1986a) study may also have both statistically and clinically significant findings. The average marital dissatisfaction score obtained for employed fathers who were high in inter-role conflict and low in personality hardiness ($M = 81.92$) was indicative of a marriage 'at risk' of dissolution (O'Leary and Turkewitz, 1978). In contrast to this, the scores indicate that all the other three groups studied (high inter-role conflict/high personality hardiness, and low inter-role conflict combined with either high or low personality hardiness) manifested adequate marital satisfaction (all M's >100).

Thus, the findings presented above show that employed mothers do not experience greater levels of inter-role conflict than employed fathers, and inter-role conflict is associated with marital dissatisfaction for employed mothers and fathers. Nonetheless, inter-role conflict is associated differently with the psychological and psychosomatic well-being of employed mothers and fathers. It would still be premature to conclude that employed wives' and employed husbands' experience inter-role conflict the same way. Indeed, our perspective of how men and women experience inter-role conflict will remain incomplete unless the societal, spousal and organizational pressures that result in inter-role conflict for employed men and employed women are considered.

There is still widespread disapproval of wives and mothers who join the labour force (see Chapter 7). Likewise, husbands frequently hold negative attitudes concerning their wives' employment, and there are data showing that this heightens wives' inter-role conflict (Beutell and Greenhaus, 1983), and exacerbates the relationship between employment status (Houseknecht and Macke, 1981) and marital functioning. When the wife or mother obtains employment, she will encounter discrimination in the organization in many cases (Heilman, 1983). This discrimination is based on the belief that her multiple roles inhibit the successful performance of her employment role, and scepticism as to whether she could balance employment and family roles adequately (Rosen, Jerdee and Prestwich, 1975). Thus, it is not surprising that Cooke and Rousseau (1984) suggest that different factors lead to inter-role conflict for employed men and women. Specifically, the primary factor responsible for the development and maintenance of inter-role conflict in females remains the traditional role women have played in the family, while for men it is the employment role. On this basis it is suggested that a separate consideration of inter-role conflict for employed men and employed women is still justified.

GOING BEYOND INTER-ROLE CONFLICT: ADDITIONAL ROLE EXPERIENCES

Recently, research on employment role experiences has broadened, encompassing questions about involvement in, satisfaction with and commitment to the dual roles of employee and homemaker by employed wives in addition to the conflict between these roles (e.g. Barling and MacEwen, 1988). A brief examination of the literature provides some indication of the extent of overlap between these differing approaches to the simultaneous experience of different roles. In one study, for example, Hornstein (1986) defined role involvement as '... a psychological commitment to a particular set or activities which, taken together, constitute a role' (p. 557). Hornstein (1986) also suggests that '... by asking subjects to indicate their level of involvement ... variations in the pattern of role commitment could be determined' (p. 557). In a different study, Yogev and Brett's (1985b) measurement of family role involvement is confounded with family role satisfaction. For example, their measure of *role involvement* included items such as 'A great satisfaction in my life comes from my role as a parent' and 'A great satisfaction in my life comes from my role as a spouse'. The conceptual overlap or contamination between these concepts becomes important in interpreting the meaning of any relationship between role experiences and marital functioning. In other words, should significant relationships emerge between these employment-related role experiences and marital functioning, the nature of the role experience that influences marital functioning would remain an open question.

The first process in clearing the conceptual confusion surrounding the various employment-related role experiences is to test whether they are discriminable. Barling and MacEwen (1988) conducted a multitrait–multimethod analysis of four employment role experiences (namely, inter-role conflict, satisfaction with, commitment to and involvement in the role of employed mother). They carefully matched their conceptual definitions of these four constructs to the way in which they are defined and used in the organizational literature. After operationalizing these constructs accordingly, their results suggested that role involvement was not discriminable from the other three constructs, but that there was strong support for the construct and discriminant validity of the other three dimensions. This means that when interpreting subsequent findings, inter-role conflict, role satisfaction and role commitment are valid, discriminable constructs when measured appropriately.

The second step in investigating the validity of these three role experiences requires an examination of whether they exert differential effects. Barling and MacEwen (1989) found that inter-role conflict is associated directly with cognitive difficulties, and indirectly with a measure relevant to job performance. However, neither commitment to nor satisfaction with the employment role was associated with either of these two variables. It remains for research to investigate whether commitment to or satisfaction with the employment role is associated in any way with marital functioning.

WIVES' SUBJECTIVE EMPLOYMENT EXPERIENCES AND MARITAL FUNCTIONING: CONCLUSION

In evaluating the effects of wives' subjective employment experiences on their own and their spouses' marital functioning, one further comparison is warranted. This involves the relative effects of wives' employment status and wives' subjective employment experiences on marital functioning. In the previous chapter, it was noted that wives' employment status was not consistently associated either with their own or their husbands' marital functioning. From research considered in the present chapter, it is clear that there is a consistent positive relationship between wives' positive experience of their employment role and marital functioning. This is consistent with the conclusion reached at the end of Chapter 4, that it is husbands' employment experiences rather than objective employment characteristics that are associated with both spouses' marital functioning.

Nonetheless, a number of issues must be considered to obtain a more comprehensive understanding of the effects of wives' experience of employment on marital functioning. First, there is much research focusing on inter-role conflict, but far fewer studies on wives' satisfaction with, and commitment to, their employment status. Because there are data showing the discriminant validity of these latter two employment role experiences (Barling and MacEwen, 1988), research should investigate whether they are differentially associated with marital functioning. This is especially relevant because inter-role conflict is indirectly associated with decrements in job-related performance (Barling and MacEwen, 1989). Yet neither satisfaction with, nor commitment to, the employment role showed similar indirect effects. Second, inter-role conflict has been operationalized on the basis of different definitions, measured with global and specific dimension using scales varying widely in format and length. Even though results across these studies are consistent, future research might profit from the development of more uniform definitions and measures (Barling and MacEwen, 1988). Third, there is very little research assessing whether wives' employment role experiences have any effect on husbands' marital functioning. Yet this is an important issue because employment role experiences such as inter-role conflict occur in the context of the marriage and the family. Lastly, there is very little research evaluating whether wives' job experiences (e.g. job satisfaction) rather than role experiences influence marital functioning. Again, this may be an important area of study given the findings of Crouter's (1984b) qualitative study on the relationship between participation in decision making and marital functioning (see Chapter 4).

Chapter 7

Maternal Employment and Children's Behaviour: New Perspectives on an Old Phenomenon

In the previous four chapters, the effects of objective and subjective employment characteristics on marital functioning were considered. Specifically, the effects of both husbands' and wives' employment status, characteristics and experiences, on both their own and their spouses' marital functioning were evaluated. The influences of parental employment characteristics and experiences are considered in Chapters 7 and 8. The effects of the mothers' employment on their children will be discussed in the present chapter, while the question of how children are influenced by their fathers' employment will be evaluated in Chapter 8.

In assessing the interdependence of employment and family systems, no issue has received as much attention as the possible effects of maternal employment on children's behaviour. The interest in the influence of maternal employment on child behaviour is not recent. In his review of the field of family studies prior to the appearance of the *Journal of Marriage and the Family* in January 1939, Broderick (1988) notes that concern about the possible effects of employed mothers on their children was already evident in the literature at that time, and there were empirical studies addressing this issue. Mathews's (1934) early manuscript based on her doctoral dissertation was followed by evaluations of adolescent daughters' reactions to (Essig and Morgan, 1946) and attitudes towards (Payne, 1956) their mothers' employment. The concern with maternal employment derives from two social factors: first, consistent with the viewpoint that equates maternal presence with maternal quality, there is a pervasive and persistent belief that maternal employment exerts detrimental effects on children; second, the increasing trend towards maternal employment has maintained an interest in the effects of maternal employment.

Consistent with the notion that our beliefs shape the way in which we conduct research and the questions we choose to ask, the ideological position that equates maternal presence with maternal quality has resulted in considerable attention being focused on the relationship between maternal employment and children's behaviour. The time, energy, involvement and commitment that are demanded by maternal employment are assumed to detract from the time, energy, involvement and commitment required for successful motherhood. This concern has been bolstered by data seemingly pointing to negative consequences of maternal employment. Two examples will suffice. First, there are findings showing that the number of mothers who choose to breast feed their infants is negatively associated with the number of mothers in the labour force (e.g. Pasternak and Ching, 1985). Second, in re-analysing data gathered during 1970 in eighteen industrialized nations, Lester (1988) found a substantial correlation ($r = 0.77$) between the number of mothers in the labour force and the national suicide rate. Yet the meaning of such correlations is open to question. For example, employed mothers may breast feed their infants less because of decreased physical access during work hours, and not because of any negative attitudes. Also, in neither of these studies is the issue of causality addressed, nor is the role of any third variable assessed. Despite the fact that the meaning of such correlations is questionable, Cochran and Bronfenbrenner (1979) suggest that work (in their terminology) is the social institution that exerts the greatest impact on childrearing.

There has been a steady increase in the number of mothers seeking employment outside of the home since the end of the Second World War. When Mathews (1934) conducted her research, she found that only 100 out of a selected sample of 568 children in the United States (i.e. 17.6%) had mothers who were employed. In contrast, some 36% of mothers of preschool children and 44% of mothers of school-aged children were employed in the United States in 1975. By March 1977, the mothers of 48% of children under the age of 18 were employed (Grossman, 1978), and four years later this figure had increased to 54% (Grossman, 1982). This indicates that by 1977, having a mother who was employed outside of the home was already the modal situation for children in the United States.

The overall increase in the prevalence of maternal employment can be appreciated from Figure 7.1. Also, although the data presented in Figure 7.1 were generated in the United States, similar trends have taken place in Britain over the same time period (Parry and Warr, 1980). Second, these data provide an underestimate of the extent to which certain demographic groups (e.g. black mothers) are employed (Johnson, 1979). Third, the trend towards an increase in the number of employed mothers will probably continue for some time: Hofferth and Phillips (1987) used data on the number of employed mothers in the United States each year between 1970 and 1985 to predict future trends in the number of either part- or full-time employed mothers. They suggest that by 1995, two-thirds of all preschool children and 75% of all school-age children will have mothers participating in the labour force. Spitze (1988) suggests that the increase will reach a plateau before the year 2000, but that the consequences of greater numbers of mothers entering the labour force will continue to be felt well into the next century. Fourth, as the number of mothers employed on a full-time basis has increased, so has the number of mothers employed on a part-time basis. The Bureau of Labour Statistics in the United States estimates that the number of mothers employed on a part-time basis increased 31% in the ten years between 1976 and 1986 (US

Bureau of Labor Statistics, 1988). Given the simultaneous increase in the number of mothers employed full-time, the increasing number of mothers in part-time employment must have been drawn from the pool of non-employed mothers, further reducing the proportion of non-employed mothers. The magnitude of this change can be appreciated from Hoffman's (1980) observation that what was once a deviant trend is now the modal pattern. Thus, ever-increasing numbers of children have mothers who are employed on a full- or part-time basis.

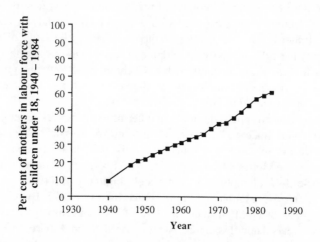

Figure 7.1   Trends in the proportion of employed mothers in the United States (from Hoffman, 1986, p.194)

Accordingly, an examination of the effects of maternal employment on children's behaviour is of concern for at least two reasons. First, it is not clear that the empirical data available support the assumption that maternal employment exerts a detrimental effect on children. Second, given the prevalence of maternal employment, there are sound practical questions motivating an empirical evaluation of the effects of maternal employment on children. For example, should any consistent effects be found, intervention, treatment and policy implications would emerge. Before entering into an evaluation of the effects of maternal employment on children, a number of directions in this literature merit consideration. These include the extent to which the effects of maternal employment have been investigated, the beliefs inherent in this research, the way in which these beliefs have shaped the research designs that have been used, and finally the way in which these beliefs have resulted in the neglect of the question of whether fathers' employment exerts similar effects on children's behaviour.

In investigating the interdependence of employment and family systems, no single issue has received as much empirical scrutiny as the relationship between maternal employment and child behaviour, and the disproportionate amount of attention devoted to this issue has continued at least since the late 1950s. For example, Etaugh (1974) reviewed 53 studies focusing on maternal employment and child behaviour reported between 1963 and 1974. Indeed, this issue has now received so much empirical attention that there are numerous published reviews spanning three decades that focus solely on the effects of maternal employment on children (e.g. Cochran and Bronfenbrenner, 1979; Etaugh, 1974; Hoffman, 1961, 1963, 1974, 1979, 1980, 1984, 1986, 1989; Kamerman and Hayes, 1982; Smith, 1981; Wallston, 1973). Because of the voluminous data available, it is no longer possible to present an in-depth discussion of all available studies on maternal employment and child behaviour in a single study. As a result, the objective of this chapter is to evaluate what is known about the effects of maternal employment on mother–child interactions and on several children's behaviours (e.g. social behaviours, scholastic performance, problem behaviours).

Until relatively recently, the belief that maternal employment exerts a detrimental effect on children's behaviour has been widespread, and largely unchallenged. This is evident from a number of sources. First, most of the childrearing books of the 1950s and 1960s expressed disapproval of the employed mother. Indeed, it was only with the 1976 revision of Benjamin Spock's classic text, *Baby and Child Care*, that maternal employment was no longer included in the section dealing with special problems that children encounter. Second, numerous magazines directed at the lay public contain articles suggesting that negative consequences ensue as a result of maternal employment (e.g. Amiel, 1985; Fallows, 1983). Third, there have been two surveys of different groups of medical professionals in the United States focusing on their perceptions of the effects of maternal employment. Heins *et al*. (1983) surveyed every paediatrician on the roster of the American Academy of Pediatrics in October 1980. They received 5758 responses, representing a 31% response rate. Heins *et al*. (1983) chose to survey paediatricians, because they are probably mothers' most important source of advice regarding children's health and development. Although Heins *et al*. (1983) conclude that paediatricians are not biased against employed mothers, it could be argued that their data indicate otherwise. Specifically, paediatricians in their study responded to a questionnaire concerning their perceptions of behavioural differences in children of employed mothers and non-employed mothers. Heins *et al*. (1983) found that paediatricians presumed that children of employed mothers fared significantly worse than children of non-employed mothers across six different dimensions, including academic and social problems, independence, attachment to the mother, susceptibility to infections, and developmental problems. With two exceptions (children of employed mothers do suffer more acute infections and do function more independently than children of homemaker mothers), the paediatricians' beliefs about these children are not supported by empirical data. It is also likely that young children of employed mothers are more susceptible to infections due to attendance at day-care centres, rather than maternal employment *per se*.

In a study conducted in 1980, Martin, Burgess and Crnic (1984) distributed questionnaires non-randomly to health professionals in Colorado (paediatricians in private practice and academic settings, paediatric house staff, family practitioners, county public health nurses and child health associates). Like Heins *et al*. (1983), therefore, Martin *et al*. (1984) focused on health professionals who would frequently encounter and advise mothers considering employment. From the 408 questionnaires returned in their study, some indication of bias against the employed mother is again apparent. Half the sample felt that maternal employment could have some benefits for the child or the mother–child relationship and only 40% of the sample believed that mothers should not be employed outside of the home. Yet 74% of the sample felt that if the mother were to be employed, it would be more beneficial to the child if she were employed on a part-time basis only. As was the case with the data from Heins *et al*.'s (1983) survey, the bias against the employed mother was more evident in males and older individuals. Given that mothers receive most of their advice concerning childrearing from the medical profession and from childrearing books, it is not surprising that Smith (1981) reports that only 44% of women believe that maternal employment exerts no harmful effects on children.

Given the beliefs of professionals concerning the potential negative effects of the employed mother, it is instructive to assess whether similar beliefs predominate among parents. Easterbrooks and Goldberg (1985) assessed whether employed mothers in a small, non-randomly selected sample believed there were positive, negative or no effects associated with their employment. They found the employed mothers and the husbands of employed mothers believed that far more positive effects, and far fewer negative effects would ensue for their children than did non-employed mothers and the husbands of non-employed mothers. Viewed in isolation, it would be possible to interpret these differences within the framework of cognitive dissonance theory. Specifically, employed and non-employed mothers hold attitudes consistent with their employment status as a strategy to reduce any guilt that would result if their beliefs and their behaviours were not congruent. However, results from the research programme of Ellen Hock suggests a more plausible explanation. She has shown that career orientation or the importance mothers attach to holding a career is relatively stable (Hock, 1980). In addition, mothers' statements within two days following childbirth as to whether they will subsequently seek employment predict whether they will do so and how well they will then balance their career and motherhood roles (DeMeis, Hock and McBride, 1986).

Social beliefs proscribe research questions that are asked, and how the questions are investigated. Research on the effects of maternal employment on children's behaviour is an example of this phenomenon. A close reading of the empirical literature would reveal that most research has investigated the presumed negative effects that maternal employment exerts on children, rather than any potential positive effects. Thus, aside from the surveys listed in Chapter 1 (namely,

General Mills American Family Report, 1981; Lauer, 1985), empirical studies have investigated whether maternal employment was associated with subsequent criminality during adolescence (McCord, McCord and Thurber, 1963). A further indication of just how this belief has limited the focus of research is the fact that the possible relationship between fathers' employment and their children's behaviour is presumed to be positive, and has been treated as a separate issue. In addition to influencing the questions asked, beliefs about maternal employment have influenced research designs. Until recently, most research in this area contrasted the behaviour of children of employed mothers with those of non-employed mothers, with the expectation that children in the former group would fare worse.

In considering the relationship between maternal employment and children's behaviour, two separate streams of research will be considered: the consequences of mothers' employment status and maternal employment experiences. In examining the consequences of maternal employment status, studies that have contrasted different behaviours and attitudes (e.g. school performance, sex-role ideology) of the children of employed and non-employed mothers will be dealt with first. Thereafter, the research focusing on the effects of maternal employment status on different aspects of the mother–child relationship, ranging from mother–child attachment to child abuse, will be examined. Lastly, studies relating mothers' subjective experiences of their employment to their children's behaviour will be examined.

MATERNAL EMPLOYMENT STATUS AND CHILDREN'S BEHAVIOUR

Children's Social Behaviour

Most research on maternal employment and children's social behaviour has focused on children's independence. Most studies consistently find that children of employed mothers are more independent than children of non-employed mothers. Moreover, this trend is consistent across all age groups ranging from toddlers (Schachter, 1981), through ten-year-olds (Gold and Andres, 1978a) and adolescents (Belsky and Steinberg, 1978; Gold and Andres, 1978b). In a study based on mothers' ratings, Gold and Andres (1978a) showed that ten-year-old children of employed mothers were better adjusted in terms of their relationships at school than the children whose mothers were not employed. Likewise, adolescents whose mothers were employed rated themselves as better adjusted at school, as having higher self-esteem and more freedom, and better personality adjustment than adolescents whose mothers are not employed (Gold and Andres, 1978b). In addition, nursery school children whose mothers are employed are also rated as better adjusted socially by their teachers than are their counterparts whose mothers are not employed (Gold and Andres, 1978c). The fact that such differences emerge when teachers (rather than mothers) provide these ratings excludes the possibility that mothers rate children negatively as a function of their own problems (e.g. depression, marital discord) rather than the child's adjustment.

Before concluding that the social behaviour of children of employed mothers is better than that of non-employed mothers, one caveat is in order. Differences between these two groups of children only emerge when specific behaviours are assessed. When global personality dimensions reflecting socioemotional adjustment are assessed, no differences emerge between these two groups (e.g. Schachter, 1981). What this suggests is that maternal employment status is not so formidable a variable, and that its effects, if any, are limited in their scope and their nature.

Children's Gender Role Stereotypes

It is often hypothesized that the children of employed mothers will manifest more egalitarian sex role stereotypes than children of non-employed mothers, especially daughters. First, compared to non-employed mothers, employed mothers may model a different set of attitudes towards female roles and different behaviours for their children than homemakers. Any modelling effect would be enhanced for employed mothers, because they are more likely than non-employed mothers to be nominated by daughters as the individual they most admire and most aspire to model from (Baruch, 1972). Second, since the 1950s, research has consistently shown that the husbands of employed mothers participate more in household chores than their counterparts whose wives are not employed (Hoffman, 1986). Consequently, as fathers, these men model a different set of behaviours, specifically non-traditional gender behaviours, from fathers whose wives are homemakers. Third, on a more direct level, employed mothers may demand more involvement in household chores from their children, thus teaching the skills required for greater independence. Of course, there are value judgements inherent in this discussion, and they should be made explicit: adoption of egalitarian gender role stereotypes and beliefs is positive. This has behavioural implications, because equal participation in household tasks by females and males would require changes by both (i.e. increases for males and decreases for females).

The first study addressing the relationship between maternal employment status and children's sex role behaviours provided data that ran contrary to the hypothesis that employed mothers exert a negative effect on their children. Specifically, from data that were collected during the 1950s and based on elementary school children, Hoffman (1963) found that employed mothers who were satisfied with their jobs went out of their way to ensure that their employment status in no way inconvenienced their children. Their children actually helped less with household chores. It is likely that Hoffman's (1963) findings, obtained from data generated in the 1950s, were a function of social forces on employed mothers, which led them to try to overcompensate their children for presumed negative effects of their absence.

Goodnow (1988) notes that the question of whether children of employed mothers perform more household chores is no longer posed. Rather it is accepted that they are more involved.

There is a gender difference in the way children participate in household tasks. Boys and girls take on somewhat different tasks when the mother is employed. While boys become involved in a wider range of household activities, girls generally become involved in more of the same activity (White and Brinkerhoff, 1981). Thus, boys become less sex typed in the tasks they assume, while girls take on more household activities that are traditionally associated with female sex-typed behaviours. Also, when the mother is employed, teenage children assume more household responsibilities than their fathers (Hedges and Barnett, 1972).

Most of the remaining data focus on attitudinal measures, and show consistently that sex role stereotyping is significantly more flexible among children and adolescents whose mothers are employed than their counterparts whose mothers are not employed (e.g. Acock, Barker and Bengtson, 1982; Gold and Andres, 1978a, b; Marantz and Mansfield, 1977; Miller, 1975; Stephan and Corder, 1985; Vogel *et al.*, 1970). There are exceptions to the finding that maternal employment is associated with more flexible gender role stereotypes. First, there are two studies in Francophone communities in Montreal where the effects of maternal employment on sex role stereotypes were minimized for nursery school children (Gold, Andres and Glorieux, 1979), and did not emerge for ten-year-old children (Gold and Andres, 1978a). In both these samples, Francophone fathers were more involved in all aspects of the child's development, and thus the effects of the mother and her employment status were reduced. With the exception of the research by Gold and her colleagues, all the other studies in which an effect of maternal employment status on children's sex role stereotyping emerged were conducted on Anglophone children. Second, Marantz and Mansfield (1977) found that maternal employment was associated only with more androgynous sex role stereotyping for daughters aged 7–8, but found no effect for 5–6-year-olds. Thus, they note that the gender roles that employed and non-employed mothers model for their daughters do not exert a uniform effect on their daughters' gender role stereotyping. Instead, Marantz and Mansfield (1977) question whether daughters' receptiveness to the influence of modelled behaviours is determined by their cognitive maturity. It is also possible that this age effect emerged in Marantz and Mansfield's (1977) study because mothers demand more independence and autonomy from 7–8-year-old children than from 5–6-year-old children.

The above studies generally show that children (but especially daughters) of employed mothers manifest more androgynous sex role stereotypes and behaviours than children whose mothers are not employed. However, Gold and Andres (1978a) noted that differences between these two groups may be a function of the mothers' employment role satisfaction rather than merely employment role status. This issue will be considered later in this chapter. Nonetheless, if the adoption of gender role biases is assumed to be negative, then the conclusion from the above findings would be that maternal employment exerts a positive effect on children.

Children's Occupational Aspirations

Closely related to children's gender role stereotyping are their occupational aspirations. There are data to show that gender role stereotypes limit the type of occupation to which an adolescent aspires (Corder and Stephan, 1984), and predict whether or not mothers prefer to be employed following the birth of their babies (McHale and Huston, 1984). Several questions have been posed regarding how maternal employment status influences the occupational aspirations of daughters. The first question is whether daughters of employed mothers are more likely to aspire to being employed themselves, and the second is whether daughters of employed mothers are less likely to aspire to occupations that are traditionally male dominated.

Stephan and Corder's (1985) study of adolescents from five different schools in a single American city provides some answers to the first question. They showed that female adolescents from dual-career families were significantly more likely to aspire to employment outside the home than were female adolescents with non-employed mothers. Moreover, Stephan and Corder's (1985) data showed that adolescent males whose mothers were employed were more likely to want their own wives to be employed outside of the home. Stephan and Corder (1985) speculate that if these two trends continue, both the number of dual earner families and the incidence of egalitarian sex role attitudes and behaviours should increase in the future. Two studies provide information relevant to the second question posed, namely whether the nature of the mother's job influences the daughter's choice of occupation. First, Breakwell, Fife-Schaw and Devereux (1988) collected data on a sample of 3160 adolescents in Great Britain to assess the direct and indirect influences that parents exert on their children's decision to enter a technologically oriented occupation. Specifically, the children of parents who were perceived to be involved in technological occupations, and to value technology themselves, were significantly more likely to aspire to technologically oriented occupations. However, this effect was reduced for daughters who were unsure of the extent to which their mothers were involved in technological jobs, or how much their mothers valued such jobs. Second, Tangri (1972) studied 200 female 'role innovators', namely, females who had an occupation in which females were under-represented considering the proportion of women in the experienced, college educated labour force. Tangri (1972) showed that although fathers' educational level was not associated with their daughters' role innovation, maternal employment status and maternal role innovation were. Specifically, even though daughters' aspirations always exceeded their mothers' occupational achievements, having an employed mother who was a role innovator was significantly associated with the acceptance of role innovation by the daughter. There were also some personality differences between the group of role innovators and the group of 'traditionals': specifically, role innovators were more likely to be independent and autonomous, variables that themselves have been associated with having an employed mother.

Children's School Achievement

If the hypothesis that employed mothers exert detrimental effects on their children because they have less time and energy to devote to them is accepted, then employed mothers would exert negative effects on their children's school performance and achievement. Employed mothers have less time and energy than non-employed mothers to direct and assist their children with schoolwork. Such concerns have been expressed for some time, and are prevalent among school administrators (see Keidel, 1970). This hypothesis has been studied across different indices of school performance and achievement.

In some studies, the children of employed mothers fare better than those of non-employed mothers. Cherry and Eaton (1977) studied the effects of maternal employment on a group of 200 socioeconomically deprived black children. In this sample, children whose mothers were employed performed better than those whose mothers were not employed on a variety of indices (e.g. spelling, and performance on the Illinois Test of Psycholinguistic Ability). Yet results from other studies show that sons of middle class employed mothers fare worse than those whose mothers are not employed. For example, in their sample of 110 middle class children from intact families that was drawn from nine different nursery schools, Gold and Andres (1978c) found that sons of employed mothers fared worse than sons of non-employed mothers on the performance subtest and full scale IQ scores on the Wechsler Preschool and Primary Scale of Intelligence (WPPSI). Similar differences did not emerge for girls. This pattern was replicated in two studies. First, in a different study by Gold and Andres (1978a) using a sample of ten-year-old, middle class children, boys whose mothers were employed again fared significantly more poorly in terms of mathematic and language performance than boys whose mothers were not employed, but no such differences emerged for girls. Likewise, Schachter (1981) showed that although there were no differences between these two groups in terms of language development, toddlers whose mothers were not employed yielded significantly higher IQ scores on the Stanford–Binet than did toddlers whose mothers were employed. However, in a further study in a middle class sample by Gold and Andres (1978c), no relationship emerged between maternal employment status and children's school performance. In another study, though, Gold and Andres (1978b) focused on the school performance of 14- to 16-year-old adolescents. Failure to find differences in subjects' school performance and achievement as a function of their mothers' employment status is most likely a function of the age of the sample. There is generally a negative correlation between children's age and parental influence over the behaviour and development of children.

Inconsistent findings with regard to school performance and achievement of children of employed and non-employed mothers is probably a function of their socioeconomic status. When socieoeconomic status has been controlled, these differences disappear. Farel (1980) contrasted the intelligence and school performance of children whose mothers were employed with those whose mothers were not employed on measures of intelligence (the WPPSI), language and general academic concepts, or task orientation. After controlling statistically for the effects of socioeconomic status (mother's level of education, family income and race), Farel (1980) concludes that there was no association between maternal employment status and intelligence or school performance. After controlling for socioeconomic status, Banducci (1967) found that high school seniors whose mothers were employed full time were not disadvantaged in terms of scholastic achievement. If anything, adolescent girls whose mothers were employed were more likely themselves to express a desire to obtain employment than those whose mothers were homemakers.

The studies cited above suggest that there is no consistent relationship between maternal employment status and children's IQ. Some studies suggest that the school adjustment and IQ performance of children of employed mothers is higher than those of non-employed mothers (Cherry and Eaton, 1977; Woods, 1972); others do not (e.g. Gold and Andres, 1978a, b; Williamson, 1970; Schachter, 1981). But perhaps a more basic question is why a relationship would be expected between maternal employment status and IQ. Given the multitude of factors that predict children's intelligence and achievement, it is unlikely that maternal employment status alone would account for any significant portion of the variance in children's intelligence. Second, even ignoring questions concerning the utility of IQ as a criterion in this context, any relationship between maternal employment status and children's intelligence, achievement and school performance is largely a function of socioeconomic status confounding maternal employment status. As such whether the mother is employed or not exerts no direct influence on children's intelligence, achievement or school performance. Instead, there are indications that children's scholastic performance and achievement (but not intelligence) are more a function of the mother's experience of her employment, and this will be considered later in this chapter.

In conclusion, then, fears that maternal employment have negative consequences for children can be discounted. On the contrary, children whose mothers are employed tend to be more independent, more flexible regarding role stereotypes and behaviours, and no less intelligent or achievement oriented than their counterparts whose mothers are homemakers. Perhaps a more important question is why researchers have continued seeking negative effects of maternal employment despite so many disconfirming studies.

One important methodological aspect in all three studies by Gold and Andres is worth noting. Specifically, they ensured that mothers who were employed either had been employed continuously since the children were born or had been employed for the past four years (Gold and Andres, 1978a, b, c). Likewise, Williamson (1970) contrasted children of non-employed mothers who had not held a job since the birth of their child and did not want to with children of mothers who had held a job for a number of years. This avoids the interpretive problem in research that fails to consider the length of time the mother has been employed, or the length of time the homemaker has not had a job

MATERNAL EMPLOYMENT STATUS AND MOTHER–CHILD INTERACTIONS

One issue frequently addressed in the literature is whether maternal employment status affects the manner in which mothers interact with their children. Given ideological beliefs underlying the fear that maternal employment would harm the child, it is not surprising that one of the central issues addressed is whether employed mothers interact less with their children. Research has also assessed whether maternal employment status is associated with the attachment relationship between mother and child, and whether employment places mothers at higher risk of engaging in physically abusive relationships with their children, presumably because women who are employed are viewed as less emotionally invested in childrearing than homemakers. There are also studies that have focused more generally on maternal employment status and mother–child interactions.

The Amount of Time Spent with Children

Before dealing with the relationship between maternal employment status and the amount of the time mothers spend with their children, it is worth while highlighting the assumption in this research. Specifically, it is assumed that the more time mothers spend with their child, the better. In other words, in this view maternal availability or maternal presence is equated with maternal quality.

Based on empirical investigations, it is apparent that employed mothers do spend less time with their children than non-employed mothers (see Goodnow, 1988). For example, Easterbrooks and Goldberg (1985) showed that on a weekday, employed mothers spend an average of 2.13 hours with their children, while non-employed mothers spent an average of 6.92 hours. McHale and Huston (1984) also showed that the number of hours mothers spend on the job is negatively associated with the amount of time spent with children. As Hoffman (1986) notes, however, the strength of the relationship between maternal employment status and the amount of time devoted to children is modest, and a number of aspects about this relationship should be noted. First, most of this research has used infants as subjects. Similar findings relating the amount of time employed mothers spend with their children may be less apparent with older children. Second, there are exceptions to the tendency for employed mothers to devote less time to their children. For example, many employed mothers consciously compensate for their employment by establishing specific times for interactions with their children. Easterbrooks and Goldberg (1985) showed that employed mothers actually spend more time with their children at the weekend than do non-employed mothers (3.29 vs 2.75 hours). Third, research findings show consistently that daughters of employed mothers are more independent and autonomous than daughters of non-employed mothers (e.g. Spitze, 1988). It is possible that autonomy and independence are mediated by the relative amount of attention children received from their mothers. Specifically, independence and autonomy may be necessitated both by the reduced time spent with mothers and greater involvement by children in household activities (e.g. Hoffman, 1986). Finally, data from a study reported by Piotrkowski and Katz (1983) provide meaning to the research findings on the effects on mother–child interactions of the amount of time mothers spend in employment. Whereas most research on maternal employment asks mothers, teachers or independent observers to rate the parent–child relationship or children's behaviour, Piotrkowski and Katz (1983) asked children themselves to rate the quality of the mother–child interaction. For example, Piotrkowski and Katz (1983) asked whether daughters' perceptions of their mothers' availability was associated with the amount of time mothers spend on their jobs. They found no significant relationship between the amount of time the mother actually spends with her daughter and the daughter's rating of the mother's availability. Piotrkowski and Katz's (1983) study suggests that an understanding of the meaning of maternal employment for children must be gleaned not only from objective analyses of the magnitude of between-group differences, nor just from the objective amount of time mothers spend with their children. Instead, in-depth interviews with the children of employed mothers are required.

Piotrkowski and Katz's (1983) results raise important questions about the effects on their children of the amount of time mothers spend in employment. Even though research consistently documents a significant relationship between the amount of time spent in employment by the mother and objective measures of her availability to her children, it might be argued that the more important criterion in this context is children's perceptions of their mothers' interpersonal availability. If Piotrkowski and Katz's (1983) results are replicated (e.g. with younger children in other socioeconomic groups), some important implications emerge. First, mothers' availability is not perceived by their children to be compromised by their employment. Second, the guilt that many mothers experience because of the objective restraints on the amount of time they have available for their children because of their employment may be unwarranted. Third, with few exceptions (e.g. Piotrkowski and Katz, 1983; Trimberger and MacLean, 1982), few studies focusing on maternal employment asked children about their perceptions of their mothers' employment. Such studies should be encouraged, however, as they may provide different insights into the effects or non-effects of maternal employment.

The Mother–Child Relationship

A number of studies have been conducted assessing the effects of maternal employment on non-temporal aspects of the mother–child relationship. A close examination of these studies reveals that by and large, it is the interaction between mothers and their infants or very young children (i.e. those typically below three years of age) that has been studied. Selection of infants and young children as subjects is consistent with the assumption that it is at this stage that the presence of the mother is critical for healthy child development. Even though small samples have been used, the results from these studies demonstrate consistently that no differences emerge between children of employed and non-employed mothers, regardless of whether maternal self-reports or external observations of mother–child interactions are used (e.g. Hoffman, 1989). For example, Mills and Stevens (1985) asked 47 mothers about the childrearing practices they used with their four-year-old children. They found that the self-reports of employed and non-employed mothers did not differ across six aspects of childrearing practices: the extent to which punishment, rewards or reason were used, the promotion of independence, the amount of spouse involvement, preference for young vs old children and rules of behaviour did not differentiate between employed and non-employed mothers. Because their data were based on maternal self-report of childrearing practices, it would be important to replicate these results using behavioural observations.

Zaslow *et al*. (1985) contrasted mother–infant interactions in two groups of employed and non-employed mothers of three-month-old infants. Like Gold and Andres (1978a, b, c) and Williamson (1970), Zaslow *et al*. (1985) ensured that none of their non-employed mothers had any intention of seeking employment. This is important as there are data showing differences among non-employed mothers according to whether they want to be employed or not (e.g. Barling, Fullagar and Marchl-Dingle, 1988; Farel, 1980). Zaslow *et al*. (1985) found that employed and non-employed mothers did not differ in their interactions with their infants.

Stith and Davis (1984) focused on five- and six-month-old children. Stith and Davis (1984) studied both the interactions between the infants of the employed mothers and the individuals who were responsible for their care during the day. Across a variety of indices of the quality of interaction between mother and infant (e.g. tactile–kinaesthetic, visual, auditory and social stimulation, positive affect, contingent vocalizations and responses to distress), there were no differences between employed and non-employed mothers. Both employed and non-employed mothers interacted in a more positive manner with the infants than the daytime caregivers.

Taken together with similar results from other studies (e.g. Hock, 1980; Schubert, Bradley-Jones and Nuttal, 1980), the concern that interaction patterns between children of employed and non-employed mothers differ can be discounted.

Nonetheless, although no differences emerge in parent–child interaction between employed and non-employed mothers, there are differences within the group of employed mothers. Consistent with previous suggestions that boys and girls are affected differently by mothers' employment status (Hoffman, 1986), there are data that suggest that employed mothers react differently to sons and daughters (Stuckey, McGhee and Bell, 1982). More specifically, employed mothers are more attentive to their daughters than their sons, while non-employed mothers are more attentive to their sons than their daughters. Other differences within the group of employed mothers will be explored in further detail in this chapter.

Mother–Child Attachment

Due to the belief that interruption of the mother–infant relationship negatively affects the child and the bonding process, a considerable amount of research has focused on the effects of maternal employment on the attachment relationship. Most of this research has investigated the attachment between mothers and very young children, typically infants under one year of age (Hoffman, 1989). Because the quality of the early attachment relationship predicts the child's subsequent social competence (Hoffman, 1986), it is important to determine whether the mother–infant attachment relationship is influenced by maternal employment.

In her review of the empirical data, Hoffman (1986) concluded that no differences emerge when comparisons are made between the attachment relationship of employed and non-employed mothers with their children. Also, it does not matter whether maternal employment status changes frequently or is stable (Owen *et al.* 1984). However, the data are not entirely consistent, as there are also reports supporting the hypothesis that less secure and more anxious attachments will be formed by children whose mothers are employed rather than homemakers. The importance of such findings is usually de-emphasized in the literature for a variety of reasons. First, methodological difficulties have hindered the interpretability of some studies. For example, Schwartz (1983) found poorer attachment relationships among children of employed mothers, yet her data also showed that mothers who were employed either full time or part time engaged in more hugging and kissing with their children than did non-employed mothers. One explanation is that the test of attachment typically used, namely the 'strange situation test', is a poor index of attachment in such contexts (Clarke-Stewart, 1989). For example, the meaning of children's behaviour on the text is ambiguous. If children whose mothers are employed do not display more anxiety when encountering strangers, and do not turn to their mothers when they enter the room after an absence, it is unclear whether this reflects rejection of the mother or greater independence of the child. Second, few studies account for mothers' attitudes and role conflicts about resuming employment (Schwartz, 1983). Third, confounding variables are rarely controlled. For example, Vaughn, Gove and Egeland (1980) showed the attachment between mother and child was compromised if the mother resumed employment before the child was twelve months old. The interpretability of findings such as this are seriously threatened by socioeconomic confounds, especially since Vaughn *et al.*'s (1980) subjects were all drawn from an economically disadvantaged group. Specifically, it is likely that there is a strong relationship between the timing of a mother's return to employment and her socioeconomic status.

The study by Barglow, Vaughn and Molitor (1987) resolves some of the problems of other studies. Barglow *et al.* (1987) controlled for those variables that are usually confounded in such studies, such as socioeconomic status, the setting in which the child spent the day, and whether the caregiver was a family member. Barglow *et al.* (1987) also used a sufficiently large sample, and found that when the mother is employed on a full-time basis outside the home from the time the child is eight months old, there is a significant increase in the probability that an insecure–avoidant attachment relationship will develop between mother and child. Barglow *et al.* (1987) emphasize, however, that only first-born children developed less secure and more avoidant relationships when their mothers were employed, and first-born children in general tend to be more dependent and anxious. Another factor in Barglow *et al.*'s (1987) study further complicates an understanding of the relationship between maternal employment status and infant–mother attachment. Specifically, unlike other studies in which no differences emerge in the attachment relationship (e.g. Chase-Lansdale and Tresch-Owens, 1987), all the children of employed mothers in Barglow *et al.*'s (1987) study were cared for in their own home each day and, therefore, would confront fewer peers and adults than children (of employed mothers) who attend day care. Consequently, it is not surprising that children of employed mothers who are cared for in their own homes would manifest more insecure attachments when facing unusual circumstances and adults with whom they are unfamiliar.

One conclusion, therefore, is that despite the fact that the employed mother spends less time with her children, the attachment relationship between mother and child is not threatened when the mother is employed (Hoffman, 1986). Several factors point to researchers continuing to focus on this issue. First, some studies (e.g. Barglow *et al.*, 1987) seemingly support the hypothesis that some children manifest more insecure and more avoidant relationships with mothers who are employed. Second, beliefs and fears will likely displace empirical findings in guiding future research agendas. For example, the fear that employed mothers who place their children in day care expose them to a variety of problems including child sexual abuse is not supported by empirical data addressing this issue (Finkelhor *et al.*, 1987).

Child Abuse

Of all the consequences that have been proposed as possible sequelae of maternal employment, none is as troubling as that of child abuse. The idea that parental employment may be associated with child abuse is not new (Cochran and

Bronfenbrenner, 1979). For example, two decades ago O'Brien (1971) provided data suggesting that fathers' job dissatisfaction and occupational underachievement were associated with child abuse. Garbarino (1976) used census data to investigate the socioeconomic predictors of child abuse in a group of mothers in New York State, and found that maternal employment was associated with child abuse. The extent to which Garbarino's (1976) study informs us about the relationship between maternal employment and child abuse is questionable, though, because he used community data (rather than individual data) as his level of analysis, and as Garbarino (1976) notes, his measurement of maternal employment was confounded with socioeconomic status. In addition, Garbarino (1976) did not differentiate empirically between child neglect and abuse. Thus, his findings probably reflect the relationship between socioeconomic status and child maltreatment in general.

Gelles and Hargreaves (1981) outline the confusion regarding the relationship between maternal employment and child abuse. Empirical support can be generated for three mutually exclusive hypotheses regarding the relationship between maternal employment status and child abuse: that employed mothers are more likely to abuse their children; that employed mothers are less likely to abuse their children; and that non-employed mothers are more likely than employed mothers to abuse their children. However, as Gelles and Hargreaves (1981) note, the amount of knowledge provided by earlier studies is limited. Over and above the problems already identified by Garbarino (1976), such studies did not isolate whether the father or the mother was the abusive parent.

Gelles and Hargreaves (1981) conducted the largest study yet on the relationship between maternal employment status and child abuse by using a nationally representative sample of 1146 families in the United States. They assessed whether maternal employment was associated with two indices of violence. The first was an 'overall violence index', and included behaviours ranging from slapping and spanking to beating up the child, and using a knife or a gun against the child. Because some of the items in this index may not result in lasting physical harm to the child, they constructed a second index, the 'child abuse index', which only included behaviours which could cause physical harm to the child, such as kicking, punching, biting the child, hitting the child with an object, beating up the child or using a knife or a gun against the child. Significant differences emerged between non-employed mothers, and mothers employed either part time or full time in terms of the overall violence index. Specifically, mothers who were not employed and those who were employed on a part-time basis yielded higher rates of overall violence than those mothers who were employed on a full-time basis. One explanation for these results is that non-employed and part-time employed mothers have more contact with their children, because they are home together more. Nonetheless, this finding provides limited information on the relationship between maternal employment and child abuse, because some of the behaviours measured (e.g. slapping or spanking) would not necessarily lead to lasting physical injury to the child, and would not be considered as child abuse by many people. The 'child abuse index' is a more accurate indicator of any effects of maternal employment status on child abuse. On this index, no significant differences emerged between non-employed mothers, and those mothers who were employed either part time or full time with regard to child abuse. Their data did show that employed mothers were more likely to be abusive if their husbands were unemployed. However, this may be a function more of the husbands' unemployment and the family stressors it creates.

In evaluating whether maternal employment status is associated with child abuse, therefore, several points are noteworthy. First, Gelles and Hargreaves's (1981) data provide a conservative test of this relationship because they excluded one- and two-year-old children from their study, despite the fact that toddlers are a high risk group for being abused. Second, the available data would suggest that there is no support for the notion that employed mothers are more likely to abuse their children than their non-employed counterparts. Third, there are now data bearing on the question of which stressors and subjective experiences of maternal employment are associated with child abuse, and they will be considered later in this chapter.

MATERNAL EMPLOYMENT STATUS: CONCLUSION

In evaluating the knowledge that we have gained from all these studies contrasting the children of employed and non-employed mothers, it can be concluded that contrary to previous concerns, no consistent adverse effects accrue to the children of employed mothers. Perhaps the most interesting aspect of this conclusion is the fact that it should come as no surprise. In 1961, Lois Hoffman summarized the prevailing knowledge of the effects of maternal employment. After acknowledging that the effects of maternal employment status differ slightly for some subgroups (e.g. across social class, sex of the child), Hoffman concluded in 1961 that:

> When these other factors are controlled, the correlates of maternal employment seem to disappear. But our present research has also taught us something else: that maternal employment is not so potent a variable that it can be used without further specification and without examination of the data separately within different subgroups. None of the studies done thus far has found meaningful differences between the children of working mothers in general and the children of non-working mothers.
>
> (Hoffman, 1961, p. 191)

It is both instructive and humbling to note that 21 years later, in further reviewing the research on the effects of maternal employment status on children, Bronfenbrenner and Crouter (1982) reached the same conclusion: in general, mothers' employment status has no systematic negative effect on children or on the mother–child relationship and, if anything, children of employed mothers manifest more egalitarian sex role stereotypes and behaviour, greater independence than those children whose mothers are not employed, and there are some subgroup differences in these findings (e.g. daughters benefit somewhat more than do sons when their mothers are employed). Perhaps what is more important from their review, however, is that Bronfenbrenner and Crouter (1982) argue that research paradigms in which the children of employed and non-employed mothers are contrasted have reached a point of diminishing returns. Stated somewhat differently, the amount of knowledge that can be generated anew from such a paradigm does not justify the conduct of such studies. Noting that such research continues unabated, Bronfenbrenner and Crouter (1982, p. 59) argue that:

> After 40 years of research, the mother's workplace still continues to be treated simply as a social address. Mothers are either present at that address for a certain number of hours per week, or they are not. That is all we know and, it would seem, all we need to know. Yet, in the light of the accumulated evidence, it should by now be obvious that a one-dimensional index of maternal employment—whether measured as a dichotomy, trichotomy, or linear metric in hours—can have only limited scientific or social significance by itself. What is needed is a more differentiated analysis of the work situation that would permit identification of specific job characteristics affecting the lives of workers as parents.

The differentiated analysis that is being called for by Bronfenbrenner and Crouter involves a focus on the employment characteristics and employment experiences of the mother, rather than just focusing on her employment status. It is to a consideration of the effects of maternal employment characteristics and experiences on the child that we now turn our attention. Before focusing on this, however, one question needs to be raised. Why is it that so long after the publication of seminal reviews (e.g. Hoffman, 1961; Stolz, 1960), and well-controlled studies (e.g. Williamson, 1970), clearly concluding that mothers who are employed exert no detrimental effects on their children, so much research continued to focus on this same issue using the same methodology for over two decades? Instead of accepting that no differences emerge favouring the children of non-employed mothers, we continue to write conclusions such as 'It is argued that failure to find differences between these two groups does not mean that there are no differences' (Jensen and Borges, 1986, p. 659). Perhaps the answer to this question lies in the powerful impact our beliefs exert. The beliefs that we hold shape the research issues we choose to investigate, the methodologies we choose to use, and the meaning we ascribe to findings from such studies. Given that research contrasting the children of employed and non-employed mothers has continued long after it has been reasonably concluded that there are no differences associated with this dichotomy, it is questionable whether these beliefs can serve any further function. Specifically, the evidence in this regard seems to suggest we may blind ourselves to consistent empirically based data that run counter to our entrenched beliefs and values.

MATERNAL EMPLOYMENT EXPERIENCE AND CHILDREN'S BEHAVIOUR

Aside from earlier calls for a consideration of the effects of the mother's employment attitudes and experiences (e.g. Hoffman, 1961), other factors also motivate a consideration of mothers' employment experiences as a causal factor in the development of parent–child relationships and child behaviour. First, extrapolating from our knowledge of the influence of employment on marital functioning, the subjective experience of employment is at least as important as objective features of employment in understanding the effects of employment on marital functioning (see Chapters 3–6). Second, given the continuing increase in the number of employed mothers, such that substantially more than 50% of all school-aged children now have mothers who are employed, an understanding of the effects of how the mothers' employment experiences influence the child becomes at least as important as an understanding of the effects of whether the mother is employed or not. Third, because employed and non-employed mothers differ systematically on numerous characteristics other than whether they currently hold a job for financial gain (e.g. socioeconomic status, race, educational level; Hoffman, 1983, 1986), any differences that do emerge between these two groups cannot necessarily be ascribed to maternal employment status alone. Fourth, related research on the effects on children separated from their mothers for a variety of reasons (hospitalization, divorce) suggests that the best predictor of post-separation maladjustment is not the separation experience itself. Instead, the quality of the family environment and the extent to which the child experienced hostility and conflict at the time of the separation are most predictive of children's post-separation adjustment (Anderson, 1980; Hetherington, Stanley-Hagan and Anderson, 1989). Finally, Bronfenbrenner and Crouter (1982) argued that previous research failed to find differences between children of employed and non-employed mothers, at least partially because the effects of maternal employment involve an extremely complex question. It is argued, however, that what really transpired is that the wrong question had been posed: instead of asking whether the children of employed mothers differ from those of non-employed mothers, which necessarily assumes uniformity of employment experiences within the group of employed mothers, we should accept the existence of considerable heterogeneity in the employment experiences of this group, and investigate whether variations in employment experiences are systematically associated with mother–child interactions and/or child behaviour. It is towards a consideration of this alternative approach to understanding the consequences of maternal employment that we now turn. The discussions so far in this chapter (and those in Chapters 3–6) have been organized in terms of the outcomes under consideration. Consistent with the conceptual focus in the remainder of this chapter, however, the discussion will be organized according to the nature of the maternal employment experience under consideration. Some of the studies that investigated the effects of mothers' employment status also considered the effects of mothers' employment experiences. As a result, some of the studies still to be discussed in this chapter allow a direct comparison of the effects of maternal employment status versus maternal employment experiences.

Mothers' Experience of the Employment Role

Two streams of research can be discerned in the studies focusing on mothers' subjective employment experiences. The first concerns the consequences of mothers' subjective experience of the employment role (e.g. inter-role conflict, role commitment, role satisfaction). The second concerns how mothers' specific job-related experiences (e.g. job satisfaction, job autonomy) influence mother–child interactions or their children's behaviour in any way. These two types of experiences will be considered separately.

Maternal employment role commitment

Perhaps the most basic variable to be investigated is whether mothers choose their roles, or are committed to their current roles, whether that be as employed mother or homemaker. Research has examined whether congruence exists between the mother's employment status and her commitment to her role either as employed mother or homemaker. The rationale underlying studies of role commitment is that confronting the frustration of a blocked employment role commitment (i.e. employed mothers who would prefer to be a homemaker, or homemakers who would prefer the employed role), day in and day out, would constitute a chronic stressor for the mother (see Chapter 2), and chronic stressors experienced by the mother are associated with child behaviour problems and maladaptive parenting (Turner and Avison, 1985).

Earlier studies operationalized role commitment in terms of employed and non-employed mothers' preference as to whether they would freely choose the employed role or not (e.g. Farel, 1980; Hoffman, 1963; Yarrow *et al.*, 1962). The results of these studies are remarkably consistent in showing that maternal employment status is not as important in predicting child behaviour or mother–child interactions as mothers' stated preference for employment. Yarrow *et al.* (1962) and Hoffman (1963) focused on the mother–child relationship as the outcome, and showed positive consequences when non-employed mothers did not wish to be employed. Farel (1980) showed that children of non-employed mothers who did not express favourable attitudes to employment manifested more age-appropriate school adjustment and competence.

In a more recent study, instead of asking employed and non-employed mothers whether they preferred to be employed or homemakers, Barling, Fullagar and Marchl-Dingle (1988) assessed employment role commitment directly. Also, maternal race was controlled experimentally, and maternal education and income were controlled statistically. Their results are consistent with those already mentioned. Although no differences emerged between the children of employed and non-employed mothers (i.e. maternal employment status exerted no effects), children whose mothers' employment status and employment commitment were not congruent (i.e. employed mothers with low employment commitment or non-employed mothers with high employment commitment) were rated as less attentive and more immature than children whose mothers employment status and employment commitment were congruent (i.e. employed with high employment commitment or homemakers with low employment commitment). These results emerged regardless of whether mothers or teachers provided the ratings of the children's social behaviours, and were consistent for boys and girls. In addition, Barling, Fullagar and Marchl-Dingle's (1988) results show that the effects of this role commitment are the same for employed and non-employed mothers. It is still not clear why children's inattention and immaturity were associated with the congruence between employment status and employment commitment while other child behaviours (e.g. conduct problems, socialized aggression, anxiety–withdrawal and psychotic behaviour) were not. Barling, Fullagar and Marchl-Dingle (1988) suggest that mother–child interactions mediate the relationship between employment role commitment and child behaviours. In other words, mother–child interactions are differentially influenced by the congruence or incongruence which in turn affect specific child behaviours, but it is not clear from their study what these parenting behaviours are. Hock and DeMeis's (in press) recent research offers one indication: they showed that maternal depression is greatest when employment role status and employment role commitment are incongruent, and maternal depression itself predicts childhood problem behaviours.

One further study addresses the effects of congruence between maternal employment status and employment commitment. Like Barling, Fullagar and Marchl-Dingle (1988), Hock (1980) did not infer mothers' role commitment from questions about preferences for, or satisfaction with, the role of homemaker or employed mother. Instead, Hock (1980) specifically measured employed and non-employed mothers' career orientations, which she defined as the level of interest expressed by the mother in career, job, occupation or herself. Although all her data are based on maternal self-reports, Hock (1980) found that non-employed mothers who were high in career orientation were more likely to perceive themselves leaving for their jobs as the cause of their infants distress upon separation than were non-employed mothers who manifested low career orientation.

In conclusion, whereas employment status exerts no effects on child behaviour (Barling, Fullagar and Marchl-Dingle, 1988; Farel, 1980), employment commitment and the congruence between maternal employment status and maternal employment commitment predict mothers' reactions to separation from their infants (Hock, 1980), the mother–child relationship (Hoffman, 1963; Yarrow *et al.*, 1962) and child behaviours (Barling, Fullager and Marchl-Dingle, 1988; Farel, 1980).

Maternal employment role satisfaction

Although there is much research on the possible effects of job satisfaction in general (e.g. Locke, 1983), there are only a few studies investigating the effects of mothers' satisfaction with their employment role on their children (Brody, Stoneman and MacKinnon, 1986; Gold and Andres, 1978a; Hoffman, 1963; Lerner and Galambos, 1985). From one study (Gold and Andres, 1978a), it is possible to contrast the effects of maternal employment role status with employment role satisfaction, while the other studies point to the effects of maternal employment role satisfaction.

As will be recalled, Gold and Andres (1978a) investigated the effects of maternal employment status on ten-year-old children. One of their salient findings was that children of employed mothers manifest sex role stereotypes and behaviours that are more egalitarian than those of children whose mothers are not employed. Gold and Andres (1978a) also collected data on employed and non-employed mothers' satisfaction with their roles. They found that when they statistically controlled for the effects of maternal role satisfaction, the effects of maternal employment status were reduced. It can be concluded from Gold and Andres's (1978a) supplementary analysis that employment role satisfaction is positively associated with children's sex role stereotypes, independent of any effects of maternal employment status. Thus, children of employed mothers who are most satisfied with their employment role manifest the most egalitarian sex role stereotypes.

This phenomenon was replicated to some extent in two other studies. Brody *et al.* (1986) showed that maternal role satisfaction was positively and significantly associated with prosocial behaviour in children between seven and nine years old, but not between their younger siblings aged 4.5 to 6.5 years old. Likewise, Woods (1972) showed that maternal employment role satisfaction was significantly associated with the personal and social adjustment of fifth grade school children. In addition, employed mothers who were satisfied with their employment status showed more affection towards the child and used milder discipline (Hoffman, 1963).

Lerner and Galambos (1985) suggested that instead of viewing maternal employment role satisfaction as a direct cause of children's behaviour, it should be viewed as a mediating variable. The basis for their assertion was the considerable body of data showing that incongruence between employment status and employment attitudes is associated with parenting behaviour (e.g. Brody *et al.*, 1986; Henggeler and Borduin, 1981; Stuckey *et al.*, 1982; Yarrow *et al.*, 1962). Lerner and Galambos (1985) speculate that this relation emerges because maternal role satisfaction is positively associated with maternal self-fulfilment and self-esteem (Lamb, Chase-Lansdale and Owen, 1979). Lerner and Galambos (1985) point to the extensive literature showing that positive parenting is associated with appropriate child behaviours.

Lerner and Galambos (1985) generated a process model wherein difficulties with child behaviours were linked with subsequent maternal role dissatisfaction, which in turn predicted maternal rejection of the child, their criterion of mother–child interaction. Finally, in this proposed model, maternal rejection predicted child behaviour one year later (see Figure 7.2). Lerner and Galambos (1985) re-analysed data from the New York Longitudinal Study to test this model empirically for the total sample, as well as separately for subgroups of employed mothers and non-employed mothers. We will focus only on the results from the total sample because results from the two subgroups were markedly similar to that of the total sample. Maternal role satisfaction exerted a direct and an indirect effect on child difficulties. Their longitudinal data showed that maternal role satisfaction (when the child was three years old) was not significantly associated with child difficulties (at age four). Instead, mother–child interaction (specifically, maternal rejection) mediated the relationship between maternal role satisfaction (when the child was three) and child difficulty one year later. Lerner and Galambos's (1985) findings should be interpreted cautiously because they were based on a relatively small sample, were collected during the 1950s, and the sample consisted mainly of middle and upper middle class women. Nonetheless, the fact that the process was comparable for employed and non-employed mothers suggests that the influence of role satisfaction, like role commitment (Barling, Fullagar and Marchl-Dingle, 1988) is consistent for employed and non-employed mothers.

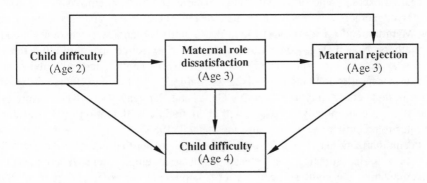

Figure 7.2   Model of indirect effects of mothers' role satisfaction in Lerner and Galambos's (1985) study

Mothers' inter-role conflict

It is widely assumed that the addition of the employment role to those already fulfilled by the mother (such as the role of spouse, mother and self) result in conflict between these roles. As will be recalled, Greenhaus and Beutell (1985) characterized inter-role conflict as arising when there is insufficient time, personal resources or too much personal strain or distress to fulfil all one's role obligations simultaneously. It is surprising that only a few studies have addressed the possible effects of maternal inter-role conflict on the mother–child relationship and children's behaviour given that inter-role conflict has a number of negative effects (see Chapter 6), and role conflict is one of the major psychological stressors that individuals encounter (see Bluen and Barling, 1988). Indeed, under certain circumstances inter-role conflict predicts clinically significant levels of marital distress for both husbands and wives (Barling, 1986a; Suchet and Barling, 1986).

There is only one published data set addressing the relationship between maternal inter-role conflict and mother–child interactions from which generalizations are possible (Gelles and Hargreaves, 1981). From their national, random sample investigating the effects of maternal employment on child abuse, Gelles and Hargreaves (1981) obtained data on a measure they referred to as 'role strain'. Because of the concern that employed mothers may be at greater risk for engaging in child abuse because of the strain caused by their dual role, they assessed the extent of role strain the mother experienced as a ratio of the domestic responsibilities the mother actually had against the amount of domestic responsibilities the mother desired. In doing so, they focused on five domestic roles: namely, money management; house maintenance and management; social activities; child supervision; and child discipline. Their results support the notion that unwanted excess domestic responsibilities are significantly associated with higher rates of child abuse, regardless of the mothers' employment status. In other words, while employed mothers were no more likely to abuse their children, undesired excess domestic responsibility experienced by both employed and non-employed mothers was negatively related to child abuse. In a re-analysis of this data set, Margolin and Larson (1988) found that a similar relationship was not yielded for fathers. Nonetheless, some caution should be exercised in interpreting these results as support for a relationship between inter-role conflict and child abuse, as issues of causality remains unresolved as Margolin and Larson (1988) note, and there is some uncertainty as to whether Gelles and Hargreaves's (1981) measure of role strain is conceptually consistent with more traditional definitions and measures of inter-role conflict (see Greenhaus and Beutell, 1985).

In summarizing her study, Schwartz (1983) points out that one of the neglected variables in investigating the effects of maternal employment experiences is maternal inter-role conflict. Schwartz (1983) directed her comments particularly towards mothers whose children were less than one year old. Apart from Gelles and Hargreaves's (1981) study, Schwartz's (1983) comments remain valid. When other studies have focused on the specific effects of inter-role conflict, they either focused on highly specific populations (e.g. divorced mothers; Johnson, 1983), on the effects of inter-role conflict on the general family environment (Anderson and Paludi, 1986), or on child care responsibilities in general (Anderson and Paludi, 1986; Johnson, 1983), excluding a specific focus on mother–child interactions. Additional research is required to provide some understanding not only of whether, but also of how, maternal inter-role conflict exerts any effects on the mother-child relationship.

Just as there is a paucity of empirical studies investigating the effects of inter-role conflict on mother–child interactions, there are also very few studies focusing on the relationship between maternal inter-role conflict and children's behaviour. In an earlier study, Baruch (1972) showed that maternal employment status alone had no influence on female college students' attitudes towards the dual career role. However, Baruch's (1972) data also revealed that female college students' attitudes towards the dual role pattern was a function of their mothers holding positive attitudes towards this role structure, and of whether their mothers had experienced any difficulty in accommodating both their employment and homemaker roles. Barling and Van Bart (1984) investigated whether children of mothers experiencing conflict between the employment and homemaker roles suffer any negative effects. In their sample of kindergarten children, they found both general and gender-specific effects. Specifically, employed mothers' inter-role conflict was negatively associated with the self-control of both their sons and their daughters. However, while mothers' inter-role conflict was associated with conduct problems in their sons but not their daughters, their inter-role conflict was associated with their daughters' but not their sons' immaturity. The finding that child gender moderates the relationship between maternal inter-role conflict and child behaviour is consistent with research showing that, in general, conduct problems may be more manifest in boys, and immaturity in girls (see Chapter 2). Also, the gender-specific findings concerning inter-role conflict are similar to those on marital conflict, which is associated with boys' conduct problems and girls' immaturity problems (Emery, 1982). However, although it is conceptually appealing to infer that inter-role conflict causes child behaviour problems or difficulties, caution should be exercised before implying any causal direction in this relationship. It is eminently possible that the existence of child behaviour problems renders the balancing of employment and homemaker roles more difficult for the mother.

In summarizing the relationship between maternal employment role experiences and child behaviour or parent–child interactions, two conclusions are justified despite the paucity of studies focusing on inter-role conflict. First, studies addressing the relationship between mother's subjective experience of her employment role, including her attitudes towards, commitment to, satisfactions with and conflicts over her employment, are consistently related to mother–child interactions and child behaviour. Specifically, more positive employment role experiences are associated positively with parent–child interactions and child behaviour. Second, the effects of mothers' experience of the employment role, whether it be commitment to the role (Barling, Fullagar and Marchl-Dingle, 1988), satisfaction with the role (Lerner and Galambos, 1985) or conflict between roles (Gelles and Hargreaves, 1981), are similar for employed and non-employed mothers.

Mothers' Experience of their Jobs

Whereas the previous section questioned the mother's experience of her employment role, this section will focus on the mother's subjective job experiences.

Perhaps the most frequently studied job attitude or experience is job satisfaction (Locke, 1983). The possibility that a mother's job satisfaction exerts some influence over her child's behaviour and development has been acknowledged for some time (e.g. Gutek *et al.*, 1981; Heyns, 1982; Hoffman, 1963). Until recently, however, generalizations from such studies have been hazardous because of conceptual problems with the way in which job satisfaction was operationalized. For example, in some studies it is not the mother's *job* satisfaction that is assessed, but rather satisfaction with the place where the job is conducted (i.e. at home or within an organization; Pasquali and Callegori, 1979). Likewise, despite their titles (e.g. Henggeler and Borduin, 1981), other studies have actually investigated maternal satisfaction with the employment role despite their claim to be measuring maternal job satisfaction.

Some studies, however, have focused specifically on maternal job satisfaction. Two of these studies concentrated on the possible effects of mothers' job satisfaction on mother–child interactions. The first of these studies focused on mother–infant interactions. Riesch (1981) showed that mothers' job satisfaction just prior to giving birth was positively associated with mother–infant interaction. In a separate study, Harrell and Ridley (1975) focused on mother–child interactions in children attending a day-care facility in a socioeconomically heterogeneous sample. Consistent with Riesch's (1981) findings, Harrell and Ridley (1975) again showed that a positive relationship existed between mother's job satisfaction and mother–child interactions. Two issues emerge from Riesch's (1981) thesis. The first issue concerns the conceptualization and operationalization of job satisfaction. As a further indication of the problems encountered in interpreting studies on job satisfaction, Riesch (1981) actually claims to have been assessing organizational commitment. However, inspection of the items comprising her measure of organizational commitment suggest strongly that job satisfaction was measured. This represents a problem of construct validity with all its attendant interpretive consequences (Cook and Campbell, 1979). The second issue relates to the detrimental consequences of the isolationism within different domains of psychology (see Chapter 1). Although job satisfaction remains the most frequently studied variable within organization psychology (Locke, 1983), its conceptualization and operationalization in Riesch's (1981) dissertation indicated that knowledge that is taken for granted in one domain may not be accessible to researchers in other domains.

The third study focused on children's behaviours as possible outcomes of mothers' job satisfaction. Barling and Van Bart (1984) investigated this issue in a group of nursery school children and their mothers. They showed that mothers' job satisfaction was significantly and positively associated with their daughters' self-control, and negatively associated with their daughters' conduct problems. However, neither of the corresponding correlations for sons was statistically significant. Barling and Van Bart (1984) note that the emergence of a gender-specific effect is consistent with data showing that fathers' job satisfaction is associated with their sons' behaviours but not with their daughters' behaviours (see Chapter 9; Barling, 1986b). Gender-specific effects also emerge in the relationship between parents' marital satisfaction and their children's behaviour (Emery, 1982).

Because of concerns expressed in the popular literature that excessive job involvement by the mother must inevitably exact a cost on children's behaviour (Amiel, 1985; Greiff and Munter, 1980a,b; Machlowitz, 1980; Rohrlich, 1980), Barling and Van Bart (1984) also investigated this issue. Contrary to speculations in the literature, however, there was no significant association between maternal job involvement and children's behaviour. At least two factors may account for this. First, speculations concerning excessive job involvement typically revolve around temporal aspects of this involvement. On the contrary, consistent with definitions within the organizational psychological literature (Brooke *et al.*, 1988), Barling and Van Bart (1984) conceptualized job involvement as the psychological identification with one's job. Second, even had temporal dimensions of job involvement been assessed, there is no conclusive support in the literature dealing with the interdependence of the family and employment for a linear relationship between the amount of time spent at one's job and the quality of family life (Bronfenbrenner and Crouter, 1982; Hoffman, 1989).

Piotrkowski and Katz (1982, 1983) conducted two studies among lower socioeconomic groups investigating the effects of mothers' job experiences on their children. In one of these studies, Piotrkowski and Katz (1983) showed that their measure of 'job-related affective state' was significantly and positively associated with daughters' reports of mother–daughter interaction. The usefulness of the finding, however, is limited. Because of the general nature of their measure of job-related experiences, it is not possible to predict from their findings which specific job experiences are associated with mother–daughter interactions, or any causal direction inherent in this relationship. Unlike most other studies investigating the interdependence of family and employment systems, Piotrkowski and Katz (1982) based their other study on a particular theoretical model. Specifically, they invoked Kohn's (1977) model which suggests that individuals assume the values of the occupation they find themselves in. In other words, individuals take on the values that will enable them best to adapt to their occupational environment and demands. In turn, these values transcend the organizational domain, and generalize to other subsystems (such as the family) in which the individual must function. Piotrkowski and Katz (1982) investigated the effect of specific job-related experiences, namely job demands, job autonomy and skill utilization on three aspects of children's scholastic behaviour—attendance, achievement and effort—as these behaviours most closely approximate the occupational environment their mothers encounter. On the basis of their theoretical model, Piotrkowski and Katz (1982) offered specific hypotheses. First, mothers' skill utilization would be positively associated with their children's scholastic achievement, presumably because mothers who have no opportunity for skill utilization on the job would not encourage similar skill use in their daughters. Second, mothers' job autonomy would be *negatively* associated with daughters' school attendance. Their rationale for this seemingly counter-intuitive hypothesis was that parents who experience close monitoring and little opportunity for autonomy on the job would perceive conformity as adaptive. As a result, this would encourage frequent school attendance by their daughters, because such attendance is indicative of conformity to the school system. Third, mothers' job demands would be positively associated with the number of homework assignments submitted by their daughters, as mothers with demanding jobs would perceive effort as adaptive and encourage similar behaviours in their daughters.

Piotrkowski and Katz's (1982) first two hypotheses obtained considerable support from their data. Mothers' skill utilization was significantly negatively associated with their daughters' achievement, but not with effort or attendance. Likewise, mothers' job autonomy was significantly and negatively associated with their daughters' school attendance, but was not associated with either achievement or effort. However, the data only provide partial support for their third hypothesis. Although mothers' job demands were significantly associated with the amount of effort expended by their daughters on English tasks, similar correlations were not yielded between mothers' job demands and the amount of effort expended on mathematics tasks. In addition, contrary to their hypotheses, job demands were associated with the two other scholastic outcomes, namely achievement and attendance. Piotrkowski and Katz's (1982) results are important not only because they demonstrate significant relationships between mothers' job experiences and child behaviours. They also isolate which maternal job experiences will influence which specific child behaviours. Moreover, Piotrkowski and Katz (1982) conducted additional analyses to exclude rival hypotheses such as selection factors (i.e. particular mothers choose specific occupations) and the influence of unmeasured variables.

Finally, in considering the effects of maternal employment experiences, two studies have focused on parental job stressors and child abuse. Both Agathonos and Stathakopoulou (1983) as well as Justice and Duncan (1978) found a large and significant relationship between job-related stressors experienced by the parent and child abuse. However, a number of elements inherent in these two studies lead to questions as to whether their results provide information concerning maternal job stressors and child abuse by the mother. First, as is the case with studies investigating unemployment and child abuse (see Chapter 9), neither Agathonos and Stathakopoulou (1983) nor Justice and Duncan (1978) specified whether the husband, the wife or both were responsible for the child abuse. Second, both these studies measured general life stressors, some of which were job related, and failed to differentiate the effects of job stressors and life stressors on child abuse. Thus, even though Agathonos and Stathakopoulou (1983) and Justice and Duncan's (1978) results are provocative and consistent with predictions, the extent to which they provide detailed information concerning mothers' job-related stressors and child abuse remains questionable.

CHILDREN'S PERCEPTIONS OF MATERNAL EMPLOYMENT

Before concluding this section on mothers' role and job experiences, one additional perspective on maternal employment should be considered. Instead of asking mothers or external observers to rate the effects of maternal employment on children, there are a few studies that have investigated children's perceptions of their mothers' employment. The importance of such a perspective can be gleaned from Piotrkowski and Katz's (1983) results. Although data from empirical studies show consistently that employed mothers spend less time with their children during the workweek, Piotrkowski and Katz (1983) found that when children of employed mothers are interviewed, they do not report experiencing their employed mothers as spending less time with them.

In possibly the earliest study that asked children about maternal employment, Selma Mathews (1934) interviewed 100 children of employed mothers and 100 children of non-employed mothers, matched in terms of age, grade, sex, school community and fathers' occupational prestige. The results of Mathews's (1934) early study are difficult to interpret because of conflicting statements she makes. For example, she documents the median happiness scores of children of employed and non-employed mothers as being 83.7 and 87.9 respectively, which she suggests 'are fairly similar' (p. 131), and says that children of employed mothers were well adjusted. Mathews then questions whether differences still exist, and concludes that 'The attitudes of the worker group were found to be less desirable than those of the non-worker group when measured by adult judgments. However, the similarity of attitudes of the two groups was striking' (p. 135). The importance of Mathews's (1934) study, however, lies not in the clarity of her findings, but rather in introducing a new perspective in viewing the effects of maternal employment on children.

King, McIntyre and Axelson (1968) questioned a large group of adolescents of employed and non-employed mothers. They found that adolescents of employed mothers viewed employment as less of a danger to the marital relationship than did adolescents whose mothers were not employed. In a more recent study, Trimberger and MacLean (1982) questioned a group of children aged nine to twelve years old concerning their perceptions of their mothers' employment. Although their data are based on a relatively small sample of 51 children, a number of their findings are noteworthy because of the absence of similar studies directly asking children for their perceptions of maternal employment. First, Trimberger and MacLean (1982) found that daughters had more knowledge about their mothers' employment than did sons, and speculate that this is associated with the closer intimacy inherent in the mother–daughter relationship. Second, contrary to widespread concern, Trimberger and MacLean (1982) found that children who spent time alone after school because of their mothers' employment-related unavailability are not more negatively disposed toward their mothers' employment than children who are not alone. From their interviews, they attribute this to the greater freedom and independence experienced by children left alone. Third, although causal inferences should be avoided, Trimberger and MacLean (1982) found significant positive relationships between a mother's attitude to her own employment, the child's attitude to his or her mother's employment, and how the child believes that he or she is influenced by the mother's employment. Although these findings should be interpreted with caution because of the relatively small sample size and absence of other studies replicating these findings, the approach of focusing on children's perceptions rather those of the mother, father or teacher alone is an avenue along which future research might profitably travel.

FUTURE DIRECTIONS FOR UNDERSTANDING AND RESEARCHING MATERNAL EMPLOYMENT

From the above discussion, three directions can be drawn. Each of these deserves some consideration, as they have considerable implications for future conceptualizing the nature and consequences of maternal employment, for policy and/or practical implications related to the increasing numbers of women in the labour force, and for the way in which research is conducted in this area.

First, considerable attention has been focused on factors that moderate the relationship either between maternal employment status and child behaviour, or maternal employment experiences and child behaviour. One longstanding example of this is the way in which the relationship between maternal employment status or maternal employment experiences and mother–child interaction is dependent on the child's sex (e.g. Hand, 1957; Mathews 1934; Stuckey *et al.*, 1982). In addition there are also data showing that the mother's educational level (Bronfenbrenner, Alvarez and Henderson, 1984) and socioeconomic class (Alvarez, 1985) moderate this relationship. Arguably, though, research could benefit more from a consideration of the factors that mediate this relationship. Assuming that maternal employment experiences are positively associated with child behaviours, the question of how a mother's employment experiences come to influence her child's behaviour needs to be answered (see Chapter 10). Bronfenbrenner *et al.* (1984) suggest that the mother's perceptions of her child may be one link between her employment status and child behaviour.

The second implication that emerges concerns practical implications and will be addressed in greater detail in Chapter 10. Past research has been motivated by the belief that negative consequences of maternal employment for the child will be uncovered if only we look hard enough. Clearly this has not transpired. Instead, employed mothers exert positive effects on their children when their experience of employment is positive. What is required now is a fundamental change in research focus and strategy, so that research can help legislators, corporate executives and practitioners understand and facilitate the conditions under which the mothers' employment experience is positive. This is especially critical given the large number of mothers currently in the labour force.

Finally, one of the primary factors motivating and sustaining the flood of research on the employed mother was the belief that this represented a deviant, unusual social role. Today, non-employed mothers are in the minority. Research might well focus on how non-employed mothers experience their roles, and influence their children and families. Because of the recent social psychological and organizational psychological research on unemployment (see Chapter 8), the experience and consequences of 'not working' are more widely understood. Frameworks adopted in attempting to understand unemployment and retirement could be used to provide a more comprehensive understanding of the experience of non-employed mothers. In any such research, it might be well to contrast both the daily and chronic effects of maternal employment and non-employment (Alpert and Culbertson, 1987)

MATERNAL EMPLOYMENT AND CHILDREN'S BEHAVIOUR: CONCLUSION

With respect to the discussion, two consistent trends are readily discernible. First, as is now widely acknowledged and accepted, data from literally countless studies show that maternal employment exerts no consistent, detrimental effects on children. Instead, if anything, the children (and especially the daughters) of employed mothers may benefit in terms of exhibiting more egalitarian sex role stereotypes and independence. Second, data derived from studies on the mother's experience of her employment role and of her job show just as consistently that when the experience of employment is positive for mothers, both their sons and their daughters benefit.

Chapter 8
Fathers' Employment and Children's Behaviour

In the previous chapter, the literature on the relationship between maternal employment status and experiences and children's behaviour was examined. In the present chapter, a related issue will be discussed: the influence of fathers' employment on their children's behaviour. In addressing this topic, contrasts and contradictions between the literatures dealing with maternal and paternal employment become apparent. First, the effects of maternal employment on children's behaviour have been considered independently of the effects of paternal employment on children's behaviour. Only one study could be located that simultaneously compared and contrasted the effects of maternal employment and paternal employment on children. Even then, the mothers and fathers in this study were not from the same dyad (Greenberger and Goldberg, 1989). Accordingly, the custom of treating maternal employment and paternal employment separately is followed in this text, not because it is believed that mothers' and fathers' employment status and employment experiences necessarily exert separate and/or different effects on their children, but because of the existence of two separate literatures. Second, while maternal employment status is widely believed to exert negative effects on children and mother–child interactions, paternal employment is viewed as positively affecting children, and paternal unemployment is perceived as negative (Bronfenbrenner and Crouter, 1982). Third, consistent with the fear that maternal employment is harmful, substantially more research has focused on the possible consequences of mother's rather than fathers' employment for children's behaviour and parent–child interactions. In sharp contrast to the wealth of speculation, theorizing and research on mothers' employment and children's behaviour, considerably less empirical research has been conducted on the effects of fathers' employment on father–child interactions and their children's behaviour.

Perhaps the major reason for this is the ideological position that initially prompted the research on maternal employment. Specifically, consistent with a 'deprivation framework', it was assumed that employment-related maternal absence was inevitably harmful to the child and the mother–child relationship. Such a belief has limited the conduct of research on the possible effects of paternal employment. In addition, this 'deprivation framework' relegates the role of the father to a lesser position than that accorded to the mother in terms of the development of the child, minimizing the father's role in all aspects of child development. Essentially, this approach assumes that fathers are detached from and disinterested in the parenting role, and fathers' employment was presumed not to affect children (Booth and Edwards, 1980). The belief that it is the job-related presence or absence of the mother that influences a child precludes an extensive examination of the effects of paternal employment on children: there are very few fathers who are voluntarily not employed. Thus, while large groups of voluntarily non-employed mothers can readily be obtained and contrasted with voluntarily employed mothers, comparably large groups of voluntarily non-employed fathers do not exist. Even if a group of fathers who voluntarily chose not to be employed could be assembled, it is likely that socio-economic status confounds, and employment commitment would limit, the validity of any results obtained.

Nonetheless, increased concern is now being expressed regarding the possible effects of paternal employment on children's behaviour and on father–child interactions. Several factors might account for this growth in interest. In the first instance, there has been an escalation of interest in the role of the father in child development in general (e.g. Booth and Edwards, 1980; Lamb, 1981, 1982). Second, the increase in the number of employed mothers may have prompted more of an interest in fathers' parenting role. Third, the shift in emphasis away from the effects of mothers' employment status towards a consideration of subjective employment experiences (see Chapter 7) has made it methodologically possible to investigate the effects of fathers' employment on their children.

As was the case when considering the effects of husbands' and wives' employment on marital functioning, and the effects of maternal employment on children, the effects of the fathers' objective employment characteristics will be considered first. Thereafter, the research investigating the hypothesis that children select occupations consistent with those held by their fathers, or with characteristics similar to those their fathers hold, will be examined. The association between fathers' subjective employment experiences and children's behaviour, and father–child interactions, will then be considered.

FATHERS' OBJECTIVE EMPLOYMENT CHARACTERISTICS AND THEIR CHILDREN

Father Absence and Children's Behaviour

There is considerable interest in the effects of father absence on all aspects of their children's development. Scores of empirical studies have been conducted contrasting the children of fathers who are present with those whose fathers are absent. The fact that research on the effects of father absence on children continues unabated is probably a function of at least three factors. First, as Hillenbrand (1976, p. 451) noted, 'Among the many stresses which assault today's American family, father absence is an increasingly frequent phenomenon'. Stevenson and

Black (1988) report that in 1982, there were more than 8 million 'single-parent' families in the United States, and that nearly 60% of children born after 1986 will spend some time in a single-parent family before they are eighteen years old. Of course, not all these single families will comprise an absent father and a mother who is present. Instead, the number of single families headed by a father is increasing. Studying the effects of father absence thus reflects an attempt to understand an important social phenomenon. The second factor that sustains an interest in father absence is the belief that father absence necessarily constitutes a burden on the family. This is reflected in Hillenbrand's (1976) statement that father absence represents a crisis for the family that demands an appropriate coping response. A third factor that maintains such research is the assumption that social policy issues can be guided directly by research findings on the consequences of father absence (Palme, 1972).

Tracing the development of the literature on father absence in general is important for an understanding of the specific effects of *employment-related* father absence on children. The effects of father absence initially focused on children whose fathers were absent due to their military service during the Second World War (Stevenson and Black, 1988). With the exception of fathers who died during active duty, such absences were typically temporary. Most of the research on father absence has not been concerned with the effects of employment-related father absence. Instead, the majority of this research has investigated the consequences of fathers' absence because of death, divorce and desertion. Before analysing studies investigating the effects of job-related father absence, therefore, it is critical to understand how different reasons for father absence (whether job related or not) affect behaviour.

Piotrkowski and Gornick (1987) proposed a framework for understanding how different types of father absence will affect families. Piotrkowski and Gornick (1987) argue that two types of job-related father absence exist, namely ordinary and extraordinary absences. In the case of ordinary job-related father absence, the absence is predictable and temporary, and usually involves stable and predictable departure and reunion rituals which help children understand and cope with the absence. On the contrary, extraordinary job-related absences exist when the weekly timing of separations (i.e. the pattern of days/nights spent at home and on the job), and the pattern of daily hours spent at home/work (i.e. at what time the father leaves and arrives home) are variable. This makes the father absence unpredictable and unstable. Piotrkowski and Gornick (1987) argue that ordinary job-related father absence does not exert any negative effects on children, whereas extraordinary job-related absence might be expected to. Barling (in press) further differentiates ordinary and extraordinary absence in terms of duration. Specifically, he includes protracted absences, such as three-month naval tours of duty (Marsella, Dubanoski and Mohs, 1974) or nine months at sea (Lynn and Sawrey, 1959) as extraordinary, regardless of whether they are regular and predictable. One additional factor not indentified by Piotrkowski and Gornick (1987) that further differentiates between ordinary and extraordinary father absence is the different emotional connotations associated with father absence due to job separations, divorce, desertion and death. For example, in cases of divorce and desertion, intrafamily conflict occurring prior to the father absence is more likely to be higher than for employment-related father absence. Likewise, when father absence is a result of death, the grief and loss experienced could not even be compared with that associated with employment-related father absence. Thus, the subjective meaning of job-related father absence is qualitatively different from other instances of father absence. Father absence constitutes a stressor. It is an objective, verifiable event. To understand its effects on children's behaviour, it is necessary to examine the subjective meaning, or the stress, associated with father absence.

In this chapter, the evaluation of the effects of father absence will be limited to studies in which the absence is job related. Single case studies or anecdotal reports from which generalization is problematic (e.g. Hood and Golden, 1979) will not be discussed. Two difficulties that are encountered in evaluating the effects of fathers' employment-related absence should be mentioned at this stage. First, in studies that have investigated the consequences of father absence for children, the reasons for the absence are either not cited at all, or are ignored (e.g. M. L. Hoffman, 1971; Sutton-Smith, Rosenberg and Landy, 1968; Svanum, Bringle and McLaughlin, 1982). Second, after excluding such investigations, very few remaining empirical studies focus exclusively on the consequences of work-related father absence.

Ordinary job-related father absence

There is only one published study that has investigated the possible consequences of ordinary job-related father absence on father–child relationships. In their study of a group of young fathers (average age = 22.9 years), McHale and Huston (1984) showed that the number of hours the fathers were absent per week because of their work was negatively associated with the extent to which they played with their infants and shared leisure time with their infants. Thus, the greater the number of hours devoted to their jobs each week, the less these fathers interacted with their infants. At the same time, though, it should be noted that the number of hours spent on the job each week by the fathers did not predict ten other aspects of the father–infant relationship in this same study. The absence of a consistent relationship here stands in contrast to findings for mothers. As noted in Chapter 7, despite a very small sample size, McHale and Huston (1984) showed that six of the same eleven mother–child interaction variables were significantly associated with time demands for the mothers of infants. It would appear, therefore, that the data support Piotrkowski and Gornick's (1987) argument concerning ordinary work-related absences: fathers' ordinary work-related absences exert no consistent effects on fathers' childrearing behaviours. One additional aspect of McHale and Huston's (1984) study is noteworthy. They refer to the number of hours worked per week as an indication of 'job involvement'. This again highlights the tendency to equate the amount of time worked with the psychological processes involved in job involvement (see Chapter 2).

There are some studies which have investigated the effects of fathers' participation in shift work schedules on their children. Because shift work interferes with the fulfilment of family roles (see Chapter 4), it might be predicted that father absence due to shift work will interfere with the father–child relationship. There are some data testing this proposition. In their earlier study, Mott *et al.* (1965) showed that parents who were involved in a shift work schedule generally felt incompetent and inadequate as parents. More specifically, fathers who were involved in an afternoon/evening shift self-reported greater difficulties with specific aspects of the father–child relationship (e.g. companionship, direction, discipline, maintenance of close relationships) than fathers involved in a day shift. Such effects were especially pronounced for fathers of younger children. Similar findings emerged in Volger *et al.*'s (1988) study: fathers involved in shift work that required them to be absent from the family during the evening or night reported poorer father–child relationships than employed fathers who were not absent from the family during the evening or night. Nonetheless, some caution should be exercised before concluding that these fathers performed more poorly than fathers who do not participate in shift work. Fathers involved in shift work may well experience greater levels of guilt concerning their childrearing adequacy because of their absence from the family at critical times. Yet there are no data showing that they differ from fathers involved in regular shifts on objective indices of parent–child interaction.

Landy, Rosenberg and Sutton-Smith (1969) analysed college students' retrospective reports on the effects on their performance of fathers' absence due to night shift work. They asked 100 female university students enrolled in an undergraduate course in developmental psychology to furnish information about their fathers' shift work history, and they obtained similar reports from the students' fathers to ascertain that the data provided by the students were accurate. On the basis of these reports, Landy *et al.* (1969) constructed five groups (20 students each), in which fathers were characterized as having been: *(a)* continuously present for all 19 years (i.e. not involved in shift work at all); *(b)* involved in shift work for between 1 and 5 years; *(c)* involved in shift work for between 6 and 10 years; *(d)* 11 or more years in shift work; or *(e)* continuously absent. A statistically significant difference emerged between these five groups, with students' quantitative performance being *higher* under conditions of father presence. However, the meaning of this difference remains ambiguous. First, Landy *et al.* (1969) computed *post hoc* analyses to isolate the groups accounting for the overall difference, and established that significant differences in female students' quantitative performance existed only between the groups whose fathers had been continuously absent and those who had been continuously present (i.e. fathers in this latter group had never engaged in shift work). It is questionable, therefore, whether the overall difference between college students who had previously been exposed to continuous father absence is attributable to their fathers' shift work history in any way. Other factors which further question the meaning and generalizability of this difference is their exclusive reliance on university students as subjects, and on retrospective data. As a result, it is not yet prudent to conclude that father absence as a function of shift work exerts a negative effect on father–child interactions (Mott *et al.*, 1965) or children's behaviour (Landy *et al.*, 1969).

Extraordinary job-related father absence

Extraordinary absences are perhaps more germane to an understanding of the effects of fathers' job-related absences on their children. First, there is little variability among fathers with respect to ordinary job-related absence, thereby precluding the possibility of finding any associated effects because of range restriction. Second, fathers are more likely than mothers to be involved in extraordinary job-related absences through *(a)* their longer working hours, *(b)* greater involvement than mothers in irregular and unpredictable patterns of working hours (i.e. greater participation in shift schedules) and *(c)* more frequent extended absences from home. In studies on prolonged father absence due to employment, the father is usually absent for a period of three months or more, often because he is a merchant sailor or employed in the military. Such studies can be characterized according to whether they concentrate on the consequence of prolonged job-related father absence on maternal attitudes and mother–child interactions, or whether they focus on effects of father absence on child behaviour. Consistent with the format followed in Chapter 7, the effects of father absence on mother–child interaction and on the mother's childrearing attitudes will be considered first. Thereafter, effects of employment-related prolonged father absence on children's behaviour will be assessed.

Marsella *et al.* (1974) hypothesized that father absence exerts an indirect impact on children through its direct effects on mothers' childrearing attitudes and behaviours. To investigate this hypothesis, they studied a group of wives whose husbands were nuclear submarine personnel, using a longitudinal design, so that they could assess the same group of wives during periods of husband presence and husband absence. They found that mothers showed significantly more maternal domination and control (e.g. strictness, intrusion, acceleration of development) under conditions of father presence rather than father absence. Their findings are consistent with Hillenbrand's (1976) study, as she also showed that maternal dominance was associated with the length of husband absence in military personnel. Marsella *et al.*'s (1974) finding may be a function of changing conditions the mother must endure during situations of father presence and absence. *(a)* Marsella *et al.* (1974) also showed that there was an increased level of marital conflict under conditions of father presence. *(b)* Beckman *et al.* (1979) showed that mothers' depression was significantly associated with their husbands' job-related presence or absence. One important implication emerges from this finding. As Marsella *et al.* (1974) recognize, because mothers' childrearing attitudes and behaviours vary depending on whether their husbands are present or absent, their children will be confronted with inconsistent maternal childrearing attitudes and behaviours. These inconsistencies may make it more difficult for the children to understand, predict and control their mothers' responses. Also, the fact that inconsistencies in father–child interactions mediate the link between fathers' unemployment and child behaviour problems (McLoyd, 1989) may guide an understanding of the effects of mothers' inconsistent childrearing on their children. Finally, however, concerns exist about the meaning and generalizability of Marsella *et al.*'s (1974) findings. Even if maternal dominance is associated with job-related husband absence, there is no indication as to whether maternal dominance is positive or negative. As a result, it is difficult to assess whether father absence is positive or negative in this context. Second, it might not be possible to generalize to the non-military population from data gathered on husbands employed in the military who undergo three-month tours of duty, or their wives because of the unique chronic stress they endure. This consideration is especially relevant given the peculiar fears that may be associated with having one's spouse on a nuclear submarine, as was the case in Marsella *et al.*'s (1974) study.

Cotterell (1986) also investigated the effects of prolonged employment-related father absence on wives' childrearing attitudes. Cotterell's (1986) study was conducted among working class families residing in four small towns in inland Australia that were geographically isolated from any large population centre. Cotterell (1986) categorized fathers as 'absent' if they had limited chances for participation in regular family activities and childrearing because of job-related absences from their family. Included in this group were fathers who participated in shift work, or travelled sizable distances which kept them away from their families for days. Unlike Marsella *et al.* (1974) who studied mothers under conditions of both husband absence and husband presence, Cotterell (1986) contrasted these 'absent' fathers with a separate group of fathers from the same geographical areas whose jobs did not require them to be absent for prolonged periods. Like Marsella *et al.* (1974), Cotterell (1986) also showed that father absence exerted a significant effect on mother–child interactions. In Cotterell's (1986) study, mothers whose husbands were frequently absent played with their children less and provided less cognitive stimulation than did mothers whose husbands were present. One plausible explanation for this finding could be the greater role load shouldered by mothers under conditions of father absence. Another explanation is that the absence was of shorter duration in Cotterell's (1986) study. Hence, mothers may not have felt the need to compensate for their spouses' job-related absence. Nonetheless, some caution should be exercised in generalizing these findings. Cotterell (1986) noted the specificity of the cultural context in which his data were collected. Within mining and rural towns in Australia, employment and home are viewed as separate functional domains, with employment being the prerogative and responsibility of the father or husband, and family obligations persisting as the duty of the mother or wife.

Thus, it would appear as though job-related father absence does exert some effect on mother–child interactions and/or childrearing attitudes. Both Marsella *et al*. (1974) and Cotterell (1986) showed significant differences in mothers' childrearing behaviours under conditions of job-related father absence and father presence. While Cotterell (1986) showed that mothers whose husbands are absent interact less with their children, Marsella *et al*. (1974) showed that mothers become more dominant when their husbands return home.

Two different studies have enquired into the question of whether consistent and prolonged work-related father absence has any effect on children's social behaviour. In a within-group analysis of military personnel and their families, Hillenbrand (1976) investigated whether the amount of job-related father absence a child had experienced was related to the child's intelligence and social behaviour. (The amount of father absence experienced ranged from 0 to 63 months in a group of 126 sixth grade school children; the average length of absence was 26 months.) Hillenbrand (1976) found that length of father absence was significantly correlated with children's quantitative ability: the longer the father absence, the *greater* the child's quantitative ability. Consistent with Marsella *et al*.'s (1974) findings from families of navy personnel, maternal dominance was positively associated with length of father absence in Hillenbrand's (1976) study. There was also a significant birth order effect, because first born children (especially males) were most likely to manifest higher levels of quantitative ability and greater perceptions of maternal dominance associated with father absence. Finally, Hillenbrand (1976) found that this general pattern of results was far stronger for sons than for daughters.

The second of the studies that investigated the effects of father absence on children's social behaviour focused on substantially more protracted absences among the families of Norwegian sailors (Lynn and Sawrey, 1959). In the group studied by Lynn and Sawrey (1959), the absentee fathers were either merchant sailors or whalers who were away from home for at least nine consecutive months of each year, and sometimes for as long as two continuous years. All fathers in this experimental group held the rank of officer and were involved in supervisory tasks. They were contrasted with a control group of fathers who were continuously present in the family, and also held supervisory jobs. Using data from structured interviews with the mothers and from structured Doll Play and Draw-a-Family tests with the children, Lynn and Sawrey (1959) found significant differences existed between the children of these two groups of fathers. Essentially, children whose fathers were continuously absent manifested less secure identification with their fathers, greater immaturity, and poorer social adjustment with their peers. It should be noted, however, that concern exists regarding the non-comparability of Lynn and Sawrey's (1959) control and experimental groups, and whether results from their samples are generalizable. To justify conclusions about the effects of job-related father absence from these two groups, they should differ only in terms of the length of absence. Yet they probably differ on numerous other factors, including the type of job, position in the organizational hierarchy, and socioeconomic status. Also, as will be considered further below, it is possible that a selection confound existed in their study (as well as most others examining extraordinary job-related father absence), because individuals with specific personality traits and/or family circumstances and expectations may be more likely to accept job conditions that require such lengthy absences from the family. Similarly, women who marry husbands knowing they will be absent either for such extended or irregular periods may not be representative of women in general. These concerns arise because the two groups studied differed from each other. The extent to which the two groups were also markedly different from the general population raises further doubts about the generalizability of the findings. While fathers in both groups engaged in some supervisory tasks as part of their jobs, it is not certain that merchant sailors and whalers can be readily contrasted with men fulfilling regular jobs, and if this argument is valid, any differences between the two groups would be artificially inflated. Together, these factors limit the extent to which any negative effects that emerge in such studies can be attributed to father absence.

From the studies reviewed above, it might be concluded that when job-related father absence is prolonged and extraordinary, negative effects accrue to the mother–child relationship, the mother's childrearing attitudes, and children's behaviour. Certainly, with only one exception (Hillenbrand, 1976), the studies reviewed above all suggest that some negative effects are associated with job-related father absence. However, methodological factors specific to each study have already been noted, suggesting that such conclusions should still be treated with caution.

There are also methodological problems common to these studies. First, with the exception of Cotterell (1986), the data on which these studies are based were collected some considerable time ago (i.e. between 1958 and 1976). It is questionable whether attitudes to job-related father absence remain the same today as they were during the period the data were collected for these studies. Second, when groups of absent fathers and present fathers are contrasted, the effects of the length of the absence are also ignored. This may be especially problematic in light of Landy *et al.*'s (1969) finding that the only two groups that differed were those of continuously absent and continuously present fathers, and Hillenbrand's (1976) finding that maternal dominance was associated with the length of the father's work-related absence.

A more important problem involves the conceptualization and operationalization of father absence. Specifically, the measures used typically ignore the meaning of the father's absence for the father, the mother and/or the child. Any research that focuses on job-related father absence follows a deficit-oriented deprivation model that is similar to that invoked in hypothesizing that maternal employment status is synonymous with maternal deprivation. As Pederson (1976) noted, such an approach cannot provide any information as to why father absence exerts negative (or in some cases, positive) effects. To obtain such information, it is critical to understand the subjective meaning of job-related father absences for children, for wives and for the fathers themselves. Although never discussed explicitly in the literature, it remains possible that some children feel the same pride in their absentee fathers' employment, as other children do when their employed fathers are continuously present. This points to the need for further research to focus on the subjective meaning of job-related father absence for the child. Likewise, in the same way that there have been calls for understanding mothers' experience of their employment and their employment role rather than focusing solely on their employment status, an understanding of what job-related absences mean to the father may facilitate predictions of its effects on children's behaviour.

INTERGENERATIONAL OCCUPATIONAL CHOICE: LIKE FATHER, LIKE SON?

In the previous section, the possibility that job-related father absence is associated with father–child interaction and/or children's behaviour was considered. In focusing further on the effects of objective characteristics of fathers' jobs on children, an additional question that has confronted social scientists in general, and sociologists and economists in particular, is whether sons tend to choose the same occupation as their fathers. The idea that sons come to resemble their fathers in meaningful domains is not new. As Troll, Bengston and McFarland (1979, p. 127) note in their review, 'Relations between generations in the family are a common theme in drama, from classical Greek theatre to today's television serials'. Before considering whether children do indeed follow in the occupational footsteps of their fathers, it should be noted that conventional wisdom suggests both positive and negative support for this hypothesis. On the one hand, there is a widespread belief that children take on the characteristics of their fathers, and this is reflected in statements such as 'like father, like son'. On the other hand, there is also widespread belief in the existence of the 'generation gap', which arises from discrepancies in the values and beliefs of parents and children, and which could predispose children to reject occupations similar to their fathers.

To some extent, interest in intergenerational occupational linkages can be traced to the transmission of social class standing within families across generations. Of greater interest from the perspective of the interaction between employment and family, however, is the question of whether children's choice of occupation is constrained or influenced in any way by that of their fathers' occupation. Fathers personify the occupational world and its roles and expectations to members of their families (Aberle and Naegele, 1952), forming an important source of children's knowledge of the occupational world (Piotrkowski and Stark, 1987). In evaluating whether fathers' choice of occupation has any effect on children in general, but more particularly on their sons, the following topics will be discussed: *(a)* studies testing the similarity between fathers' and sons' occupational preferences and choices, including characteristics of fathers' occupations that influence their sons' choice of occupation, occupational success and social behaviour; and *(b)* mediators between fathers' occupation and sons' occupation.

Similarities between Fathers' and Sons' Occupational Choices

Numerous studies have been conducted assessing the similarity between fathers' occupational choice and that of their sons. The results of these studies show that the likelihood of sons pursuing the same occupation as their fathers vastly exceeds chance. In those cases where children follow different occupations from that of their fathers, they typically enter an occupation with higher socioeconomic prestige.

One of the earlier studies that focused on this issue was conducted by Nelson (1939), who focused on a large sample of college students ($N = 3211$). Unlike many other studies, however, Nelson (1939) focused on the occupational choices of both males and females together. Nelson's (1939) data clearly demonstrate the trend for sons to enter the same occupations as their fathers. For example, Nelson (1939) noted that seven of 54 bankers' children themselves chose banking, a number far exceeding chance expectations given the extensive variety of possible occupational choices open to them. Likewise, 124 children of the 570 fathers involved in commerce chose commerce for themselves. Nelson (1939) notes that in some occupations (namely, dentistry and the ministry), the probability of children following in the footsteps of their fathers would have been even greater had the sample excluded daughters.

Since then, other studies have replicated and extended Nelson's (1939) earlier findings. Unlike Nelson (1939), Jensen and Kirschner (1955) did not study a sample of university students. Instead, they reported data obtained from representative sample of 8000 heads of households in six cities across the United States. Jensen and Kirschner (1955) showed that sons followed their fathers' occupations in five of the ten occupational classifications they used in their study. Also, fathers with manual occupations tended to have sons with manual occupations. The same was true of fathers and sons in non-manual occupations. Where discrepancies occurred between fathers' and sons' occupations, they were attributable to sons progressing further up the occupational hierarchy relative to their fathers. Aberle and Neaegele (1952) investigated the relationship between the prestige of fathers' jobs and their sons' occupational choice. They found that when fathers were asked about their sons' future occupations, fathers initially denied having any specific aspirations for their children. However, on further questioning, it became apparent that any occupation chosen by the son was acceptable to the father as long as it was a middle class, professional or business occupation. Moreover, they note that no father visualized downward mobility for his son.

Reinhardt (1970) extended the general question of occupational linkages between father and son by investigating whether sons who enter an occupation similar to that of their father are more likely to experience success in their career. Reinhardt (1970) collected data from 105 military jet pilots whose performance was rated as outstanding. His data highlight additional effects of father's occupations on their sons. Specifically, not only had fathers of two-thirds of the superior jet pilots served in the military themselves, but 85% of them had been affiliated with the same division. Because it may be argued that occupational linkages are specific to instances of career success, it is interesting to note that Reinhardt (1970) also investigated occupational inheritance among 70 career failures. (Career failure was indicated when the jet pilot was grounded because of unsatisfactory performance or withdrew voluntarily from flying.) Again, his data provide strong support for the occupational inheritance hypothesis. In sharp contrast to the pattern yielded in the successful group, only 3% of the fathers of the career failures were active or former military pilots. Because so many of the studies on the intergenerational transmission of occupation have focused on children regarded as successful (e.g. university students and graduates), Reinhardt's (1970) data on career failures within the military is especially important.

Werts's (1968) study is noteworthy because of the extremely large sample from which his data were collected. Specifically, his study of 70 015 males who entered college in 1961 replicated earlier results (Nelson, 1939; Jensen and Kirschner, 1955). In addition, Werts (1968) also raised an issue that will be pursued further in this chapter: the data showing a link between fathers' and sons' occupations provides no information as to how such linkages emerge between father and son.

From these studies, it seems clear that with respect to occupational choice, there is a highly significant statistical tendency for sons to follow in the footsteps of their fathers. Also, Chopra (1967) has shown that similar results are obtained in India, excluding the possibility that the occupational linkage phenomenon is culturally specific. However, these research studies raise questions that are at least as interesting and important as those that they answer. First, while fathers influence the occupational choice of their children, mothers do not (Mortimer, Lorence and Kumka, 1986). Likewise, daughters' career/vocational choice is not influenced by either of their parents in the same way as that of sons (Aberle and Naegele, 1952). One possible reason for this is the restricted range of mothers' occupations because fewer jobs have traditionally been open to them (at least relative to husbands). Second, socioeconomic status is confounded in these studies, and it remains to be seen whether similar effects emerge when socioeconomic status is controlled. Third, these studies provide no indication of which specific aspects (e.g. objective or subjective) of the fathers' occupation influence their sons. Finally, given the existence of a pattern of intergenerational transmission of occupation, just how this transmission or inheritance takes place is a critical question that remains to be answered (Aldous *et al.*, 1979). Given the significant association between a father's occupation and the occupational choice of his son, it is important to identify the processes that mediate the relationship between fathers' and sons' occupational choices. The possible ways in which such influence might occur are numerous. For example, Piotrkowski and Stark (1987, p. 3) note that:

... children can acquire occupational knowledge directly. As they listen to their parents talk about their jobs, as they see their parents come home tired after a hard day at work, as they spend time at parents' workplaces, they may develop feelings and ideas about work.

However, on the basis of the knowledge currently available on occupational linkage, other processes responsible for the linkage between father and son cannot be excluded as explanations for the similarity between fathers' and sons' occupational choice.

Mediating the Influence of Fathers' Occupational Choice

One of the routes through which the transmission of occupational choice between father and son might occur is via direct attempts on the part of the father to influence his son. It is possible that fathers engage in deliberate, conscious behaviours to bias their children's occupational choices. There is one study testing this hypothesis. Breakwell, Fife-Schaw and Devereux (1988) asked 3160 teenagers in England whether their parents had attempted to influence their career choice, and whether or not such attempts were successful. Their data show that although the teenagers reported that parents did try to influence their choice of career directly, the teenagers further reported that these attempts were not successful. However, Breakwell *et al.*'s (1988) results may underestimate the effects of deliberate attempts by fathers to influence their sons. First of all, it would seem that the best way of assessing whether parents influence their teenagers' choices would not be to simply ask the teenage children. They might be most inclined to deny that parents influence their behaviour in any way. Second, Breakwell *et al.* (1988) did not separate their sample by gender of parent and child, even though data from different studies show that sons are more predisposed to occupational inheritance than daughters, and that intergenerational transmission of occupation does not occur between mother and son. Nonetheless, the possibility that intergenerational transmission of occupation occurs because of direct attempts by either parent is not supported at this stage.

One alternative approach is to focus on facets of fathers' occupation that influence sons' choice of occupation. One of Mortimer's (1974) earlier studies on the intergenerational transmission of occupations addresses this issue. In this analysis, Mortimer (1974) analysed data from the Michigan Student Study, a longitudinal investigation of students attending the University of Michigan. Mortimer (1974) coded parental occupation in accordance with census classifications, and focused on three work values or experiences: autonomy, the nature of the reward system inherent in the occupation (i.e. intrinsic or extrinsic) and the predominant role served by the occupation. Her focus on values or experiences as mediating variables was motivated by Kohn's (1969) hypothesis that the values that a father espouses will influence his own attitudes and behaviour. In turn, these attitudes and behaviours will influence father–son interactions, and will be communicated to sons. In general, Mortimer's (1974) results replicate the findings mentioned earlier in which sons' occupational preferences matched their fathers' occupations. More importantly, Mortimer's (1974) data showed that when sons do not inherit their fathers' occupations exactly, they prefer occupations that reflect similar value structures to those inherent in their fathers' occupations. Functional similarity is important in this respect, as sons of dentists and scientists who did not prefer their fathers' occupations expressed a greater interest in medicine, and there was little movement away from the scientific/medical field. Similarly, sons of teachers overchose engineering, accounting and scientific-oriented professions, all of which require the interpretation of information. Likewise, there was a disproportionate likelihood of choosing one's father's occupation when that occupation reflected considerable autonomy. This suggests the importance of the role of relevant work values in the transmission of occupations between father and son. In a subsequent re-analysis of this data set, Mortimer (1976) showed that the same results emerged even after the effects of fathers' and mothers' education, fathers' occupational status and family income were controlled statistically.

Barclay, Stilwell and Barclay (1972) extended the notion that facets of the fathers' occupation influence children. Barclay *et al.* (1972) followed Holland's (1966) theory of vocational development, which suggests that an individual's choice of occupation provides a reflection of his or her interests and values; in turn, these interests and values influence social interaction. Barclay *et al.* (1972) investigated whether fathers' vocational preferences were associated with their sons' social behaviours as rated by themselves, their teachers and peers. Their results showed that the values inherent in fathers' occupation were consistent with the social behaviour of both sons and daughters.

There are also some studies which demonstrate that the closeness of the father–son relationship mediates the influence of fathers' occupations on their sons. Before discussing these studies, it should first be noted that the quality of the father–son relationship is associated with the nature of the father's occupation. With regard to occupational success, Reinhardt (1970) showed that only 9% of his successful pilots reported paternal deprivation during childhood. In contrast, 73% of this successful group suggested that the father was the more significant parent. Indeed, Reinhardt (1970) noted that successful pilots reported that their fathers had spent so much time with them and engaged in so many joint activities that he was initially doubtful about the veracity of the data. Of the unsuccessful pilots, 20% experienced prolonged paternal deprivation during the pre-college years. Reinhardt's (1970) conclusions would have been strengthened had inferential statistics been used. In a second study, Mortimer (1976) showed that the father–son relationship was significantly closer when fathers' held professional rather than business occupations. Nonetheless, these differences just failed to achieve statistical significance when the effects of socioeconomic status were excluded, suggesting that they were a function of socioeconomic confounds. The closeness of the father–son relationship was significantly associated with extrinsic work values for sons whose fathers engaged in business careers, but was significantly associated with intrinsic work values for sons whose fathers occupied professional careers. These specific relationships may be a function of the values that are important within each of these two occupational groups. From these data, it is apparent that the nature of the father' occupation is associated with the closeness of the father–son relationship.

Mortimer (1976) also ascribes to the quality of the father–son relationship a mediating function in the association between fathers' occupation and son's career preference. In one of a series of studies investigating the occupational linkage hypothesis, Mortimer (1976) suggested that the intergenerational transmission of occupational values between father and son is more likely to occur under conditions of close father–son relationships. Based on data collected from 1200 male students entering the University of Michigan during 1962 and 1963, Mortimer (1976) showed that when fathers were in high status business occupations, their sons avoided academic careers. Instead, these sons chose business and legal careers. On the contrary, when fathers occupied low status business careers, their sons selected non-business-oriented occupations if a close father-son relationship existed. Mortimer (1976) further showed that the closeness of the father–son relationship was dependent on the prestige and functional focus of the father's occupation. Mortimer and her colleagues examined this issue (namely, the joint effects of these mediating factors) in more detail in two subsequent reports (Mortimer *et al.* 1986; Mortimer and Kumka, 1982). The source of the data for these two reports was the same as those of Mortimer's previous research namely the Michigan Student Study. However, these latter two reports went beyond the earlier research by controlling socioeconomic status and grade point average (as an indicator of intelligence; Mortimer and Kumka, 1982), and exploring differences between professional and business groups. Also, the two reports documented the effects of occupational linkages on different dimensions of career attainment, entailing the proposal and testing of a causal model of factors that mediate the effects of fathers' occupational status and prestige on their sons' occupational attainments. Direct paths were found between intrinsic values and job autonomy, extrinsic values and income, and people-oriented values and the social content of the job (cf. Piotrkowski and Katz, 1982). Mediated effects of fathers' occupation on sons' career attainment also emerged. The link between the closeness of the father–son relationship and intrinsic work values was mediated by sons' self-competence, while sons' work involvement mediated the link between the father–son relationship and people-oriented values. Also, sons' extrinsic work values were directly influenced by the father–son relationship. The closeness of the father–son relationship itself was directly influenced by fathers' socioeconomic status (fathers' occupational prestige, educational level and family income) (see Figure 8.1). What is especially noteworthy is that the model was supported using longitudinal data: data on sons' occupational attainments were obtained ten years after the various predictor variables.

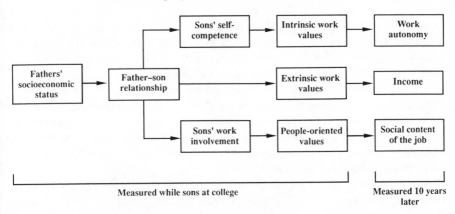

Figure 8.1   Indirect paths between fathers' and sons' occupations in Mortimer *et al.*'s (1986) longitudinal data

Some clarification about the terms used in this model is in order. What Mortimer *et al.* refer to as 'job involvement' probably reflects 'career salience'. To assess job involvement, college students rated the importance they expected different areas of life (one of which was a career or occupation) to have for them after they left college. The term 'father–son relationship' was referred to as 'paternal support' by Mortimer *et al.* (1986). To assess this, they used two items measuring the son's perception of *(a)* the father's understanding/empathy of his son and *(b)* the son's feeling of closeness to his father.

There is consistent support for the hypothesis concerning occupational linkage between father and son. In general, this is an important conclusion, because it runs counter to Troll *et al.*'s (1979) general conclusion that there is only meagre empirical evidence in general for the intergenerational transmission of values and characteristics between parents and children. It should be noted, however, that Troll *et al.* paid scant attention in their general review to the issue of intergenerational transmission of occupational values and characteristics. Nonetheless, a number of questions remain to be answered. First, the range of mediating factors that have been investigated remains limited. Other factors that should be investigated include paternal job dissatisfaction (Barling, 1986b; Mortimer, 1976). The occupational linkage process breaks down when children with close relationships to their fathers realize that their fathers are dissatisfied with their jobs or their occupations. Second, there are exceptions to the pattern of intergenerational transmission. Many children do not choose to follow in their fathers' occupational footsteps. Third, several methodological problems which beset research on intergenerational transmission limit the magnitude of any association between generations. Measurement typically occurs at one point in time only, data are invariably retrospective, only one data source is used (typically children), and predictor or mediating variables are usually investigated independently of each other rather than integrated in an overall model.

In addition, the possibility of bidirectional causality between father and son is not acknowledged, aggregate measures of association (percentage agreement) are usually computed rather than within-family analyses (i.e. individual fathers and their sons), samples are usually limited to university students or other successful individuals, and the reliability of occupational coding typically remains unreported. Fourth, it is worth noting that most of the data on which these studies are based were collected some time ago. Even recently published articles (e.g. Mortimer *et al*., 1986; Mortimer and Kumka, 1982) are based on data collected in the 1960s. It remains to be seen whether support for the occupational linkage hypothesis emerges when more recent data are analysed.

Finally, most of the research has investigated occupational linkages between father and son. While there are data showing that similar results do not emerge when the mothers' occupation is considered (Mortimer *et al*., 1986), the reasons for these differences are not well understood. Even though explanations involving the salience of role modelling have been invoked (see Mortimer *et al*., 1986), it remains unclear why employed mothers should exert little effect on the occupational choice of their children, especially their daughters. One possibility for this is that the extent to which mothers' choice of occupations was restricted in previous generations is no longer as limiting a factor for their daughters. The consequence of this is that daughters now have a larger range of occupations from which to choose, and this limits the magnitude of any statistical association between maternal occupation and their daughters' occupational choice.

FATHERS' SUBJECTIVE WORK EXPERIENCES AND THEIR CHILDREN'S BEHAVIOUR

The first issue examined in this chapter was the effects of fathers' job-related absence on their children. Thereafter, the effects of the type of occupation the father holds were considered. In so doing, the focus was on objective characteristics of the fathers' occupation. Although some account was taken of the fathers' subjective employment characteristics in considering whether specific job-related values (namely intrinsic, extrinsic and people-oriented values) mediate the relationship between the nature of fathers' occupation and their sons' occupational preferences, fathers' subjective employment experiences now become the principal focus.

The nature of the subjective job experiences that will be considered differ somewhat from those considered with respect to occupational linkages. Specifically, in considering occupational linkages, the focus was on occupationally relevant values, although there was limited consideration of the role of job satisfaction (Mortimer, 1976). On the contrary, the focus now moves specifically to employment experiences such as job dissatisfaction, the amount of autonomy inherent in the fathers' job, job stress and inter-role conflict.

Fathers' Job Dissatisfaction

As indicated in the previous chapter, there is considerable speculation and some data concerning the relationship between mothers' job satisfaction, mother–child interaction and child behaviour. Some research has considered whether fathers' job dissatisfaction fulfils a similar role in childrearing and child development (Cochran and Bronfenbrenner, 1979; Mortimer, 1976).

Honzik (1967) conducted one of the earlier studies assessing the effects of fathers' job satisfaction on children, exploring its relationship with children's intelligence. Honzik (1967) based her analyses on data initially collected as part of the Guidance Study at the Institute of Human Development in Berkeley, California. In this study, a representative sample of children born between 1928 and 1929 were followed for 30 years. Consistent with the findings on occupational linkages, Honzik (1967) found that while there was a relationship between paternal occupational satisfaction and intelligence for sons, no significant relationships emerged for daughters. Honzik (1967) followed the children until they were 30 years of age, and showed that this pattern of differential results for sons and daughters remained consistent across each of the sixteen occasions the sample was tested. Honzik's (1967) findings stimulate more questions than they can answer. First, she did not define 'occupation satisfaction', and this variable was probably confounded both by occupational success and socioeconomic status. Second, even in the presence of statistically significant relationships between fathers' job satisfaction and their sons' intelligence, it remains unclear why children's intelligence was associated with their fathers' job satisfaction. Possibly, the measure of job satisfaction reflected career success, which itself is associated with the father's intelligence to some extent. Finally, just how fathers' job satisfaction comes to influence their children, in other words, what factors mediate the effects of fathers' job satisfaction on children's behaviour, remains vague.

Barling (1986b) also investigated the effects of fathers' job dissatisfaction on their children, focusing on their children's social behaviours. He found that fathers' job dissatisfaction was associated with children's conduct problems and hyperactivity. Barling (1986b) also investigated perceived organizational climate and job involvement, but found no effects. Two aspects of these findings are notable, as they strengthen the veracity of the findings. First, Barling (1986b) controlled statistically for fathers' level of education in an attempt to excise the effects of socioeconomic status. Second, teacher reports of children's behaviour were used because of the biases that may be introduced (e.g. social desirability, autocorrelation) when parents report on their children and their own behaviour. Again, however, the issue of how job satisfaction affects specific behaviours, and why it is only job satisfaction remains unanswered.

One hypothesis that has been advanced to account for this process is that job dissatisfaction influences the way in which fathers interact with their children. In turn, it is the nature and quality of such father–child interactions that directly affect child behaviour (cf. Barling, Fullagar and Marchl-Dingle, 1988; Lerner and Galambos, 1985). Thus, in the present context, it is suggested that the existence of close father–child relationships enables children to recognize their fathers' job dissatisfaction and to appreciate its negative effects on their fathers (Barling, 1986b; Piotrkowski and Stark, 1987). Two separate empirical questions derive from this hypothesis. The first is whether a relationship does indeed exist between fathers' job dissatisfaction and father–child interactions. If this question is answered in the affirmative, the second question that emerges is whether these father–child interactions in turn influence children's behaviour. It is possible to pinpoint studies in the literature that have investigated each of these two issues. Grossman, Pollack and Golding (1988) assessed the role of fathers' job satisfaction and job involvement in predicting different aspects of the father–son relationship among five-year-old children. The two most striking findings were that the only significant predictor of the amount of time the father spent with his child on the weekend was his job satisfaction, and that this effect was negative: the greater the job satisfaction, the less time the father spent playing with the child. Moreover, the magnitude of this correlation ($r = -0.68$) was almost twice as large as the next highest correlations (those between fathers' occupation and fathers' socioeconomic status on the one hand and the amount of time spent with the child on the weekend on the other; $r = 0.38$ not significant). Consistent with this, fathers' job satisfaction was also the strongest predictor ($r = -0.53$) of the average amount of time the father spent playing with the child on a typical day. Although the difference in the magnitude of the correlation between fathers' job satisfaction and the other predictors was not as great in this instance, fathers' job satisfaction was again the most significant predictor of the amount of time spent in playing with the child. These results partially replicated Feldman, Nash and Aschenbrenner's (1983) result. They found that job dissatisfaction and low job salience predicted greater levels of playfulness between fathers and their infants aged six to eight months. However, because there is some uncertainty as to the construct validity or meaning of their job salience and job satisfaction variables, their results are somewhat more difficult to interpret.

Although job involvement did not predict either the amount of time spent on weekends or the amount of time spent playing by the father with his child/ren in Grosssman *et al.*'s (1988) study, the direction of the relationship between job satisfaction and both these aspects of the father–child relationship is consistent. Specifically, higher job satisfaction was associated with *less* time spent by the father with the child at the weekend, and *less* time spent by the father playing with the child (Grossman *et al.*, 1988). Nonetheless, considering these relationships in isolation would provide a truncated perspective of the association between employment experiences and the father-child relationship. As Grossman *et al.* (1988) note, both the quantity and the quality of the father–son relationship must be considered before a comprehensive understanding of the effects of fathers' employment experiences on sons' behaviour can be attained. Grossman *et al.* (1988) also focused on the connection between employment experiences and the quality of the father–child relationship. They showed that job satisfaction was significantly and positively associated with the extent to which fathers supported attempts at autonomy and affiliation by their children. These results are consistent with other studies investigating the relationship between fathers' job satisfaction and qualitative aspects of the father–child relationship. For example, Kemper and Reichler (1976b) showed that fathers' job satisfaction predicted the extent to which they positively rewarded their children, while their job dissatisfaction predicted their use of punishment. In addition, data from McKinley's (1964) earlier study provide some support for the notion that fathers' job satisfaction is positively associated with qualitative aspects of the father–son relationship. Even though McKinley (1964) relied on children to report retrospectively on the level of the father's job satisfaction, the quality of the father–child relationship suffered when the father was dissatisfied with his job. McKinley (1964) found that across all levels of socioeconomic status, fathers who were more dissatisfied with their jobs were more hostile in their interactions with their children, and used more severe disciplinary techniques.

From these studies, it is possible to suggest that two consistent patterns exist. Fathers who are satisfied with their jobs devote less time to their children. However, before it is inferred or concluded from this that fathers' job satisfaction exerts a general negative impact on the father–child relationship, it must be noted that the quality of the time spent with their children is positively associated with fathers' job satisfaction. Now that a consistent association has been established between a father's job satisfaction and the father–child relationship, the second empirical question to be answered is whether the father–child relationship mediates the link between fathers' job experiences and child behaviour. In other areas, parent–child interactions mediate the effects of unemployment on children's behaviour (McLoyd, 1989), and parents' marital dissatisfaction on the child (Emery, 1982). Emery (1982) suggested that under conditions of high marital dissatisfaction and conflict, children who have a close relationship with either parent are less likely to be affected negatively by the marital conflict. In other words, a close parent–child relationship would buffer the child against any negative effects that may follow from parental dissatisfaction. An alternative explanation consistent with literature on the effects of parents' subjective employment experiences on children (see Piotrkowski and Stark, 1987) is that it is perhaps through such close parent–child relationships that children will come to learn and appreciate the conditions their parents must endure. As a result, a close relationship with a father who is dissatisfied with his job will exacerbate any negative impact on the child. There is only one study in which this issue was assessed empirically.

Barling (1986b) investigated these contrasting hypotheses in a group of 161 fathers who were employed full time, and used a composite index of the father–child relationship reflecting the frequency with which certain activities took place. Specifically, the items assessed the extent to which the father played with or laughed with, read to, explained or taught things to, and hugged or held the child.

After statistically controlling for the effects of the fathers' educational level (as a criterion of socioeconomic status), Barling (1986b) showed that the father–child relationship moderated the effects of fathers' job satisfaction on teacher ratings of children's hyperactivity and conduct problems. Specifically, under conditions of a close father–child relationship, fathers' job dissatisfaction was associated with significantly higher levels of both hyperactivity and conduct problems. On the other hand, when fathers were dissatisfied with their jobs but the father–child relationship was not as close, scores for hyperactivity and conduct problems were significantly lower. This finding provides some support for Piotrkowski and Stark's (1987) suggestion that information about fathers' jobs and their sons' reactions to their jobs are conveyed through a close father–child relationship. Therefore, instead of buffering any negative effects of job dissatisfaction on the child (Emery, 1982), knowledge about fathers' job dissatisfaction would be transmitted to children overtly or covertly through such a relationship.

It should be noted, however, that the father–child relationship did not moderate the effects of fathers' job dissatisfaction on other child outcomes such as children's personality problems, immaturity or subcultural delinquency. First, these results parallel results from the literature on marital dissatisfaction and distress, where it is found consistently that marital dissatisfaction affects conduct problems (especially in boys), but not any these other three dimensions of behaviour (e.g. Emery, 1982). Second, it is possible that the children in Barling's (1986b) study were too young to manifest subcultural delinquency problems. Third, it is clear that the effects of different subjective employment experiences are transmitted to children through diverse mediating variables. It remains for future research to identify the precise nature of these mediating mechanisms. This is critical not only from a theoretical position, but also from a pragmatic perspective. It is doubtful whether it is possible to prevent large-scale job dissatisfaction. To ameliorate any negative effects of job dissatisfaction, therefore, it would be beneficial to be able to isolate the processes through which fathers' job dissatisfaction (and, of course, employed mothers' job dissatisfaction) exerts negative influences on children. For example, in the same way that research has investigated depression as an outcome of employment experiences for mothers (Hock and DeMeis, in press), and this depression in turn may mediate the relationship between mothers' employment experiences and children's behaviour (see Chapter 7), research should assess whether similar processes occur with fathers.

Fathers' General Employment Experiences

In considering the effects of fathers' subjective employment experiences, most research has focused on their job satisfaction. There has been some research endeavouring to isolate the effects of subjective employment experiences other than job satisfaction on children's behaviour. Unlike the research on the fathers' job dissatisfaction, research focusing on fathers' general subjective employment experiences has focused exclusively on its effects on the childrearing attitudes and behaviours, or the father–child relationship.

One study reported by Coburn and Edwards (1976) partially replicated findings of the study conducted on employed mothers by Piotrkowski and Katz (1982; see Chapter 7). Coburn and Edwards (1976) considered the relationship between the perceived degree of autonomy in one's job, and childrearing attitudes and values. Based on a sample of 875 male non-self-employed workers in British Columbia, Canada, Coburn and Edwards (1976) found that men who experienced higher levels of autonomy on the job valued self-control and independence for their children more than their counterparts experiencing low levels of job-related autonomy. Men experiencing lower levels of job-related autonomy were more likely to value obedience and good manners by their children than their counterparts who were high in job-related autonomy. Piotrkowski and Katz (1982) showed that mothers' autonomy on the job was negatively associated with children's voluntary attendance at school, whereas the mothers' skill utilization was positively associated with their children's scholastic achievement. Both studies support Kohn's (1969) hypothesis that job-related values are consistent with childrearing values. However, the causal nature of the relationship is unclear. While it is possible that occupations mould values, it is equally possible, as Coburn and Edwards (1976) note, that individuals choose occupations that are consistent with their pre-existing value system.

The experience and consequences of inter-role conflict for fathers and husbands have received substantially less attention than mothers' inter-role conflict. In one of the few studies that focused on inter-role conflict among men, Baruch and Barnett (1986b) investigated the effects of inter-role conflict on various aspects of fathers' participation in activities with their children. Their results demonstrate that fathers' participation in child care tasks (such as taking the child to a birthday party, the doctor or dentist, attendance at teacher interviews, cleaning up the child's room) was significantly associated with fathers' feelings that they required more time for their careers, and that family roles and employment roles interfered with each other.

There is some concern about the effects of negative employment experiences for fathers on their children. In particular, there are suggestions of an association between negative job stress and child abuse (Agathonos and Stathakopoulou, 1983; Justice and Duncan, 1978). Such an hypothesis would be consistent with findings already mentioned, namely that fathers' job dissatisfaction is associated with greater levels of father–child hostility (McKinley, 1964) and punishment of children, particularly of daughters (Kemper and Reichler, 1976b). In this context, child abuse would reflect an extraordinarily maladaptive form of parent–child interaction. However, the exact meaning of the findings of the studies cited above concerning a relationship between negative job stress and child abuse remains uncertain. Justice and Duncan present insufficient details (e.g. on their sample, their method or their analyses) to justify any conclusive statements. Agathonos and Stathkopoulou (1983) mainly focused on general life stress, while the nine items in their stress measure covered too wide a range to be readily interpretable. For example, it contained items on being fired, being unemployed for more than one month, retirement (and it is dubious whether such an item would be relevant to a group of individuals who had recently abused their children), and a change in job-related conditions. An inspection of these items also does not answer whether they assessed daily, acute or chronic job stressors (Pratt and Barling, 1988), or even job-related stressors. Perhaps most importantly, while Agathonos and Stathakopoulou (1983) found differences between abusive and non-abusive parents on general life stress, similar differences were not yielded in terms of job stress. In addition, from the perspective of the current discussion, neither Justice and Duncan (1978) nor Agathonos and Stathakopoulou (1983) stipulated whether they interviewed the mother or the father, or which parent was abusive. One other study purporting to investigate the relationship between fathers' job experiences (rather than job stress) and child abuse suffers from many of the same problems and thus remains uninterpretable. Specifically, O'Brien (1971) showed that violence was more likely to occur in families where husbands were underachieving in the dual role of worker/earner. However, like the previous studies cited, O'Brien (1971) provides insufficient information as to who was perpetrating the violence (i.e. the mother or the father) and also fails to separate family violence on the basis of whether wife abuse or child abuse occurred.

Consequently, some consistency exists in the findings of studies focusing on the effects of fathers' subjective work experiences on their children. While fathers' job satisfaction was associated with less time devoted to children, both job satisfaction and general employment experiences positively influenced the father–child interactions. However, there is no empirical support for the hypothesis that job stress is associated with child abuse.

FATHERS' EMPLOYMENT AND THEIR CHILDREN: CONCLUSION

In reviewing the effects of fathers' employment on their children, a number of topics should be considered. These include a contrast of the effects of objective and subjective employment characteristics, a contrast of the effects of mothers' and fathers' employment on their children, the need to focus on specific employment experiences, the nature of the research designs used and the need for further research in this area that targets specific attention on causal inferences.

With regard to the first issue, namely the relative effects of fathers' objective and subjective job characteristics on their children, the data are quite clear. There is no empirical support for the belief that fathers' ordinary job-related absences exert negative effects on mother–son interactions or on children's behaviour. However, some studies indicate that fathers' extraordinary job-related absences may exert negative effects on children, but methodological problems (e.g. selection factors, non-comparability of control and experimental groups) need to be resolved before this conclusion is warranted. Fathers' subjective employment experiences consistently predict both father–son interactions as well as children's behaviour.

Specifically, although positive employment experiences are related to decreased time spent with children, positive employment experiences (job satisfaction in particular) are associated with closer father–son relationships and more appropriate behaviour on the part of children. Fathers' occupational choice appears to influence their sons' occupational preferences. The research of Mortimer and her colleagues (Mortimer, 1974, 1976; Mortimer and Kumka, 1982; Mortimer *et al.*, 1986) underlines the importance of fathers' personal work values as direct and indirect influences in the process of occupational linkages. Again, therefore, the data are consistent with the notion that it is fathers' subjective work experiences that exert effects on their children, especially sons.

The second issue that emerges from this chapter is whether mothers' and fathers' employment status and experiences exert similar and/or different effects on their children. It is suggested that the similarities between the effects of mothers' and fathers' employment status and employment experiences far outweigh any differential influence that they may exert on parent–child interactions and children's behaviour. Specifically, ordinary work-related absence of the mother or the father exerts no consistent detrimental influence. While extraordinary job-related parent absences (e.g. unpredictable shift schedules, prolonged absences) may exert some influences—this is more likely to be a function of the scheduling or amount of absence rather than a function of the work itself. On the other hand, when employment is experienced positively by either the mother or the father, the quality of parent–child relationships and children's behaviour is enhanced. The one exception to the conclusion that fathers' and mothers' employment exerts comparable effects follows from the literature on occupational linkages. While the effects of fathers' occupational choices and preferences on their sons have been documented, there is no support for similar effects between fathers and daughters, or mothers and their sons and daughters. Yet this is not attributable to the absence of such effects as much as it is attributable to the fact that such research has not been reported in the literature. Possibly, mothers are involved in a more restricted range of occupations than fathers, while the range of occupations open to their daughters is expanding, as a result of which linkages between mothers and daughters are less likely to be significant. As well, there may be different effects regarding the influence of mothers' employment status, especially on their daughters. As noted in the previous chapter, the children of employed mothers are themselves more likely to seek employment than children of non-employed mothers. Furthermore, in the same way that the values inherent in the fathers' occupation affect sons' occupational choice, similar effects are apparent between mothers and daughters (Breakwell *et al.*, 1988; Tangri, 1972).

Accordingly, it is fitting at this stage to call for a *rapprochement* between these two literatures. Because mothers' and fathers' employment experiences exert similar effects on their interactions with their children and on their children's behaviour, the more important question is whether the effects of mothers' and fathers' employment experiences are additive. In other words, what are the combined effects of mothers' and fathers' employment experiences on their children? If mothers and fathers both experience their jobs positively, is effect on their children greater than when only one parent is satisfied with his or her work? Alternatively, what are the effects on children if one parent is satisfied with his or her job, yet the other parent is extremely dissatisfied? Reconceptualizing the effects of parental employment experiences on children in this way is now especially important because of the large number of mothers now employed, and the considerable role accorded to the mother as a role model to her children. In addition, such a reconceptualization would extend the notion of the 'family work day' (Kingston and Nock, 1985; Nock and Kingston, 1984) away from a consideration of the joint amount of time worked by parents each day towards a consideration of the simultaneous effects of both parents' job experiences.

Third, based on the research of Piotrkowski and Katz (1982) and Coburn and Edwards (1976), it is apparent that focusing on specific job experiences (e.g. autonomy) may provide explanations as to why some parental job experiences influence specific child behaviours. Given that a general link between parental employment experiences and child behaviour has been established, it remains for research to isolate why specific employment experiences are tied to particular parent–child interactions and child behaviours.

The level of sophistication of the research addressing fathers' employment is worthy of attention. Attempts at conceptual modelling that characterize recent research on occupational linkages between father and son, or that characterize the research on employment experiences and marital functioning (see Chapters 3–6) are not evident in the research on fathers' subjective employment experiences using univariate approaches. It is likely that this reflects the recency with which fathers' subjective employment experiences have generated concern. Nonetheless, presentation of more complex models and the use of multivariate statistics would strengthen our understanding of the processes involved.

Lastly, in any research on the influence of either mothers' or fathers' employment experiences, it remains to be seen whether parental employment experiences *cause* changes in their interactions with their children, or in their children's behaviour. One alternative is that 'problem' children detract from their parents' attention, effort and success on the job, making it is less likely that they will be satisfied with their jobs. Yet with very few exceptions (e.g. Mortimer and Kumka, 1982; Mortimer *et al.*, 1986), the literature on both mothers' and fathers' employment experiences is characterized by cross-sectional research designs which do not allow alternative hypotheses such as this to be tested. This issue will be considered further in Chapter 10.

Chapter 9
Unemployment and Family Functioning

Our nation continues to grapple with a deep depression that colors and shapes all aspects of American life.... These economic conditions are taking their toll on the health of our nation's citizens. Unemployment, in particular, touches every aspect of family and community life, resulting in higher divorce rates, increased incidence of alcoholism and drug abuse, child and spouse abuse, and juvenile delinquency.

(US Senator, D. Riegle, 1982, p. 1113)

There can be very little doubt that unemployment constitutes one of the major social problems confronting society today. A number of factors combine to magnify the problem. First, it is not just individuals who are affected by unemployment. Instead, families and even entire communities are affected by unemployment. Second, although the unemployment rate in most westernized societies in the latter part of the 1980s has generally been lower than in the preceding ten years, unemployment still directly affects millions of families. Third, rates of unemployment fluctuate continuously, forcing constant individual, family and community adaptation. Fourth, widespread unemployment means that adolescents must question whether they can realistically expect to be employed on completion of their schooling. Employment can no longer be considered a 'right' accorded to all. A poignant interchange from one of the earlier meetings between former US President Ronald Reagan and Soviet General Secretary Gorbachev illustrates the larger social question this raises. After Reagan had harangued Gorbachev about what he regarded as the pathetic human rights record of the USSR, Gorbachev responded that the record of the United States was nothing to be proud of because millions of people are unemployed in the United States. In contrast, Gorbachev countered that in the USSR employment is viewed as a fundamental human right.

A review of the literature reveals that large-scale unemployment is by no means a recent phenomenon in the Western world, and that there is a long history of interest by social scientists and politicians in unemployment that continues unabated today. For example, Fryer and Payne (1986) note that Taylor's (1909) early *Bibliography of Unemployment and the Unemployed*, which refers to some 800 books, pamphlets, documents and articles, has been criticized because its ahistorical perspective ignored the fact that unemployment had already been a problem for three centuries. In the twentieth century, the large-scale unemployment that has afflicted the United States, Britain and most European countries, first within the 1930s and again in the 1970s and early 1980s stimulated an enormous body of research on the consequences of unemployment.

CONTRASTING UNEMPLOYMENT IN THE 1930s AND 1980s

There are two separate literatures examining the relationship between unemployment and the family, which can be distinguished on the basis of the two different time periods in which they were generated, namely the 1930s and the 1980s. In comparing the two literatures on unemployment, numerous authors have raised questions as to whether research conducted during the 1930s can guide an understanding of current unemployment (e.g. Fryer and Payne, 1986; Jahoda, 1982; Thomas, McCabe and Berry, 1980). First, the subjective experience of unemployment during these two time periods may be distinct, on both a psychological and a financial level. Second, the methodologies used to study unemployment and the family within each of these time periods varied considerably. Because of these differences, it is critical to examine these characteristics with a view to ascertaining whether generalizations from the research conducted during the 1930s can direct research investigating, or guide an understanding of the current effects of unemployment on the family. Third, the prevalence of unemployment was substantially higher during the 1930s than during the 1980s. It was not uncommon for average unemployment levels to exceed 30% during the 1930s, and to range between 10% and 15% during the early 1980s in the United States, the United Kingdom and Europe. In presenting these statistics, it is critical to note that unemployment statistics are invariably inaccurate and comparisons between countries and regions across time periods are hazardous. First, the definition of unemployment varies widely between countries. Some countries require that an individual actively seeks employment to be regarded as unemployed, others no longer regard an individual as unemployed after a period of one year, in which case the individual is placed on the welfare role. Second, governments can manipulate the definition of unemployment to change its apparent prevalence for their own political purposes, for example by arbitrarily including or excluding seasonal unemployment or students seeking vacation employment. Third, official statistics ignore individuals who are involuntarily working part time, or who have stopped seeking employment because they are so discouraged. Consequently, most official unemployment statistics should be regarded as underestimates, and have been for some considerable time. This problem is not specific to the experience of unemployment in the 1980s. Indeed, George Orwell had already noted this very same problem in his 1937 book, *The Road to Wigan Pier*.

The overall rate and community-specific rate of unemployment may be extremely significant in determining the way in which individuals are affected, possibly because unemployed individuals may look to their community for a social comparison group to help account for their experience and guide their future expectations. For example, in one recent study no differences emerged between employed and unemployed individuals in terms of marital satisfaction (Kessler, Turner and House, 1987). The authors suggested that no differences occurred in this study because individuals viewed their unemployment as beyond their personal control, because this study was conducted in a Michigan community experiencing unusually high levels of unemployment. Likewise, 1970 census data from Denmark show that the risk of mortality from earlier unemployment is moderated significantly by local unemployment levels: mortality is highest following unemployment in communities where the unemployment rate is high (Iversen *et al.*, 1987). It is also possible that reactions to unemployment within a community suffering from high levels of unemployment will be tempered by differing expectations for employment.

A further difference between the unemployment of the 1930s and that of the 1980s is financial. There was little if any unemployment insurance during the 1930s. The effects of husbands' unemployment were magnified by the fact that very few wives were employed during this period. Hence when husbands lost their jobs, the family had no income. In contrast, most individuals who lost their jobs during the 1980s retained at least a portion of their income for some time (e.g. one year) either through unemployment insurance systems (e.g. Batt, 1983; Thomas *et al.*, 1980) or through spousal salaries if both spouses had been employed. As a result, the experience of financial hardship altered dramatically between these two periods. This distinction is critical, because the experience of economic hardship and the experience of unemployment are different. Hence, economic hardship and unemployment may exert different influences on family functioning. In other words, economic hardship exerts effects independent of unemployment.

The severity of the overall effects of economic hardship on the family during the 1930s can be adequately described using a few of the examples cited by Jahoda (1982), most of which would be unheard of today. First, in some communities with high levels of unemployment, malnutrition affected 21% of school children. Second, daily caloric intake in families of the employed averaged 2705 contrasted with 1951 in unemployed families. In two communities in which unemployment was extremely high, 57% and 76% of the children were under normal weight. Third, in one Polish community, less than half the children had shoes, and over 50% of the children of mineworkers were absent from school because of a lack of adequate clothing. The implications of these statistics for family functioning are many. Aside from any adverse health, scholastic or social consequences for the children, the position and perceived status of the father/husband as breadwinner was severely threatened. Traditional roles may have been reversed at times, with fathers staying at home and mothers accepting full-time employment. In sharp contrast, largely because of the experience in the 1930s, unemployment insurance and social welfare schemes had been introduced in most countries by the 1980s, and the financial effects of unemployment have been reduced somewhat.

On a methodological level, the studies conducted in the 1930s have often been characterized as inadequate. The problem here is not the quantity of studies conducted. Indeed, there were many longitudinal investigations (e.g. Bakke, 1933, 1940; Elder, 1974). Most of these studies, however, relied solely on qualitative analyses and few used comparison groups of employed individuals. Although case studies are still used in the 1980s (e.g. Binns and Mars, 1984; Briar, 1978; Clark, 1987; Fagan, 1979; Hartley, 1987; Marsden and Duff, 1975), most current studies on the effects of unemployment on the family are more consistent with the positivist tradition, and hence use quantitative methods and control groups of employed individuals. In addition, perhaps consistent with the most salient issue at the time, most of the earlier investigations focused primarily on the economic consequences of unemployment, with fewer investigations of the effects of unemployment on marital and/or family functioning (e.g. Angell, 1936; Cavan and Ranck, 1938; Komarovsky, 1940).

Numerous societal changes since the 1930s further limit the extent to which the results from early studies can guide current knowledge and understanding of the effects of unemployment on marriage and the family. For example, contrasted with the social situation prevailing during the 1930s, in particular the perceived and actual power of the husband, gender-related social attitudes have become more egalitarian. Consequently, job loss might now be less devastating to the position of the husband in the marriage and family, as his presumed loss of power and inadequacy as family breadwinner would be seen as less important.

Despite these differences between the two time periods, it would be premature to discard completely the findings from studies conducted on the consequences of unemployment for the family during the 1930s. Instead, findings from the 1930s can still be used to suggest which questions must be answered in the 1980s. Also, Fineman (1983) states that it is only through qualitative studies that the phenomenological experience of the unemployed can be appreciated, and the 1930s provided several detailed qualitative studies. Further, some of the most important research on the effects of unemployment on the family (specifically, on children) consists of longitudinal data initially collected during the 1930s, and aspects of those data continue to be re-analysed (e.g., Elder, 1974; Elder and Caspi, 1988).

It is the aim of this chapter to consider the effects of unemployment on family functioning. Consistent with the convention followed throughout this book, the influence of unemployment on marital functioning will be considered first, followed by effects of parental unemployment on parent–child interaction and children's behaviour. However, two subjects should be addressed beforehand: why unemployment is expected to exert widespread negative effects on the family, and the effects of unemployment on other aspects of personal functioning.

UNEMPLOYMENT AS A MAJOR PSYCHOSOCIAL STRESSOR

It is clear that unemployment is a psychosocial stressor associated with considerable psychological strain (Fryer and Payne, 1986; Warr, Jackson and Banks, 1988).

The most dominant themes that emerge in attempts to explain the stressful nature of unemployment include unemployment as a major life event, and unemployment as a role stressor or psychosocial transition. Within the major life events approach to stress, unemployment is held to be a major stressor. In constructing their *Organizational Change Inventory*, Sarason and Johnson (1979) included unemployment as one of the major events. Although unemployment is not one of the events on Sarason's *Life Events Schedule* (Sarason, Johnson and Siegel, 1978), both retirement and being fired from work are included. In addition, negative consequences frequently associated with unemployment (e.g. financial difficulties, change in social activities, marital problems, illness) are assessed directly.

Unemployment also fits the definition of a role stressor. Warr (1984a, b) describes the considerable role changes and readjustment required when moving between employment and unemployment (e.g. Jackson *et al.*, 1983). In turn, these role transitions precipitate major life crises because of the personal role redefinitions required and the instability and unpredictability that they generate. Consistent with a role transition perspective, Archer and Rhodes (1987) compare the psychological significance of job loss to the process of bereavement because of the significance of the employment role. Finally, Baum, Fleming and Reddy (1986) submit that unemployment is generally stressful because of the actual loss and perceptions of loss of control at the time of the job loss, and the subsequent development of learned helplessness.

Whatever the mechanism involved, unemployment is a chronic stressor. This is an important point, because it follows that, like other chronic stressors (e.g. Dew *et al.*, 1987), its effects will endure for some time (Pratt and Barling, 1988). Perhaps the enormity of unemployment as a chronic role stressor can best be appreciated from Warr's (1984a, pp. 425–6) statement that:

> ... the transition from employment to unemployment is more than the removal of features of the employed role, such as a reduction in money or in required tasks. It also involves introduction of features of a new role as unemployed person, many of which are unpleasant, and it brings with it changes in the number and content of other roles which are not themselves directly linked to occupational issues. Finally, these three types of change generate instability and unpredictability, experienced loss of personal control, a need to cope through the acquisition of new perspectives and skills, and a requirement to resolve questions about oneself which may otherwise never be raised.

UNEMPLOYMENT AND PSYCHOLOGICAL WELL-BEING

Before considering the effects of unemployment on marital functioning and child behaviour, it will be helpful to summarize the results of the voluminous body of research on unemployment and psychological well-being. While many studies assess the effects of unemployment on aspects of psychological well-being, there are far fewer studies focusing on the effects of unemployment on the family.

Consequently, the results of these more general studies may help in guiding the way in which the effects of unemployment on the family are approached. It is also likely that the effects of unemployment on individuals' psychological distress mediate the influence of unemployment on the family (e.g. Liem and Liem, 1988). Several aspects of individual well-being that may be influenced by unemployment will be considered briefly. These include self-esteem, depression and mortality, anxiety and alcohol use.

A number of relatively unequivocal conclusions can be made concerning the psychological consequences of unemployment because of the vast number of studies conducted with large samples, many of which used longitudinal designs. As a group, unemployed individuals fare more poorly than employed individuals on virtually all aspects of psychological functioning (Fryer and Payne, 1986; Warr, 1984a, b; Warr *et al.*, 1988). More specifically, findings suggest consistently that unemployed individuals as a group are more depressed than their employed counterparts, and that depression follows unemployment (e.g. Feather and O'Brien, 1986; Patton and Noller, 1984; Tiggemann and Winefield, 1984). Oliver and Pomicter (1981) showed that the predictors of depression differed for unemployed and employed individuals. Specifically, employment potential in the following year and both objective financial status and subjective financial concerns were predictive of depression for unemployed individuals, but not for currently employed individuals. Research findings generally show a similar trend between employed and unemployed individuals with regard to self-esteem. Although some studies find no differences in self-esteem between these two groups (e.g. Gurney, 1980; Hartley, 1980), Fryer and Payne (1986) suggest that is due to the use of global measures of self-esteem (e.g. Hartley, 1980), and they note that when specific aspects of self-esteem are measured, unemployed individuals score consistently worse than their employed individuals (Feather and O'Brien, 1986). Unemployment is also associated with cognitive difficulties such as attention and concentration problems (Fryer and Warr, 1984) among working class men.

A related issue is whether unemployment is associated with an increased risk of mortality. Data from two studies based on national census data support the link between unemployment and mortality. Moser and his colleagues (Moser, Fox and Jones, 1984; Moser and Goldblatt, 1986) showed that unemployment increased the risk of mortality by 20–23% in England and Wales. Iversen *et al.* (1987) based their analyses on the 1970 census data collected in Denmark on 2 million employed individuals, and 22 000 unemployed individuals. They showed that being unemployed on 9 November 1970 increased the risk of death by 40–50% over the next decade after controlling for marital status and occupation. The two most significant causes of death for this high-risk group were suicides and accidents.

A large body of research focuses on the anxiety of unemployed individuals. Findings from this area are informative because the questionnaire used in many of these studies, namely Goldberg's (1972) twelve-item General Health Questionnaire (GHQ), allows inferences to be drawn about the clinical meaning of findings:

individuals scoring equal to or greater than 3 are at risk of manifesting clinically significant anxiety problems. Results from both cross-sectional and longitudinal analyses suggest that unemployed individuals have significantly higher anxiety levels than employed individuals, and that the process of becoming unemployed significantly increases anxiety levels (e.g. Jackson *et al.*, 1983). Warr (1984b) examined findings from studies using the twelve-item GHQ and found that in four studies, between 54% and 62% of the unemployed samples scored 3 or more, in contrast to employed samples, in which the range was 15% to 25%. Even though Fryer and Payne (1986) argue that these figures overestimate the psychiatric risk, unemployed individuals still remain at greater risk of developing psychiatric symptoms.

One final area worthy of consideration is whether unemployed individuals consume more alcohol than their employed counterparts. Despite the belief that unemployed individuals consume more alcohol, and are more likely to be alcoholic than their unemployed counterparts, results do not necessarily support the notion that there are differences between employed and unemployed individuals in terms of the amount of alcohol consumed (e.g. Cook *et al.*, 1982; Smart, 1979). Three recent studies shed more light on this phenomenon. Warr and Payne (1983b) asked middle class and lower class men in Britain how their behaviour had changed since they had become unemployed. Overall, they retrospectively reported a significant *decrease* in the amount of alcohol they consumed. Iversen and Klausen (1986) conducted a longitudinal study in Sweden, in which they examined patterns of alcohol consumption among a group of shipyard workers seven months prior to their layoffs, and then again eighteen months after their layoff. Of the 100 workers initially tested, those who remained unemployed were significantly more likely to have *decreased* their alcohol consumption, while those who had regained employment were more likely to have increased their consumption after their re-employment. Iversen and Klausen (1986) suggest two possible explanations for this. First, unemployed individuals may reduce their alcohol consumption because they have less money available to spend on alcohol. Second, the social groups in which unemployed individuals used to drink were primarily work related, and may have disintegrated subsequent to their job loss. In a separate study using a large random sample in Great Britain, irrespective of the amount of alcohol consumed, unemployed individuals had far more hazardous drinking styles than employed individuals (Crawford *et al.*, 1987). In other words, because they were more likely to binge drink, any particular drinking episode was potentially dangerous.

The results of these three studies suggest, therefore, that men consume less alcohol during periods of unemployment. However, their pattern of drinking may become more risky. In this sense, the effects of unemployment on alcohol consumption may still mediate the relationship between unemployment and marital functioning, because alcohol abuse exerts negative effects on marital satisfaction (Dunn *et al.*, 1987) and is a correlate of family violence (O'Leary, 1988). The importance of these general indices of psychological well-being will be discussed again later in this chapter, when their possible role as mediating factors in the relationship between unemployment and family functioning are considered.

UNEMPLOYMENT AND MARITAL FUNCTIONING

In examining the relationship between unemployment and marital functioning, it is worth noting the predominant assumption on which such investigations are founded. Specifically, irrespective of when the particular studies were conducted, most research on the consequences of unemployment for marital functioning assumes that unemployment exerts detrimental effects not only on the unemployed individuals but also on both partners within the relationship. Two points about this assumption are noteworthy. First, it provides an indication of the acceptance of an open systems perspective in the literature. Second, there is a gender-specific bias, because the research investigates the effects of *husbands'* unemployment on their wives. Recall from Chapter 7, however, that negative effects are presumed to emerge when wives are employed.

Unemployment and Marital Functioning: Earlier Studies

Mirra Komarovsky's (1940) *The Unemployed Man and His Family* is perhaps the most well-known case study focusing on the effects of unemployment and marital functioning. Komarovsky's study is worth considering in some detail as it is similar to other case studies conducted during the 1930s, and since that time. Komarovsky (1940) interviewed a relatively small sample (59 families of 89 who were approached) drawn from an industrial area just outside of New York City during the winter of 1935–36. Each member of the family was interviewed privately. Parents received $1.00 each, and children 50 cents for their participation, and all were guaranteed that their responses were confidential. Adults were interviewed for between two and four hours each, and children for about one hour. Interestingly, sex biases are evident in the location of the interviews. Mothers were interviewed mainly at home, fathers were frequently interviewed '... over a glass of beer in a nearby restaurant'(p. 6), while interviews with the children were conducted '... in a drug store over an ice-cream' (p. 6). Notes were taken after the interview, and the length of each record for the entire family ranged between 25 and 70 typewritten pages (with an average of 35 pages).

Consistent with prevailing social beliefs and stereotypes of the time, Komarovsky (1940) was interested in the effects of unemployment on husbands' authority, status and power within the family. Her hypothesis was that unemployment would lead to a deterioration in the husbands' control and authority, and she was further interested in the consequences of such a deterioration. One of the biases inherent in the interpretation of and generalizations from case studies such as the one conducted by Komarovsky (1940) is immediately apparent from her analysis of whether there was a deterioration in the husbands' status. Komarovsky states that 'Unemployment does tend to lower the status of the husband' (p. 23), but immediately points out that 'It has had this effect in 13 out of 58 families included in the study' (p. 23). An examination of Komarovsky's Table 1 further shows that while no husband's status increased because of his unemployment, there was no change in status for 44 of the husbands. Yet Komarovsky then provides detailed analyses, using long quotations, of three of the thirteen families where there was evidence of a deterioration in the husbands' authority and status.

Komarovsky (1940) also analysed factors that precipitated a deterioration in the husband's power, and suggests that the husband's diminished breadwinner role, the increase in the amount of time he spent at home, and changes within the husband consequent to his unemployment precipitated his diminished status and authority within the marriage. Nonetheless, it would be interesting to determine which psychological factors were present in the 44 husbands who did not manifest any deterioration in authority or status. Also, more recent studies suggest that the additional amount of time spent at home by the husband does not necessarily lead to a deterioration in marital functioning (e.g. Brinkerhoff and White, 1978). In fact, Thomas *et al*. (1980) showed that 15% of the men in their study reported that their marital relationships had improved since their job loss.

Komarovsky (1940) was also interested in the consequences of deteriorations in the husbands' status and authority for specific aspects of the marital relationship. Thirty-eight of the 59 couples provided information on their sexual relationship during their husbands' unemployment. Of these, sixteen showed no change in their sexual relationship. The remaining 22 all evidenced a worsening of the sexual relationship; in four of these couples, all sexual contact ceased when the husband lost his job. When asked for their reasons for the decline, eight of the couples mentioned causes not related to the experience of unemployment, for example ill-health or ageing of the couple. (However, Komarovsky's conclusion that ill-health was not related to the experience of unemployment might be re-evaluated in light of subsequent research suggesting that an increase in psychosomatic symptoms is a consistent consequence of unemployment; Fryer and Payne, 1986). The remaining fourteen couples all mentioned factors related to their unemployment. Specifically, eleven mentioned the fear of pregnancy and its associated financial burdens, two wives referred to a loss of respect for their husbands because of their unemployment, and the remaining wife alluded to her 'general anxiety' Clearly, very few couples attributed decreases in their sexual contact to the husbands' perceived loss of authority and power within the family.

One characteristic of the sample which would limit the generalizability of any findings is the definition of unemployment. Komarovsky (1940) reports 'duration of relief' (p. 134) for the sample as follows: 4 men had been unemployed for one year, 12 for two years, 14 for three years, 21 for four years and 8 for five years. Most research on unemployment today would focus on individuals who were unemployed for two years or less, and many legal definitions of unemployment would exclude individuals who had been without a job for more than a year (at which time they are placed on welfare), thereby excluding them from such studies. Also, because the duration of employment is associated with its consequences in general (Fryer and Payne, 1986; Warr, 1984a, b), as well as with marital functioning (Atkinson, Liem and Liem, 1986), this represents a significant difference from the situation in the 1980s.

Since Komarovsky (1940) reported the results of her case study, there have been many studies in the literature that either directly or indirectly investigate the possible effects of unemployment on marital functioning using the case study approach (e.g. Binns and Mars, 1984; Briar, 1978; Fagan, 1979; Hartley, 1987; Marsden and Duff, 1975). In keeping with recent reviews (e.g. Fryer and Payne, 1986), these studies will not be examined further. This is not to imply that such qualitative studies are without value. On the contrary, they can provide unique insights into the phenomenological experience of unemployment. However, as Fryer and Payne (1986) argue, the way in which these studies have been conducted and reported does not provide for ready comparisons across different studies and samples, thereby limiting their utility when attempting to generalize from their findings. Only when qualitative research is based on techniques that facilitate such comparisons (e.g. Van Maanen, Dabbs and Faulkner, 1982) will an integration of the findings from case studies be possible.

Unemployment and Marital Functioning: Studies from the 1980s

Marital adjustment

There are several studies in which the global marital adjustment of employed and unemployed men has been contrasted. Although Friedemann (1986) investigated both unemployment and economic stress, she only reports a significant positive correlation between economic stress and marital problems. The meaning of this relationship remains unclear because no findings are presented as to whether marital problems are higher in the unemployed sample than in the employed sample, regardless of economic distress. Moreover, the nature of the marital problems under consideration remain obscure because scores on this variable were derived from a set of unstated, open-ended questions in an interview.

In their study of 89 families, Brinkerhoff and White (1978) contrasted unemployed with employed individuals (62% of their sample were unemployed). Although Brinkerhoff and White (1978) explicitly acknowledged that marital satisfaction is a multidimensional construct, they chose only to investigate global marital satisfaction. Neither spouse's marital satisfaction differed from husbands' unemployment status. Also, Brinkerhoff and White (1978) found no relationship between total family income from all sources and either spouse's marital satisfaction. However, husband unemployment and total family income exerted a significant additive effect on husbands' marital satisfaction. Specifically, unemployed husbands whose family income was low were significantly more dissatisfied with their marriages than any of the other three groups (viz. unemployed husbands with an acceptable family income, or employed husbands irrespective of their income). A similar interaction effect did not emerge for wives.

One problem with Brinkerhoff and White's (1978) investigation is their sole focus on a global criterion of marital satisfaction. Larson (1984) focused more broadly in his comparison of 40 employed males and 41 males who had been unemployed for approximately six months. All 81 men held or had held blue collar jobs in the construction or meat processing industry. In this study, in which wives were also surveyed, Larson (1984) compared the two groups in terms of global as well as specific aspects of marital satisfaction. He found significant differences regarding total marital adjustment between the employed and unemployed groups. After controlling for educational level, the adjusted mean score for the unemployed group was 107.98, and that of the employed group was 114.07 on Spanier's Dyadic Adjustment Scale. Larson (1984) further analysed the marital adjustment of these two groups by contrasting their scores on the subscales of Spanier's (1976) Dyadic Adjustment Scale. No significant differences emerged in terms of the Satisfaction, Cohesion or Affection subscales. In contrast, the scores of the unemployed individuals were significantly lower than their employed counterparts on the Consensus subscale (adjusted M's 47.86 vs 51.81). Two aspects of Larson's (1984) findings are particularly noteworthy. First, the use of the Dyadic Adjustment Scale subscales enabled Larson to isolate which specific aspect of marital adjustment was influenced by unemployment. As can be seen, the affective component of marital adjustment was not related to the men's unemployment. However, unemployed husbands reported less consensus in their marriages, suggesting more disagreements and arguments in relationships in which the husband is unemployed. Second, although the differences between these two groups in total adjustment and consensus were statistically significant, it is questionable whether the magnitude of these differences was clinically significant. First, the dyadic adjustment score of the unemployed group was within one standard deviation of Spanier's (1976) married sample (i.e. the sample Spanier was using as the 'normal' group), and was substantially higher than the mean score of Spanier's (1976) group of divorced individuals. Second, although the adjusted mean Consensus score of the unemployed group was within one standard deviation of Spanier's (1976) divorced group, Larson's (1984) employed group scored within one standard deviation of both Spanier's (1976) divorced and married groups.

In terms of more specific indices of marital adjustment, Larson (1984) also investigated whether there were any differences in marital communication between their two groups. Employed husbands were significantly more satisfied with the perceived quality of marital communication than were their unemployed counterparts, again after controlling for the effects of educational level (adjusted M's = 101.37 vs 92.12 respectively). Some caution should be exercised in interpreting and generalizing from this finding concerning marital communication, however, because like other studies, Larson's (1984) measures of marital communication and marital adjustment may well have been highly correlated (e.g. Suchet and Barling, 1986), and the magnitude of the difference between the two groups may not be sufficient to indicate a meaningful or clinical difference (as opposed to a statistical difference). Furthermore, this finding needs to be replicated because there are no other studies focusing on marital communication among the unemployed.

When Atkinson *et al.* (1986) contrasted different indices of marital functioning among employed and unemployed husbands, they found that unemployed husbands experienced poorer marital quality than their employed counterparts. Consistent with studies showing that the duration of unemployment is associated with psychological distress (e.g. Fryer and Payne, 1986; Warr, 1984a, b) Atkinson *et al.* (1986) showed that the duration of unemployment was also associated with marital distress. Specifically, marital support decreased as the number of weeks of unemployment increased. As predicted, these results suggest that unemployment is a chronic stressor, and its effects on marital functioning will last as long as the stressor itself, as long as there is any concern that the effects of the stressor are not yet over, or that the stressor may recur.

Marital role performance

There is speculation that major role changes occur when husbands lose their jobs, especially if wives then seek and obtain employment. There are at least two ways of investigating the effects of unemployment on marital role performance: first, by contrasting the participation of employed and unemployed husbands in household tasks; and, second, by assessing whether any role changes occur following husbands' job loss. Despite curiosity about the effects of unemployment on marital role performance, there are only three investigations directly contrasting the marital role performance of employed and unemployed individuals and their spouses. As part of a larger study of change in social behaviours following unemployment in England, Warr and Payne (1983b) studied 196 working class and 203 middle class, married white men who had been unemployed for between six and twelve months. They were interested in the amount of domestic work completed by husbands, and investigated five specific domestic behaviours: namely, completion of household tasks; shopping for food and other household articles; child care; and preparing meals for oneself or others. From their subjects' retrospective accounts, Warr and Payne (1983b) concluded that both working class and middle class men increased their participation in all these activities after they lost their jobs. In a second study, Warr (1984c) focused exclusively on a larger sample of unemployed, working class men, and found the same pattern: males increased their participation in domestic activities following their job loss.

In investigating the household division of labour following unemployment, Shamir (1986) used both research strategies described above. First, he compared groups of unemployed and employed men and women, and then reported data from a six-month longitudinal analysis of the unemployed men in the same sample. Shamir (1986) focused on eleven household tasks among employed (*n* = 159) and unemployed (*n* = 126) men and women in Israel. Over and above those household tasks included in Warr's studies (Warr and Payne, 1983b; Warr, 1984c), Shamir (1986) also investigated more specific household tasks such as planning meals, cleaning and taking out the garbage, playing with and helping children with their homework, household and car repairs and maintenance, and participation in decision making concerning family finances. Not surprisingly, women performed more household tasks than men, irrespective of unemployment status. Shamir's (1986) cross-sectional data also provided support for the notion that unemployed individuals assume more household responsibilities than their employed counterparts, irrespective of gender. However, this effect pertained only to some of the tasks considered, namely shopping, cleaning the house and taking out the garbage, and handling financial matters. Shamir's (1986) longitudinal analysis replicated his and Warr and Payne's (1983b) cross-sectional studies. Shamir (1986) recontacted his unemployed sample six months after the first survey, and found a statistically significant trend for re-employed men and women to decrease their participation in household tasks. Two observations from Shamir's (1986) data provide further insights into the role performance of unemployed individuals. First, when unemployed individuals increased their role performance, the new tasks fulfilled were primarily solitary in nature (e.g. shopping, cleaning, handling finances); they did not necessarily lead to increased interaction between the spouses. Second, unemployment did not bring about major role reversals between spouses of the nature and magnitude depicted in some qualitative studies (e.g., Hartley, 1987; Kaufman, 1982).

Data from Liem and Liem's (1988) longitudinal panel study in the Boston area further replicate the above studies. While their earlier analyses suggested that both spouses initially perceived that husbands decreased their marital role performance following unemployment (Atkinson *et al.*, 1986), Liem and Liem (1988) later found that when objective role performance was assessed, the earlier findings (Shamir, 1986; Warr, 1984c; Warr and Payne, 1983b) were replicated. Husbands' objective marital role performance increased immediately following unemployment, and continuing unemployment was associated with increased participation in household tasks by the unemployed husband.

At least two explanations might account for the fact that unemployed men participate more in household responsibilities. First, unemployed men may simply have more time available to them, and this is consistent with data showing that shift workers who are at home during the day complete more marital roles. Second, husbands share more in household responsibilities as the ratio of husbands' and wives' contributions to total family income approach equality (Barling, in press). Thus it can be predicted that if husbands lose their income their participation in household tasks will increase, especially if their wife is employed. Nevertheless, regardless of the factors prompting this phenomenon, any changes in husbands' objective role performance may be of some clinical significance, given research findings showing that their marital role performance is associated with marital satisfaction.

Spouse abuse

As is evident from Senator Riegle's (1982) statement at the beginning of this chapter, the belief that unemployment results in family violence is widespread. A typical quote from one of the numerous articles that appeared in lay publications during the early 1980s reflects on the link between unemployment, alcohol use and family violence:

> Daytime drinking is on the rise throughout the industrial states, and one of the predictable results is an increase in family abuse. 'They sit in the tavern all day and then head home to kick the wife and kids around', says Don Brook's wife, Diane. 'I don't know whether there is more violence, but I do know the severity has increased', adds Jo Sullivan of Range Women's Advocates in Chisholm, Minn. 'It's no longer the pushes and shoves and slaps. Now it's the stitches, the wired jaws, the broken ribs.'
>
> (Newsweek, 1983, p. 34)

Two different methodologies have been used to investigate the relationship between unemployment and spouse abuse. First, studies have focused on whether women in hospital emergency rooms or shelters for battered women are more likely to have husbands who are unemployed than women who are not abused. Second, studies have used large-scale, randomly selected samples to assess whether there is any relationship between unemployment and spouse abuse. The belief that unemployment was associated with spouse abuse initially gained considerable popularity from studies examining women who sought refuge at shelters for abused women (e.g. Fitch and Papantonio, 1983; Gayford, 1975; Lewis, 1987). Gayford's (1975) study serves as an example of this research paradigm. Gayford (1975) studied 100 women who had been severely and repeatedly physically abused by their husband (e.g. 44 of the women had lacerations, seventeen of which were caused by razors, knives or broken bottles; all had been hit with clenched fists; 59 were repeatedly kicked; and weapons were used in 42 cases, usually the first available object). When these women were interviewed, they were all receiving shelter at a variety of social welfare agencies. Among other questions, these 100 women were asked about their husbands' employment history. Eleven of the wives reported that their husbands were 'mostly' unemployed, eighteen were 'frequently' unemployed, and nineteen were 'occasionally' unemployed. In other words, 48% had husbands with some experience of unemployment. The fact that the rates of unemployment in this sample are far higher than those reported within the general population is taken to indicate that unemployment is associated with physical aggression against one's spouse.

Several factors cast doubt on the validity of such findings. First, as with other studies employing a similar methodology, the use of self-selected samples of women seeking shelter from abusive marital relationships certainly limits the generalizability of the results. Second, it is unclear whether the unemployed men in the sample were *currently* experiencing unemployment. If there is indeed a relationship between unemployment and spouse abuse, including employed men in the unemployed sample would provide an underestimate of the relationship between unemployment and spouse abuse. Third, by identifying only those women who had suffered 'severe' physical aggression, it is possible that Gayford (1975) may have again provided an underestimate of the number of unemployed husbands who physically abuse their partners. More widely accepted criteria of physical aggression would certainly include slapping, shoving, pushing and throwing objects—acts that do not necessarily have to be repeated frequently (e.g. O'Leary *et al.*, 1989; Straus, 1979).

It is critical to note, therefore, that results from studies using a different methodology also yield support for the existence of an association between unemployment and spouse abuse. Straus, Gelles and Steinmetz (1980) interviewed 2143 intact families in a national probability sample in the United States. There were a number of indications from their study that unemployment status is associated with spouse abuse. First, the extent of violence by the husband against the wife was twice as great in families where the husband was unemployed rather than employed (8% vs 4%). Second, Straus *et al.* (1980) also investigated physical aggression by wives against husbands. Although the precipitating causes may be varied (e.g. unemployed husbands and wives are together at home more; unemployed husbands' perceived power and status is reduced), physical aggression by the wife on the husband occurred in 14% of marriages where the husband was unemployed. In contrast, physical aggression by the wife against the husband occurred in 4% of marriages where the husband was employed. Third, physical aggression between spouses, irrespective of who perpetrated the aggression and who was the victim, was uniformly greater when the husband was employed on a part-time basis only (12% and 13%). Thus, aggression against one's spouse was higher in individuals employed on a part-time basis than among those who were unemployed. Finally, two points should be noted. All these rates of physical abuse were obtained using an index of spouse abuse that included aggressive acts which might not cause physical injury (e.g. slapping, shoving, pushing). Also, Straus and Gelles (1986) conducted a second national probability sample a decade later, and replicated the general finding that spouse abuse is higher among unemployed individuals.

Despite the fact that studies using different methodologies suggest strongly that unemployment is associated with spouse abuse, some issues remain unresolved. Because these issues will be discussed again when considering unemployment and child abuse, they will be mentioned only briefly at this stage. First, the causal role of unemployment needs to be clarified. Research on unemployment and spouse abuse has been cross-sectional or retrospective in nature, and the possibility that third variable effects such as objective economic hardship or perceived financial strain moderate or mediate this relationship cannot be excluded. Likewise, it is not known whether unemployment causes new instances of physical aggression between spouses who had previously not engaged in any physical aggression towards each other, whether it triggers pre-existing problems or causes an increase in the severity of current physical aggression. Second, the research treats unemployment as a homogeneous experience, even though one of the most significant advances in understanding unemployment has been Jahoda's (1982) conceptualization of the heterogeneity in the experience of unemployment. Thus, not all individuals who lose their jobs become physically aggressive. On the contrary, most certainly do not, and there are anecdotal reports that cohesion between spouses sometimes increases following unemployment (e.g. Thomas *et al*., 1980). Identifying factors which make some marital partners more resilient to marital problems in the face of unemployment would have considerable conceptual and treatment implications.

Marital dissolution

One final question regarding unemployment is whether it is associated with marital dissolution or divorce (Briar, 1978; Ray and McLoyd, 1986). South (1985) notes that the existence of such a relationship would appear to be one of the most rigorously confirmed phenomena in the area of family sociology. A positive relationship between unemployment and divorce is often presumed to exist because of the severity of the stress associated with unemployment, and because the magnitude of zero-order correlations between unemployment and divorce is often substantial (e.g. $r = 0.91$, South, 1985). Yet at least three factors detract from the credibility of this association. First, there are very few published empirical studies on the relationship between unemployment and marital instability. Second, even when data indicate higher separation and divorce rates among unemployed compared to employed groups (a ratio of 7:2 in Liem and Liem's 1988 study), such findings have to be treated cautiously because of the small sample sizes on which such data are based. Third, while neither negating nor diminishing the severity of the stress experienced during unemployment, obtaining a costly divorce may be less likely during periods of unemployment when income is reduced. Fourth, interpretive problems arise because different countries, states or provinces require different time intervals before a divorce is granted. Lastly, any conclusions from prior research investigating this issue may be outdated because they refer to periods covering 1867–1906, 1920–1943 and the late 1940s.

Using data available from the US Department of Health, Education and Welfare for the years 1947 to 1979 inclusive, South (1985) investigated whether a relationship exists between unemployment and divorce in the post Second World War era. Data on the unemployment rate over the same period was obtained from the Departments of the Census and Commerce. South's (1985) data offered support for the hypothesis that unemployment is positively associated with divorce. First, the bivariate correlation between the unemployment rate in a particular year and divorce rate in the following year was positive and significant ($r = 0.48$) across the years 1947–79. South (1985) computed a series of multiple regression analyses in which three confounding variables were controlled statistically: divorce rates the year before; the percentage of the population between the ages of 20 and 29 (the age group experiencing the highest divorce rate during the 1960s); and the female labour force participation rate. The data then strongly supported the original hypothesis: unemployment was still associated with divorce rates one year later. South (1985) further speculated that divorce rates may react more to *changes* in the economy, that is, improvements or deteriorations in the unemployment rate. The data showed that an increase in the annual unemployment rate was followed by increases in the rate of divorce. South (1985) further investigated whether change in the gross national product (GNP) as an indicator of macroeconomic health, was associated with divorce. Again, change in the GNP was associated with subsequent divorce after controlling for the three confounding variables mentioned above. The direction of this relationship was as predicted: namely, divorce rates increased more sharply during times of economic contraction than during periods of economic growth.

In interpreting these results, a number of issues must be borne in mind. First, South (1985) cautions that while statistically significant, the three indicators used (namely the unemployment rate, annual change in the unemployment rate and GNP) are substantially less predictive of divorce than the age structure of the sample, female labour force participation and prior divorce rates. Second, because of the nature of South's (1985) data, inferences are only possible at the aggregate level; conclusions at the individual level cannot be justified. Also, although most unemployed individuals do not divorce, no research has isolated factors that predict which unemployed individual will choose to divorce. Different methodologies focusing at the individual rather than the aggregate level are required to identify mediating factors between unemployment and subsequent marital instability (e.g. Barling *et al.*, 1989). Third, because unemployment and divorce rates very across communities, future research should focus on more specific geographic regions. This is of added importance because of the way in which community unemployment rates moderate marital satisfaction (Kessler *et al.*, 1987) and mortality (Iversen *et al.*, 1987) following unemployment. Lastly, the use of a one-year time lag in South's (1985) study may be problematic. Although this choice may have been constrained by practical limitations imposed by archival data, changes in economic conditions occur more rapidly (e.g. monthly; Steinberg, Catalano and Dooley, 1981). Hence, providing a measure of the annual change in unemployment may conceal a wide variation in unemployment rates during that year. This would limit the likelihood of obtaining significant relationships between unemployment and marital dissolution.

Unemployment and Marital Functioning: Conclusion

In summary, unemployment does not exert uniformly negative effects on all aspects of marital functioning. Instead, the effects of unemployment differ across separate areas of marital functioning. First, there is little consistency in the way in which marital satisfaction covaries with unemployment; some reports indicate greater marital dissatisfaction among unemployed groups, and others show no differences between employed and unemployed groups with respect to marital satisfaction. These inconsistencies occur when global measures of marital satisfaction are used; yet not when specific aspects of marital functioning are studied. Second, marital role performance increases during times of unemployment for husbands and wives, and decreases on re-employment. Third, the risk of spouse abuse is associated with the unemployment rate, but the role of unemployment in family violence will be considered further in the next section. Lastly, increases in the unemployment rate, or negative changes in GNP are associated with marital dissolution.

UNEMPLOYMENT, PARENT–CHILD INTERACTIONS AND CHILD BEHAVIOUR

There is no shortage of speculation about the negative effects of parental unemployment on parent–child interactions. Two examples of this will suffice. First, in his book *The Reckoning*, an historical analysis of the automobile industry in the United States, David Halberstam (1986) comments on the social sequelae of high unemployment in Michigan:

> There was pain in daily existence as the lives of thousands of citizens collapsed. There were more broken homes, households where the men could no longer face the fact that they had failed as providers and simply left. Social welfare agencies reported a dramatic climb in cases of wife and child beating. There was a major increase in suicides. The school system printed up small guide books for students whose parents were unemployed, telling them how to handle certain situations, warning them that their fathers were likely to be shorter of temper.
>
> (Halberstam, 1986, p. 51)

Second, it is also widely believed that unemployment is associated with emotional or psychological child abuse, and such a belief is perpetuated in the popular press and lay magazines. For example, statements such as 'Parents whose lives are full of stresses, including unemployment, alcohol or drug abuse, and social isolation, are more likely than others to mistreat their children' (*Newsweek*, 1988) are not uncommon.

A review of the available literature on parental unemployment reveals some interesting trends. First, research has focused much attention on the effects of unemployment on parent–child relationships, especially on child abuse. More attention has focused on physical than on psychological child abuse or child neglect.

Second, in contrast to the belief that maternal employment exerts a negative effect on children (see Chapter 1), paternal *unemployment* is expected to exert negative effects on parent–child relationships and children's behaviour. Third, the belief that unemployment places the child at physical is so widespread that one would expect research to reflect beliefs about the relation between unemployment and child abuse. Yet this is not the case; there is relatively little published empirical research on this topic. Finally, the effects of unemployment on parent–child interaction and children's behaviour have typically been considered separately, with comparatively less emphasis on the effects of unemployment on children's behaviour. Consequently, they will be considered separately in this chapter. This practice does not imply that they are separate conceptually. On the contrary, if parental unemployment is associated with child abuse, the child's experience of being abused may in turn result in child behaviour problems.

Child Abuse

It is assumed that children whose parents are unemployed are at risk of physical abuse, and research has addressed this assumption (see Belsky, 1980; Ray and McLoyd, 1986). As already noted, support for an association between unemployment and spouse abuse was derived from studies using two different research strategies. These same two strategies (namely, the use of shelter samples and random samples) have also been used to study the link between unemployment and child abuse. Essentially, two questions have been asked about the link between unemployment and child abuse: is unemployment higher among physically abusive parents, and is child abuse higher in groups of unemployed parents? In addition, a third strategy used to study the effects of parental unemployment on child abuse is to assess whether changes in community unemployment rates are associated with community-wide rates of child abuse.

Like research on unemployment and marital functioning, initial interest in the possibility of a statistical association between unemployment and child abuse was stimulated by observations of physically abused children and their parents who presented in hospital emergency rooms or other social welfare agencies. For example, although he presented no absolute statistics, Galdston (1965) observed that of children who appear in hospital emergency rooms having suffered severe physical abuse at the hands of their parents, 'Many of the fathers were unemployed or worked part-time' (p. 442). In a later study, Cater and Easton (1980) examined the hospital records of 80 children who had clearly been physically abused. They found that relative to the extent of unemployment in the normal population, the father was unemployed in a disproportionate number of cases in their sample, namely 30%.

Gil (1971) used a variation of this approach. Instead of focusing on small samples of individuals seeking shelter within one geographic region, he examined all cases of child abuse that were reported through legal channels within the United States during 1967 and 1968, involving almost 13 000 incidents of physical child abuse. These data were extended by case studies of almost 1400 incidents reported during 1967 in a representative sample of 39 cities and counties. As in the Cater and Easton (1980) study, significantly more of these these fathers were unemployed than would be expected in a normal population. Specifically, 12% of the fathers were unemployed at the time of the abusive incident, and almost half had been unemployed during the year prior to the abusive incident. This finding is supported by Light's (1973) subsequent re-analysis of Gil's (1971) data. After controlling for the effects of biased reporting that Light identified in Gil's (1971) study, the father's unemployment status remained the single most important factor differentiating between children who had been abused and index children (i.e. those who had not).

Such studies are plagued with methodological problems which limit the generalizability of their findings in a manner similar to studies investigating the role of unemployment in samples of physically abused wives. Hence, the fact that similar findings emerge when large-scale, random samples are examined is of some importance. As part of their national probability sample of 2143 families, Straus *et al.* (1980) also investigated the relationship between unemployment and child abuse. Of the 2143 families in their sample, 1146 had children between the ages of three and seventeen living at home, and it was this subsample that they used to examine whether parental unemployment was associated with child abuse. Irrespective of whether the target sample consisted of unemployed parents or abused children, a link between parental unemployment and child abuse exists. Specifically, while physical abuse by either parent occurred in 14% of the families in which the father was employed on a full-time basis, 22% of the families in which the father was unemployed were characterized by physical child abuse (Straus *et al.*, 1980). Straus *et al.* (1980) may have underestimated the extent of physical child abuse in their study, because they studied children who might be least at risk of suffering from physical aggression by either or both of their parents. Specifically, the risk of child abuse is highest for children under the age of three, yet Straus *et al.* (1980) excluded children who were less than three years old. Nonetheless, the finding that families in which the father is unemployed are more likely to be characterized by child abuse was replicated a decade later (Straus and Gelles, 1986). In terms of understanding the effects of employment status, it is worth noting that physical child abuse occurred in 27% of the homes where the father was employed on a part-time basis, the highest of all the rates reported. Similarly, spouse abuse was highest when the husband was employed on a part-time basis. An understanding of why this should occur is essential, but research on part-time employment in the organizational literature is perhaps too recent to be able to provide answers (Rotchford and Roberts, 1982).

Steinberg *et al.* (1981) noted that previous studies investigating unemployment and economic conditions on the one hand, and child abuse and neglect on the other, cannot disentangle causal direction because of the cross-sectional nature of such studies. Accordingly, they used a longitudinal aggregate technique in which *changes* in economic condition, including changes in the unemployment rate, were used to predict subsequent community-wide levels of child abuse with a lag of between one and three months. Moreover, because both unemployment and child abuse rates differ between communities, they conducted within-community analyses in two socioeconomically different communities. Steinberg *et al.* (1981) argue further that using a community as its own control means that socioeconomic levels are controlled, and third variable confounds are rendered less credible because they are stable across short time periods within large communities. Steinberg *et al.* (1981) chose not only to investigate monthly change in unemployment rates, but also investigated the role of changes in the overall size of the workforce within the two communities. They did so because the unemployment rate includes not only individuals who have been laid off involuntarily, but also individuals who voluntarily withdrew from their organizations, those who chose not to accept employment that was inconsistent with their expectations, as well as those individuals who had been fired. Because the definition of unemployment is so general and its operationalization somewhat erratic, they noted that the unemployment rate sometimes increases at the same time as the size of workforce, although there was no significant correlation between these two measures in their study. Finally, Steinberg *et al.* (1981) separated child abuse from neglect. Other studies investigating economic conditions (including unemployment) have either combined neglect and abuse (e.g. Garbarino, 1976), or failed to investigate neglect.

Steinberg *et al.* (1981) found that unemployment was *not* significantly associated with child abuse in either of the two communities they investigated. After controlling for the variance attributable to prior levels of child abuse within the community, the size of the workforce was a significant predictor of child abuse two months later. More specifically, reductions in the size of the workforce predicted increased reports of child abuse two months later. The results relating to the prediction of child neglect were not as consistent. Although unemployment again did not explain changes in reports of neglect, the size of the workforce significantly predicted changes in neglect in one of the two communities they studied. The community in which no significant pattern emerged exhibited considerable change in neglect, as evidenced by the large variability in the data relative to its low mean, a situation which statistically reduces the probability of obtaining significant findings within this community. Steinberg *et al.* (1981) note that the relationship that did emerge between the size of the labour force and neglect two months later in the other community is consistent with the interpretation that reports of neglect are more likely when parents are away working or looking for a job.

Several issues emerge from Steinberg *et al.*'s (1981) study. First is the failure to support the link between unemployment and child abuse, particularly because other studies have found such a link (e.g. Cater and Easton, 1980; Galdston, 1965; Gil, 1971; Light, 1973; Straus *et al.*, 1980; Straus and Gelles, 1986). Steinberg *et al.* (1981) argue that measures of unemployment used in previous studies may be flawed, because individuals may have been classified as unemployed even though they did not fit the usual definition of unemployed. Their index of the size of the workforce more accurately captured the nature of the stressor of interest, namely *changes* in macroeconomic conditions. Because the direction of this result was such that *decreases* in the size of the workforce were followed by *increases* in reports of child abuse on an aggregate level in both communities, the hypothesis that adverse economic conditions are linked with child abuse two months later is supported. Second, as Steinberg *et al.* (1981) themselves note, because they used aggregated community data, care must be taken not to commit the 'ecological fallacy'. In other words, their findings cannot be used to address the question of whether there is any systematic within-person association between changes in economic conditions and child abuse. Hence, it is not possible to conclude that it is individuals whose economic conditions worsen who subsequently abused their children. Nonetheless, the fact that the significant effect was replicated for changes in economic conditions (1) across two different communities and (2) after controlling statistically for the possibility that child abuse precedes changes in economic conditions enhances the external validity of their findings. Third, Steinberg *et al.* (1981) assessed child abuse and neglect separately, and showed that the economic changes only consistently affected child abuse. Finally, Steinberg *et al.*'s (1981) data are consistent with other findings showing a two- to three-month lag between economic downturns and psychiatric disturbance in adults (Catalano and Dooley, 1977; Frank, 1981).

The studies considered here are consistent in finding a relationship between economic downturns and the number of reported cases of child abuse. One problem with the interpretation of this link has already been mentioned, namely that of the ecological fallacy (which, it should be noted, is equally relevant in considering aggregate level community data on unemployment and divorce; South, 1985). A related problem with all these studies is that the identity of the abusive parent is typically ignored. Specifically, abused children may be more likely to have fathers who are unemployed, and fathers who are unemployed are more likely to have children who have been physically abused than fathers who are employed. Yet none of this research identifies whether the child was physically abused by the mother or the father (or even someone other than the parents). As a result, it cannot be concluded on the basis of these findings that unemployed fathers are more likely to physically abuse their children. Rather, a more appropriate conclusion is that children from families in which the father is unemployed are more likely to be abused. To investigate whether unemployment is linked with child abuse on an individual level, a different methodology would be required, in which individuals are monitored during periods when their employment status changes. Such research could be extended in a number of meaningful ways. The effects of unemployment and economic change on psychological and physical abuse against children should both be assessed, but separately. At the same time, because of increases in reports of sexual abuse, future research might investigate whether unemployment or adverse changes in economic conditions are associated with the sexual abuse of children.

Finally, other issues must be addressed in considering the meaning of the relation between unemployment and child abuse. First, one of the most important questions that should be dealt with in any within-subject design is why the vast majority of unemployed parents, or parents whose economic conditions change for the worse, do not resort to child abuse. In other words, such studies should identify psychological and social factors that enhance personal resilience in the face of negative economic changes and conditions. Second, the issue of causality must be confronted. Despite the consistency in findings, and even if unemployment or changes in the size of the workforce *precede* increases in child abuse, none of these studies points to the existence of a *causal* relationship. For example, it is quite possible that other factors (i.e. 'third variable' effects) account both for an individual's unemployment as well as the enactment of child abuse. The results from Layton and Eysenck's (1985) longitudinal study of school-leavers provides one example of how such third variable effects might operate. They tested a large group of sixteen-year-old male pupils while still at school. Layton and Eysenck (1985) showed that the psychoticism measure of the Eysenck Personality Questionnaire (but not scores from the extraversion, neuroticism or lie subscales) was a significant predictor of future unemployment status. They conclude that this finding is not surprising. Individuals scoring higher on their psychoticism subscale would be more 'immature, irresponsible, troublesome, solitary, hostile, anti-authoritarian, independent, non-conformist, querulous and generally difficult to handle' (Layton and Eysenck, 1985, p. 388), characteristics that would not serve an individual well in the job environment. Importantly, some of these personality attributes (e.g. immaturity, irresponsibility, troublesomeness, solitary nature, hostility and being difficult to control) also characterize individuals who abuse their children. Third, investigators have focused on whether unemployed individuals are more likely to abuse their children, or abused children are more likely to have parents who have lost their jobs. In such investigations, the samples used consist of individuals seeking or receiving assistance from social welfare agencies. Such individuals are more visible and typically hold less social power. Lower socioeconomic status people come into contact with social agencies more than high socioeconomic status people. Therefore, it may appear as though more lower socioeconomic status parents are unemployed and abuse their children. Yet when socioeconomic levels are controlled, this link may not be supported. Finally, unemployed fathers spend more time with their children, as do unemployed husbands with their wives. As such, it is also possible that any link between unemployment and family violence is a function of the increased physical and interpersonal contact between parent and child, or between spouses, that is brought about by unemployment.

Parent–Child Interactions

The studies considered so far on unemployment and parent–child interactions all focused on child abuse. A second focus of enquiry has been directed at understanding the effects of unemployment on parent–child interactions in general (see McLoyd, 1989). Radin and her colleagues (Harold-Goldsmith, Radin and Eccles, in press; Radin and Harold-Goldsmith, 1989; Radin and Greer, 1987) have examined the way in which fathers' unemployment bears upon their general relationships with their children. There are suggestions that the father–child relationship may improve during periods of paternal unemployment, especially if the amount of contact between father and child is increased (Ray and McLoyd, 1986). It is important to move beyond a perspective that only considers possible negative consequences of unemployment for the father–child relationship.

Radin and Harold-Goldsmith (1989), Radin and Greer (1987) and Harold-Goldsmith *et al.* (in press) all showed that working class and lower middle class unemployed fathers were more involved in various aspects of childrearing than were their employed counterparts. Radin and Greer (1987) quantified these differences, showing that unemployed fathers were the primary care givers of their children for 49% of the week contrasted to employed fathers, who fulfilled the same capacity for less than half that time (23% of the week). In searching for an explanation for these findings, Radin and Harold-Goldsmith (1989) empirically contrasted three hypotheses: (1) unemployed fathers become more involved with their children because resource allocation between spouses when the father is unemployed approaches unity; (2) irrespective of unemployment status, husbands with a more traditional sex role ideology will be less involved with their children than those with a more liberal sex role ideology; and (3) unemployed husbands will participate more in childrearing because they have greater demands placed on them and time available to meet those demands. Support for all three hypotheses emerged in the group of employed fathers. However, only sex role ideology predicted the extent of unemployed fathers' involvement with their children. Confidence in these findings would have been strengthened had a larger sample of unemployed fathers ($n > 17$) been tested. Radin and Harold-Goldsmith's (1989) findings only address the issue of whether unemployed fathers spent more time interacting with their children then do employed fathers. Harold-Goldsmith and Radin (1989) also investigated whether unemployment was associated with the *quality* as well as the *quantity* of father–child interactions. They found that while unemployed fathers spent more time interacting with their children, the quality of their interactions suffered in comparison to that of employed fathers. Radin and Harold-Goldsmith (1989) also obtained observational data of father–child interactions, and showed that employed fathers were more nurturant towards their children than unemployed fathers. These findings are interesting in light of the data on fathers' job satisfaction. As noted in the previous chapter, fathers who are satisfied with their jobs spend less time with their children during the work week, but fathers' job satisfaction is positively associated with the quality of parent–child interactions (e.g. Grossman *et al.*, 1988; McKinley, 1964). Again, however, the relatively small samples used in Radin and Harold-Goldsmith's (1989) study of working and lower middle class fathers (31 employed fathers, 14 unemployed) suggest that these findings should be replicated with larger samples to enhance their generalizability.

Although it examined economic hardship rather than unemployment, one further study requires some attention. First, this particular study was generated from the Oakland Growth Study (see Elder, 1974), and the longitudinal nature of the data obtained is unusual and makes for some intriguing speculation. Second, this particular study examined mediational processes underlying the link between unemployment and children's behaviour. Beginning in 1931, the mental, social and physical development of 167 normal, fifth grade children from five different schools in Oakland, California was studied until 1939. Describing the significance of their study, Elder, Nguyen and Caspi (1985) state that 'the Great Depression can be viewed as a natural field experiment that created an exogenous change in the social and economic situations of families and altered the developmental context of children' (p. 362). A number of aspects of Elder *et al.*'s (1985) findings are interesting. First, Elder *et al.* (1985) partialled out the effects of social class, thereby minimizing the effect of socioeconomic status on their results. Second, there were no significant correlations between mothers' income loss and the extent to which the father was rejecting, indifferent to and supportive of his adolescent children. On the contrary, consistent with other studies (see McLoyd, 1989), these three father–child behaviours were significantly associated with the extent of income loss suffered by the father, suggesting that income loss exerted its effects through its influence on the father, not on the mother. Third, father–child relationships mediated the effect of fathers' financial difficulties on their daughters' behaviour, but not on their sons' behaviour. Lastly, it should be borne in mind that Elder *et al.* (1985) did not study the effects of unemployment but rather the effects of economic hardship. As a result, it remains to be seen whether the process model specified by Elder *et al.* (1985) also explains the association between unemployment and child–parent relations. This is a particularly important concern for at least two reasons. First, on the basis of adolescents' self-reports, Lempers, Clark-Lempers and Simons (1989) have shown that subjective economic hardship influences depression and loneliness in adolescents through the mediating effects of diminished parental nurturance and the use of inconsistent disciplinary practices. Second, Harold-Goldsmith *et al.* (in press) have shown that *perceived* or *subjective* financial distress is a better predictor of father–child interactions than unemployment status, i.e. merely contrasting employed and unemployed individuals.

Children's Behaviour

The possibility that children's behaviour changes as a function of their parents' unemployment has long been the subject of speculation (Elder, 1974). Empirical research investigating this possibility, however, has not benefited from as much attention. Although there is a considerable body of literature empirically assessing whether children's physical health, social behaviour and/or scholastic performance is a function of objective economic hardship (e.g. Elder and Caspi, 1988; Jahoda, 1982; Moen, Kain and Elder, 1983), there is a dearth of research investigating the specific effects of unemployment controlling for financial difficulties. In this section, effects attributable mainly to unemployment will be presented.

Before discussing the research on unemployment and children's behaviour, one gender-specific bias implicit in this research merits emphasis. Invariably, this research focuses on fathers who are unemployed; there are no studies assessing mothers' involuntary unemployment, and its possible consequences for children. Yet considering the number of males and females in the labour force, a disproportionately greater number of women are unemployed (Taylor, 1988), and economic strain may be greater for women (Perrucci and Targ, 1988). Thus, the assumptions surrounding fathers' unemployment and mothers' employment reflect a gender bias: while mothers' daily *absence* from the home because of employment is assumed to exert negative effects on the children (see Chapters 1 and 7), it is fathers' daily *presence* because of unemployment that is assumed to exert negative effects on children. The basis of this assumption is that negative effects ensue when parents move away from socially prescribed roles.

One reason for expecting unemployment to influence children's behaviour derives from the obvious presence of the father in the home on a daily basis. Over and above the fact that this increases the amount of contact between father and child, there would be psychological and social pressures on the father, for example because societal norms expect him to be at work, unless he is a shift worker, on vacation or sick. Violation of socially prescribed roles may induce conflict for the father, particularly if the conflict is relevant to his breadwinner or parenting roles. Other psychological factors associated with unemployment may also exert negative effects on children. First, the family structure and dynamics might change considerably when the father is unemployed. In addition, the traditional division of labour changes in families where the father is unemployed (e.g. Shamir, 1986; Warr and Payne, 1983b; Warr, 1984c), especially if the wife becomes employed. Second, as Piotrkowski and Stark (1987) noted, children learn about the world of paid work through the experiences and emotions their parents convey implicitly, and talk about explicitly. Presumably, fathers transmit their unemployment experiences in the same way. Pautler and Lewko (1987) expand on this, noting that children and adolescents perceive and comprehend aspects of their parents' world, including the world of work. Research findings support the notion that by the age of eleven, children have an intuitive grasp of the economy, which includes an understanding of the limitations of their parents' economic position (Siegel, 1980). More specifically, even preschool children whose fathers are unemployed have a greater understanding of the meaning of unemployment than their counterparts whose fathers are employed (Radin and Greer, 1987).

Some studies have investigated how children's exposure to, or indirect experience with, paternal unemployment contributes to their general concerns and anxieties. Pautler and Lewko (1984) contrasted two large groups of grade 6, 9 and 12 children and adolescents whose parents were either unemployed (N = 209) or employed (N = 284). Four specific domains of concern to these children were identified, namely concerns about school, family, family economics and economics. There were no meaningful differences in either the school, family or economic domains. However, children who had some familial exposure to unemployment exhibited far greater concerns in the family economic domain. The specific items that were of concern to these children included 'My father being out of work for a long time' and 'My father losing his job'. This finding is noteworthy, because it indicates the effects of exposure to unemployment may not generalize to other domains.

There are other data which suggest that exposure to unemployment increases children's worries. Specifically, there are two studies using large groups of fifth and sixth grade children which contrasted their worries during the 1930s (Pinter and Lev, 1940) with those in 1977 (Orton, 1982). Contrasting children's concerns across these two time periods provides some indication of whether differences in community levels of unemployment are associated with children's worries and concerns. For comparative purposes, it should be noted that these two studies used essentially the same items as Pautler and Lewko (1984). Although the extent to which children were concerned with school remained stable across the two time periods, boys from Pinter and Lev's (1940) earlier sample were far more concerned about economic issues than were boys in Orton's (1982) sample, although there were no corresponding differences for girls. On a global level, therefore, children's exposure to unemployment through their parents' unemployment is positively associated with their level of concern, but the effect on their concern is domain specific. In other words, the results of these three studies suggest that instead of generalizing, the effects of exposure to unemployment are limited to economic or job-related worries.

Moen (1983) has suggested that unemployment may exert long-term effects on children, in that exposure to parental unemployment affects children's future expectations about their own likelihood of obtaining employment, expectations as to what employment can provide them with, and work values and beliefs. To investigate the possible effects of unemployment on work values on children, it is first necessary to show that differences exist in the work values and attitudes of employed and unemployed adults. O'Brien and Kabanoff (1979) randomly sampled 0.5% of the total population of metropolitan Adelaide, Australia, producing samples of 74 unemployed and 1383 employed individuals. They showed that the work or employment-related values of employed individuals differed significantly. Specifically, unemployed individuals expressed less value in influence, autonomy and interactions at work, and wanted less pressure from their jobs. Thus, if children and adolescents do learn about the world of paid work at least partially through interactions with their parents (e.g. Piotrkowski and Stark, 1987), then a reasonable case may be made to support the notion that the children of employed and unemployed parents would be exposed to different work values.

Two studies have been conducted to investigate whether adolescents' work values are influenced by parents' unemployment (Dowling and O'Brien, 1981; Isralowitz and Singer, 1986). Although these studies were conducted in different countries (Australia and the United States, using cross-sectional and longitudinal designs respectively), both studies showed that parental unemployment exerted no influence on children's work values. These results may seem counter to findings showing that children whose fathers are unemployed (*a*) are more concerned about family/economic issues (Paulter and Lewko, 1984), (*b*) have a greater understanding of the meaning of unemployment (Radin and Greer, 1987), and (*c*) possess work values that vary with parental unemployment. One possible explanation that will be pursued in more detail later in this chapter is that transmission of parental values to children and adolescents does not occur automatically. Instead, to understand when parents' unemployment impinges on their adolescents' work values requires a focus on the psychological processes that might mediate this relationship. Perhaps parents' unemployment only impinges on their adolescents' work values when there is a close relationship between parent and adolescent. In other words, it is through a close father–child relationship that an appreciation of the fathers' unemployment experiences could be transmitted.

Despite the wealth of speculation that children of the unemployed are necessarily negatively affected, there is very little empirical research directly contrasting the behaviour of children of employed and involuntarily unemployed parents. Madge (1983) found no differences between younger children of employed and unemployed parents in terms of verbal intelligence or achievement scores on the California Achievement Test. Likewise, there were no differences between unemployed and employed fathers regarding the extent to which they cognitively stimulated their children. Yet children of unemployed fathers, and especially sons, held lower perceptions of their own cognitive abilities. Friedemann (1986) showed no differences in peer relationships between these two groups, although children of unemployed parents did tend to experience more extreme positive and negative scores. Although Radin and Greer (1987) showed that young children (particularly sons) of unemployed fathers were absent from school more frequently than children whose fathers were employed, their small sample size suggests that this finding be investigated more in the future.

UNEMPLOYMENT, PARENT–CHILD INTERACTIONS AND CHILD BEHAVIOUR: CONCLUSION

On the one hand, there is consistent support for the notion that unemployment affects parent–child interactions, particularly in as much as children whose fathers are unemployed are more likely to be physically abused. Yet aside from concerns about unemployment and economic issues, there are very few behavioural differences between the children of employed and unemployed parents. Consistent with research on subjective economic hardship (Elder *et al.*, 1985; Lempers *et al.*, 1989), it might be worthwhile for future research to focus on parent–child relationships and psychosocial processes that mediate the relationship between unemployment and child behaviour problems. Thus, Paulter and Lewko's (1984) suggestion that differences between the children of employed and unemployed fathers '... contrast sharply with the idyllic, Pollyannish view of childhood as a worry-free, carefree time of life' (p. 16), while not necessarily incorrect, is at best premature.

UNEMPLOYMENT AND FAMILY FUNCTIONING: AN AGENDA FOR FUTURE RESEARCH AND THEORY

In reviewing the studies that have been conducted on unemployment and marital functioning, parent–child interactions and child behaviour, several common issues emerge. Three issues have considerable implications for the way in which the nature of unemployment is conceptualized, and its effects understood. These include the need to focus on the subjective experience of unemployment rather than unemployment status alone (Jahoda, 1982), factors that mediate the relationship between unemployment and family functioning (McLoyd, 1989), and the precise role (i.e. precipitating or exacerbating function) of unemployment on any subsequent family functioning. After considering these two major issues, additional avenues for future research will be identified.

The Subjective Experience of Unemployment

Studies focusing on the effects of unemployment on family functioning have been based on a research paradigm in which employed and unemployed individuals (or their families) are contrasted. The inherent assumption within this approach (whether by default or design) is that there is considerable homogeneity in the experience *within* each of these two groups, yet substantial variation *between* these two groups. However, this assumption and the implications it holds for conceptualizing the nature of unemployment and directing the way in which possible effects of unemployment and family functioning are studied, can be challenged on at least three grounds.

First, one of the consistent conclusions reached so far in this text is that both husbands' and wives' subjective employment experience is a better predictor of family functioning than is their objective employment status. Likewise, fathers' and mothers' employment experiences are better predictors of their children's behaviour than is their employment status. The research already described suggests that when employed and unemployed individuals are contrasted, the relationship between unemployment family functioning is not substantial. One reason for this could be that the variation within each of these two groups is similar to, or exceeds, the variation between the two groups. Unemployment does not exert uniform effects either on marital functioning or on the father–child relationship (Ray and McLoyd, 1986). Instead, people respond differently to unemployment, with some people faring better following unemployment. Thus, the empirical data also point to the notion that there is considerable variation in the way in which unemployed individuals experience their unemployment. Consequently, it might be interesting to investigate whether variations in the experience of unemployment can enhance our understanding of the relationship between unemployment and family functioning.

A third and more important reason for focusing on the subjective meaning of unemployment derives from the work of Marie Jahoda (1982). Arguably, one of the more meaningful developments in understanding the nature of unemployment has developed from Jahoda's (1982, 1988) conceptualization of the manifest and latent functions of employment of which people are potentially deprived during unemployment. Because of the importance of Jahoda's (1982) contribution and their implications for understanding the nature and effects of unemployment, the manifest and latent functions of employment and their consequences will be described. According to Jahoda (1982), employment fulfils one manifest function, in that it enables individuals to accumulate sufficient financial assets to meet their needs. Certainly there is a vast literature showing that poverty in general, and poverty arising because of unemployment, is negatively associated with psychological well-being and family functioning (Moen *et al.*, 1983). Although this manifest function of employment is not psychological in nature, there is research showing that the perceived or subjective financial strain caused by job loss negatively affects personal family functioning. For example, financial concerns are associated with self-esteem, depression, psychological symptoms and physical health in older, unemployed professionals (Mallinckrodt and Fretz, 1988) and retired individuals (Krause, 1987). Perhaps more to the point, Kessler *et al.* (1987) provide an additional perspective on the role of perceived financial strain. In a group of randomly selected unemployed individuals in an area of the United States in which unemployment was rife, they found that perceived financial strain mediated the relationship between unemployment and physical health and psychological well-being. When the effects of perceived financial strain were controlled statistically, unemployed individuals functioned at a level similar to that of a group of employed individuals (Kessler *et al.*, 1987). Kessler *et al.* (1987) further showed that marital strain did not mediate the relationship between unemployment and psychological health and physical symptoms. Given the absence of other studies, it would have been interesting had they chosen to investigate whether perceived financial strain mediated the relationship between unemployment and marital strain.

Even more important from a psychological perspective are the latent functions of employment, and the consequences of their deprivation. The foremost of the latent functions of employment is the provision of a time structure for the individual. Employment's role in providing a time structure has long been recognized, but frequently taken for granted. For example, Freud considered the way in which employment provides a temporal structure to be of such importance that he maintained work was a major factor linking people with reality (Jahoda, 1982). Much earlier, in Shakespeare's *Antony and Cleopatra* (IV, iv), Antony points to this particular function of employment when he says that 'To business that we love we rise betime, And go to't with delight'. In addition, numerous recent studies show significant relationships between the extent to which unemployed individuals maintain some structure to their day and positive psychological well-being (e.g. Brenner and Bartell, 1983; Feather and Bond, 1983; Hepworth, 1980; Swinburne, 1981).

A second latent function of employment identified by Jahoda (1982) is the social contact gained via employment. The growing body of research showing the importance of social networks and social support for individual psychological well-being attests to the significance of such social contacts (Cohen and Wills, 1985; Jackson, 1988). Although it might be argued that family relations can fulfil needs for social contacts in the absence of employment, Jahoda (1982) argues that it is precisely because family relations are more emotionally laden, that non-familial relationships assume such importance. Thus it is important to take note of one recent study conducted by Jackson (1988). First, he showed that although the overall size of an individual's network remains constant in the first two months following unemployment, the structure of the network changes; unemployed individuals turned more to their families and less to their friends for social support. This highlights the importance of Moen's (1980) proposition that we should measure the effects of unemployment on the family rather than any individual family member. Second, network size did not change, although the amount of contact between unemployed individuals and non-family members decreased. Third, Jackson (1988) showed that, in general, family members were more inclined to provide expressive or emotional support rather than information support. This is important given findings that different types of support may exert different effects (Barling, MacEwen and Pratt, 1988).

Related to the provision of social contacts is the third latent function of employment, namely the sense of purpose that emanates from involvement in a collective enterprise. During periods of unemployment, individuals are deprived of the regular activity afforded by employment, and may suffer psychological distress as a result. Finally, Jahoda (1982) notes that employment provides the individuals with a sense of personal identity and social status. Self-esteem suffers and psychological depression increases significantly during unemployment.

Several implications emerge from the conceptualization of the manifest and latent functions of employment. The foremost implication concerns the way in which unemployment is typically conceptualized as a homogeneous experience. On the contrary, there is considerable variation in the way in which individuals perceive and experience their unemployment. Given this heterogeneity, it is apparent that individuals respond differently to unemployment. The failure to find consistent differences between employed and unemployed groups with respect to family functioning may reflect the failure to account for these within-group differences. Second, a perspective to the unemployment experience as being heterogeneous has considerable ramifications for the conduct of research. To continue contrasting the marital and family functioning of employed and unemployed individuals will result in little benefit. Instead, studies of how marital and family functioning are associated with different unemployment experiences are needed. Third, research should assess whether each of the latent functions impinge on marital and family functioning in a unique or an additive manner.

Nonetheless, although Jahoda (1982) has provided what is probably the most extensive model of the subjective experience of unemployment, her model is not exhaustive. In a later article, Jahoda (1988) emphasizes how an understanding of mental health or positive resilience could further explain why some unemployed individuals do not react negatively to their unemployment. Additional factors may further explain the subjective experience of unemployment. Archer and Rhodes (1987) suggest that the process of adjustment to loss is central, and emphasize the feelings of bereavement that would follow the loss of one's job. The possible advantages of such refinements are further illustrated by Parke and Collmer (1975), who suggest that the extent to which the job loss was sudden and/or predictable might be most important in accounting for physical violence by parents against their children. Parke and Collmer's (1975) suggestion calls attention to the need to consider any acute stressors inherent in the unemployment process.

If this call to reconceptualize unemployment is heeded, methodological consequences would ensue. An examination of the subjective experience of unemployment (rather than unemployment status) requires the use of within-group designs in which individual variations in the manifest and latent functions of employment are assessed.

Mediators of the Relationship between Unemployment and Family Functioning

As was the case with the relationship between objective employment attributes and subjective employment experiences on the one hand, and family functioning on the other, the magnitude of the relationship between unemployment and family functioning is low. One likely cause of this is the way in which unemployment has been conceptualized and operationalized, i.e. the assumption of no variation within the unemployed group. Also, the psychological processes that mediate the relationship between unemployment and family functioning have not been identified and incorporated into research. The failure to isolate mediating factors is of particular importance in this context. Specifically, while the magnitude of relationships between unemployment and family functioning has not been remarkable, the relationship between unemployment and various indices of psychological distress, such as self-esteem and depression, is more consistent across studies and generally stronger than those studies in which indices of family functioning are the outcome (Fryer and Payne, 1986). Given that depression, for example, is a robust and consistent correlate of marital functioning (Beach and O'Leary, (1986), it is possible that depression mediates the relationship between unemployment and marital functioning. Moreover, because unemployment is implicated in depression, and depression may even be causally associated with marital dissatisfaction for men, the mediating role of depression is suggested. This hypothesis becomes all the more plausible given Atkinson *et al.*'s (1986) findings. They showed husbands' hostility, depression and psychosomatic symptoms mediated the relationship between unemployment and marital role performance, marital support and marital cohesion. Specifically, unemployment predicted each of these three mediators. In turn, specific reactions to job loss predicted supportive behaviours within the marital relationship.

In their subsequent analysis of the same data set, Liem and Liem (1988) tested whether husbands' emotional state (primarily depression) mediated the relationship between unemployment and family functioning, or whether family functioning mediated the relationship between unemployment and emotional state. They suggested that the results provide support for the notion that emotional state mediated the relationship between unemployment and marital functioning, but caution is warranted in interpreting and generalizing from the findings of their panel study. Even though Dew *et al.* (1987) found that husbands' psychological reactions to their job loss influenced their spouses' and families' reactions, the results on which Liem and Liem (1988) based their conclusion did not achieve statistical significance ($p < 0.11$).

Thus, in attempting to account more comprehensively for the relationship between unemployment and either marital functioning, or child behaviours, future research might focus on psychological processes that mediate this relationship. One area for such research is the father–child relationship. McLoyd (1989) concludes that fathers' unemployment exerts the most negative effect on child behaviour when fathers become more disciplinarian and inconsistent in their parenting following unemployment. It has also been suggested that marital distress might mediate the relationship between unemployment and father–child relationships, or between unemployment and child behaviour problems (Ray and McLoyd, 1986). Certainly there are data from the clinical literature supporting this position, in that marital distress and conflict is associated with both child behaviour problems and inappropriate parent–child interactions (Emery, 1989).

Does Unemployment Cause or Uncover Family Distress?

One of the major issues that has attracted the attention of researchers interested in the consequences of unemployment is the precise role of unemployment in predicting any subsequent disorder (e.g. Dooley and Catalano, 1980). The specific issue here is whether unemployment is sufficient in itself to bring about subsequent change (e.g. Brenner, 1975), or whether unemployment interacts with other personal and/or situational variables in effecting such change (e.g. Kessler *et al.*, 1987). There is support for both these positions, in that unemployment predicts psychological distress, and that psychological distress is exacerbated by social and personal factors, such as economic downturns and major life stressors (e.g. Aldwin and Revenson, 1986; Kessler *et al.*, 1987). Support for this latter position also derives, for example, from Rutter (1981), who suggests that individuals are more at risk of psychological distress when they are confronted by multiple rather than single stressors or crises.

In evaluating whether unemployment causes or uncovers family distress, the question of whether the quality of marital and/or family functioning prior to unemployment moderates the effects of unemployment looms large. Komarovsky (1940) reported that those marriages that were most at risk of dissolution following the unemployment of the male breadwinner were also those most fraught with marital problems prior to the experience of unemployment. Other earlier case studies produced similar evidence (e.g. Angell, 1936; Cavan and Ranck, 1938). Some commentators further suggested that unemployment exacerbates prior levels of marital functioning. Thus, where marital problems existed prior to unemployment, these problems will be exacerbated during and following unemployment; and unemployment might enhance the quality of a marriage that was already functioning positively prior to unemployment (Moen *et al.*, 1983; Ray and McLoyd, 1986). In a similar vein, O'Brien (1985) notes that there were already indications from research conducted during the 1930s that prior work attitudes (e.g. job satisfaction) moderate the impact of unemployment. Thus, taken together with the results from more general studies showing the moderating effects of personal resilience and/or social factors (Aldwin and Revenson, 1986; Kessler *et al.*, 1987), research focusing on unemployment and family functioning might profitably investigate what role prior marital satisfaction and family functioning fulfils in the way in which individuals and families adapt to unemployment.

Apart from these three suggestions taken from the research already discussed, five additional avenues for research on unemployment and family functioning emerge from more general research on the nature and consequences of unemployment. First, findings from the research of Brockner and his colleagues (e.g. Brockner, 1988; Brockner *et al.*, 1987) show consistently that it is not only individuals who are laid-off who are affected by unemployment. Instead, 'survivors' of layoffs are also affected. Although this research programme has been directed primarily at understanding the survivors' work attitudes and behaviours, it might be worth while investigating whether the layoff of one's close work colleagues engenders any effects beyond the work environment, specifically on the family because of the concerns and guilt raised among the survivors. Whether the fear of losing one's own job has any role in this process is also worthy of some consideration.

One recent trend in the workplace, which may be partially a function of the consequences of lingering unemployment, is the increasing frequency of underemployment. Burris (1983) describes underemployment as arising when individuals accept jobs for which their qualifications exceed the requirements of the job. Understanding the consequences of underemployment might help unravel the relationship between unemployment and family functioning. First, task complexity is one job characteristic that is associated with psychological well-being (e.g. Hackman and Oldham, 1980; Warr, 1987a, b). In underemployment and unemployment, task complexity is typically absent. Second, like unemployment, underemployment leads to feelings of psychological distress. For example, Kaufman (1982) found that 20% of individuals who accepted jobs, following unemployment, that left them functionally underemployed described their lives as having changed drastically for the worse. Yet only 5% of professionals who remained unemployed or were re-employed at an appropriate level reported similar feelings. Hence, it might be informative for future research to assess whether the experience of underemployment is associated in any way with marital and family functioning. The experience of part-time employment may parallel that of underemployment with its decreased demand on task complexity. It might also be interesting to investigate whether the experience of part-time employment is associated with family functioning. This is especially relevant because of data showing that spouse abuse was 50% higher (12% vs 8%) among part-time employed than unemployed men in Straus *et al.*'s (1980) random sample, and that child abuse is also highest among parents employed on a part-time basis.

Third, with very few exceptions (e.g. Elder, 1974; Komarovsky, 1940), the data discussed in this chapter were derived from contrasted group studies using questionnaires that facilitated comparisons between employed and unemployed individuals and their families. As already noted, case studies focusing only on unemployed individuals were excluded because their use of qualitative analyses made interpretation of the results within studies, and comparisons of findings between studies, extremely difficult. Yet there is little doubt that a phenomenological approach would contribute to a more comprehensive understanding of the relationship between unemployment and family functioning (e.g. Fineman, 1983). What is required in this context, however, is the use of a technique in these qualitative studies that would facilitate such analyses and comparisons (e.g. Van Maanen *et al.*, 1982).

Another item for the agenda of future research on unemployment and the family concerns the subjects of such studies. Almost invariably, research on the effects of unemployment on the family continues to focus exclusively on whether the father is unemployed, unless the unemployed individual is the mother within a single-parent family. Even in the latter case, the independent variable of interest would then typically be poverty rather than the experience of unemployment. Yet the limitations of this approach become apparent when it is realized that in terms of the number of men and women in the labour force, a disproportionate number of women are unemployed (Taylor, 1988). This suggests that future research should focus more attention on unemployed wives and mothers. In any such research, differentiating between individuals who do not have a job because of non-employment (e.g. homemakers) rather than unemployment (see Chapter 2) would be critical because of the different subjective experiences associated with non-employment and unemployment.

One final issue concerns the use of longitudinal research in studies of unemployment in general, and unemployment and family functioning in particular. While there are longitudinal studies on the consequences of unemployment (e.g. Jackson *et al*., 1983), with few exceptions (e.g. Elder, 1974; Liem and Liem, 1988; Perrucci and Targ, 1988) most studies focusing on the effects of unemployment on family functioning have utilized cross-sectional designs. Cross-sectional designs limit the extent to which causal issues can be addressed in non-experimental studies. One notable example of this is the research on paternal unemployment and child behaviour. While the consequences of unemployment on child behaviour may appear to be modest, Moen (1980) has proposed that the consequences of early exposure to paternal unemployment will become most pronounced when the child reaches adulthood. At that time, individuals who were exposed to parental unemployment may manifest employment values and attitudes that are inappropriate in terms of functioning in current work environments. This hypothesis has not been tested adequately.

The suggestion that the prolonged effects of early exposure to unemployment be investigated gains considerable support from Elder's (1974) analysis of the Oakland Growth Study data. Elder's (1974) analyses showed that adolescents whose fathers became unemployed exhibited significantly better adjustment later in life. For example, they performed better at school, were more likely to enter college and were more satisfied with their lives, their marriages and their jobs. Elder and his colleagues (Moen *et al*., 1983) suggest that exposure to unemployment forces the child or adolescent to confront new tasks and challenges, the benefits or drawbacks of which may only become apparent later in life. For example,

> ... older children were called upon for household activities as families shifted toward a more labor intensive economy (Elder, 1974). Adult-like responsibilities became more a part of the lives of both boys and girls. Boys tended to seek gainful employment, while girls helped with domestic responsibilities, including child care, meal preparation, house cleaning, sewing and ironing. The involvement of boys in work roles accelerated their liberation from parental controls.
>
> (Moen *et al*., 1983, pp. 231–2).

They referred to this as the 'downward extension' hypothesis, suggesting that while the increased role pressures brought to bear on first born sons may bring about negative effects at the time, positive benefits will emerge some time in the future. There is some support for this proposition in Hillenbrand's (1976) study on the effects of prolonged job-related father absence. For first-born children, especially sons, higher levels of quantitative achievement were positively associated with job-related father absence. Nonetheless, the important point here is that the way in which unemployment affects children may change over the life course, and to understand such effects, longitudinal studies tracking behaviours over the course of the life span are required.

UNEMPLOYMENT AND FAMILY FUNCTIONING: CONCLUSION

In conclusion, unemployment exerts no consistent effects on global marital satisfaction. However, marital role performance increases during unemployment, and decreases when employment is regained. Also, both spouse abuse and marital dissolution are associated with unemployment. There are very few differences between the children of employed and unemployed fathers. However, unemployment affects parent–child interactions in general and child abuse in particular, and there are indications that any effects of unemployment on children's behaviour are mediated by father–child interactions. In all these results, issues of causality remain to be resolved. Last, one of the major advances in understanding the effects of unemployment has been the provision of models that enable a focus on the subjective meaning of unemployment.

Chapter 10

Employment, Unemployment and Family Functioning: Concluding Thoughts

It is fitting at this stage to summarize and evaluate just what is known about the link between employment and family functioning, the implications of this knowledge, and what is still to be learned. Also, conceptual research and practical implications of this knowledge will be considered. An appropriate point of departure is to re-examine the three assumptions that were identified in the first chapter.

ASSUMPTION 1: UNIDIRECTIONAL EFFECTS OF EMPLOYMENT ON FAMILY LIFE

As stated initially, it is widely believed that employment influences family functioning. It is true that research findings support this belief, but research has not disconfirmed the alternative assumption that family functioning influences employment. There are some data showing that family factors influence the individual's functioning in the organization. Perhaps this can be illustrated best with examples from research on absenteeism. Tracing the historical development of research on absenteeism. Johns and Nicholson (1982) noted that until the late 1970s, it was held that an analysis of organizational conditions would be sufficient to uncover the causes of absenteeism. This ignored the fact that when people are absent from the organization, they are present elsewhere. Johns and Nicholson (1982) argued that our focus must include factors outside of the workplace in predicting absence, because traditional predictors of organizational withdrawal behaviours (i.e. tardiness, absence and turnover), such as job dissatisfaction, are insufficient. Satisfied employees still absent themselves from the job when personal incentives are more attractive, or family conditions more compelling than the incentives or punishments attached to job absence. Perhaps the most obvious example of the influence of family factors on job attendance is the presence of a sick child at home. The data show consistently that this particular family situation results in absenteeism from the job, especially for mothers (e.g. Northcott, 1983; Salkever, 1980, 1982). Morgan and Herman (1976) identified other family-related factors that are perceived as motivating and justifying absence from the organization, and these included family activities, attendance at family functions and home maintenance.

Very little research has been designed so that bidirectional effects can be detected. One notable exception to this is Lerner and Galambos's (1985) analysis of the interdependence of maternal role satisfaction and child behavioural difficulties. They analysed data collected over a two-year period, and found that child difficulties measured when the child was two years old predicted maternal role dissatisfaction when the child was three. In turn, maternal role dissatisfaction at that stage predicted children's behavioural difficulties one year later (see Figure 7.2).

The assumption of a unidirectional effect of employment on family functioning has severely restricted the way in which the relationship is conceptualized, and the manner in which research has investigated this relationship. Simply stated, the alternative assumption that there is a bidirectional relationship between employment and family functioning has virtually been ignored (Gutek *et al.*, 1988). Assumptions also guide the way in which results are interpreted. Most of the research on employment and family functioning has been of a cross-sectional nature. Even though cross-sectional data cannot justify causal inferences, significant correlations between employment factors and family functioning are still taken as support for a unidirectional effect.

An additional threat to the assumption of a unidirectional effect is that no relationship exists between employment and family functioning. There may be studies reporting no effects of employment on family functioning. However, because journal editors are far more disposed to publish significant findings than null results (Mahoney, 1976), studies showing no association between employment and family functioning are unlikely to be published. Instead, their destination is far more likely to be the proverbial file drawer.

ASSUMPTION 2: EMPLOYMENT EXERTS AN INEVITABLY NEGATIVE EFFECT ON FAMILY LIFE

As will be recalled, the starting assumption was that employment invariably exerts negative effects on family functioning. Yet this assumption is not fully supported by research findings. First, positive correlations between, for example, job satisfaction and marital satisfaction have been misread. While it is true that a positive correlation between these two variables means that individuals experiencing job dissatisfaction also experience marital dissatisfaction, this interpretation is incomplete because it ignores the fact that individuals who are satisfied with their jobs are likely to be satisfied with their marriages. Hence, the assumption that employment is bad for the family has led to incomplete readings of research findings. Second, some research findings show that employment experiences are not linked to marital functioning. For example, Greenhaus *et al.* (1987) found that high levels of job performance do not necessarily compromise accountants' marital satisfaction. Barling, Bluen and Moss (1988) showed that job-related achievement striving did not jeopardize medical practitioners' marital satisfaction. Third, even when job stress is associated with marital dissatisfaction, interpreting these results to mean that employment negatively affects family functioning ignores third variable effects. For example, Barling and Rosenbaum (1986) found that negative job stress was associated with marital dissatisfaction. Yet negative affect or depression may function as a third variable here: negative affect has been implicated as a causal factor in negative job stress (Brief *et al.*, 1988) as well as marital dissatisfaction (Beach *et al.*, 1988; Chapter 9). Hence, disregarding third variable effects may result in an inaccurate interpretation of such relationships.

ASSUMPTION 3: SEX BIASES IN THE LINK BETWEEN WORK AND FAMILY LIFE

One issue that has been raised throughout this text is the existence of a gender bias inherent in the presumed link between employment and family functioning. One example of this is the existence of separate literatures dealing with the effects of fathers' employment and mothers' employment on children. The continued existence of these separate literatures reflects an assumption that mothers' employment and fathers' employment exert different effects on their children. In an era when gender differences are no longer taken for granted, it is critical to evaluate whether any assumptions about gender differences can be justified empirically.

On one level, it might be claimed that men and women have similar organizational experiences. Specifically, despite Hall's (1972) earlier observation about gender-biased differences in the experience of inter-role conflict, recent findings suggest that men and women manifest similar levels of inter-role conflict (see Chapter 6). Yet for several reasons, it is argued strongly that such a position disregards reality. First, job-related pressures still differ markedly for men and women. Women still experience considerable discrimination throughout their career. During school, males' and females' exposure to different role models, and to the sex-typed nature of occupations, may bias children's vocational expectations. Farmer (1971) even questions if high school boys and girls are exposed to the same vocational decision-making process during guidance lessons. During the job selection process, females are discriminated against: regardless of qualifications, men are typically judged more suitable and more qualified for jobs than are women, and men are more likely to receive higher starting salaries (Heilman, 1983). Discrimination against women continues within the organization. Compared to men, women are less likely to be offered training opportunities, less likely to receive promotion and salary increases, and their successful performances are less likely to result in appropriate rewards (Heilman, 1983). Second, although men and women now report similar levels of inter-role conflict, mothers still have simultaneously to balance home and job responsibilities more frequently than fathers. This discrepancy between attitudes and behaviours is made clear from a study of a random sample of Edmonton households in 1979 (Northcott, 1983).

Although there were no gender differences in response to the statement that 'In a marriage, it is just as much a man's responsibility to care for children as it is a women's' (Northcott, 1983, p. 390), mothers were far more likely to stay home with a sick child regardless of whether they were employed full time or part time than were fathers. This reinforces the finding that while attitudes regarding appropriate gender-based parenting behaviours have changed, and may be more egalitarian, fathers still differ substantially from mothers in the extent to which they are involved in family tasks and responsibilities (Moore and Hofferth, 1979; Presland and Antill, 1987).

This argument can be extended. While there are no differences in the levels of inter-role conflict experienced, its predictors and consequences are not consistent for men and women. Voydanoff (1988) found that job-related factors such as work role conflict and ambiguity predicted employment/family conflict for men but not for women, as did involvement in weekend work or a non-day shift. Yet the strength of the relationship between employment/family conflict and the age of the youngest child in the family (presumably a measure of family role responsibilities) was far greater for women than for men. With regard to outcomes, inter-role conflict is equally associated with marital satisfaction for men and women (Barling, 1986a; Suchet and Barling, 1986), but unwanted household responsibilities predict child abuse (Margolin and Larson, 1988) and health problems (Barling and Janssens, 1984) for women but not for men. Likewise, the paths between inter-role conflict and psychological well-being differ for men and women (Sekaran, 1985).

One gender-biased assumption is not valid. As often stated, fathers' employment is believed to be beneficial for children, but mothers' employment is detrimental. While questions continue as to whether mothers should be employed, there is no similar questioning as to whether fathers should be employed. Yet the data show consistently that mothers' and fathers' employment experiences exert similar effects on their children. Specifically, fathers' and mothers' positive employment experiences are positively correlated with children's behaviour.

Thus, a dilemma exists in determining how to deal with the gender bias in the way men and women experience the link between employment and family. Do we reflect the situation as it is, or do we reflect the situation as we would like it to be? In other words, do we draw the conclusion from social and organizational reality that men and women continue to be treated differently in organizations, or do we infer from empirical findings with respect to inter-role conflict that there are no differences between how men and women experience their employment? There are costs and benefits associated with either alternative. Deciding that there are no differences is an attractive alternative because it appears less discriminatory, but it ignores the differences in social and organizational pressures on men and women. One way to resolve this dilemma is by recognizing that differences still exist, and designing one's research accordingly, while simultaneously acknowledging explicitly that one's value and objective is that of equal treatment for men and women in society and its institutions.

CONCEPTUAL ISSUES IN THE INTERDEPENDENCE BETWEEN FAMILY AND EMPLOYMENT

It is clear by know that there is an abundance of studies investigating the link between family functioning and employment. Several conceptual consequences emerge from existing knowledge about the link between family functioning and employment. These include the need for considering and contrasting the role of subjective and objective employment factors, mediational models, multiple stressor models, the importance of an open systems approach, causal issues in the relationship between employment and the family, and the contribution of the framework specified in Chapter 2 concerning different types of stressors and stress. Taking explicit cognisance of these consequences in future research and theorizing might hasten the day when a viable and comprehensive conceptual framework can be proposed.

Objective and Subjective Employment Characteristics

As evident throughout the text, there is no shortage of studies investigating the link between objective employment attributes (e.g. shift work, mothers' employment status, the amount of time spent on the job) and family functioning. In general, the results of these studies are consistent: objective employment attributes do not exert a meaningful effect on family functioning. Recently, the importance of investigating subjective employment experiences has been emphasized, and the results from this series of studies all point in the same direction: taking account of subjective employment experiences enhances the prediction of family functioning. Clearly, future research can no longer afford to overlook the critical role of subjective employment experiences, and a more appropriate approach would be to study the effects of objective and subjective employment aspects in the same study.

Mediation Models

One of the more important advances in investigations into the link between employment and the family has been the proposal and testing of mediational models. This is perhaps best illustrated by the advances provided by Parasuraman *et al.*'s (1989) recent study. As noted in Chapter 5, research has consistently failed to document a direct association between wives' employment status and husbands' marital satisfaction. Parasuraman *et al.* (1989) proposed and investigated a mediational model suggesting that wives' employment status exerts indirect effects on husbands' marital satisfaction through its direct effects on husbands' inter-role conflict and satisfaction with child care arrangements. They found no association between wives' employment status and marital functioning, but their data supported the mediating role of satisfaction with child care arrangements although not inter-role conflict. As such, Parasuraman *et al.*'s (1989) study advances knowledge about the link between employment status and marital satisfaction. Several studies testing mediational models (e.g. Barling *et al*., 1989; Barling and MacEwen, 1989; Lerner and Galambos, 1985; Mortimer *et al*., 1986; Sekaran, 1985) have also resulted in a more comprehensive understanding of the link between employment and family functioning. Also, although they did not explicitly test a mediational model, Jackson and Maslach's (1982) results point to the need for understanding indirect effects. They showed that police officers' burnout, an index of job-related strain, was negatively associated with marital and family functioning. Consequently, knowledge of the association between employment and the family will be furthered if relevant mediating variables are identified.

Multiple Stressors

With very few exceptions, statistically significant associations between employment and family are modest in magnitude. One reason for this is that no single employment variable is powerful enough to exert a profound effect on family functioning. Also, many other factors besides employment contribute to family functioning. When a combination of employment and/or personal factors is investigated, the prediction of family functioning is enhanced. This calls for a multiple stressors model, where the combined effects of several, simultaneous stressors or events are investigated. One example involves the effects of parental employment experiences on children. Studies invariably investigate the effects of either mothers' employment or fathers' employment separately. Yet there may be an additive effect on children's behaviour if both parents experience their employment negatively. An inspection of the marital functioning literatures also supports the need for a multiple stressor model. Specifically, the causes or predictors of marital functioning are numerous and diverse. This leads naturally into a discussion on the need for an open systems model in understanding the link between family functioning and employment.

The Need for an Open Systems Model

There are several reasons why an open systems model is needed to understand the link between family and employment functioning. These include the need to investigate mediating factors outside the employment and family systems, and the need to focus on multiple stressors. The causes of marital functioning cannot be located exclusively within the employment domain, and an explanation of the experience of employment requires a focus beyond that of the family. All this points to the fact that focusing only on job and family factors will result in an incomplete perspective of their relationship. It should be noted, however, that adoption of an open systems framework has clear implications for the identification of an initial causal determinant linking employment and family. Once it is accepted that all personal, family and employment systems and subsystems constantly impinge on each other, and are in a continual state of flux, the identification of an initial causal determinant in any chain would be difficult, if not impossible.

Daily Acute and Chronic Job Stressors

In Chapter 2, a framework for differentiating between different types of stressors was offered. The objective was to provide a means of predicting the duration and timing of any outcome or strain, as well as the effectiveness of different coping strategies. In retrospect, that framework has proved useful in integrating and understanding the link between employment and family functioning. Given the importance of a framework that would enable predictions about time lags between events and their outcomes (Campbell *et al.*, 1982; Gollob and Reichardt, 1987), and an understanding of how coping strategies interact with family and employment, further tests of this framework are in order. To evaluate the predictions of that framework more appropriately, studies undertaking specific *a priori* tests of its hypotheses are now required.

Causal Issues in the Link between Family and Employment

There is little doubt that inferences regarding the causal link between employment and family functioning are premature. One of the reasons for this is that with few exceptions (Barling *et al.*, 1989; Barling and MacEwen, 1989; Brett and Reilly, 1988; Lerner and Galambos, 1985; MacEwen and Barling, 1988a; Marsella *et al.*, 1974), previous studies have relied exclusively on data collected at a single point in time. Hence, it is crucial that future data be collected on a longitudinal basis wherever possible.

There is a further reason for exercising caution in implying any causal effects of employment on family functioning. One question that has often been posed is whether unemployment is sufficient to cause any effects on marital functioning, or whether unemployment uncovers pre-existing problems (Dooley and Catalano, 1980). Komarovsky's (1940) early findings suggested that marital functioning was enhanced after unemployment if it was positive beforehand. In contrast, marital functioning was most threatened after unemployment where there had been pre-existing marital problems. A similar pattern is now emerging from more recent reports. Elder and Caspi (1988) found in the re-analysis of their data collected during the Great Depression that emotional instability only deteriorated for individuals already showing signs of instability. Warr, Jackson and Banks (1988) noted a similar pattern for individuals' health problems before and after a layoff. A recent study on the effects of a short-term strike replicate this pattern. Vispo and Shine (1985) found that the effects of perceived financial stress during a strike were most pronounced where, in their words, 'the marriage was already shaky' (p. 115). Thus, the list of predictors of how employment influences marital functioning must include prior marital functioning. In a separate context, Grant *et al.* (1987, p. 231) reached the same conclusion, as can be understood from the title of their article 'Life events do not predict symptoms: symptoms predict symptoms'. Finally, as mentioned previously, failure to account for third variables such as depression (e.g. Brief *et al.*, 1988) in accounting for the relationship between job stressors and marital functioning reduces the extent to which causal inferences are possible. Until depression is accounted for in this case, it is possible that the link between job stressors and marital functioning is spurious, in other words, it results because of the effect of depression on job stressors and marital functioning.

If a theory specifying the link between employment and the family is to be achieved, it is critical that any causal networks be investigated. Nonetheless, the obstacles to doing so should not be underestimated. Identifying the initial causal factor in the link between employment and the family may be as problematic as resolving the chicken and the egg dilemma.

IMPLICATIONS FOR RESEARCH ON EMPLOYMENT AND THE FAMILY

For knowledge about the link between employment and family functioning to advance, it is critical that the methodologies used facilitate causal inferences. The methodology most suited to this objective would be either a true experimental design, or a quasi-experimental design (Cook and Campbell, 1979). In true experimental designs, individuals are assigned randomly to control and experimental groups; in quasi-experimental designs, individuals are placed in either an experimental or control group on a non-random basis. Despite the advantages these two methodologies have for causal inferences, they are not readily applicable to studying employment and family linkages, where random assignment to groups is not always possible, and tests of multiple predictors of employment or family functioning often require non-experimental designs. Thus, correlational designs will continue to predominate in this area. One way to advance understanding of the causal link between family functioning and employment using correlational designs is to collect longitudinal data from which causal inferences are possible. Causal inferences can be strengthened in these cases if two conditions are fulfilled. First, because the strength of any effect is dependent on the appropriateness of the time lag, it is critical that the time period between assessments is based on an understanding of precisely when effects are expected to become manifest. As Gollob and Reichardt (1987, p. 82) note cogently in a different context:

> ... different time lags typically have different effect sizes. For example, the effects of taking 2 aspirin on reducing headache pain may be zero 2 min after ingestion, may be substantial after 30 min, may be near maximum after 2 or 3 hours, may be much reduced after 5 hours, and may be zero again after 24 hours.

Thus, the advantages of repeated measurements is apparent, and the *reasons* for the amount of time that lapses between the two testing phases may be a more important consideration than the *quantity* of time elapsing. Second, causal inferences about the link between two variables are reinforced to the extent that confounding effects are excluded. Because experimental control is difficult to achieve in this situation, control should be exerted by statistically partialling out any confounding effects.

Until now, considerable mention has been made of the need to focus on mediating variables. Future research on the relationship between employment and family functioning will also be enhanced by explicitly considering variables that moderate this relationship. One avenue for this research is to continue to assess the role of gender as a moderating variable. This would address differences in the link between employment and family functioning for males and females. Other possible moderating variables include objective characteristics of employment (e.g. whether individuals are involved in shift work, flexible work schedules, overtime work) and subjective employment experiences (e.g. whether the relationship between employment and family functioning is consistent across different levels of job involvement; see Innes and Clarke, 1985). It is also worth considering the role of social support or personality factors such as hardiness as possible moderators, as findings from such research isolate the coping techniques that are effective, and have considerable implications for treatment and intervention strategies.

CLINICAL VS STATISTICAL EFFECTS OF EMPLOYMENT ON FAMILY FUNCTIONING

To some extent, the above issue have been considered throughout this text. Although the magnitude and direction of the relationship between employment experiences and family functioning has also been considered throughout this text, one issue that has not been addressed is the *meaning* of these relationships. As already noted, the magnitude of the relations between employment or unemployment on the one hand, and family functioning on the other, are modest at best. This remains true even when the additive effects of different employment experiences are examined (e.g. Barling, 1984). From one perspective, these modest relations should be expected, because employment represents only one of the numerous predictors of family functioning. Nevertheless, there are some important exceptions to this pattern, which raise the issue of whether employment exerts effects on marital functioning that are statistically significant but of limited applied meaning, or whether some employment experiences exert effects on marital functioning that are both statistically significant and of some clinical consequence. Findings from four separate research topics show the situations under which employment characteristics and experiences exert clinically relevant effects on family functioning. These include the effects of (1) inter-role stressors on marital functioning, (2) job stressors, (3) status incongruency on physical aggression between marital partners, and (4) maternal employment role commitment on children's behavioural problems.

Two separate studies have found that inter-role conflict is associated with marital dissatisfaction scores suggestive of a marriage at risk for dissolution. Fathers reporting high levels of inter-role conflict and low levels of personality hardiness achieved marital satisfaction scores within the distressed range (M = 81.9) of Locke and Wallace's (1959) Short Marital Adjustment Test (Barling, 1986a). Those experiencing high levels of inter-role conflict and high hardiness, or low levels of inter-role conflict regardless of their hardiness, manifested adequate marital satisfaction (all M's >106.61). In a separate investigation, Suchet and Barling (1986) showed a somewhat similar pattern using the same index of marital functioning: employed mothers reporting high inter-role conflict and little support from their spouses also yield scores indicative of a marriage at risk (M = 79.67). On the contrary, independent of the level of spouse support, employed wives low in inter-role conflict manifested satisfactory marital adjustment, as did employed wives high in inter-role conflict who received instrumental and emotional support from their husbands (all M's >100). Two aspects of these studies are noteworthy. First, the alternative hypothesis that marital dissatisfaction leads to inter-role conflict was tested and excluded subsequently in a short-term longitudinal analysis (MacEwen and Barling, 1988a). Second, these two studies provide some insight as to how the effects of high levels of inter-role conflict could be treated on an individual level. For example, knowing how social support functions to protect individuals experiencing high levels of inter-role conflict from negative marital functioning could provide some direction for individual treatment.

There is some empirical support for the notion that job stressors are associated with spouse abuse (MacEwen and Barling, 1988b). Nonetheless, although the variance accounted for in spouse abuse is minimal, the possible clinical meaning of this finding should not be underestimated. There was a one-year time lag between the assessment of stress and marital aggression, and although marital aggression is relatively stable (O'Leary *et al.*, 1989), the initial stress accounted for 1% of the variance in marital aggression *after* partialling out the variance (51%) attributable to prior levels of marital aggression. The relations between job-related attributes and marital aggression have been addressed in another way. Although wives' occupational status does not place them at any greater risk for being abused, the risk of experiencing psychological and physical abuse (including abuse that is life threatening) increases when wives' jobs are of a higher prestige than their husbands' jobs. Specifically, Hornung *et al.* (1981) found that when husbands' job prestige was similar to wives', the relative risk for the wife to be psychologically abused, physically abused or to experience life-threatening abuse was 0.97, 0.69 and 0.17 respectively. In contrast, when wives' occupational achievement exceeds that of their husbands', these relative risk rates are 1.03, 1.29 and 1.46 respectively. This indicates that where the wife is occupationally superior to her husband, the likelihood that she will experience physical aggression of life-threatening severity is 1.46 times greater than those situations in which there is occupational consistency between spouses. Lastly, in the same way that wives' employment status places them at no greater risk for experiencing spouse abuse, mothers' employment status does not jeopardize children's well-being. Yet in one study, when mothers' employment status was not congruent with their employment role commitment, teachers rated their children as at least as inattentive and immature as Quay and Peterson's (1983) sample of 24 clinic children (Barling, Fullagar and March-Dingle, 1988). Inattention and immaturity scores for children whose mothers' employment status and commitment were congruent were similar to those of Quay and Peterson's (1983) normal sample. These studies illustrate that under certain conditions, employment stressors and experiences do exert a clinically meaningful influence on some aspects of marital and family functioning.

PRACTICAL IMPLICATIONS

Given the current state of knowledge about the link between employment and the family, several strategies can be identified that might increase the likelihood that employment experiences and family functioning influence each other positively. These approaches can be differentiated with respect to their target, i.e. whether intervention is directed at the societal, organizational, government or family/individual level.

Societal Interventions

To some extent, what are truly necessary are interventions aimed at clarifying public misconceptions regarding the effects of employment on family functioning. Articles based on assumptions rather than empirical data continue to appear in popular magazines (e.g. Amiel, 1985; Fallows, 1983). These articles perpetuate prevailing fears, myths and misconceptions. To some extent, professionals and academics involved in this area have been remiss in not correcting misconceptions. Even though modifying social attitudes and beliefs is extremely difficult, such a preventive approach might counteract misconceptions regarding interactions between employment and the family.

It might be most appropriate to target children by providing them with more appropriate information regarding the 'world of paid work' well before they enter the labour force. Children are already recipients of this information. As Piotrkowski and Stark (1987) observe, children learn about the meaning of paid work through observations of their employed parents. It may be worth while to consider a more direct approach similar to that used to inform children about the meaning of divorce, and help them cope with its consequences. It this context, 'bibliotherapy' has been used extensively. Specifically, picture books, source books and novels concerning the meaning of divorce that are relevant for different age groups abound. The availability of similar sources of information regarding the nature of employment and unemployment, and their consequences for the family may be useful in providing children with an accurate conception of employment. One example of this is Cleary's (1977) book *Ramona and Her Father*. In this particular book appropriate for junior elementary school children, Ramona's father is laid off, and Cleary (1977) captures much of the meaning of unemployment for the family. For example, the initial shock is illustrated well, as is the uncertainty about the future, perceived financial strain and its consequences for all family members, and the additional family role responsibilities assumed by the father. More direct techniques could also be used to inform high school students of the range of vocational opportunities open to them. For example, Farmer (1971) suggests that appropriate vocational decision-making procedures be taught in high school guidance courses.

Organizations and the Well-being of their Members and Members' Families

The question of whether organizations are responsible for the psychological and physical well-being of their employees and their families is not new. Indeed, it is a question that has frequently been posed by academics and columnists in many sources, especially during the 1980s (e.g. Castro, 1988; McCroskey, 1982; *US News and World Report*, 1980). More specifically, Ivancevich, Matteson and Richards (1985) ask pointedly 'Who is liable for stress on the job?', and suggest that the organization is, at least from a legal viewpoint. Consistent with this view, there are guidelines in the literature for the implementation of specific programmes by organizations (e.g. Kater, 1985; Segal, 1984). Most remarkable is that despite the considerable attention focusing on this issue, there have been relatively few attempts by organizations to implement such programmes, and even fewer attempts to assess systematically whether the programmes achieve their stated objectives. Examples of two organizational programmes, namely company sponsored child care and employee assistance programmes, will be used to illustrate this situation.

One of the initial catalysts underlying the introduction of company sponsored child care programmes was the belief that they would help the organization fulfil its moral responsibilities to its labour force. Yet the reasons for organizations providing child care opportunities (whether on-site or not) are more instrumental and self-serving: Friedman (1986) notes that American organizations are involved in child care because of the benefits that may accrue to the organization. Because child care would presumably make it easier for employees to balance their parenting and employment roles, it is argued that companies which provide such facilities would be able to attract, recruit and retain valuable employees because of their enhanced public image and the increased company commitment and job satisfaction of their employees. Also, such companies would enjoy lower absenteeism, tardiness and accident rates. Yet despite the plethora of literature on the effects of day care on the child (see Clarke-Stewart, 1989), there are few controlled studies on the effects of child care on organizational functioning (Miller, 1984; Phillips, 1984). This may be a critical shortcoming. As will be noted below, the widespread implementation of company sponsored child care probably hinges more on empirical demonstrations of the benefits for organizations than on arguments about moral responsibility.

The experience with employment assistance programmes parallels that of child care centres. In their various forms, employment assistance programmes represent attempts to confront personal problems that are manifest directly or indirectly at the workplace, regardless of whether or not they affect job performance. In particular, employment assistance programmes have been established to confront problems such as alcohol and drug abuse, smoking, weight control and blood pressure. Yet again, however, while it is believed that these programmes benefit those organizations that provide them, there is no body of empirical data currently available to substantiate this belief (Miller, 1986; Weiss, 1987). As was the case with child care facilities, the lack of empirical data is particularly problematic because employee assistance programmes are unlikely to be introduced without supporting data. One notable exception to the lack of company initiated programmes is flexible work schedules. As noted in Chapter 3, governments were intent on introducing flexible work schedules because of transportation problems and the need to get more mothers back into the labour force during the 1970s. In the United States, the government was particularly interested in the effects of flexible work schedules, and mandated that any federal government department introducing flexible work schedules had to conduct research on its effects. As a result, there is a wealth of relevant data that has guided government policy and motivated organizations to introduce such programmes

Thus, two final points should be noted. First, American organizations and labour unions have been conspicuous in not adapting to the demands of the modern family, and are only now beginning to shoulder some of the responsibility for including relevant policies and procedures in their compensation packages. In this respect, American organizations have lagged behind their European counterparts (Cooke, 1989; Raabe and Gessner, 1988). Cooke (1989) notes that efforts in this direction in America would benefit tremendously from studying and emulating the successful experiences of European companies. In particular, European programmes have been far more wide-ranging than typical American programmes, and have included company sponsored child care programmes, maternity and parental leave, child allowances, care for sick children and family members, and assistance with transportation and housing. Second, interest has been expressed in the factors that motivate organizations to consider such programmes. Hall and Richter (1988) maintain that until executives understand that the link between family and employment is not a 'woman's problem' (p. 214), and appreciate the potential rewards that accrue to the organization following implementation of such programmes, they will remain unwilling to consider strategies targeted at the interdependence of employment and family. In their study of 276 employers in America, McNeely and Fogarty (1988) found that financial advantages to the organization and the employee were viewed as the most powerful incentives for implementing such programmes. When they were asked what they would like to know most about the experiences of other companies with employment/family programmes, they again referred to the cost effectiveness of these programmes (e.g. cost, productivity, absence, job satisfaction, recruitment and turnover). Hence, social scientists should investigate the benefits to the organization and the individual of such programmes.

Government Policies to Help Employees Balance Jobs and Families

Because organizations seem either unwilling or unable to confront the family needs of their employees voluntarily, it is necessary to look to other sources. One alternative source is the government. Through legislated incentives and/or punishments, governments have at their disposal the means for motivating organizations to implement programmes (a) to assist employees cope with the stress involved in balancing family and employment responsibilities, and (b) to enhance organizational functioning (Cooke, 1989). Yet at least in the United States, government policies have lagged behind the changes and needs of the family. Social scientists may be in a position to assist government (and organizations) by providing research that is relevant to policy decisions (Stipek and McCroskey, 1989). The example of flexible work schedules cited previously illustrates this point.

Interventions Targeted at the Individual or Family

The individual employee and his or her spouse and/or children remain the most obvious target for any intervention or treatment. There are several reports in the literature of such attempts. It is not within the scope of this discussion to describe in detail or evaluate these clinical interventions. These programmes are outlined here merely to display the range of issues that have been addressed. For example, based on research findings on maternal employment, Etaugh (1984) derived a series of suggestions as to how to address or treat any problems children encounter as a result of their mother's employment. Most of the remaining literature has addressed the problems of adults. For example, there are programmes for dealing with burnout (Glicken, 1983), with the stress generated when either spouse is involved in business travel (Culbert and Renshaw, 1972), with the stress associated with being an employed mother (Long and Haney, 1988), and with challenges to marital functioning that may emerge when both spouses are employed (Yogev, 1983). In an interesting case study, Siegerman (1983) describes the treatment for depression in a 71-year-old man who had been forced to accept mandatory retirement.

The problem, therefore, does not rest with the lack of suggestions, or actual interventions to help individuals and family members better balance the demands of employment and family responsibilities. The problem lies in getting organizations to implement such programmes. However, other problems arise when individuals are targeted for 'treatment'. First, accepting that individuals should be offered some kind of 'treatment' assumes that inter-role conflict, for example, is an 'abnormal' problem. Extreme caution should be exercised, however, in labelling inter-role conflict as a 'problem' that requires 'treatment'. It is not surprising that individuals experience difficulty balancing employment and family demands given the lack of social, organizational and governmental resources at their disposal. Therefore, societal values and organizational procedures are more appropriate targets for 'treatment'. Second, with the exception of programmes (e.g. job training) directed specifically at high risk groups (e.g. hard-core unemployed), intervention attempts targeted at the individual level are not consistent with the notion of prevention. As Farmer (1971) notes, the individual counselling approach requires that one wait for a problem to emerge. Finally, as was the case with child care and employee assistance programmes, there have been very few attempts to evaluate systematically those programmes implemented to induce the required changes (e.g. Long and Haney, 1988).

One final point regarding intervention is in order. It has been noted that identifying the initial causal stressor or event may be difficult if not impossible given the interactive nature of open systems. At the same time, however, the same open systems perspective implies that intervention attempts aimed at any point within the system will affect all substystems.

SOME REMAINING EMPLOYMENT/FAMILY ISSUES

Trying to predict the questions that are likely to be asked in the future is a risky undertaking at any time. However, based on the literature available and on current societal trends, several topics relevant to employment and the family that must be confronted can be isolated. These include the experience of non-employed individuals, retirees, part-time employees, and the possible effects of increasing technological and electronic sophistication at the workplace.

People who are not employed do indeed work, and vary in how they subjectively experience their work. Occupational theories have proved to be useful in understanding the non-paid work of homemakers (e.g. Tinsley and Tinsley, 1989). In the same way, employment models (Jahoda, 1982) and job characteristics models (Hackman and Oldham, 1980; Warr, 1987a, b) may be useful in describing and understanding the experience of homemakers. There is some empirical support for investigating the contribution of employment, job and occupational theories to an understanding of the meaning and consequences of homemakers' role and work experiences. As noted in Chapter 7, the consequences of maternal employment role experiences are consistent regardless of whether mothers are employed or not (e.g. Barling, Fullagar and March-Dingle, 1988; Lerner and Galambos, 1985).

Employment and occupational theories may also be useful in understanding the meaning and consequences of another form of non-employment, namely retirement. Like unemployment, there is a tendency for psychological and physical well-being to be compromised when the individual retires, but this does not hold true for everyone (McGoldrick and Cooper, 1985). Also, in the same way that the psychological well-being of individuals who experience involuntary unemployment can be predicted by the extent to which they continue to fulfil the manifest and latent functions of employment (Jahoda, 1982), so may the extent to which retirement was voluntary predict retirees' well-being.

Emerging societal trends may also present new issues that need to be investigated and understood. One social trend of increasing significance during the 1980s has been the rise in the number of people who are employed on a part-time basis. To date, not enough is known about the experience of part-time employment (Rotchford and Roberts, 1982). This may be especially important given the counterintuitive findings regarding employment status and family violence. Specifically, rates of both spouse abuse (Straus *et al.*, 1980) and child abuse (Gelles and Hargreaves, 1981) are higher for individuals employed on a part-time basis than for those who are unemployed or employed full time. It remains to be seen why such a relationship emerges, and whether part-time employment affects other aspects of family functioning. Until more is known about the nature and meaning of part-time employment, it would be premature to advise mothers with young children to accept part-time rather than full-time employment, on the assumption that part-time employment is less stressful than full-time employment, but more satisfying than non-employment (Martin *et al.*, 1984).

Another trend which may affect the link between employment and the family involves the increasing use of computerized technology in organizations. With the increasing use of computers, facsimile machines, cordless telephones and the like, it is often suggested that people will be more inclined to do their paid work at home. Commuting and parking problems make this possibility even more attractive (Schwartz, Tsiantar and Springen, 1989). If such a change does take place, the implications for employment/family linkages would be considerable: Recall that Jahoda (1982) suggested that the type of social support received on the job (typically informational) is fundamentally different from that offered by the family (usually emotional). Employment offers a different and important source of alternative support. However, massive changes along these lines are unlikely for several reasons. First, following the introduction of computers in the late 1970s and early 1980s, similar arguments about a move away from the office were advanced, but widespread changes did not follow. Second, one of the prevalent beliefs about paid work is that its meaning derives from the fact that it occurs within an organizational, social and group context (Bucholz, 1978). Third, the belief that doing one's job from home would enable individuals to balance the demands of family and employment may not be realistic. For example, devoting full attention to one's job at home still requires that alternative child care be available (Schwartz *et al.*, 1989). Lastly, one prerequisite for career advancement is that individuals are visible within the organization (Cooper and Cliff, 1985).

CONCLUSION

Given continuing pressures that affect the way in which individuals balance their employment and family responsibilities, the voluminous amount of research on employment and family will continue, if not increase. Undoubtedly, our understanding of the interdependence has progressed tremendously because of this, especially over the past decade. This is important: from a conceptual perspective, a more comprehensive understanding about the link between employment and family functioning is in the offing. On a pragmatic level, governments and organizations are waiting and asking for more comprehensive models and data answering their specific concerns. If these are forthcoming, they are more likely to welcome change and actively assist in its implementation.

References

Aberle, D.F., and Naegele, K.D. (1952). Middle-class fathers' occupational role and attitudes toward children. *American Journal of Orthopsychiatry*, **22**, 366–78.

Acock, A.C., Barker, D., and Bengston, V.L. (1982). Mother's employment and parent–youth similarity. *Journal of Marriage and the Family*, **44**, 441–55.

Agathonos, H., and Stathakopoulou, N. (1983). Life events and child abuse: A controlled study. In J. Leavitt (ed.), *Child Abuse and Neglect: Research and Innovations in NATO Countries*, pp. 83–91. Kluwer, Netherlands.

Aldous, J. (1969a). Occupational characteristics and males' role performance in the family. *Journal of Marriage and the Family*, **31**, 707–12.

Aldous, J. (1969b). Wives' employment status and lower-class men as husband–fathers: Support for the Moynihan thesis. *Journal of Marriage and the Family*, **31**, 469–76.

Aldous, J. (1981). *Two paychecks: Life in Dual-Career Families*. Sage, California.

Aldous, J., Osmond, M.W., and Hicks, M.W. (1979). Men's work and men's families. In W.R. Burr *et al.* (eds), *Contemporary Theories About the Family*. Vol. 1: *Research-Based Theories*, pp. 227–56. Macmillan, New York.

Aldwin, C.M., and Revenson, T.A. (1986). Vulnerability to economic stress. *American Journal of Community Pyschology*, **14**, 161–75.

Allen, R.E., and Keaveny, T.J. (1979). Does the work status of married women affect their attitudes toward family life? *Personnel Administrator*, **24**, 63–6.

Alpert, D., and Culbertson, A. (1987). Daily hassles and coping strategies of dual-earner and nondual-earner women. *Psychology of Women Quarterly*, **11**, 359–66.

Alvarez, W.F. (1985). The meaning of maternal employment for mothers and their perceptions of their three-year old children. *Child Development*, **56**, 350–60.

American Psychiatric Association, (1987). *Diagnostic and Statistical Manual of Mental Disorders–Revised*. American Psychiatric Association, Washington, D C.

Amiel, B. (1985). Dilemma of the working parent. *MacLean's* 23 December, 5.

Anand, V. (1975). The flexible hours concepts. *Accountancy*, **86**, 92–4.

Anderson, C.W. (1980). Attachment in daily separations: Reconceptualizing day care and maternal employment issues. *Child Development*, **51**, 242–5.

Anderson, C.R., Hellriegel, D., and Slocum, J.W. (1977). Managerial response to environmentally induced stress. *Academy of Management Journal*, **20**, 260–72.

Anderson-Kulman, R.E. (1986). Working mothers and the family context: Predicting positive coping. *Journal of Vocational Behavior*, **28**, 241–53.

Angell, R.C. (1936). *The Family Encounters the Depression*. Scribner, New York.

Archer, J., and Rhodes, V. (1987). Bereavement and reactions to job loss: A comparative review. *British Journal of Social Psychology*, **26**, 211–24.

Aring, C.D. (1974). Work. *American Journal of Psychiatry*, **131**, 901.

Atkinson, T., Liem, R., and Liem, J.H. (1986). The social costs of unemployment: Implications for social support. *Journal of Health and Social Behavior*, **27**, 317–31.

Avery-Clark, C. (1986). Sexual dysfunction and disorder patterns of working and nonworking wives. *Journal of Sex and Marital Therapy*, **12**, 93–107.

Bailey, J.M., and Bhagat, R.S. (1987). Meaning and measurement of stressors in the work environment: An evaluation. In S.V. Kasl and C.L. Cooper (eds), *Stress and Health: Issues in Research Methodology*, pp. 207–29. Wiley, Chichester.

Bakke, E.W. (1933). *The Unemployed Man*. Nisbet, London.

Bakke, E.W. (1940). *Citizens without Work*. Yale University Press, New Haven.

Banducci, R. (1967). The effect of mother's employment on the achievement, aspirations, and expectations of the child. *The Personnel and Guidance Journal*, **46**, 263–7.

Barclay, J.R., Stilwell, W.E., and Barclay, L.K. (1972). The influence of paternal occupation on social interaction measures in elementary school children. *Journal of Vocational Behavior*, **2**, 433–46.

Barglow, P., Vaughn, B.E., and Molitor, N. (1987). Effects of maternal absence due to employment on the quality of infant–mother attachment in a low-risk sample. *Child Development*, **58**, 945–54.

Barling, J. (1984). Effects of husbands' work experiences on wives' marital satisfaction. *The Journal of Social Psychology*, **124**, 219–25.

Barling, J. (1986a). Interrole conflict and marital functioning amongst employed fathers. *Journal of Occupational Behaviour*, **7**, 1–8.

Barling, J. (1986b). Fathers' work experiences, the father–child relationship and children's behaviour. *Journal of Occupational Behaviour*, **7**, 61–6.

Barling, J. (in press). Employment and marital functioning. In F.D. Fincham and T. Bradbury (eds), *The Psychology of Marriage: Conceptual, Empirical and Applied Perspectives*. Praeger, New York.

Barling, J., and Barenbrug, A. (1984). Some personal consequences of flexitime work schedules. *Journal of Social Psychology*, **123**, 137–8.

Barling, J., Bluen, S.D., and Fain, R. (1987). Psychological functioning following an acute disaster. *Journal of Applied Psychology*, **72**, 683–90.

Barling, J., Bluen, S.D., and Moss, V. (1988). Type A behavior and marital dissatisfaction: Disentangling the effects of achievement striving and impatience-irritability. Manuscript submitted for publication.

Barling, J., and Charbonneau, D. (1989). Disentangling the relationship between Type A behaviour, performance and health. Manuscript submitted for publication.

Barling, J., Fullagar, C., and Marchl-Dingle, J. (1987). Employment commitment as a moderator of the maternal employment status/child behavior relationship. *Journal of Occupational Behavior*, **9**, 113–22.

Barling, J., and Janssens, P. (1984). Work stressors, gender differences and psychosomatic health problems. *South African Journal of Psychology*, **14** (2), 50–3.

Barling, J., and MacEwen, K.E. (1988). A multitrait–multimethod analysis of four maternal employment role experiences. *Journal of Organizational Behavior*, **9**, 335–44.

Barling, J., and MacEwen, K.E. (1989). Maternal employment experiences, attention problems and behavioral performance: A mediational model. Manuscript submitted for publication.

Barling, J., MacEwen, K.E., and Pratt, L.I. (1988). Manipulating the type and source of social support: An experimental investigation. *Canadian Journal of Behavioral Science*, **20**, 140–53.

Barling, J., and Milligan, J. (1987). Some psychological consequences of striking: a six month longitudinal study. *Journal of Occupational Behaviour*, **8**, 127–38.

Barling, J., and Rosenbaum, A. (1986). Work stressors and wife abuse. *Journal of Applied Psychology*, **71**, 346–8.

Barling, J., Tetrick, L.E., and MacEwen, K.E. (1989). Linking work stress to marital instability. Manuscript under preparation.

Barling, J., and Van Bart, D. (1984). Mothers' subjective employment experiences and the behaviours of their nursery school children. *Journal of Occupational Psychology*, **57**, 49–56.

Barling, J., O'Leary, K.D., Jouriles, E.N., Vivian, D., and MacEwen, K.E. (1987). Factor similarity of the Conflict Tactics Scales across samples, spouses and sites: Issues and implications. *Journal of Family Violence*, **2**, 37–53.

Barnett, R.C. (1982). Multiple roles and well-being: A study of mothers of preschool age children. *Psychology of Women Quarterly*, **7**, 175–8.

Bartolome, F. (1983). The work alibi: When it's harder to go home. *Harvard Business Review*, March–April, 67-74.

Bartolome, F., and Evans, P.A.L. (1980). Must success cost so much? *Harvard Business Review*, March–April, 137–48.

Baruch, G.K. (1972). Maternal influences upon college women's attitudes toward women and work. *Developmental Psychology*, **6**, 32–7.

Baruch, G.K., and Barnett, R.C. (1986a). Role quality, multiple role involvement, and psychological well-being in midlife women. *Journal of Personality and Social Psychology*, **51**, 578–85.

Baruch, G.K., and Barnett, R.C. (1986b). Consequences of fathers' participation in family work: Parents' role strain and well-being. *Journal of Personality and Social Psychology*, **51**, 983–92.

Batt, W.L. (1983). Canada's good example with displaced workers. *Harvard Business Review*, **61**, 6-22.

Baum, A., Fleming, R., and Reddy, D.M. (1986). Unemployment stress, locus of control, reactance and learned helplessness. *Social Science and Medicine*, **22**, 509–16.

Baum, A., Gatchel, R.J., and Schaeffer, M.A. (1983). Emotional, behavioral, and physiological effects of chronic stress at Three Mile Island. *Journal of Consulting and Clinical Psychology*, **51**, 565–72.

Beach, S.R.H., Nelson, G.M., and O'Leary, K.D. (1988). Cognitive and marital factors in depression. *Journal of Psychopathology and Behavioral Assessment*, **10**, 93–105.

Beach, S.R.H., and O'Leary, K.D. (1986). The treatment of depression occurring in the context of marital discord. *Behavior Therapy*, **17**, 43–9.

Becker, M.A., and Byrne, D. (1984). Type A behavior and daily activities of young married couples. *Journal of Applied Social Psychology*, **14**, 82–8.

Beckman, K., Marsella, A.J., and Finney, R. (1979). Depression in the wives of nuclear submarine personnel. *American Journal of Psychiatry*, **136**, 524–6.

Beehr, T.A. (1985). The role of social support in coping with organizational stress. In T.A. Beehr and R.S. Bhagat (eds), *Human Stress and Cognition in Organizations*, pp. 375–98. John Wiley, New York.

Beehr, T.A., and Franz, T.M. (1987). The current debate over the meaning of job stress. In J.M. Ivancevich and D.C. Ganster (eds), *Job Stress: From Theory to Suggestion*, pp. 5–18. Haworth Press, New York.

Bell, R.A., Daly, J.A., and Gonzales, M.C. (1987). Affinity-maintenance in marriage and marital satisfaction. *Journal of Marriage and the Family*, **49**, 445–54.

Belsky, J. (1980). Child maltreatment: An ecological perspective. *American Psychologist*, **35**, 320–35.

Belsky, J., and Steinberg, L.D. (1978). The effects of day-care: A critical review. *Child Development*, **49**, 929–49.

Beutell, N. J., and Greenhaus, J.H. (1983). Integration of home and nonhome roles: Women's conflict and coping behavior. *Journal of Applied Psychology*, **68**, 43–8.

Bey, D.B., and Lange, J. (1974). Waiting wives: Women under stress. *American Journal of Psychiatry*, **131**, 283–6.

Binns, D., and Mars, G. (1984). Family, community and unemployment: A study in change. *Sociological Review*, **32**, 662–95.

Blaney, N.T., Brown, P., and Blaney, P.H. (1986). Type A, marital adjustment and life stress. *Journal of Behavioral Medicine*, **9**, 491–502.

Blood, R.O., and Hamblin, R. L. (1958). The effect of the wife's employment on the family power structure. *Social Forces*, **36**, 347–52.

Blood, R.O., and Wolfe, D.M. (1960). *Husbands and Wives: The Dynamics of Married Living*. The Free Press, Illinois.

Bluen, S.D., and Barling, J. (1988). Psychological stressors associated with industrial relations. In C.L. Cooper and R. Payne (eds), *Causes, Coping and Consequences of Stress at Work*, pp. 175–205. Wiley, Chichester.

Bluen, S.D., Barling, J., and Burns, W. (1989). Predicting job satisfaction and depression using the impatience-irritability and achievement striving dimensions of type A behavior. *Journal of Applied Psychology* (in press).

Bohen, H., and Viveros-Long, A. (1981). *Balancing Job and Family Life*. Temple University Press, Philadelphia.

Bolger, N., DeLongis, A., Kessler, R.C., and Wethington, E. (1989). The contagion of stress across multiple roles. *Journal of Marriage and the Family*, **51**, 175–84.

Booth, A. (1979). Does wives' employment cause stress for husbands? *The Family Coordinator*, **28**, 445–9.

Booth, A., and Edwards, J.N. (1980). Fathers: The invisible parent. *Sex Roles*, **6**, 445–56.

Booth, A., Johnson, D.R., White, L., and Edwards, J.N. (1984). Women, outside employment and marital instability. *American Journal of Sociology*, **90**, 567–83.

Booth-Kewley, S., and Friedman, H.S. (1987). Psychological predictors of heart disease: A quantitative review. *Psychological Review*, **101**, 343–62.

Bosch, L., and de Lange, W.A.M. (1987). Shift work in health care. *Ergonomics*, **30**, 773–91.

Bossard, J.H.S., and Boll, E.S. (1966). *The Sociology of Child Development*, 4th edn. Harper and Row, New York.

Bowen, G.L. (1987). Wives' employment status and marital adjustment in military families. *Psychological Reports*, **61**, 467–74.

Breakwell, G.M., Fife-Schaw, C., and Devereux, J. (1988). Parental influence and teenagers' motivation to train for technological jobs. *Journal of Occupational Psychology*, **61**, 79–88.

Brenner, M.H. (1975). Trends in alcohol consumption and associated illnesses: Some effects of economic changes. *American Journal of Public Health*, **65**, 1279–92.

Brenner, S.O., and Bartell, R. (1983). The psychological impact of unemployment: A structural analysis of cross sectional data. *Journal of Occupational Psychology*, **56**, 129–36.

Brett, J.M. (1982). Job transfer and well-being. *Journal of Applied Psychology*, **67**, 450–63.

Brett, J.M., and Reilly, A.H. (1988). On the road again: Predicting the job transfer decision. *Journal of Applied Psychology*, **73**, 614–20.

Briar, K.H. (1978). *The Effect of Long Term Unemployment on Workers and Their Families*. San Francisco, CA.

Brief, A.P., Burke, M.J., George, J.M., Robinson, B.S., and Webster, J. (1988). Should negative affectivity remain an unmeasured variable in the study of job stress? *Journal of Applied Psychology*, **73**, 193–8.

Brinkerhoff, D.B., and White, L.K. (1978). Marital satisfaction in an economically deprived population. *Journal of Marriage and the Family*, **40**, 259–67.

Broadbent, D.E. (1985). The clinical impact of job design. *British Journal of Clinical Psychology*, **24**, 33–44.

Brockner, J. (1988). The effects of work layoffs on survivors: Research, theory and practice. *Research in Organizational Behavior*, **10**, 213–55.

Brockner, J., Grover, S., Reed, T., Dewitt, R., and O'Malley, M. (1987). Survivors' reactions to layoffs: We get by with a little help for our friends. *Administrative Science Quarterly*, **32**, 526–41.

Broderick, C.B. (1988). To arrive where we started: The field of family studies in the 1930s. *Journal of Marriage and the Family*, **50**, 569–84.

Broderick, J.E., and O'Leary, K.D. (1986). Contributions of affect, attitudes and behavior to marital satisfaction. *Journal of Consulting and Clinical Psychology*, **54**, 514–17.

Brody, G.H. Stoneman, Z., and MacKinnon, C.E. (1986). Contributions of maternal child rearing practices and play contexts to sibling interactions. *Journal of Applied Developmental Psychology*, **7**, 225–36.

Bronfenbrenner, U., Alvarez, W.F., and Henderson, C.R. (1984). Working and watching: Maternal employment status and parents' perceptions of their three-year old children. *Child Development*, **55**, 1362–78.

Bronfenbrenner, U., and Crouter, A.C. (1982). Work and family through time and space. In S.B. Kamerman and C.D. Hayes (eds), *Families that Work: Children in a Changing World*, pp. 39–83. National Academy Press, Washington, DC.

Brooke, P.P., Russell, D.W., and Price, J. L. (1988). Discriminant validation measures of job satisfaction, job involvement and organizational commitment. *Journal of Applied Psychology*, **73**, 139–45.

Bucholz, R.A. (1978). An empirical study of contemporary beliefs about work in American society. *Journal of Applied Psychology*, **63**, 219–27.

Buik, S. (1988). Interrole conflict, integrative social support, hardiness, and marital adjustment among dual-employment couples. Unpublished Honours Thesis, Department of Psychology, Queen's University, Kingston, Ontario, Canada.

Bullock, R.P. (1952). *Social Factors Related to Job Satisfaction: A Technique for the Measurement of Job Satisfaction*. Ohio State University Press, Columbia, Ohio.

Burden, D.S. (1986). Single parents and the work setting: The impact of multiple job and homelife responsibilities. *Family Relations*, **35**, 37–43.

Burke, R.J., and McKeen, C.A. (1988). Work and family: What we know and what we need to know. Working paper 88-15, School of Business, Queen's University, Kingston, Canada.

Burke, R.J., and Weir, T. (1976). Relationship of wives' employment status to husband, wife and pair satisfaction and performance. *Journal of Marriage and the Family*, **38**, 279–87.

Burke, R.J., and Weir, T. (1980). The type A experience: Occupational and life demands, satisfaction and well-being. *Journal of Human Stress*, **6**, 28–38.

Burke, R.J., Weir, T., and DuWors, R.E. (1979). Type A behavior of administrators and wives' reports of marital satisfaction and well-being. *Journal of Applied Psychology*, **64**, 57–65.

Burke, R.J., Weir, T., and DuWors, R.E. (1980a). Work demands on administrators and spouse well-being. *Human Relations*, **33**, 253–78.

Burke, R.J. Weir, T., and DuWors, R.E. (1980b). Perceived type A behaviour of husbands' and wives' satisfaction and well-being. *Journal of Occupational Behaviour*, **1**, 139–50.

Burke, W.W. (1988). From the editor. *Academy of Management Executive*, **2**, 184.

Burris, B.H. (1983). The human effects of underemployment. *Social Problems*, **31**, 96–110.

Butler, E.W., McAllister, R.J., and Kaiser, E.J. (1973). The effects of voluntary and involuntary residential mobility on females and males. *Journal of Marriage and the Family*, **35**, 219–27.

Callan, V.J. (1987). Adjustment of mothers and childless wives. *Journal of Marriage and the Family*, **49**, 847–56.

Campbell, A., Converse, P.E., and Rodgers, W.L. (1976). *The Quality of American Life*. Russell Sage Foundation, New York.

Campbell, J.P., Daft, R.L., and Hulin, L.L. (1982). *What to Study: Generating and Developing Research Questions*. Sage, Palo Alto, California.

Carruthers, N.E., and Pinder, C.C. (1983). Urban geographic factors and location satisfaction following a personnel transfer. *Academy of Management Review*, **26**, 520–6.

Caspi, A., Bolger, N., and Eckenrode, J. (1987). Linking person and context in the daily stress process. *Journal of Personality and Social Psychology*, **52**, 184–95.

Castro, J. (1988). Home is where the heart is. *Time*, 3 October, 46.

Catalano, R., and Dooley, C.D. (1977). Economic predictors of depressed mood and stressful life events in a metropolitan community. *Journal of Health and Social Behavior*, **18**, 292–307.

Cater, J.I., and Easton, P.M. (1980). Separation and other stress in child abuse. *The Lancet*, 972–4.

Cavan, R., and Ranck, K. (1938). *The Family and the Depression*. University of Chicago Press, Chicago.

Chase-Lansdale, P.L., and Tresch-Owen, M. (1987). Maternal employment in a family context: Effects on infant–mother and infant–father attachments. *Child Development*, **58**, 1505–12.

Cherlin, A. (1979). Work life and marital dissolution. In G. Levinger and O.C. Motes (eds), *Divorce and Separation: Context, Causes and Consequences*, pp. 151–66. Basic Books, New York.

Cherry, F.F., and Eaton, E.L. (1977). Physical and cognitive development in children: Low income mothers working in the child's early years. *Child Development*, **48**, 158–66.

Chisholm, R.F., Kasl, S.V., and Mueller, L. (1986). The effects of social support on nuclear worker responses to the Three Mile Island accident. *Journal of Occupational Behaviour*, **7**, 179–94.

Chopra, S.L. (1967). A comparative study of achieving and underachieving students of high intellectual ability. *Exceptional Children*, 631–4.

Clark, D.Y. (1987). Families facing redundancy. In S. Fineman (ed.), *Unemployment: Personal and Social Consequences*, pp. 97-117. Tavistock, London.

Clark, R.A., Nye, F.I., and Gecas, V. (1978). Husbands' work involvement and marital role performance. *Journal of Marriage and the Family*, **40**, 9–21.

Clarke-Stewart, K.A. (1989). Infant day care: Maligned or malignant. *American Psychologist*, **44**, 266–73.

Cleary, B. (1977) *Ramona and Her Father*. William Morrow, New York.

Clegg, C., Wall, T., and Kemp, N. (1987). Women on the assembly line: A comparison of main and interactive explanations of job satisfaction, absence and mental health. *Journal of Occupational Psychology*, **60**, 273–87.

Coburn, D., and Edwards, V.L. (1976). Job control and child rearing values. *Canadian Review of Sociology and Anthropology*, **13**, 337–44.

Cochran, M.M., and Bronfenbrenner U. (1979). Child rearing, parenthood, and the world of work. In C. Kerr and J.M. Rosow (eds), *Work in America*, pp. 138–54. Van Nostrand, New York.

Cohen, S., and Wills, T.A. (1985). Stress, social support and the buffering hypothesis. *Psychological Bulletin*, **98**, 310–57.

Cook, A.H. (1989). Public policies to help dual-earner families meet the demands of the work world. *Industrial and Labor Relations Review*, **42**, 201–15.

Cook, D.G., Cummins, R.O., Bartley, M.J., and Shaper, A.G. (1982). Health of unemployed middle-aged men in Great Britain. *Lancet*, **1**, 1290.

Cook, T.D., and Campbell, D.T. (1979). *Quasi-Experimentation: Design and Analysis Issues for Field Settings*. Houghton Mifflin, Boston.

Cooke, R.A., and Rousseau, D.M. (1984). Relationship of life events and personal orientations to symptoms of strain. *Journal of Applied Psychology*, **68**, 446–58.

Cooper, W.H., and Cliff, L.H. (1985). Getting noticed. Working paper 85-18R, School of Business, Queen's University, Kingston, Canada.

Corder, J., and Stephan, C.W. (1984). Females' combination of work and family roles: Adolescents' aspirations. *Journal of Marriage and the Family*, **46**, 391–402.

Cotterell, J.L. (1986). Work and community influences on the quality of child rearing. *Child Development*, **57**, 362–74.

Crawford, A., Plant, M.A., Kreitman, N., and Latcham, R.W. (1987). Unemployment and drinking behaviour: Some data from a general population survey of alcohol use. *British Journal of Addiction*, **82**, 1007–16.

Crosby, F. (1984). Job satisfaction and domestic life. In M.D. Lee and R.B. Kanungo (eds), *Management of Work and Personal Life: Problems and Opportunities*, pp. 138–54. Praeger, New York.

Crosby, F.J. (1987). *Spouse, Parent, worker: On Gender and Multiple Roles*. Yale University Press, New Haven.

Crouter, A.C. (1984a). Spillover from family to work: The neglected side of the work–family interface. *Human Relations*, **37**, 425–42.

Crouter, A.C. (1984b). Participative work as an influence on human development. *Journal of Applied Development Psychology*, **5**, 71–90.

Culbert S.A., and Renshaw, J.R. (1972). Coping with the stresses of travel as an opportunity for improving the quality of work and family life. *Family Process*, 321–37.

Davidson, L.M., and Baum, A. (1986). Chronic stress and post-traumatic stress disorders. *Journal of Consulting and Clinical Psychology*, **54**, 303–8.

Davidson, L.M., Fleming, R., and Baum, A. (1984). Chronic stress, catecholamines and sleep disturbance at Three Mile Island. *Journal of Human Stress*, Summer, 75–83.

DeLongis, A., Folkman, S., and Lazarus, R.S. (1988). The impact of daily stress on health and mood: Psychological and social resources as mediators. *Journal of Personality and Social Psychology*, **54**, 486–95.

DeMeis, D.K., Hock, E., and McBride, S.L. (1986). The balance of employment and motherhood: Longitudinal study of mothers' feelings about separation from their first-born infants. *Developmental Psychology*, **22**, 627–32.

Dew, M.A., Bromet, E.J., and Schulberg, H.C. (1987). A comparative analysis of two community stressors' long-term mental health effects. *American Journal of Community Psychology*, **15**, 167–84.

Ditto, W.B. (1982). Daily activities of college students and the construct validity of the Jenkins Activity Survey. *Psychosomatic Medicine*, **44**, 537–43.

Dooley, D., and Catalano, R. (1980). Economic change as a cause of behavioral disorder. *Psychological Bulletin*, **87**, 450–68.

Dowling, P., and O'Brien, G.E. (1981). The effects of employment, unemployment and further education upon the work values of school leavers. *Australian Journal of Psychology*, **33**, 185–95.

Draughn, P.S. (1984). Perceptions of competence in work and marriage of middle-age men. *Journal of Marriage and the Family*, **46**, 403–9.

Dunham, R.B. (1977). Shift work: A review and theoretical analysis. *Academy of Management Review*, **2**, 624–34.

Dunham, R.B., Pierce, J.L., and Castaneda, M.B. (1987). Alternative work schedules: Two field quasi experiments. *Personnel Psychology*, **40**, 215–46.

Dunkel-Schetter, C., Folkman, S., and Lazarus, R.S. (1987). Correlates of social support receipt. *Journal of Personality and Social Psychology*, **53**, 71–80.

Dunn, N.J., Jacob, T., Hummon, N., and Sedhauer, R.A. (1987). Marital stability in alcoholic-spouse relationships as a functions of drinking pattern and location. *Journal of Abnormal Psychology*, **96**, 99–107.

Dunnette, M.D. (1973). *Work and Nonwork in the Year 2001*. Brooks/Cole, Monterey, California.

Dyer, W.G. (1956). A comparison of families of high and low job satisfaction. *Marriage and Family Living*, **18**, 58–60.

Easterbrooks, M.A., and Goldberg, W.A. (1985). Effects of early maternal employment on toddlers, mothers and fathers. *Developmental Psychology*, **21**, 774–83.

Eckenrode, J. (1984). Impact of chronic and acute stressors on daily reports of mood. *Journal of Personality and Social Psychology*, **46**, 907–18.

Eden, D. (1982). Critical job events, acute stress, and strain: A multiple interrupted time series. *Organizational Behavior and Human Performance*, **30**, 312–29.

Elder, G.H. (1974). *Children of the Great Depression*. University of Chicago Press, Chicago.

Elder, G.H., and Caspi, A. (1988). Economic stress in lives: Developmental perspectives. *Journal of Social Issues*, **44** (4), 25–46.

Elder, G.H., Nguyen, T.V., and Caspi, A. (1985). Linking family hardships to children's lives. *Child Development*, **56**, 361–75.

Emery, R.E. (1982). Interpersonal conflict and the children of discord and divorce. *Psychological Bulletin*, **92**, 310–30.

Emery, R.E. (1989). Family violence. *American Physchologist*, **44**, 321–8.

Emery, R.E., and O'Leary, K.D. (1982). Children's perceptions of marital discord and child adjustment. *Journal of Abnormal Child Psychology*, **10**, 11–24.

Emery, R.E., Binkoff, J.E., Houts, N.L., and Carr, E.G. (1983). Children as independent variables: Some clinical implications of child effects. *Behavior Therapy*, **14**, 398–412.

Essig, M., and Morgan, D.H. (1946). Adjustment of adolescent daughters of employed women. *Journal of Educational Psychology*, **37**, 219–33.

Etaugh, C. (1984). Effects of maternal employment on children: A review of recent research. *Merrill–Palmer Quarterly*, **20**, 71–98.

Etaugh, C. (1984). Effects of maternal employment on children: Implications for the family therapist. In J.C. Hansen and S.H. Cramer (eds), *Perspectives on Work and the Family*, pp. 16–39. Aspen, Rockville, Maryland.

Evans, P.A.L., and Bartoleme, F. (1980). *Must Success Cost So Much?* Grant McIntyre, London.

Fagan, L.H. (1979). Unemployment and family crisis. *New University Quarterly*, 66–74.

Fallows, D. (1983). What daycare can't do, *Newsweek*, 10 January, 8.

Farel, A.M. (1980). Effects of preferred maternal roles, maternal employment, and sociodemographic status on school adjustment and competence. *Child Development*, **51**, 1179–86.

Farmer, H.S. (1971). Helping women to resolve the home–career conflict. *Personnel and Guidance Journal*, **49**, 795–801.

Farrington, K. (1986). The application of stress theory to the study of family violence: Principles, problems and prospects. *Journal of Family Violence*, **1**, 131–47.

Feather, N.T., and Bond, M.J. (1983). Time structure and purposeful activity among employed and unemployed university graduates. *Journal of Occupational Psychology*, **56**, 241–54.

Feather, N.T., and O'Brien, G.E. (1986). A longitudinal study of the effects of employment and unemployment on school-leavers. *Journal of Occupational Psychology*, **59**, 121–44.

Feldman, S.S., Nash, S.C., and Aschenbrenner, B.G. (1983). Antecedents of fathering. *Child Development*, **54**, 1628–36.

Fendrich, M. (1984). Wives' employment and husbands' distress: A meta-analysis and a replication. *Journal of Marriage and the Family*, **46**, 871–9.

Field, T., Healy, B., Goldstein, S., Perry, S., and Bostell, D. (1988). Infants of depressed mothers show 'depressed' behavior even with nondepressed adults. *Child Development*, **59**, 1569–79.

Fineman, S. (1983). Work meanings, non-work, and the taken-for-granted. *Journal of Management Studies*, **20**, 143–58.

Finkelhor, D., Williams, L.M., Burns, N., and Kalinowski, M. (1987). The incidence of sexual abuse in day care: 1983–1985. Third Annual Family violence conference, New Hampshire, July.

Fitch, F.J., and Papantonio, A. (1983). Men who batter; Some pertinent characteristics. *Journal of the American Association*, **171**, 180–2.

Fortune (1987). Executive guilt: Who's taking care of the children? 16 February, 30.

Fox, S., and Krausz, M. (1987). Correlates of relocation of intention and emotional responses to an Israeli plant relocation. *Journal of Occupational Behavior*, **8**, 325–38.

Frances, A., and Gale, L. (1973). Family structure and treatment in the military. *Family Process*, **12**, 171–8.

Frank, J.A. (1981). Economic change and mental health in an uncontaminated setting. *American Journal of Community Psychology*, **9**, 395–410.

Frese, M., and Okonek, K. (1984). Reasons to leave shiftwork and psychological and psychosomatic complaints of former shift workers. *Journal of Applied Psychology*, **69**, 509–14.

Friedemann, M.L. (1986). Family economic stress and unemployment: Children's peer behavior and parents' depression. *Child Study Journal*, **16** (2), 125–2.

Friedman, D.E. (1986). Child care for employees' kids. *Harvard Business Review*, **64**, 28–37.

Friedman, M., and Rosenman, R.H. (1974). *Type A Behavior and Your Heart*. Wildwood House, London.

Friend, J.G., and Haggard, E.A. (1948). *Work Adjustment is Related to Family Background: A Conceptual Basis for Counselling*. Oxford University Press, London.

Fryer, D., and Payne, R. (1986). Being unemployed: A review of the literature on the psychological experience of unemployment. In C.L. Cooper and I.T. Robertson (eds), *International Review of Industrial and Organizational Psychology*, pp. 235–78. John Wiley, Chichester.

Fryer, D., and Warr, P. (1984). Unemployment and cognitive difficulties. *British Journal of Clinical Psychology*, **23**, 67–8.

Gaesser, D.L., and Whitbourne, S.K. (1985). Work identity and marital adjustment in blue-collar men. *Journal of Marriage and the Family*. **47**, 747–51.

Galdston, R. (1965). Observations of children who have been physically abused and their parents. *American Journal of Psychiatry*, **121**, 440–3.

Gans, H.J. (1972). Vance Packard misperceives the way most American movers live. *Psychology Today*, **6** (4), 20–8.

Garbarino, J. (1976). Preliminary study of some ecological correlates of child abuse: The impact of socioeconomic stress on mothers. *Child Development*, **47**, 178–85.

Garbarino, J., Guttman, E., and Seeley, J.W. (1986). *The Psychologically Battered Child*. Jossey-Bass, San Francisco.

Gault, W.S. (1984). Real estate realities. *Personnel Journal*, **63**, 30–1.

Gayford, J.J. (1975). Wife battering: A preliminary survey of 100 cases. *British Medical Journal*, **1**, 194–7.

Gelles, R.J., and Hargreaves, E.F. (1981). Maternal employment and violence toward children. *Journal of Family Issues*, **2**, 509–30.

General Mills American Family Report, 1980–81 (1981). *Families at Work: Strengths and Strains*. General Mills, Minneapolis.

Gennard, J. (1981). The effects of strike activity on households. *British Journal of Industrial Relations*, **19**, 327–44.

Gerber, L.A. (1983). *Married to their Careers: Career and Family Dilemmas in Doctors' Lives*. Tavistock Publications, New York.

Gil, D.G. (1971). Violence against children. *Journal of Marriage and the Family*, **33**, 637–48.

Gilbert, L.A., and Rachlin, V. (1986). Women and men together but equal: Issues in dual career marriages. Paper presented at the meetings of the American Psychological Association, 1986.

Glicken, M.D. (1983). A counseling approach to employee burnout. *Personnel Journal*, **62**, 222–8.

Gold, D., and Andres, D. (1978a). Development comparisons between ten-year-old children with employed and nonemployed mothers. *Child Development*, **49**, 75–84.

Gold, D., and Andres, D. (1978b). Comparisons of adolescent children with employed and nonemployed mothers. *Merrill–Palmer Quarterly*, **24**, 243–54.

Gold, D., and Andres, D. (1978c). Relations between maternal employment and development of nursery school children. *Canadian Journal of Behavioral Science*, **10**,

Gold, D., Andres, D., and Glorieux, J. (1979). The development of Francophone nursery school children with employed and nonemployed mothers. *Canadian Journal of Behavioral Science*, **11**, 168–73.

Goldberg, D.P. (1972). *The Detection of Psychiatric Illness by Questionnaire*. Oxford University Press, Oxford.

Gollob, H.F., and Reichardt, C.S. (1987). Taking account of time lags in causal models. *Child Development*, **58**, 80–92.

Goodman, P.S. (1979). *Assessing Organizational Change: The Rushton Quality of Work Experiment*. Wiley, New York.

Goodnow J.J. (1988). Children's household work: Its nature and functions. *Psychological Bulletin*, **103**, 5–26.

Gover, D.A. (1963). Socio-economic differential in the relationship between marital adjustment and wife's employment status. *Marriage and Family Living*, **35**, 452–8.

Grant, I., Patterson, T., Olshen, R., and Yager, J. (1987). Life events do not predict symptoms: Symptoms predict symptoms. *Journal of Behavioral Medicine*, **10**, 231–40.

Greenberger, E., and Goldberg, W.A. (1989). Work, parenting and the socialization of children. *Developmental Psychology*, **25**, 22–35.

Greenberger, E., Goldberg, W.A., Crawford, T.J., and Granger, J. (1988). Beliefs about the consequences of maternal employment for children. *Psychology of Women Quarterly*, **12**, 35–59.

Greenhaus, J.H., Bedeian, A.G., and Mossholder, K.W. (1987). Work experiences, job performance, and feeling of personal and family well-being. *Journal of Vocational Behavior*, **31**, 200–15.

Greenhaus, J.H., and Beutell, N.J. (1985). Sources of conflict between work and family roles. *Academy of Management Review*, **10**, 76–88.

Greiff, B.S., and Munter, P.K, (1980a). *Tradeoffs: Executive, Family and Organizational Life*. Signet, New York.

Greiff, B.S., and Munter, P.K. (1980b). Can a two-career family live happily ever after? *Across the Board*, **17** (9), 40–7.

Gross, R.H., and Arvey, R.D. (1977). Marital satisfaction, job satisfaction, and task distribution in the homemaker job. *Journal of Vocational Behavior*, **11**, 1–13.

Grossenbacher-Boss, P., McCubbin, H.I., and Lesteram, G. (1979). The corporate executive wife's coping patterns in response to routine husband–father absence. *Family Process*, **18**, 79–86.

Grossman, A.S. (1978). Children of working mothers, March 1977. *Monthly Labor Review*, 30–3.

Grossman, A.S. (1982). More than half of all children have working mothers. *Monthly Labor Review*, **105** (2), 41–3.

Grossman, F.K. Pollack, W.S., and Golding, E. (1988). Fathers and children: Predicting the quality and quantity of fathering. *Developmental Psychology*, **24**, 82–91.

Gurin, G., Veroff, J., and Feld, S. (1960). *Americans View their Mental Health: A Nationwide Survey*. Basic Books, New York.

Gurney, R.M. (1980). Does unemployment effect the self-esteem of school-leavers? *Australian Journal of Psychology*, **32**, 175–82.

Gutek, B.A., Nakumara, C.Y., and Nieva, V.F. (1981). The interdependence of work and family roles. *Journal of Occupational Behavior*, **2**, 1–16.

Gutek, B.A., Repetti, R.L., and Silver, D.L. (1988). Non-work roles and stress at work. In C.L. Cooper and R. Payne (eds), *Causes, Coping and Consequences of Stress at Work*, pp. 141–74. Wiley, Chichester.

Haavio-Mannila, E. (1971). Satisfaction with family, work, leisure and life among men and women. *Human Relations*, **24**, 585–601.

Hackman, R.J., and Oldham, G.R. (1980). *Work Redesign*. Reading, MA: Addison-Wesley.

Hageman, M.J.C. (1978). Occupational stress and marital relationships. *Journal of Police Science and Administration*, **6**, 402–12.

Halberstam, D. (1986). *The Reckoning*. Morrow, New York.

Hall, D.T. (1972). A model of coping with role conflict. *Administrative Science Quarterly*, **4**, 471–86.

Hall, D.T., and Gordon, F.E. (1973). Career choices of married women: Effects on conflict, role behavior and satisfaction. *Journal of Applied Psychology*, **58**, 42–8.

Hall D.T., and Richter, J. (1988). Balancing work life and home life: What can organizations do to help? *Academy of Management Executive*, **1**, 213–23.

Hand, H. (1957). Working mothers and maladjusted children. *The Journal of Educational Sociology*, **30**, 245–6.

Harold-Goldsmith, R., Radin, N., and Eccles, J.S. (in press). Objective and subjective reality: The effects of job loss and financial stress on fathering behaviors. *Family Perspectives*.

Harrell, J.E., and Ridley, C.A. (1975). Substitute child care, maternal employment and the quality of mother–child interaction. *Journal of Marriage and the Family*, **37**, 556–64.

Harris, M. (1979). Keeping a working marriage working. The combined demands of jobs, home and children can strain the two-income family. Here's how couples cope. *Money*, 44–8.

Hartley, J. (1980). The impact of unemployment upon the self-esteem of managers. *Journal of Occupational Psychology*, **53**, 147–55.

Hartley, J., (1987). Managerial unemployment: The wife's perspective and role. In S. Fineman (ed.), *Unemployment: Personal and Social Consequences*, pp. 118–37. Tavistock, New York.

Haynes, S.G., Feinleib, M., Levine, S., Scotch, N., and Kannel, W.B. (1978). The relationship of psychological factors to coronary heart disease in the Framingham study. *American Journal of Epidemiology*, **107**, 384–402.

Hedges, J.N., and Barnett, J.K. (1972). Working women and the division of household tasks. *Monthly Labor Review*, **95**, 9-14.

Heilman, M.A. (1983). Sex bias in work settings: The lack of fit model. In L.L. Cummings and B. Staw (eds), *Research in Organizational Behavior*, Vol. 5, pp. 269–98. JAI Press, Connecticut.

Heins, M., Stillman, P., Sabers, D., and Mazzeo, J. (1983). Attitudes of pediatricians toward maternal employment. *Pediatrics*, **72**, 283–90.

Henggeler, S.W., and Borduin, C.M. (1981). Satisfied working mothers and their preschool children. *Journal of Family Issues*, **2**, 322–35.

Hepworth, S.J. (1980). Moderating factors of the psychological impact of unemployment. *Journal of Occupational Psychology*, **53**, 139–45.

Herman, J.B., and Gyllstrom, K.K. (1977). Working men and women: Inter-and intrarole conflict. *Psychology of Women Quarterly*, **1**, 319–33.

Hersch, S.B. (1977). *The Executive Parent*. Sovereign Books, Washington DC.

Hetherington, E.M., Stanley-Hagan, M., and Anderson, E.R. (1989). Marital transitions: A child's perspective. *American Psychologist*, **44**, 303–12.

Heyns, B. (1982). The influence of parents' work on children's achievement. In S.B.

Kamerman and C.D. Hayes (eds), *Families that Work: Children in a Changing World*, pp. 229–67. National Academy Press, Washington, DC.

Hicks, W.D., and Klimoski, R.J. (1981). The impact of flexitime on employee attitudes. *Academy of Management Journal*, **24**, 333–41.

Hillenbrand, E.D. (1976). Father absence in military families. *The Family Coordinator*, 451–8.

Hobfoll, S.E., and London, P. (1986). The relationship of self-concept and social support to emotional distress among women during war. *Journal of Social and Clinical Psychology*, **4**, 189–203.

Hobfoll, S.E., and Walfisch, S. (1984). Coping with a threat to life: A longitudinal study of self concept, social support and psychological distress. *American Journal of Community Psychology*, **12**, 87–100.

Hock, E. (1980). Working and nonworking mothers and their infants: A comparative study of maternal caregiving characteristics and infant social behavior. *Merrill-Palmer Quarterly*, **26**, 79–100.

Hock, E., and DeMeis, D. (in press). Depression in mothers of infants: The role of maternal employment. *Child Development*.

Hofferth, S.L., and Phillips, D.A. (1987). Child care in the United States, 1970–1995. *Journal of Marriage and the Family*, **49**, 559–71.

Hoffman, L.W. (1961). Effects of maternal employment on the child. *Child Development*, **32**, 187–97.

Hoffman, L.W. (1963). Effects on children: Summary and discussion. In F.I. Nye and L.W. Hoffman (eds), *The Employed Mother in America*. Rand McNally, Chicago.

Hoffman, L.W. (1974). Effects of maternal employment on the child: A review of the research. *Developmental Psychology*, **10**, 204–28.

Hoffman, L.W. (1979). Maternal employment: 1979. *American Psychologist*, **34**, 859–65.

Hoffman, L.W. (1980). The effects of maternal employment on the academic attitudes and performance of school-aged children. *School Psychology Review*, **9**, 319–36.

Hoffman, L.W. (1984). Work, family, and the socialization of the child. In R.D. Parke (ed.), *The Review of Child Development Research*, Vol. 7, pp. 41–60. University of Chicago Press, Chicago.

Hoffman, L.W. (1986). Work, family and the child. In M.S. Pollock and R. O. Perloff (eds), *Psychology and Work: Productivity, Change and Employment*, pp. 173–220. American Psychological Association, Washington, DC.

Hoffman, L.W. (1989). Effects of maternal employment in the two-parent family. *American Psychologist*, **44**, 283–92.

Hoffman, M.L. (1971). Father absence and conscience development. *Developmental Psychology*, **4**, 400–6.

Holahan, C.K., and Gilbert, L.A. (1979a). Interrole conflict for working women: Careers versus jobs. *Journal of Applied Psychology*, **64**, 86–90.

Holahan, C.K., and Gilbert, L.A. (1979b). Conflict between major life roles: Women and men in dual career couples. *Human Relations*, **32**, 451–67.

Holland, J.L. (1966). *The Psychology of Vocational Choice*. Blaisdell, Waltham, Massachusetts.

Holman, T.B. (1981). The influence of community involvement on marital quality. *Journal of Marriage and the Family*, **43**, 143–9.

Holmes, T.H., and Rahe, R.H. (1967). The social readjustment rating scale. *Journal of Psychosomatic Research*, **11**, 213–18.

Honzik, M.P. (1967). Environmental correlates of mental growth: Prediction from the family setting at 21 months. *Child Development*, **38**, 337–64.

Hood, J., and Golden, S. (1979) Beating time/making time: The impact of work scheduling on men's family roles. *The Family Coordinator*, **28**, 575–82.

Hooley, J.M., Richters, J.E., Weintraub, S., and Neale, J.M. (1987). Psychopathology and marital distress: The positive side of positive symptoms. *Journal of Personality and Social Psychology*, **96**, 27–33.

Hoppock, R. (1935). *Job Satisfaction*. Harper and Row, New York.

Hornstein, G.A. (1986). The structuring of identity among midlife women as a function of their degree of involvement in employment. *Journal of Personality*, **54**, 551–75.

Hornung, C.A., and McCullough, B.C. (1981). Status relationships in dual-employment marriages: Consequences for psychological well-being. *Journal of Marriage and the Family*, **43**, 125–41.

Hornung, C.A., McCullough, B.C., and Sugimoto, T. (1981). Status relationships in marriage: Risk factors in spouse abuse. *Journal of Marriage and the Family*, **43**, 675–92.

House, J.S. (1987). Chronic stress and chronic disease in life and work: Conceptual and methodological issues. *Work and Stress*, **1**, 129–34.

Houseknecht, S.K., and Macke, A.S. (1981). Combining marriage and career: The marital adjustment of professional women. *Journal of Marriage and the Family*, **43**, 651–61.

Innes, J.M., and Clarke, A. (1985). Job involvement as a moderator variable in the life events stress–illness relationship. *Journal of Occupational Behaviour*, **6**, 299–303.

Iris, B., and Barrett, G.V. (1972). Some relations between job and life satisfaction and job importance. *Journal of Applied Psychology*, **50**, 301–4.

Isralowitz, R.E., and Singer, M. (1986). Unemployment and its impact on adolescent work values. *Adolescence*, **21**, 145–58.

Ivancevich, J.M., and Ganster, D.C. (1987). *Job Stress: From Theory to Suggestion*. Haworth, New York.

Ivancevich, J.M., Matteson, M.T., and Richards, E.P. (1985). Who's liable for stress on the job? *Harvard Business Review*, **63**, 60–5.

Iverson, L., Anderson, O., Anderson, P.K., Christofferson, K., and Keiding, N. (1987). Unemployment and mortality in Denmark, 1970–1980. *British Medical Journal*, **295**, 879–84.

Iverson, L., and Klausen, H. (1986). Alcohol consumption among laid off workers before and after closure of a Danish shipyard: A two year follow up study. *Social Science and Medicine*, **22**, 107–9.

Jackman, M. (1984). *The Macmillan Book of Business and Economic Quotations*. Macmillan, New York.

Jackson, P.R. (1988). Personal networks, support mobilization and unemployment. *Psychological Medicine*, **18**, 397–404.

Jackson, P.R., Stafford, E.M., Banks, M.H., and Warr, P.B. (1983). Unemployment and psychological distress in young people: The moderating role of employment commitment. *Journal of Applied Psychology*, **68**, 525–35.

Jackson, S.E. (1983). Participation in decision making as a strategy for reducing job-related strain. *Journal of Applied Psychology*, **68**, 3–19.

Jackson, S.E., and Maslach, C. (1982). After-effects of job-related stress: Families as victims. *Journal of Occupational Behaviour*, **3**, 63–77.

Jackson, S.E., Zedeck, S., and Summers, E. (1985). Family life disruptions: Effects of job-induced structural and emotional interference. *Academy of Management Journal*, **28**, 574–86.

Jahoda, M. (1982). *Employment and Unemployment: A Social-Psychological Analysis*. Cambridge University Press, New York.

Jahoda, M. (1988). Economic recession and mental health: Some conceptual issues. *Journal of Social Issues*, **44**, 13–24.

Jandorf, L., Deblinger, E., Neale, J.M., and Stone, A.A. (1986). Daily versus major life events as predictors of symptom frequency: A replication study. *The Journal of General Psychology*, **113**, 205–18.

Jans, N.A. (1982). The nature and measurement of job involvement. *Journal of Occupational Psychology*, **55**, 57–68.

Jensen, L., and Borges, M. (1986). The effect of maternal employment on adolescent daughters. *Adolescence*, **21**, 659–66.

Jensen, P.G., and Kirchner, W.K. (1955). A national answer to the question, 'Do sons follow their fathers' occupations?' *Journal of Applied Psychology*, **39**, 419–21.

Johns, G., and Nicholson, N. (1982). The meanings of absence: New strategies for theory and research. In B. Staw and L.L. Cummings (eds), *Research in Organizational Behavior*, Vol. 4, pp. 127–72. JAI Press, Connecticut.

Johnson, B.L. (1979). Changes in marital and family characteristics of workers, 1970–78. *Monthly Labour Review*, 49–52.

Johnson, D.R., White, L.K., Edwards, J.N., and Booth, A. (1986). Dimensions of marital quality–toward methodological and conceptual refinement. *Journal of Family Issues*, **7**, 31–49.

Johnson, F.A., Kaplan, E.A., and Tusel, D.J. (1979). Sexual dysfunction in the 'two-career' family. *Medical Aspects of Human Sexuality*, 7–17.

Johnson, P.J. (1983). Divorced mothers' management of responsibilities: Conflicts between employment and child care. *Journal of Family Issues*, **4**, 83–103.

Johnson, V.E., and Masters, W.H. (1976). Contemporary influences on sexual response–The work ethic. *The Journal of School Health*, **46**, 211–15.

Jones, A.P., and Butler, M.C. (1980). A role transition approach to the stresses of organizationally induced family role disruption. *Journal of Marriage and the Family*, **42**, 367–76.

Jones, S.B. (1973). Geographic mobility as seen by the wife and mother. *Journal of Marriage and the Family*, **35**, 210–18.

Jouriles, E.N., Pfiffner, L.J., and O'Leary, S.G. (1988). Marital conflict, parenting and toddler conduct problems. *Journal of Abnormal Child Psychology*, **16**, 197–206.

Justice, B., and Duncan, D.F. (1978). How do job-related problems contribute to child abuse? *Occupational Health and Safety*, **47**, 42–5.

Kahn, R.L. (1981). *Work and Health*. Wiley, New York.

Kahn, R.L., Wolfe, D.M., Quinn, R.P., Snoek, J.D., and Rosenthal, R.A. (1964). *Role Stress: Studies in Role Conflict and Ambiguity*. Wiley, New York.

Kalin, R., and Lloyd, C.A. (1985). Sex role identity ideology and marital adjustment. *International Journal of Women's Studies*, **8**, 32–9.

Kamerman, S.B., and Hayes, C.D. (1982). *Families that Work: Children in a Changing World*. National Academy Press, Washington, DC.

Kanter, R.M. (1977). *Work and Family in the USA: A Critical Review and Agenda for Research and Policy*. Russell Sage Foundation, New York.

Kater, D. (1985). Management strategies for dual-career couples. *Journal of Career Development*, 75–80.

Katz, D., and Kahn, R.L. (1978). *The Social Psychology of Organizations*, 2nd edn. Wiley, New York.

Kaufman, H.G. (1982). *Professionals in Search of Work: Coping with the Stress of Job Loss and Underemployment*. Wiley, New York.

Kazdin, A.E. (1975). Characteristics and trends in applied behavior analysis. *Journal of Applied Behavior Analysis*, **8**, 332.

Keegan, D.L., Sinha, B.N., Merriman, J.E., and Shipley, C. (1979). Type A behaviour pattern. *Canadian Journal of Psychiatry*, **24**, 724–30.

Keenan, A., and Newton, T.J. (1985). Stressful events, stressors and psychological strains in young professional engineers. *Journal of Occupational Behaviour*, **6**, 151–6.

Keidel, K.C. (1970). Maternal employment and ninth grade achievement, Bismarck, North Dakota. *The Family Coordinator*, **19**, 95–7.

Keith, P.M., and Schafer, R.B. (1983). Employment characteristics of both spouses and depression in two-job families. *Journal of Marriage and the Family*, **45**, 877–84.

Keith, P.M., and Schafer, R.B. (1985). Role behavior, relative deprivation and depression among women in one and two job families. *Family Relations*, **34**, 22–33.

Kelly, K.E., and Houston, B.K. (1985). Type A behaviour in employed women: Relationship to work, marital and leisure variables, social support, stress, tension and health. *Journal of Personality and Social Psychology*, **48**, 1067–79.

Kemper, T.D., and Reichler, M.L. (1976a). Work integration, marital satisfaction and conjugal power. *Human Relations*, **29**, 929–44.

Kemper, T.D., and Reichler, M.L. (1976b). Father's work integration and types and frequencies of rewards and punishments administered by fathers and mothers to adolescent sons and daughters. *The Journal of Genetic Psychology*, **129**, 207–19.

Kessler, R.C., and McRae, J.A. (1982). The effects of wives' employment on the mental health of married men and women. *American Sociological Review*, **47**, 216–27.

Kessler, R.C. Turner, J.B., and House, J.S. (1987). Intervening processes in the relationship between unemployment and health. *Psychological Medicine*, **17**, 949–61.

Khaleque, A., Wadud, N., and Chowdhury, M. (1988). Work attitudes, strain and mental health of employed mothers in Bangladesh. *Work and Stress*, **2**, 41–7.

Killien, M., and Brown, M.A. (1987). Work and family roles of women: Sources of stress and coping strategies. Paper presented at the 1986 Western Society for Research in Nursing Conference in Portland, Oregon.

Kim, J.S., and Campagna, A.F. (1981). Effects of flexitime on employee attendance and performance: A field experiment. *Academy of Management Journal*, **24**, 729–41.

King, K., McIntyre, J., and Axelson, L.J. (1968). Adolescents' views of maternal employment as a threat to the marital relationship. *Journal of Marriage and the Family*, **30**, 633–7.

Kingston, P.W., and Nock, S.L. (1985). Consequences of the family work day. *Journal of Marriage and the Family*, **47**, 619–29.

Kobasa, S.C. (1982). The hardy personality: Toward a social psychology of stress and health. In G.S. Sanders and J. Suls (eds). *Social Psychology of Health and Illness*. Lawrence Erlbaum, New Jersey.

Kobasa, S.C., and Puccetti, M.C. (1983). Personality and social resources in stress resistance. *Journal of Personality and Social Psychology*, **45**, 839–50.

Kogi, K. (1985). Introduction of the problems of shiftwork. In S. Folkard and T.H. Monk (eds), *Hours of Work: Temporal Factors in Work-Scheduling*, pp. 165–84. Wiley, Chichester.

Kohn, M.L. (1969). *Class and Conformity*. University of Chicago Press, Chicago.

Kohn, M.L., and Schooler, C. (1983). *Work and Personality: An Inquiry into the Impact of Social Stratification*. Albex, Norwood, New Jersey.

Komarovsky, M. (1940). *The Unemployed Man and His Family: The Effect of Unemployment upon the Status of Men in 59 families*. Arno Press, New York.

Komarovsky, M. (1987). *Blue-Collar Marriage*. Yale University Press, New Haven.

Kopelman, R.E. Greenhaus, J.H., and Connolly, T.F. (1983). A model of work, family and interrole conflict: A construct validation study. *Organizational Behavior and Human Performance*, **32**, 198–215.

Krause, N. (1984). Employment outside the home and women's psychological well-being. *Social Psychiatry*, **19**, 41–8.

Krause, N. (1987). Chronic financial strain, social support and depressive symptoms among older adults. *Psychology and Aging*, **2**, 185–92.

Krause, N., and Geyer-Pestello, H.F. (1985). Depressive symptoms among women employed outside the home. *American Journal of Community Psychology*, **13**, 49–67.

Kriegsmann, J.K., and Hardin, D.R. (1974). Does divorce hamper job performance? *The Personnel Administrator*, **19**, 26–9.

Lacy, W.B., Bokemeier, J.L., and Shepard, J.M. (1983). Job attribute preferences and work commitment of men and women in the United States. *Personnel Psychology*, **36**, 315–29.

Ladewig, B.H., and McGee, G.W. (1986). Occupational commitment, a supportive family environment, and marital adjustment: Development and estimation of a model. *Journal of Marriage and the Family*, **48**, 821–9.

Lamb, M.E. (1981). *The Role of the Father in Child Development*. Wiley, New York.

Lamb, M.E. (1982). Parental influences on early socio-emotional development. *Journal of Child Psychology and Psychiatry*, **23**, 185–90.

Lamb, M.E., Chase-Lansdale, L., and Owen, M.T. (1979). The changing American family and its implications for infant development: The sample case of maternal employment. In M. Lewis and L.A. Rosenblum (eds), *The Child and its Family*, pp. 267–91. Plenum, New York.

Landy, F., Rosenberg, B.G., and Sutton-Smith, B. (1969). The effect of limited father absence on cognitive development. *Child Development*, **40**, 941–4.

Lang, D., and Markowitz, M. (1986). Coping, individual differences and strain: A longitudinal study of short-term role overload. *Journal of Occupational Behaviour*, **7**, 195–206.

Lantos, B. (1943). Work and the instincts. *International Journal of Psychoanalysis*, **24**, 114–19.

Larson, J.H. (1984). The effect of husband's unemployment on marital and family relations in blue collar families. *Family Relations*, **33**, 503–11.

Lauer, H. (1985). Jobs in the 1980's: A sourcebook for policy makers. In D. Yankelovich, H. Zetterberg, B. Strumpel, and M. Shanks (eds), *The Work at Work*, pp. 237–407. Octagon Books, New York.

Lawler, E.E., Nadler, D.A., and Cammann, C. (1980). *Organizational Assessment: Perspectives on the Measurement of Organizational Behavior and the Quality of Work Life*. Wiley, New York.

Laws, J.L. (1971). A feminist review of marital adjustment literature: The rape of the Locke. *Journal of Marriage and the Family*, **33**, 483–519.

Layton, C., and Eysenck, S. (1985). Psychoticism and unemployment. *Personality and Individual Differences*, **6**, 387–90.

Lempers, J.D., Clark-Lempers, D., and Simons, R.L. (1989). Economic hardship, parenting, and distress in adolescence. *Child Development*, **60**, 25–39.

Lerner, J.V., and Galambos, N.L. (1985). Maternal role satisfaction, mother–child interaction and child temperament: A process model. *Developmental Psychology*, **21**, 115–64.

Lester, D. (1988). Economic factors and suicide. *The Journal of Social Psychology*, **128**, 245–8.

Lewis, B.Y. (1987). Psychosocial factors related to wife abuse. *Journal of Family Violence*, **2**, 1–10.

Lewis, R.A., and Spanier, G.B. (1979). Theorizing on the quality and stability of marriage. In W.R. Burr, R. Hill, F.I. Nye and I.L. Reiss (eds), *Contemporary Theories about the Family*, Vol. 2, pp. 268-94. The Free Press, New York.

Liem, R., and Liem, J.H. (1988). Psychological effects of unemployment on workers and their families. *Journal of Social Issues*, **44**, 87–105.

Light, R. (1973). Abused and neglected children in America: A study of alternative policies. *Harvard Educational Review*, **43**, 356–98.

Locke, E.A. (1983). The nature and course of job satisfaction. In M.D. Dunnette (ed.), *Handbook of Industrial and Organizational Psychology*, pp. 1297–350. Wiley, New York.

Locke, H.J., and Mackeprang, M. (1949). Marital adjustment and the employed wife. *American Journal of Sociology*, **54**, 536–8.

Locke, H.J., and Wallace, K.M. (1959). Short marital-adjustment and prediction tests: Their reliability and validity. *Marriage and Family Living*, **21**, 251–5.

Lockhart, L.L. (1987). Effect of race and social class on the incidence of marital violence. *Journal of Marriage and the Family*, **49**, 603–10.

Locksley, A. (1980). On the effects of wives' employment on marital adjustment and companionship. *Journal of Marriage and the Family*, **42**, 337–45.

Lodahl, T.M., and Kejner, M. (1965). The definition and measurement of job involvement. *Journal of Applied Psychology*, **49**, 24–33.

London, M., Crandall, R., and Seals, G.W. (1977). The contribution of job and leisure satisfaction to quality of life. *Journal of Applied Psychology*, **62**, 328–34.

Long, B.C., and Haney, C.J. (1988). Coping strategies for working women: Aerobic exercise and relaxation interventions. *Behavior Therapy*, **19**, 75–83.

Long, N., Slater, E., Forehand, R., and Fauber, R. (1988). Continued high or reduced interparental conflict following divorce: Relation to young adolescent adjustment. *Journal of Consulting and Clinical Psychology*, **56**, 467–9.

Loo, R. (1986). Post-shooting stress reactions among police officers. *Journal of Human Stress*, Spring, 27–31.

Lynn, D.B., and Sawrey, W.L. (1959). The effects of father-absence on Norwegian boys and girls. *Journal of Abnormal and Social Psychology*, **59**, 258–62.

MacEwen, K.E., and Barling, J. (1988a). Interrole conflict, family support and marital adjustment of employed mothers: A short term, longitudinal study. *Journal of Organizational Behavior*, **9**, 241–50.

MacEwen, K.E., and Barling, J. (1988b). Multiple stressors, violence in the family of origin and marital aggression. *Journal of Family Violence*, **3** 73–88.

Machlowitz, M. (1980). *Workaholics: Working with Them, Living with Them*. Addison-Wesley, Massachusetts.

MacIntosh, H. (1968). Separation problems in military moves. *American Journal of Psychiatry*, **125**, 156–61.

Madge, N. (1983). Unemployment and its effects on children. *Journal of Child Psychology and Psychiatry*, **24**, 311–19.

Mahoney, M.J. (1976). *Scientist as Subject: The Psychological Imperative*. Ballinger Publishing Co, Cambridge, Massachusetts.

Maklan, D.H. (1977). *The Four-Day Workweek: Blue Collar Adjustment to a Nonconventional Arrangement of Work and Leisure Time*. Praeger, New York.

Mallinekrodt, B., and Fretz, B.R. (1988). Social support and the impact of job loss on older professionals. *Journal of Counseling Psychology*, **35**, 281–6.

Mann, P.A. (1972). Residential mobility as an adaptive experience. *Journal of Consulting and Clinical Psychology*, **39**, 37–42.

Marantz, S.A., and Mansfield, A.F. (1977). Maternal employment and the development of sex role stereotyping in five to eleven year old girls. *Child Development*, **48**, 668–73.

Maret, E., and Finlay, B. (1984). The distribution of household labor among women in dual-earner families. *Journal of Marriage and the Family*, **46**, 357–64.

Margolin, L., and Larson, O.W. (1988). Assessing mothers' and fathers' violence toward children as a function of their involuntary participation in family work. *Journal of Family Violence*, **3**, 209–24.

Marks, S.R. (1977). Multiple roles and role strain: Some notes on human energy, time and commitment. *American Sociological Review*, **41**, 921–36.

Marsden, D., and Duff, E. (1975). *Workless: Some Unemployed Men and their Families*. Pergamon, England.

Marsella, A.J. Dubanoski, R.A., and Mohs, K. (1974). The effects of father presence and absence upon maternal attitudes. *The Journal of Genetic Psychology*, **125**, 257–63.

Martin, H.P., Burgess, D., and Crnic, L.S. (1984). Mothers who work outside the home and their children: A survey of health professionals' attitudes. *Journal of the American Academy of Child Psychiatry*, **23**, 472–8.

Martin, J.A., and Ickovics, J.R. (1987). The effects of stress on the psychological well-being of army wives: Initial findings from a longitudinal study. *Journal of Human Stress*, **13**, 108–15.

Martin, M.J., Schumm, W.R., Bugaighis, M.A., Jurich, A.P., and Bollman, S.R. (1987). Family violence and adolescents' perceptions of outcomes of family conflict. *Journal of Marriage and the Family*, **49**, 165–71.

Mashal, M. (1985). The development and validation of an interrole strain questionnaire for dual worker couples. Unpublished Ph.D. dissertation, Queen's University, Kingston, Ontario.

Maslach, C., and Jackson, S.E. (1979). Burned-out cops and their families. *Psychology Today*, May, 59–62.

Mathews, S.M. (1934). The effect of mothers and out of home employment upon their children's ideas and attitudes. *Journal of Applied Psychology*, **19**, 116–36.

Mathews, K.A. (1982). Psychological perspectives on the Type A behavior pattern. *Psychological Bulletin*, **91**, 293–323.

McAllister, R., Butler, E., and Kaiser, E. (1973). The adjustment of women to residential mobility. *Journal of Marriage and the Family*, **35**, 197–204.

McCord, J., McCord, W., and Thurber, E. (1963). Effects of maternal employment on lower-class boys. *Journal of Abnormal and Social Psychology*, **67**, 177–82.

McCroskey, J. (1982). Work and families: What is the employer's responsibility? *Personal Journal*, **61**, 30–8.

McGee, G.W., Goodson, J.R., and Cashman, J.F. (1987). Job stress, job dissatisfaction: Influence of contextual factors. *Psychological Reports*, **61**, 367–75.

McGoldrick, A.E., and Cooper, C.L. (1985). Stress at the decline of one's career: The act of retirement. In T.A. Beehr and R.S. Bhagat (eds), *Human Stress and Cognition in Organizations*, pp. 177–201. Wiley, New York.

McHale, S.M., and Huston, T.L. (1984). Men and women as parents: Sex role orientations, employment, and parental roles with infants. *Child Development*, **55**, 1349–61.

McKain, J.L. (1973). Relocation in the military: Alienation and family problems. *Journal of Marriage and the Family*, **35**, 205–9.

McKinley, F.G. (1964). *Social Class and Family Life*. Free Press, New York.

McLoyd, V.C. (1989). Socialization and development in a changing economy: The effects of paternal job and income loss on children. *American Psychologist*, **44**, 293–302.

McNeely, R.L., and Fogarty, B.A. (1988). Balancing parenthood and employment: Factors affecting company receptiveness of family-related innovations in the workplace. *Family Relations*, **37**, 189–95.

Meadow, D. (1988). Managing social work problems. In G.M. Gould and M.C. Smith (eds), *Social Work in the Workplace*, pp. 152–69. Springer, New York.

Meeks, S., Arnkoff, D.B., Glass, C.R., and Notarius, C. (1986). Wives' employment status, hassles, communication and relational efficacy: Intra vs. extra relationship factors and marital adjustment. *Family Relations*, **35**, 249–55.

Meier, S.T. (1987). An unconnected special issue. *American Psychologist*, **42**, 881.

Mertensmeyer, C., and Coleman, M. (1987). Correlates of inter-role conflict in young rural and urban parents. *Family Relations*, **36**, 425–9.

Miller, L.E., and Weiss, R.M. (1982). The work/leisure relationship: Evidence for the compensatory hypothesis. *Human Relations*, **35**, 763–71.

Miller, R.E. (1986). EAP research then and now. *Employee Assistance Quarterly*, **2**, 49–86.

Miller, S.M. (1975). Effects of maternal employment on sex role perception, interests and self esteem in kindergarten girls. *Developmental Psychology*, **11**, 405–6.

Miller, T.I. (1984). The effects of employer–sponsored child care on employee absenteeism, turnover, productivity, recruitment or job satisfaction: What is claimed and what is known. *Personnel Psychology*, **37**, 277–89.

Mills, B.C., and Stevens, A. (1985). Employed and nonemployed mothers: Differences in parental child rearing practices. *Early Child Development and Care*, **22**, 181–94.

Moen, P. (1980). Measuring unemployment: Family considerations. *Journal of Human Stress*, **33**, 183–92.

Moen, P. (1983). Unemployment, public policy, and families: Forecasts for the 1980s. *Journal of Marriage and the Family*, **45**, 751–60.

Moen, P., Kain, E.L., and Elder, G.H. (1983). Economic conditions and family life: Contemporary and historical perspectives. In R.R. Nelson and F. Skidmore (eds), *American Families and the Economy: The High Costs of Living* pp. 213–59. National Academy Press, Washington DC.

Moore, K.A., and Hofferth, S.L. (1979). Effects of women's employment on marriage: Formation, stability and roles. *Marriage and Family Review*, **2**, 27–36.

Morgan, L.G., and Herman, J.B. (1976). Perceived consequences of absenteeism. *Journal of Applied Psychology*, **61**, 738–42.

Mortimer, J.T. (1974). Patterns of intergenerational occupational movements: A smallest–space analysis. *The American Journal of Sociology*, **79**, 1278–99.

Mortimer, J.T. (1976). Social class, work and the family: Some implications of the father's occupation for familial relationships and sons' career decisions. *Journal of Marriage and the Family*, **38**, 241–56.

Mortimer, J.T. (1980). Occupation–family linkages as perceived by men in the early stages of professional and managerial careers. In H.Z. Lopata (ed.), *Research in the Inter-weave of Social Roles: Women and Men*, Vol. 1, Jai Press, Greenwich, Connecticut, pp. 99–117.

Mortimer, J.T., and Kumka, D. (1982). A further examination of the 'Occupational Linkage hypothesis'. *The Sociological Quarterly*, **23**, 3–16.

Mortimer, J.T., Lorence, J., and Kumka, D.S. (1986). *Work, Family, and Personality: Transition to Adulthood*. Ablex, Norwood, New Jersey.

Moser, K.A., Fox, A.J., and Jones, D.R. (1984). Unemployment and mortality in the OPCS longitudinal study. *Lancet*, **ii**, 1324–8.

Moser, K.A., and Goldblatt, P.O. (1986). Unemployment and mortality: Further evidence from the OPCS longitudinal study, 1971–81. *Lancet*, **i**, 365–7.

Mott, F.L., and Moore, S.F. (1979). The causes of marital disruption among young American women: An interdisciplinary perspective. *Journal of Marriage and the Family*, **41**, 355–65.

Mott, P.E., Mann, F.C., McLoughlin, Q., and Warwick, D.P. (1965). *Shift Work*. University of Michigan Press, Ann Arbor.

Mugford, S.K. (1980). Wife occupational superiority and marital troubles: A comment on Richardson's 'test' of the hypothesis. *Journal of Marriage and the Family*, **42**, 243–6.

Near, J.P., Rice, R.W., and Hunt, R.G. (1980). The relationship between work and nonwork domains: A review of empirical research. *Academy of Management Review*, **5**, 415–29.

Nelson, E. (1939). Fathers' occupations and student vocational choices. *School and Society*, **50**, 572–6.

Neuman, S.G. (1978). Wife, mother, teacher, scholar, and sex object: Role conflicts of a female academic. *Intellect*, 302–6.

Newsweek (1980). The superwoman squeeze. 19 May, 72.

Newsweek (1983). Left out. 21 March, 26.

Newsweek (1986). A mother's choice. 31 March, 46.

Newsweek (1987). Not tonight dear. 26 October, 64.

Newsweek (1988). Emotional child abuse, 3 October, 48.

Nock, S.L., and Kingston, P.W. (1984). The family work day. *Journal of Marriage and the Family*, **46**, 333–43.

Noe, R.A., Steffy, B.D., and Barber, A.E. (1988). An investigation of the factors influencing employees' willingness to accept mobility opportunities. *Personnel Psychology*, **41**, 559–80.

Nord, W.R. (1977). Job satisfaction reconsidered. *American Psychologist*, **32**, 1026–53.

Northcott, H.C. (1983). Who stays home? Working parents and sick children. *International Journal of Women's Studies*, **6**, 387–94.

Novaco, R.W., Stokols, D., Campbell, J., and Stokols, J. (1979). Transportation stress and community psychology. *American Journal of Community Psychology*, **7**, 361–30.

O'Brien, G. E. (1985). Distortion in unemployment research: The early studies of Bakke and their implications for current research on employment and unemployment. *Human Relations*, **38**, 877–94.

O'Brien, G.E., and Kabanoff, B. (1979). Comparison of unemployed and employed workers on work values, locus of control and health variables. *American Psychologist*, **14**, 143–54.

O'Brien, J.E. (1971). Violence in divorce prone families. *Journal of Marriage and the Family*, **33**, 692–8.

O'Leary, K.D. (1984). Marital discord and kids: Problems, strategies, methodologies and results. In A. Doyle, D. Gold, and D.S. Moskowitz (eds), *Children in Families under Stress*, pp. 35–46. Jossey-Bass, San Francisco.

O'Leary, K.D. (1988). Physical aggression between spouses: A social learning perspective. In V.B. van Hasselt, R.L. Morrison, A.S. Bellack, and M. Hersen (eds), *Handbook of Family Violence*, pp. 31–55. Plenum, New York.

O'Leary, K.D., and Turkewitz, H. (1978). Methodological errors in marital and child treatment research. *Journal of Consulting and Clinical Psychology*, **66**, 747–58.

O'Leary, K.D. Barling, J., Arias, I., Rosenbaum, A., Malone, J., and Tyree, A. (1989). Prevalence and stability of physical aggression between spouses: A longitudinal analysis. *Journal of Consulting and Clinical Psychology*, **57**, 263–8.

Oliver, J.M., and Pomicter, C. (1981). Depression in automotive assembly-line workers as a function of unemployment variables. *American Journal of Community Psychology*, **9**, 507–12.

Olson, K.R., and Schellenberg, R.P. (1986). Farm stressors. *American Journal of Community Psychology*, **14**, 555–69.

Orden, S.R., and Bradburn, N.M. (1969). Working wives and marriage happiness. *American Journal of Sociology*, **74**, 392–407.

Orthner, D.K., and Axelson, L.J. (1980). The effects of wife employment on marital sociability. *Journal of Comparative Family Studies*, **11**, 531–45.

Orton, G.L. (1982). A comparative study of children's worries. *The Journal of Psychology*, **110**, 153–62.

Orwell, G. (1937). *The Road to Wigan Pier*. Harcourt Brace, New York.

Owen, M.T., Easterbrooks, M.A., Chase-Lansdale, L., and Goldberg, W.A. (1984). The relation between maternal employment status and the stability of attachments to mother and to father. *Child Development*, **55**, 1894–1901.

Packard, V. (1972). *A Nation of Strangers*. David McKay Company, New York.

Palme, O. (1972). The emancipation of man. *Journal of Social Issues*, **28**, 237–46.

Parasuraman, S., Greenhaus, J.H., Rabinowitz, S., Bedeian, A.G., and Mossholder, K.W. (1989). Work and family variables as mediators of the relationship between wives' employment and husbands' well-being. *Academy of Management Journal*, **32**, 185–201.

Parke, R.D., and Collmer, C.W. (1975). Child abuse: An interdisciplinary analysis. In E.M. Hetherington (ed.), *Review of Child Development Research*, Vol. 5, pp. 509–90. University of Chicago Press, Chicago.

Parry, G. (1987). Sex-role beliefs, work attitudes and mental health in employed and non-employed mothers. *British Journal of Social Psychology*, **26**, 47–58.

Parry, G., and Warr, P.E. (1980). The measurement of mothers' work attitudes *Journal of Occupational Psychology*, **53**, 245–52.

Parsons, T. (1959). The social structure of the family. In R.N. Amshen (ed.), *The Family: Its Function and Destiny*, pp. 241–74. Harper and Brothers, New York.

Pasquali, L., and Callegari, A.I. (1978). Working mothers and daughters' sex role identification in Brazil. *Child Development*, **49**, 902–5.

Pasternak, B., and Ching, W. (1985). Breast feeding decline in urban China: An exploratory study. *Human Ecology*, **13**, 433–66.

Patton, W., and Noller, P. (1984). Unemployment and youth: A longitudinal study. *Australian Journal of Psychology*, **36**, 399–413.

Pautler, K.J., and Lewko, J.H. (1984). Children's worries and exposure to unemployment: A preliminary investigation. *Canada's Mental Health*, 14–38.

Pautler, K.J., and Lewko, J.H. (1987). Children's and adolescents' views of the work world in times of economic uncertainty. In J.H. Lewko (ed.), *How Children and Adolescents View the World of Work*. Jossey-Bass, California.

Payne, R. (1956). Adolescents' attitudes towards the working wife. *Marriage and Family Living*, **18**, 345–8.

Payne, R., Jick, T.D., and Burke, R.J. (1982). Whither stress research? An agenda for the 1980s. *Journal of Occupational Behavior*, **3**, 131–45.

Pederson, F.A. (1976). Does research on children reared in father-absent families yield information on father influences? *The Family Coordinator*, **25**, 459–64.

Perucci, C.C., and Targ, D.B. (1988). Effects of a plant closing on marriage and family life. In P. Voydanoff and L.C. Majka (eds), *Families and Economic Distress: Coping Strategies and Social Policy*, pp. 55–71. Sage, California.

Peyrot, M., McMurray, J.F., and Hedges, R. (1988). Marital adjustment to adult diabetes. *Journal of Marriage and the Family*, **59**, 363–76.

Philliber, W.W., and Hiller, D.V. (1983). Relative occupational attainments of spouses and later changes in marriage and wife's work experience. *Journal of Marriage and the Family*, **45**, 161–70.

Phillips, D. (1984). Day care: Promoting collaboration between research and policy making. *Journal of Applied Developmental Psychology*, **5**, 91–113.

Pietromonaco, P.R., Manis, J., and Frohardt-Lane, K. (1986). Psychological consequences of multiple social roles. *Psychology of Women Quarterly*, **10**, 373–82.

Pietromonaco, P.R., Manis, J., and Markus, H. (1987). The relationship of employment to self-perception and well being in women: A cognitive analysis. *Sex Roles*, **17**, 467–77.

Pinter, R., and Lev, J. (1940). Worries of school children. *The Journal of Genetic Psychology*, **56**, 67–76.

Piotrkowski, C.S. (1979). *Work and the Family System*. MacMillan, New York.

Piotrkowski, C.S., and Gornick, L.K. (1987). Effects of work-related separations on children and families. In *The Psychology of Work and Loss*, pp. 267–299. Jossey-Bass, California.

Piotrkowski, C.S., and Katz, M.H. (1982). Indirect socialization of children: The effect of mothers' jobs on academic behaviors. *Child Development*, **53**, 1520–9.

Piotrkowski, C.S., and Katz, M.H. (1983). Work experience and family relations among working-class and lower-middle class families. *Research in the Interweave of Social Roles: Jobs and Families*, **3**, 187–200.

Piotrkowski, C.S., Rapaport, R.N., and Rapaport, R. (1987). Families and work. In M.B. Sussman and S.K. Steinmetz (eds), *Handbook of Marriage and the Family*, pp. 251–83. Plenum, New York.

Piotrkowski, C.S., and Stark, E. (1987). Children and adolescents look at their parents' jobs. In J.H. Lewko (ed.), *How Children and Adolescents View the World of Work*, pp. 3–19. Jossey-Bass, California.

Pleck, J.H. (1983). Husbands paid work and family roles: Current research issues. *Research in the Interweave of Social Roles: Jobs and Families*, Vol. 2. JAI Press, Greenwich, Connecticut.

Pleck, J.H. (1985). *Working Wives/Working Husbands*. Sage, California.

Pleck, J.H. (1986). Employment and fatherhood: Issues and innovative policies. In M.E. Lamb (ed.), *The Father's Role: Applied Perspectives*, pp. 385–412. Wiley, New York.

Pleck, J.H., Staines, G.L., and Lang, L. (1980). Conflicts between work and family life. *Monthly Labor Review*, 29–32.

Pond, S.B., and Green, S.B. (1983). The relationship between job and marriage satisfaction within and between spouses. *Journal of Occupational Behavior*, **4**, 145–55.

Pooyan, A., and Eberhardt, B. (1987). Farm stress and its relationship with farmers' attitudes and health. Paper presented at the American Psychological Association Convention, New York.

Pratt, L.I., and Barling, J. (1988). Differentiating between daily events, acute and chronic stressors: A framework and its implications. In J.R. Hurrell, L.R. Murphy, S.L. Sauter, and C.L. Cooper (eds), *Occupational Stress: Issues and Developments in Research*, pp. 41–53. Taylor and Francis, London.

Presland, P., and Antill, J.K. (1987). Household division of labour: The impact of hours worked in paid employment. *Australian Journal of Psychology*, **39**, 273–91.

Presser, H.B. (1986). Shift work among American women and child care. *Journal of Marriage and the Family*, **48**, 551–64.

Presser, H.B. (1988). Shift work and child care among young dual-earner American parents. *Journal of Marriage and the Family*, **50**, 133–48.

Presser, H.B., and Cain, V.S. (1983). Shift work among dual-earner couples with children. *Science*, **219**, 876–9.

Price, R.H. (1985). Work and community. *American Journal of Community Psychology*, **13**, 1–12.

Prinz, R.J., De Rosset-Myer, E., Holden, E.W., Tarnowski, K.J., and Roberts, W.A. (1983). Marital disturbance and child problems: A cautionary note regarding hyperactive children. *Journal of Abnormal Child Psychology*, **11**, 393–9.

Quay, H.C., and Peterson, D.R. (1983). Revised behavior problem checklist. Unpublished manuscript, Box 248074, University of Miami, Coral Gables, Florida, 33124.

Raabe, P.H., and Gessner, J. (1988). Employer family-supportive policies: Diverse variations on the theme. *Family Relations*, **37**, 196–202.

Radin, N., and Greer, E. (1987). Father unemployment and the young child. Paper presented at the biennial meeting of the Society for Research in Child Development. Baltimore, April.

Radin, N., and Harold-Goldsmith, R. (1989). The involvement of selected unemployed and employed men with their children. *Child Development*, **60**, 454–9.

Ray, S.A., and McLoyd, V.C. (1986). Fathers in hard times: The impact of unemployment and poverty on paternal and marital relations. In M.E. Lamb (ed.), *The Father's Role: Applied Perspectives*, pp. 339–83. Wiley, New York.

Reinhardt, R.F. (1970). The outstanding jet pilot. *American Journal of Psychiatry*, **127**, (6), 32–6.

Renshaw, J.R. (1976). An exploration of the dynamics of the overlapping worlds of work and family. *Family Process*, 143–65.

Richardson, J.G. (1979). Wife occupational superiority and marital troubles: An examination of the hypothesis. *Journal of Marriage and the Family*, **41**, 63–72.

Ridley, C.A. (1973). Exploring the impact of work satisfaction and involvement on marital interaction when both partners are employed. *Journal of Marriage and the Family*, **35**, 229–37.

Riegle, D.W. (1982). The psychological and social effects of unemployment. *American Psychologist*, **37**, 1113–15.

Riesch, S.K. (1981). Occupational commitment, role conflict and the quality of mother-child interaction. *Dissertation Abstracts International*, **42** (4-B), 1395–6.

Robbins, B. (1939). Neurotic disturbances in work. *American Journal of Psychiatry*, **2**, 333–42.

Robinson, N., and Heller, R.F. (1980). Experience with the Bortner questionnaire as a measure of Type A behaviour in a sample of UK families. *Psychological Medicine*, **10**, 567–71.

Rohrlich, J.B. (1980), *Work and Love: The Crucial Balance*. Harmony Books, New York.

Rosen, B., Jerdee, T.H., and Prestwich T.L. (1975). Dual-career marital adjustment: Potential effects on discriminatory managerial attitudes. *Journal of Marriage and the Family*, **37**, 565–72.

Rosen, L.N., and Moghadam, L.Z. (1988). Social support, family separation, and well-being among military wives. *Behavioral Medicine*, 64–70.

Rosenfield, S. (1980). Sex differences in depression: Do women always have higher rates? *Journal of Health and Social Behavior*, **21**, 33–42.

Ross, C.E., and Huber, J. (1985). Hardship and depression. *Journal of Health and Social Behavior*, **26**, 312–27.

Rotchford, N.L., and Roberts, K.H. (1982). Part-time workers as missing persons in organizational research. *Academy of Management Review*, **7**, 228–34.

Rousseau, D.M. (1978). Relationship of work to nonwork. *Journal of Applied Psychology*, **63**, 513–17.

Ruble, D.N., Fleming, A.S., Hackel, L.S., and Stangor, C. (1988). Changes in the marital relationship during the transition to first time motherhood: Effects of violated expectations concerning division of household labor. *Journal of Personality and Social Psychology*, **55**, 78–87.

Rutenfranz, J., Colquhoun, W.P., Knauth, P., and Ghata, J.N. (1977). Biomedical and psychological aspects of shift work. *Scandinavian Journal of Work and Environmental Health*, **3**, 165–82.

Rutter, M. (1981). Stress, coping and development: Some issues and some questions. *Journal of Child Psychology and Psychiatry*, **22**, 323–56.

Salkever, D.S. (1980). Effects of children's health on maternal hours of work: A preliminary analysis. *Journal of Human Resources*, 156–66.

Salkever, D.S. (1982). Children's health problems and maternal work status. *Journal of Human Resources*, **27**, 94–109.

Sarason, I.G., and Johnson, J.H. (1979). Life stress, organizational stress, and job satisfaction. *Psychological Reports*, **44**, 75–9.

Sarason, I.G., Johnson, J.H., and Siegel, J.M. (1978). Assessing the impact of life change: Development of the Life Experiences Survey. *Journal of Consulting and Clinical Psychology*, **46**, 932–46.

Schachter, F.F. (1981). Toddlers with employed mothers. *Child Development*, **52**, 958–64.

Schaeffer, M.H., Street, S.W., Singer, J.E., and Baum, A. (1988). Effects of control on the stress reactions of commuters. *Journal of Applied Social Psychology*, 18, 944–57.

Schein, E.H. (1980). *Organizational Psychology*, 3rd ed. Prentice Hall, New Jersey.

Schubert, J.B., Bradley-Johnson, S., and Nuttal, J. (1980). Mother–infant communication and maternal employment. *Child Development*, 51, 246–9.

Schumm, W.R., and Bugaighis, M.A. (1986). Marital quality over the marital career: Alternative explanations. *Journal of Marriage and the Family*, 48, 165–8.

Schwartz, H.S. (1982). Job involvement as obsession-compulsion. *Academy of Management Review*, 7, 429–32.

Schwartz, J., Tsiantar, D., and Springen, K. (1989). Escape from the office. *Newsweek*, 24 April, 58–60.

Schwartz, P. (1983). Length of daycare attendance and attachment behavior in eighteen month old infants. *Child Development*, 54, 1075–8.

Schweiger, D.M., and Leana, C.R. (1986). Participation in decision making. In E.A. Locke (ed.), *Generalizing from Laboratory to Field Settings*, pp. 147–66. Lexington Books, Massachusetts.

Segal, S. (1984). The working parent dilemma. *Personnel Journal*, 63, 50–6.

Seidenberg, R. (1973). *Corporate Wives–Corporate Casualties?* Amacom, New York.

Sekaran, U. (1985). The paths to mental health: An exploratory study of husbands and wives in dual-career families. *Journal of Occupational Psychology*, 58, 129–37.

Sell, R.R. (1983). Transferred jobs: A neglected aspect of migration and occupational change. *Work and Occupations*, 10 (2), 179–206.

Shakespeare, W. (1977). *Antony and Cleopatra*. Penguin, New York.

Shamir, B. (1983). Some antecedents of work–nonwork conflict. *Journal of Vocational Behavior*, 23, 98–111.

Shamir, B. (1986). Protestant work ethic, work involvement and the psychological impact of unemployment. *Journal of Occupational Behavior*, 7, 25–38.

Shamir, B. (1987). Unemployment and household division of labor. *Journal of Marriage and the Family*, 48, 195–206.

Shreve, A. (1982). Careers and the lure of motherhood. *New York Times Magazine*. 21 November, 38.

Siegel, M. (1980). *Cops and Women*. Tower Publications, New York.

Siegerman, C.B. (1983). Psychotherapy of the elderly: Case #8. *Journal of Geriatric Psychology*, 16, 83–5.

Smart, R.E. (1979). Drinking problems among employed, unemployed and shift workers. *Journal of Occupational Medicine*, 21, 73.

Smilgis, M. (1987). Trapped behind the wheel. *Time*, 20 July, 62–3.

Smith, D.S. (1985). Wife employment and marital adjustment: A cumulation of results. *Family Relations*, 34, 483–90.

Smith, E.J. (1981). The working mother: A critique of the research. *Journal of Vocational Behavior*, 19, 191–211.

Snowden, L.R., Schott, T.L., Awalt, S.J., and Gillis-Knox, J. (1988). Marital satisfaction in pregnancy. *Journal of Marriage and the Family*, 50, 325–34.

South, S.J. (1985). Economic conditions and the divorce rate: A time-series analysis of the postwar United States. *Journal of Marriage and the Family*, 47, 31–41.

Spanier, G.B. (1976). Measuring dyadic adjustment: New scales for assessing the quality of marriage and similar dyads. *Journal of Marriage and the Family*, 38, 15–28.

Spanier, G.B., and Lewis, R.A. (1980). Marital quality: A review of the seventies. *Journal of Marriage and the Family*, 42, 825–39.

Spence, J.T., Helmreich, R.L., and Pred, R.S. (1987). Impatience versus achievement strivings in the Type A pattern: Differential effects on students' health and academic achievement. *Journal of Applied Psychology*, 72, 522–8.

Spence, J. T., Pred, R.S., and Helmreich, R.L. (1989). Achievement strivings, scholastic aptitude, and academic performance: A follow up to 'Impatience versus Achievement Strivings in the Type A pattern'. *Journal of Applied Psychology*, **74**, 176–8.

Spitze, G. (1988). Women's employment and family relations: A review. *Journal of Marriage and the Family*, **50**, 595–610.

Spitze, G., and South, S.J. (1985). Women's employment, time expenditure and divorce. *Journal of Family Issues*. **6**, 307–29.

Spitze, G., and Waite, L.J. (1981). Wives' employment: The role of husbands' perceived attitudes. *Journal of Marriage and the Family*, **43**, 117–24.

Spock, B. (1976). *Baby and Child Care*. Simon and Schuster, Markham, Ontario.

Staines, G.L. (1980). Spillover versus compensation: A review of the literature on the relationship between work and nonwork. *Human Relations*, **33**, 111–29.

Staines, G.L. (1986). Men's work schedule and family life. In R.A. Lewis and M.B. Sussman (eds), *Men's Changing Roles in the Family*, pp. 43–65. Haworth, New York.

Staines, G.L., and Pleck, J.H. (1983). *The Impact of Work Schedules on the Family*. Institute for Social Research, Ann Arbor, Michigan.

Staines, G.L., and Pleck, J.H. (1984). Nonstandard work schedules and family life. *Journal of Applied Psychology*, **69**, 515–23.

Staines, G.L., and Pleck, J.H. (1986). Work schedule flexibility and family life. *Journal of Occupational Behaviour*, **7**, 147–53.

Staines, G.L., Pottick, K.J., and Fudge, D.A. (1985). The effects of wives' employment on husbands' job and life satisfaction. *Psychology of Women Quarterly*, **9**, 419–24.

Staines, G.L., Pottick, K.J., and Fudge, D.A. (1986). Wives' employment and husbands' attitudes towards work and life. *Journal of Applied Psychology*, **71**, 118–28.

Staines, G.L. Pleck, J.H., Shepard, L.J., and O'Connor, P. (1978). Wives' employment status and marital adjustment: Yet another look. *Psychology of Women Quarterly*, **3**, 90–120.

Staw, B.M. (1984). Organizational behaviour: A review and reformulation of the field's outcome variables. *Annual Review of Psychology*, **35**, 627–66.

Steinberg, L.D., Catalano, R., and Dooley, D. (1981). Economic antecedents of child abuse and neglect. *Child Development*, **52**, 975–85.

Steinberg, L., and Silverberg, S.B. (1987). Marital satisfaction in middle stages of family life cycle. *Journal of Marriage and the Family*. **49**, 751–60.

Stephan, C.W., and Corder, J. (1985). The effect of dual career families on adolescents' sex role attitudes, work and family plans and choices of important others. *Journal of Marriage and the Family*, **47**, 921–9.

Stevenson, M.R., and Black, K.N. (1988). Paternal absence and sex-role development: A meta-analysis. *Child Development*, **59**, 793–814.

Stipek, D., and McCroskey, J. (1989). Investing in children: Government and workplace policies for parents. *American Psychologist*, **44**, 416–23.

Stith, S.M., and Davis, A.J. (1984). Employed mothers and family day-care substitute caregivers: A comparative analysis of infant care. *Child Development*, **55**, 1340–8.

Stokes, J.P., and Peyton, J.S. (1986). Attitudinal differences between full-time homemakers and women who work outside the home. *Sex Roles*, **15**, 299–331.

Stokols, D., Novaco, R.W., Stokols, J., and Campbell, J. (1978). Traffic congestion, Type A behavior and stress. *Journal of Applied Psychology*, **63**, 467–80.

Stolz, L.M. (1960). Effects of maternal employment on children: Evidence from research. *Child Development*, **31**, 749–63.

Stone, A.A. (1987). Event content in a daily survey is deferentially associated with concurrent mood. *Journal of Personality and Social Psychology*, **52**, 56–8.

Stone, A.A., Reed, B.R., and Neale, J.M. (1987). Changes in daily event frequency precede episodes of physical symptoms. *Journal of Human Stress*.

Straus, M.A. (1979). Measuring intrafamily conflict and violence: The Conflict Tactics (CT) Scale. *Journal of Marriage and the Family*, **41**, 75–86.

Straus, M.A., and Gelles, R.J. (1986). Societal change and change in family violence from 1975 to 1985 as revealed by two national surveys. *Journal of Marriage and the Family*, **48**, 465–79.

Straus, M.A., Gelles, R.J., and Steinmetz, S.K. (1980). *Behind Closed Doors*. Anchor Press, New York.

Strube, M.J. (1988). The decision to leave an abusive relationship: Empirical evidence and theoretical issues. *Psychological Bulletin*, **104**, 236–50.

Stuckey, M.F., McGhee, P.E., and Bell, N.J. (1982). Parent–child interaction: The influence of maternal employment. *Developmental Psychology*, **18**, 635–44.

Suchet, M., and Barling, J. (1986). Employed mothers: Interrole conflict, spouse support and marital functioning. *Journal of Occupational Behaviour*, **4**, 167–8.

Sutton-Smith, B., Rosenberg, B.G., and Landy, F. (1968). Father absence effects in families of different sibling compositions. *Child Development*, **39**, 1213–21.

Svanum, S., Bringle, R.G., and McLaughlin, J.E. (1982). Father absence and cognitive performance in a large sample of six-to eleven-year old children. *Child Development*, **53**, 136-43.

Swinburne, P. (1981). The psychological impact of unemployment on managers and professional staff. *Journal of Occupational Psychology*, **54**, 47–64.

Tangri, S.S. (1972). Determinants of occupational role innovation among college women. *Journal of Social Issues*, **28**, 177–99.

Taylor, F.I. (1909). *A Bibliography of Unemployment and the Unemployed*. P.S. King and Son, London.

Taylor, M. (1988). A gender-based analysis of the consequences of employed reductions on well-being: Plant workers in two Newfoundland fishing outports. *Canadian Journal of Community Mental Health*, **7**, 67–80.

Terborg, J.R. (1985). Working women and stress. In T.A. Beehr and R.S. Bhagat (eds), *Human Stress and Cognition in Organizations*, pp. 245–86. John Wiley, New York.

Thomas, L.E., McCabe, E., and Berry, J.E. (1980). Unemployment and family stress: A reassessment. *Family Relations*, **29**, 517–24.

Thomas, S., Albrecht, K., and White, P. (1984). Determinants of marital quality in dual-career couples. *Family Relations*, **33**, 513–21.

Thoresen, R.J., and Goldsmith, E.B. (1987). The relationship between army families' financial well-being and depression, general well-being, and marital satisfaction. *The Journal of Social Psychology*, **127**, 545–7.

Tiggemann, M., and Winefield, A.H. (1984). The effects of unemployment on the mood, self esteem, locus of control, and depressive affect of school-leavers. *Journal of Occupational Psychology* **57**, 33–42.

Tinsley, H.E.A., and Tinsley, D.J. (1989). Reinforcers of the occupation of homemaker: An analysis of the need-gratifying properties of the homemaker occupation across stages of the homemaker life cycle. *Journal of Counseling Psychology*, **36**, 189–95.

Toufexis, A. (1985). The perils of dual careers. *Time*, 69.

Trist, E.L., Higgin, G.W., Murray, H., and Pollock, A.B. (1965). *Organizational Choice*. Tavistock, London.

Trimberger, R., and MacLean, M.J. (1982). Maternal employment: The child's perspective. *Journal of Marriage and the Family*, **44**, 469–75.

Troll, L., Bengston, V., and McFarland, D. (1979). Generations in the family. In W.R. Burr, R. Hill, F.I. Nye, and I.L. Reiss (eds), *Contemporary Theories about the Family: Research-Based Theories*, Vol 1, pp. 127–61. Free Press, New York.

Turner, R.J., and Avison, W. R. (1985). Assessing risk factors for problem parenting: The

significance of social support. *Journal of Marriage and the Family*, **47**, 881–92.
Tuthill, M. (1980). Marriage and a career: No easy choices and a good chance of divorce. *Nation's Business*.
Ulbrich, P.M. (1988). The determinants of depression in two-income marriages. *Journal of Marriage and the Family*, **50**, 121–31.
US News and World Report (1980). Jobs and family: The walls were down. June, 57.
US Bureau of Labor Statistics (1988). Moms move to part-time careers. *Newsweek*, 15 August, 64.
Van Maanen, J., Dabbs, J.M., and Faulkner, R.R. (1982). *Varieties of Qualitative Research*. Sage, California.
Vaughn, B.E., Gove, F.L., and Egeland, B. (1980). The relationship between out-of-home care and the quality of infant–mother attachment in an economically disadvantaged population. *Child Development*, **51**, 1203–14.
Verbrugge, L.M. (1983). Multiple roles and physical health of women and men. *Journal of Health and Social Behavior*, **24**, 16–30.
Veroff, J., Douvan, E., and Kulka, R.A. (1981). *The Inner American: A Self Portrait from 1957 to 1976*. Basic Books, New York.
Vinokur, A., and Selzer, M.K. (1975). Desirable versus undesirable life events: Their relationship to stress and mental disorder. *Journal of Personality and Social Psychology*, **32**, 329–37.
Vispo, R.H., and Shine, D. (1985). Strike and stress in a maximum security hospital. *Psychiatric Quarterly*, **57**, 111–20.
Vogel, S.R., Broverman, I.K., Broverman, D.W., Clarkson, F.E., and Rosenkrantz, P.S. (1970). Maternal employment and perceptions of sex roles among college students. *Developmental Psychology*, **3**, 384–91.
Volger, A., Ernst, G., Nachreiner, F., and Hanecke, K. (1988). Common free time of family members under different shift systems. *Applied Ergonomics*, **19**, 213–18.
Voydanoff, P. (1987). *Work and Family Life*. Sage, California.
Voydanoff, P. (1988). Work role characteristics, family structure demands, and work/family conflict. *Journal of Marriage and the Family*, **50**, 749–61.
Voydanoff, P., and Kelly, R.F. (1984). Determinants of work-related family problems among employed parents. *Journal of Marriage and the Family* **46**, 881–92.
Walker, A.J. (1985). Reconceptualizing family stress. *Journal of Marriage and the Family* **47**, 827–37.
Walker, E.J. (1976). Till business us do part? *Harvard Business Review*, 94–101.
Walker, J. (1985). Social problems of shiftwork. In S. Folkard and T. Monk (eds), *Hours of Work: Temporal Factors in Work-scheduling*. Wiley, New York, pp. 211–25.
Wallston, B. (1973). The effects of maternal employment on children. *Journal of Child Psychiatry*, **14**, 18–95.
Warr, P. (1983). Work, jobs and unemployment. *Bulletin of the British Psychological Society*, **36**, 305–11.
Warr, P. (1984a). Work and employment. In P.J. Drenth, H. Thierry, P.J. Willems and C.J. Wolff (eds), *Handbook of Work and Organizational Psychology*, Vol. 1, pp. 413–43. Wiley, New York.
Warr, P. (1984b). Job loss, unemployment and psychological well-being. In V.L. Allen and E. Van de Vliert (eds), *Role Transitions*, pp. 263–85. Plenum, New York.
Warr, P. (1984c). Reported behaviour changes after job loss. *British Journal of Social Psychology*, **23**, 271–5.
Warr P. (1987a). Job characteristics and mental health. In P. Warr (ed.), *Psychology of Work*, pp. 247–69. Penguin, London.
Warr, P. (1987b). *Work, Unemployment and Mental Health*. Clarendon Press, Oxford.

Warr, P., Jackson, P., and Banks, M. (1988). Unemployment and mental health: Some British studies. *Journal of Social Issues*, **44**,(4) 47–68.

Warr, P., and Parry, G. (1982a). Paid employment and women's psychological well-being. *Psychological Bulletin*, **91**, 498–516.

Warr, P., and Parry, G. (1982b). Depressed mood in working-class mothers with and without paid employment. *Social Psychiatry*, **17**, 161–5.

Warr, P., and Payne, R. (1983a). Affective outcomes of paid employment in a random sample of British workers. *Journal of Occupational Behavior*, **4**, 91–104.

Warr, P., and Payne, R. (1983b). Social class and reported changes in behavior after job loss. *Journal of Applied Social Psychology*, **13** 206–22.

Warren, L.W., and McEachren, L. (1983). Psychosocial correlates of depressive symptomatology in adult women. *Journal of Abnormal Psychology*, **92**, 151–60.

Watson, D., Pennebaker, J.W., and Folger, R. (1987). Beyond negative affectivity: Measuring stress and satisfaction in the workplace. In J.M. Ivancevich and D.C. Ganster (eds), *Job Stress: From Theory to Suggestion*, pp. 141–58. Haworth Press, New York.

Webster's New Collegiate Dictionary, (1977). A. Merriam Webster, Springfield, Massachusetts.

Wedderburn, A.A.I. (1981). Is there a pattern in the value of time off work? In A. Reinberg, N. Vieux and P. Andlauer (eds), *Night and Shift Work: Biological and Social Aspects*. Pergamon Press, Oxford.

Weiss, R.M. (1987). Writing under the influence: Science versus fiction in the analysis of corporate alcoholism programs. *Personnel Psychology*, **40**, 341–56.

Weissman, M.M., and Paykel, E.S. (1972). Moving and depression in women. *Society*, **9**, 24–8.

Weller, L., and Rofe, Y. (1988). Mixed and homogeneous marriages in Israel. *Journal of Marriage and the Family*, **50**, 245–54.

Werts, G.E. (1968). Paternal influence on career choice. *Journal of Counseling Psychology*, **15**, 48–52.

White, L.K., and Brinkeroff, D.B. (1981). The sexual division of labor: Evidence from childhood. *Social Forces*, **60**, 170–81.

Wilensky, H. (1960). Work, careers and social integration. *International Social Science Journal*, **12**, 543–60.

Williamson, S.Z. (1970). The effects of maternal employment on the scholastic performance of children. *Journal of Home Economics*, **62**, 609–13.

Winett, R.A., and Neale, M.S. (1980a). Results of experimental study on flexitime and family life. *Monthly Labor Review*, 29–32.

Winett, .R.A., and Neale, M.S. (1980b). Modifying settings as a strategy for permanent, preventive behavior change. In R. Karoly and J.J. Steffen (eds), *Improving Long-Term Effects in Psychotherapy*. Gardner Press, New York.

Wolfe, D.A. Jaffe, P., Wilson, S.K., and Zak, L. (1985). Children of battered women: The relation of child behavior to family violence and maternal stress. *Journal of Consulting and Clinical Psychology*, **53**, 657–65.

Woods, M.B. (1972). The unsupervised child of the working mother. *Developmental Psychology*, **6**, 14–25.

Work, C.P., Witkin, G., Moore, N.J., and Golden, S. (1987). Jam sessions. *US News and World Report*, 7 September, 20–7.

Yarrow, M.R., Scott, P., Deleeuw, L., and Heinig, C. (1962). Childrearing in families of working and non-working mothers. *Sociometry*, **25**, 122–40.

Ybarra, L. (1982). When wives work: The impact on the Chicano family. *Journal of Marriage and the Family*, **44**, 169–78.

Yogev, S. (1981). Do professional women have egalitarian marital relationships? *Journal of Marriage and the Family*, **43**, 865–71.

Yogev, S. (1983). Dual-career couples: Conflicts and treatment. *American Journal of Family Therapy*, **11**, 38–44.

Yogev, S., and Brett, J. (1985a). Perceptions of the division of housework and child care and marital satisfaction. *Journal of Marriage and the Family*, **47**, 609–18.

Yogev, S., and Brett, J. (1985b). Patterns of work and family involvement among single- and dual-earner couples. *Journal of Applied Psychology*, **70**, 754–68.

Young, M., and Wilmott, P. (1973). *The Symmetrical Family*. Pantheon, New York.

Zaslow, M.J., Pedersen, F.A., Suwalsky, J.T.D., Cain, R.L., and Fivel, M. (1985). The early resumption of employment by mothers: Implications for parent–infant interaction. *Journal of Applied Developmental Psychology*, **6**, 1–16.

Zedeck, S. (1987). Work, family and organizations: An untapped research triangle. Presidential address to Division 14 of the American Psychological Association, August, New York City.

Zedeck, S., Jackson, S.E., and Summers, E. (1983). Shift work schedules and their relationship to health, adaptation, satisfaction and turnover intention. *Academy of Management Journal*, **26**, 297–310.

Author Index

Subject Index